Easy Works 3 for Windows™

Sandra E. Eddy

Easy Works 3 for Windows

Library of Congress Catalog No.: 94-65334

ISBN: 1-56529-755-5

97 96 95 94 6 5 4 3 2 1

Interpretation of the printing code: the rightmost double-digit number is the year of the book's printing; the rightmost single-digit number, the number of the book's printing. For example, a printing code of 94-1 shows that the first printing of the book occurred in 1994.

Publisher: David P. Ewing

Associate Publisher: Corinne Walls

Publishing Director: Lisa A. Bucki

Managing Editor: Anne Owen

Product Marketing Manager: Ray Robinson

Credits

Acquisitions Editors
Thomas F. Godfrey III
Nancy Stevenson

Product Director
Steven M. Schafer

Production Editor
Barbara K. Koenig

Editors
Susan Shaw Dunn
Patrick Kanouse

Technical Editor
Richard F. Brown

Book Designer
Amy Peppler-Adams

Cover Designer
Jay Corpus

Production Team:
Angela Bannan
Claudia Bell
Anne Dickerson
Bob LaRoche
Elizabeth Lewis
Andrea Marcum
Nanci Sears Perry
Linda Quigley
Amy L. Steed
Michael Thomas
Lillian Yates

Indexer:
Michael Hughes

Composed in *Stone Serif* and *MCPdigital* by Que Corporation

About the Author

Sandra E. Eddy, the author of several computer books, specializes in writing about Windows and Windows applications. She is cofounder of The Eddy Group, Inc., a computer book and technical writing company.

For eight years, Ms. Eddy was both a manager of technical writers and a technical writer for a major software company.

Acknowledgments

Thanks to all the people at Que who contributed their talents to this project. Special thanks go to Lisa Bucki, the Publishing Director; Steve Schafer, the Product Director; Barbara Koenig, the Production Editor; and Tom Godfrey and Nancy Stevenson, the Acquisitions Editors.

Many thanks to Richard Brown, the Technical Editor, who made this book as accurate and thorough as possible.

Contents at a Glance

Contents

Part III: Using the Word Processor 64

Part IV: Formatting a Document 80

Part V: Using the Spreadsheet 128

Introduction

What You Can Do with Works for Windows

Microsoft Works for Windows is an integrated program that combines word processing, spreadsheet, database, and communications applications—or *tools*—into one user-friendly, easy-to-use program. You can use the Works tools to create and edit a variety of documents and, using the Communications tool, to send them to other computers.

Using Works for Windows, you can:

- *Create letters, memoranda, proposals, and reports.* With a typewriter, pressing a key leaves a permanent imprint of a character on your paper. To correct a mistake, you have to use correction fluid or retype the page from the beginning. With Works, you see the text and data on-screen. You can easily correct any typographical errors before you print the document.
- *Insert, rearrange, or delete text, data, rows, and columns.* From any location in your document, you can insert and delete text or data. You can create a document by starting in the middle and then going back later to add the introduction, titles, headings, and summary in any order.
- *Check spelling.* Before you print any Works file, you can run a spelling check to search for misspellings. You can even leave spelling errors for Works to catch so that you can concentrate on writing instead of spelling.
- *Make formatting changes.* With Works, you can easily change margins, tabs, and other formatting options. Experiment with the settings until the document appears as you want it. You can emphasize parts of a file by applying boldface and italics. You can also use a different font (typeface) and font size.
- *Search for text and data.* You can search your document for a particular word, phrase, or piece of data. For example, you can move quickly to the section of your document that contains the phrase *to summarize* in order to add a point.
- *Search and replace text and data.* You can replace text and data in a document quickly and easily. For example, you can change all occurrences of *lamp* to *lighting fixture.*

- *Preview your document before you print.* You can magnify parts of your document in a preview window for a closer look at your text and graphics. Then you can close this window to edit your document before printing it.

- *Copy or move information from one document to another and from one application to another.* All the Works tools provide Copy, Cut, and Paste commands to facilitate copying and moving. Using the drag-and-drop feature, you can drag information from one location on-screen to another.

- *Create spreadsheets in which you can write simple formulas to add, subtract, multiply, and divide.* You tell Works the numbers to use, and Works calculates the results correctly every time. If you copy formulas to other locations, Works automatically changes the formulas to reflect their new location.

- *Make changes and recalculate automatically.* You can change, add, or delete data, and Works will recalculate the results automatically.

- *Create charts that show a picture of selected data.* You can easily change the chart type, add titles, and change colors and patterns.

- *Build flexible databases.* If a client moves or an invoice changes, you don't have to create a new form. You can easily update the existing record on-screen.

- *Sort records in many different ways and retrieve selected records.* Works lets you sort a client list, for instance, according to ZIP code so that mailings are easier to compile. You can sort a phone list in alphabetical order by last name. You can sort by state so that you can instantly see the names of all your customers who live in South Carolina.

- *Contact other computers to swap information.* Works enables you to send your documents to others—in your work group, in your network, or even across the country.

Task Sections

The Task sections include numbered steps that tell you how to accomplish certain tasks, such as using Works' menus or printing a file. The numbered steps walk you through a specific example so that you can learn the task by actually doing it.

Big Screen

At the beginning of each task is a large screen shot that shows how the computer screen will look after you complete the task. Sometimes the screen shot shows a feature discussed in that task, such as a toolbar button.

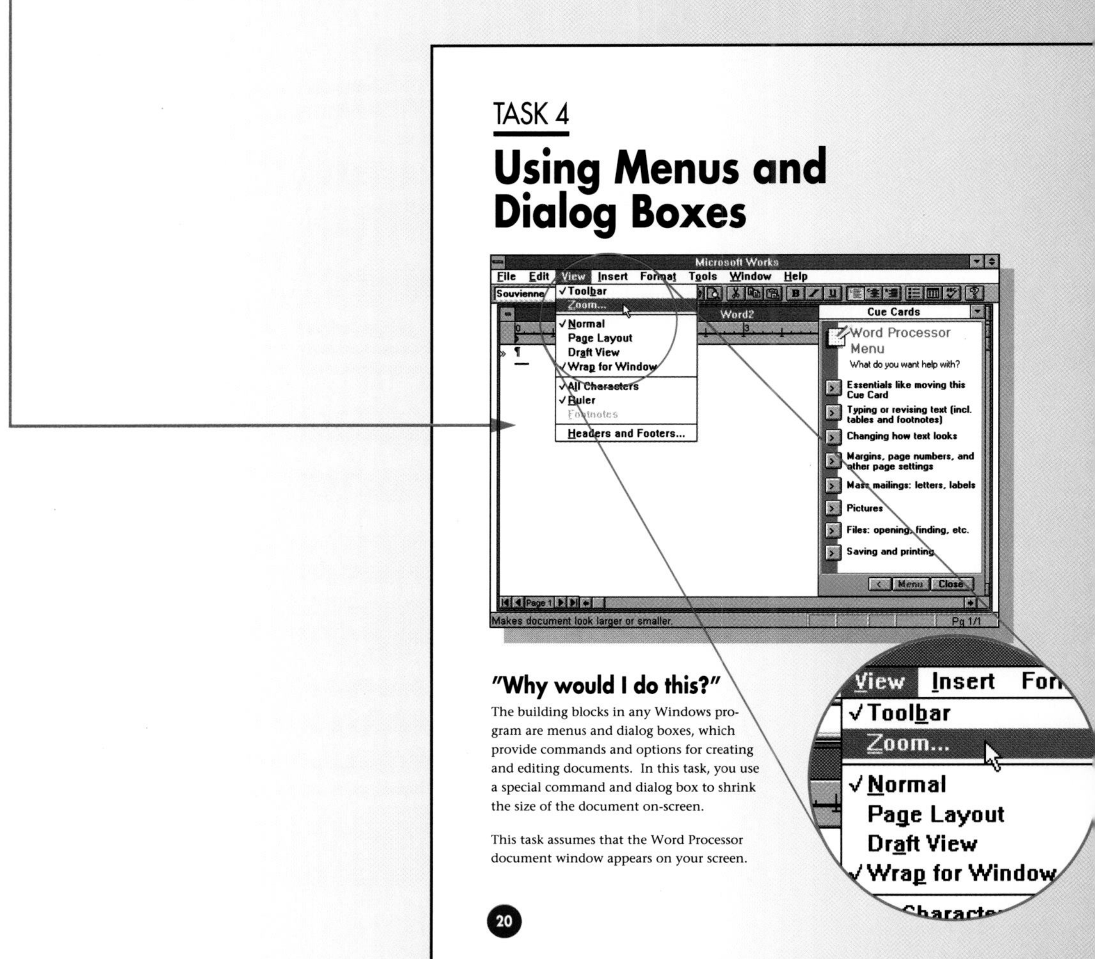

Step-by-Step Screens

Each task includes a screen shot for each step of a procedure. The screen shot shows how the computer screen looks at each step in the process.

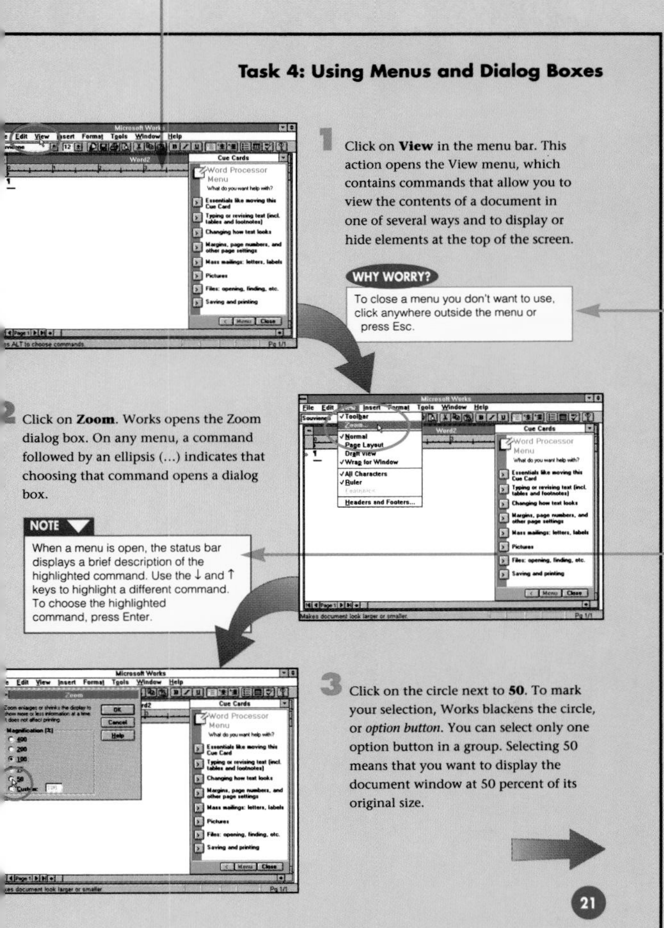

Task 4: Using Menus and Dialog Boxes

1 Click on **View** in the menu bar. This action opens the View menu, which contains commands that allow you to view the contents of a document in one of several ways and to display or hide elements at the top of the screen.

WHY WORRY?

To close a menu you don't want to use, click anywhere outside the menu or press Esc.

2 Click on **Zoom**. Works opens the Zoom dialog box. On any menu, a command followed by an ellipsis (...) indicates that choosing that command opens a dialog box.

NOTE

When a menu is open, the status bar displays a brief description of the highlighted command. Use the ↓ and ↑ keys to highlight a different command. To choose the highlighted command, press Enter.

3 Click on the circle next to **50**. To mark your selection, Works blackens the circle, or *option button*. You can select only one option button in a group. Selecting 50 means that you want to display the document window at 50 percent of its original size.

21

Why Worry? Notes

You may find that you performed a task, such as opening a menu, that you didn't want to do after all. The Why Worry? notes tell you how to undo certain procedures or how to get out of a situation, such as pressing Esc to close a menu.

Other Notes

Many tasks include short notes that tell you a little more about certain procedures. These notes define terms, explain other options, point out shortcuts, and so on.

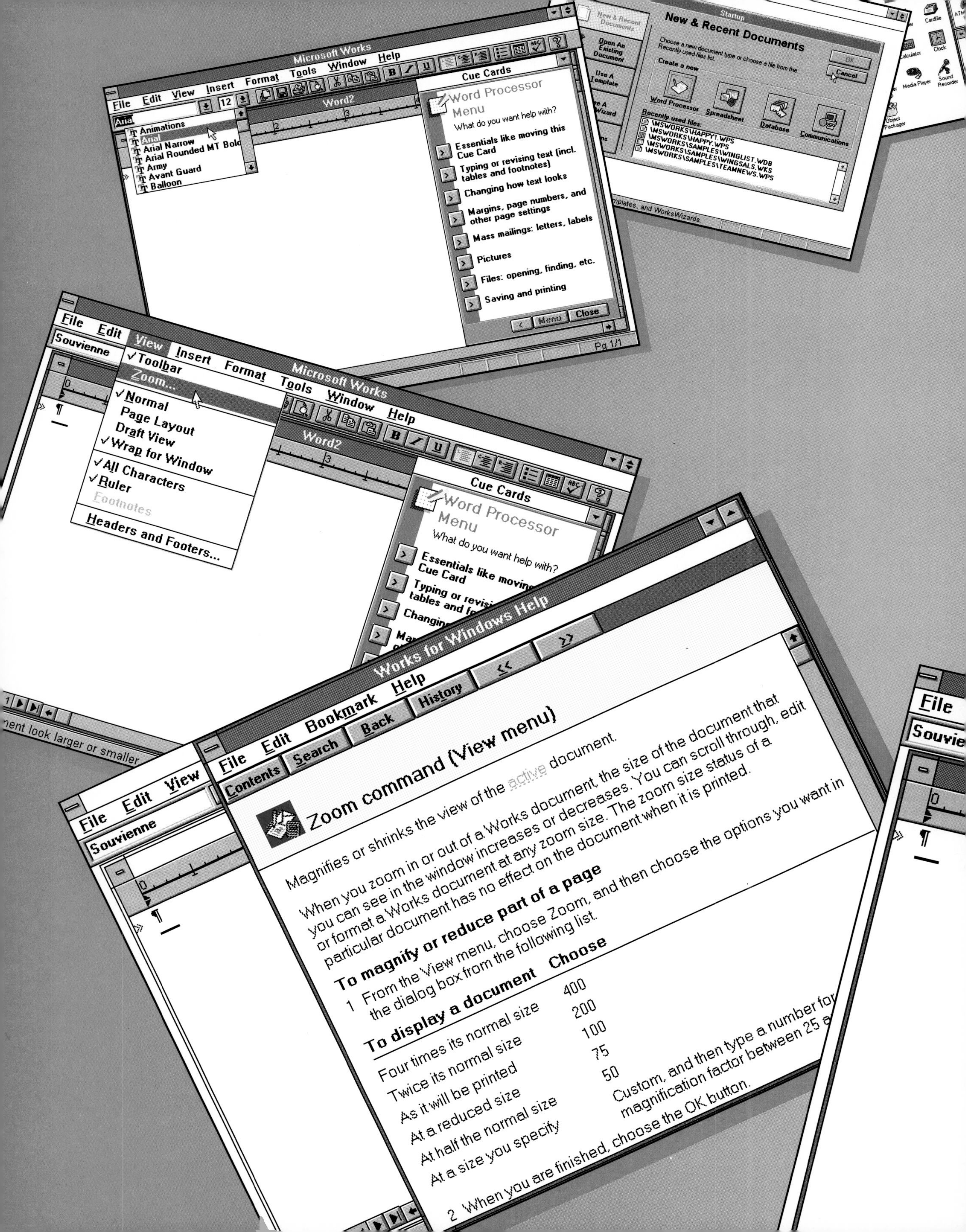

Microsoft Works
File Edit View Insert Format Tools Window Help
Word2
Cue Cards
Word Processor Menu
What do you want help with?
Essentials like moving this Cue Card
Typing or revising text (incl. tables and footnotes)
Changing how text looks
Margins, page numbers, and other page settings
Mass mailings: letters, labels
Pictures
Files: opening, finding, etc.
Saving and printing
Menu Close
Pg 1/1
Animations
Arial
Arial Narrow
Arial Rounded MT Bold
Army
Avant Guard
Balloon
Startup
New & Recent Documents
Choose a new document type or choose a file from the Recently used files list.
Create a new
Word Processor Spreadsheet Database Communications
Recently used files:
\MSWORKS\HAPPY1.WPS
\MSWORKS\HAPPY.WPS
\MSWORKS\SAMPLES\WINGLIST.WDB
\MSWORKS\SAMPLES\WINGSALS.WKS
\MSWORKS\SAMPLES\TEAMNEWS.WPS
OK
Cancel
Open An Existing Document
Use A Template
Templates, and WorksWizards.
Toolbar
Zoom...
Normal
Page Layout
Draft View
Wrap for Window
All Characters
Ruler
Footnotes
Headers and Footers...
Souvienne
Works for Windows Help
File Edit Bookmark Help
Contents Search Back History << >>
Zoom command (View menu)
Magnifies or shrinks the view of the active document.
When you zoom in or out of a Works document, the size of the document that you can see in the window increases or decreases. You can scroll through, edit or format a Works document at any zoom size. The zoom size status of a particular document has no effect on the document when it is printed.
To magnify or reduce part of a page
1 From the View menu, choose Zoom, and then choose the options you want in the dialog box from the following list.
To display a document Choose
Four times its normal size 400
Twice its normal size 200
As it will be printed 100
At a reduced size 75
At half the normal size 50
At a size you specify Custom, and then type a number for magnification factor between 25 a
2 When you are finished, choose the OK button.

PART I

Running Works for Windows

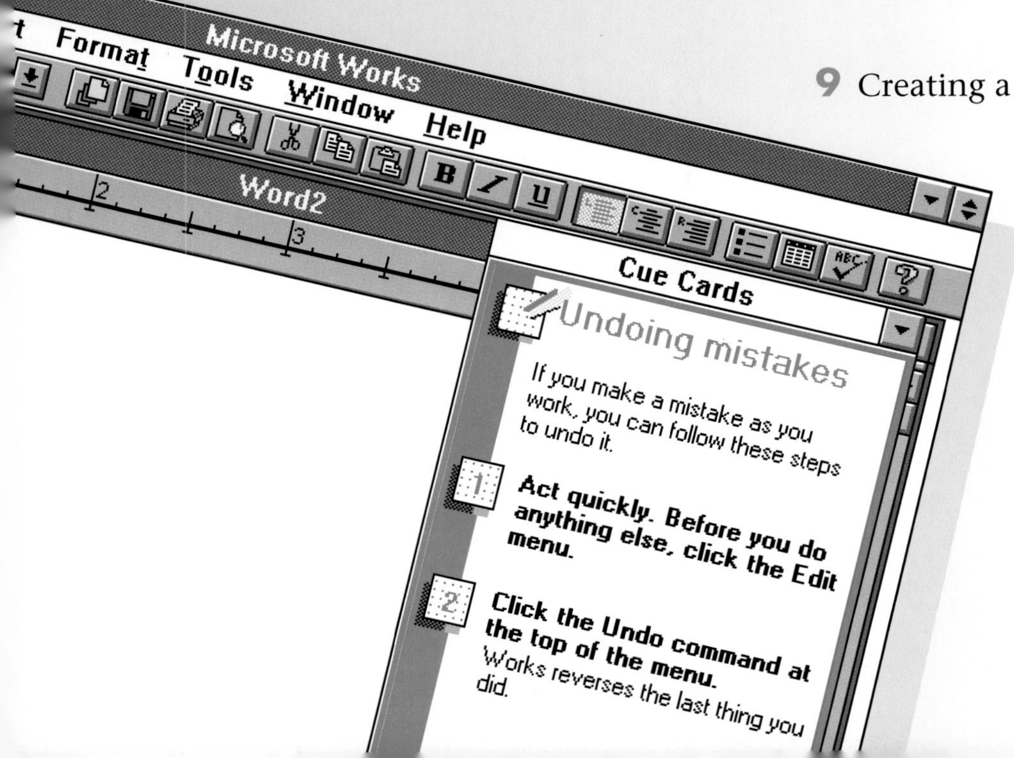

Part I of this book provides information about Microsoft Works for Windows basics. Before you create your first document, spreadsheet, or database, and before you start your first communications session, you should find out about the fundamentals of Works.

Undoing mistakes

If you make a mistake as you work, you can follow these steps to undo it.

1 **Act quickly. Before you do anything else, click the Edit menu.**

2 **Click the Undo command at the top of the menu.** Works reverses the last thing you did.

☞ If the menu says Cannot Undo and is dimmed, Works can't undo the mistake.

Done >

< Menu Close

In this part, you'll start and exit Works. Before you read on, make sure that Works is installed on your hard disk drive. You should have a Works program group or program icon in your Windows Program Manager window. To learn how to install Works, see your Works documentation.

You'll discover how to start a Works tool, and you'll learn about the basic elements of any Works window. You'll find out about the toolbar, menus, and commands.

In this part, you'll also learn how to get help in Works. You'll use Works' help facility and Cue Cards. You'll also discover how to use AutoStart templates and WorksWizards to create files. In Works, you'll find that help is always at your fingertips—just a click or two and you'll find out about Windows features and functions.

Dialog boxes are the small windows in which you do a great deal of your work while in any Windows application. In dialog boxes, you'll specify options, change measurements, and start operations. Some of the elements of dialog boxes are:

- *Group*. A group of related items surrounded by a border.
- *Text box*. A rectangular box in which you type information such as a file name or a measurement. One way of finding out whether a box is a text box is to look at the insertion point. An insertion point that looks like a flashing I indicates a text box.

- *Check box*. A square box that contains an ×, is clear, or is gray. To select a check box, click in the box; an × appears. To deselect a check box, click in the box; the × disappears. A gray check box indicates that your selection includes both choices (selected and deselected); for example, if you select a paragraph that contains both italicized and unitalicized text, the Italic check box would be gray. You can check as many check boxes in a group as you want.
- *List box*. A list of available choices, such as file names, directories, fonts, point sizes, and so on. To select an item in a list, click on it. If the list is long, there might be a scroll bar on the right side of the list for scrolling through your choices. Drop-down list boxes must be opened before you can see the list. Text/List box combinations allow you to either type your choice or select it from a list.

- *Option buttons*. A round button that is either filled or empty. In a group of option buttons, you can choose only one. Some dialog boxes have more than one group of option buttons.
- *Command buttons*. Action buttons you click to carry out a command or action. OK and Cancel are the two most common command buttons. Clicking on OK indicates that you have finished working in the dialog box and want Works to act on all the options you selected. Clicking on Cancel means that you want to "back out" of using the dialog box without implementing any options. If a command button has a heavier border than other command buttons in the dialog box, it is the default button. To select the default button, either click on it or press Enter.

The tasks in this part provide the building blocks for the rest of this book.

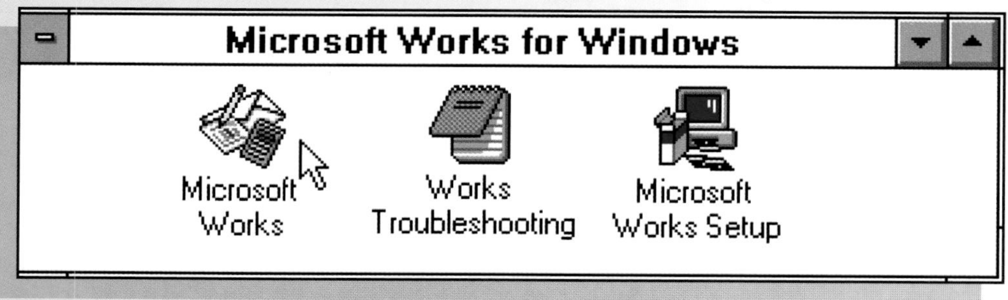

TASK 1

Starting and Exiting Works for Windows

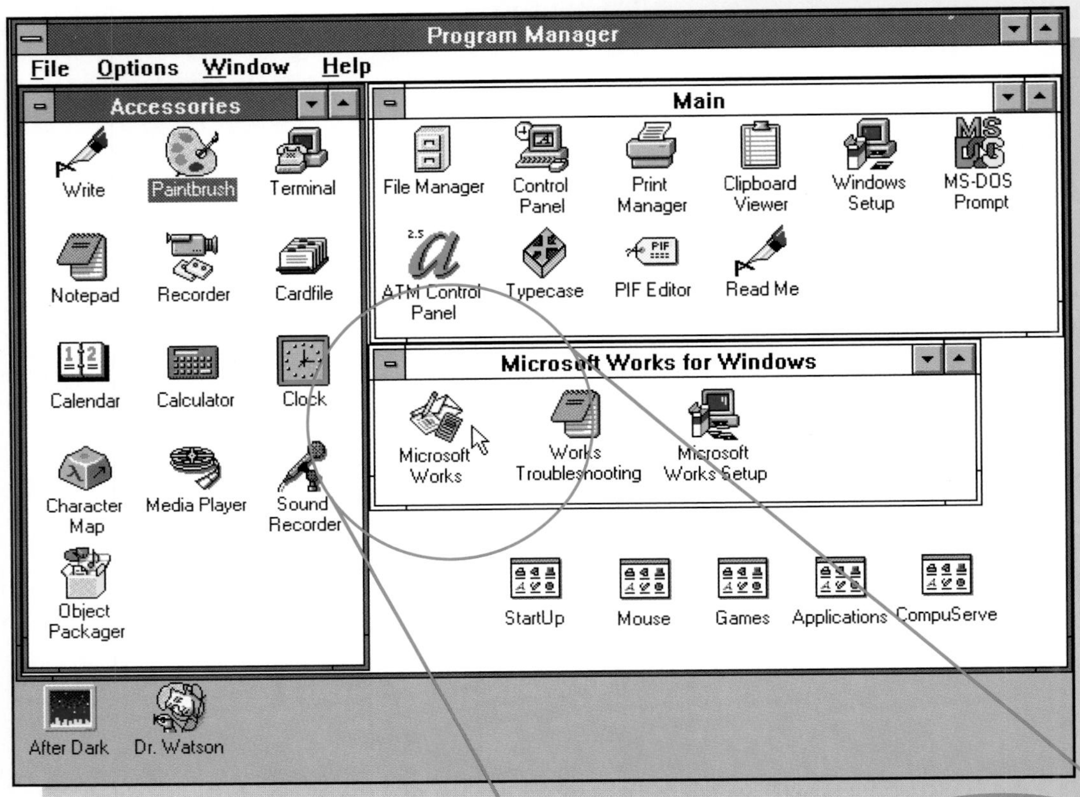

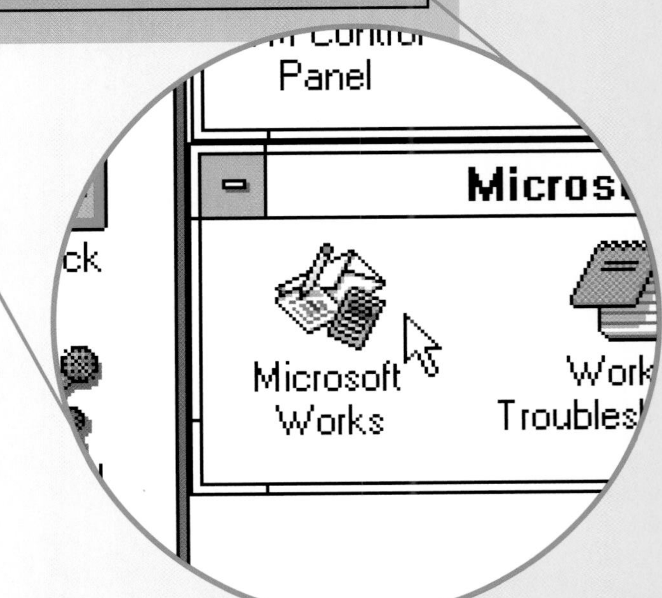

"Why would I do this?"

Starting Works is easy to do. It's just about as easy as turning on your television or radio. When you have completed your work in Works, you can exit Works and return to Windows' Program Manager. We'll start Works right now. Then we'll exit Works.

This task assumes that you have turned on your computer and monitor and have started Microsoft Windows. The starting window—Program Manager—is on your screen.

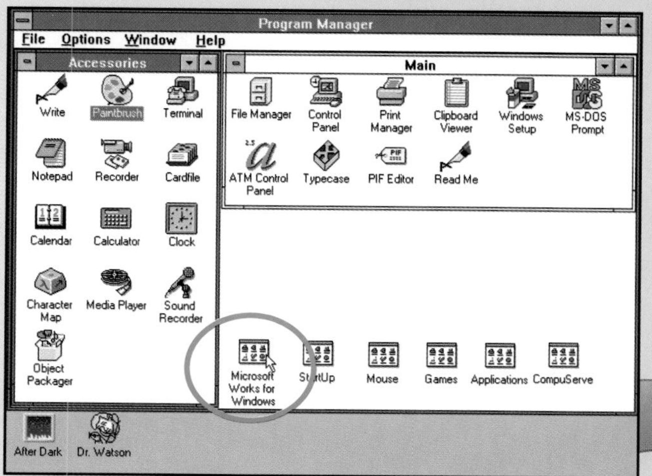

1 Double-click on the *group icon* for Microsoft Works for Windows. This icon represents the *program group* in which you stored Works when installing the program. Move the mouse pointer to the group icon and double-click by pressing the left mouse button twice in rapid succession; this opens a *program group window,* where Microsoft Windows stores programs.

2 Double-click on the *program icon* for Microsoft Works. This step starts the Works program. Each time you start the program, an introduction screen with your name and program information appears, followed by the Startup dialog box for New & Recent Documents.

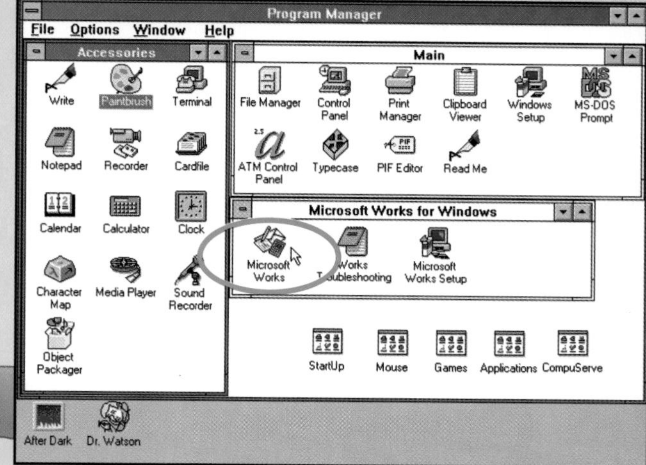

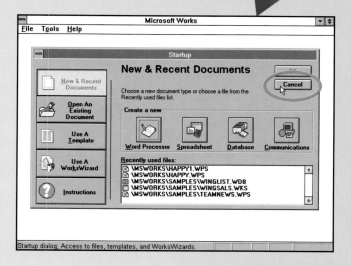

3 Click on the **Cancel** button. Clicking on the Cancel button closes a dialog box without saving any of the changes you made in that dialog box.

Task 1: Starting and Exiting Works for Windows

4 Click on **File** in the menu bar. This step opens the File menu, which contains Works' file management commands.

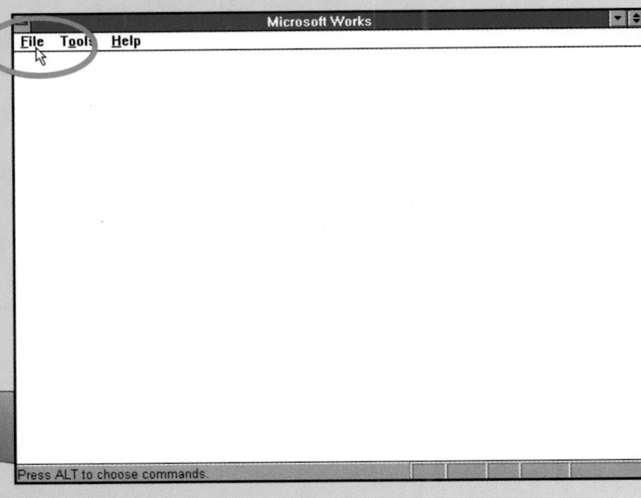

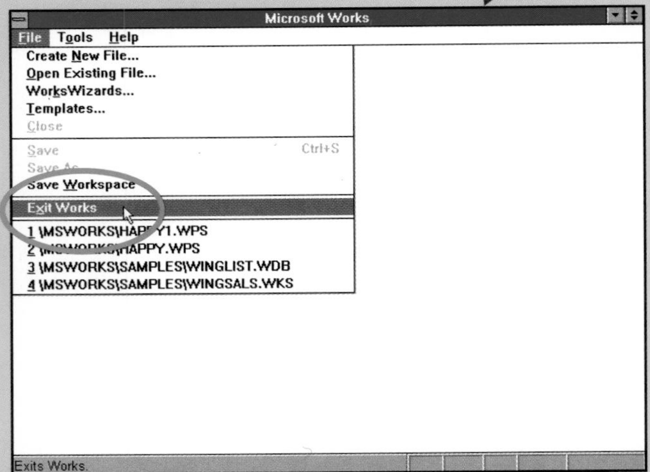

5 Click on the **Exit Works** command. This step closes the Works application window. You return to the Program Manager window.

NOTE

Before you exit Works, you should save each file you worked on during that work session. If you forget to save your work, Works prompts you to save; however, you can exit Works without saving your work.

NOTE

Microsoft Works provides a quick way to exit the program: double-click on the Control menu button. This button is in the top left corner of the Works application window. You return to the Windows Program Manager. This shortcut replaces steps 4 and 5.

TASK 2

Starting a Tool

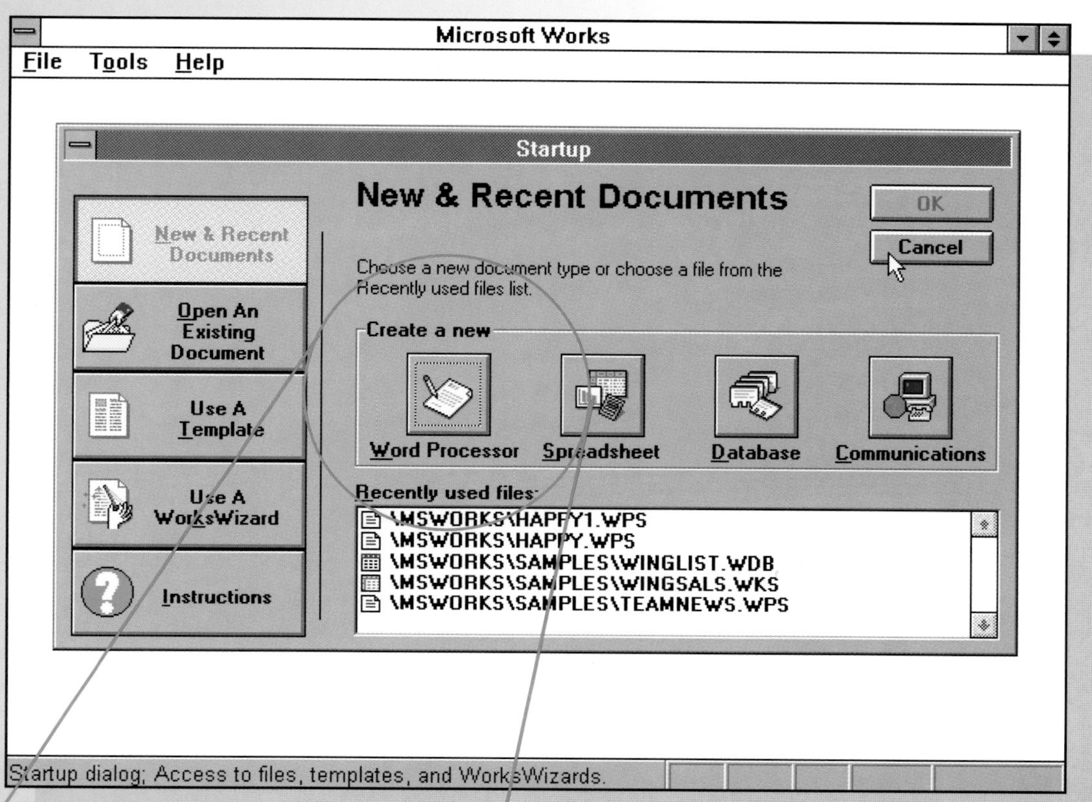

"Why would I do this?"

Opening a Microsoft Works *tool*—one of the Works applications—is the first step in creating a document, spreadsheet, or database file, or in starting a communications session. This action opens a window and allows you to use Works menus and toolbars.

In this task, you will start the Word Processor tool. Then you'll be able to learn more about Works menus and toolbars.

Task 2: Starting a Tool

1 In Windows' Program Manager, double-click on the *program icon* for Microsoft Works in the Microsoft Works for Windows group window. After the introduction screen, the Startup dialog box for New & Recent Documents appears.

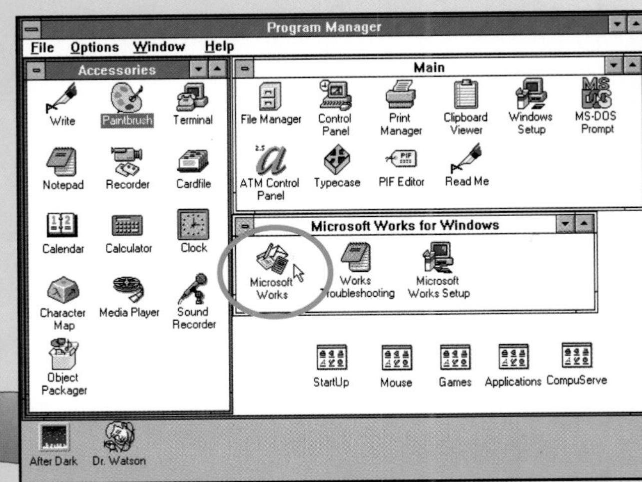

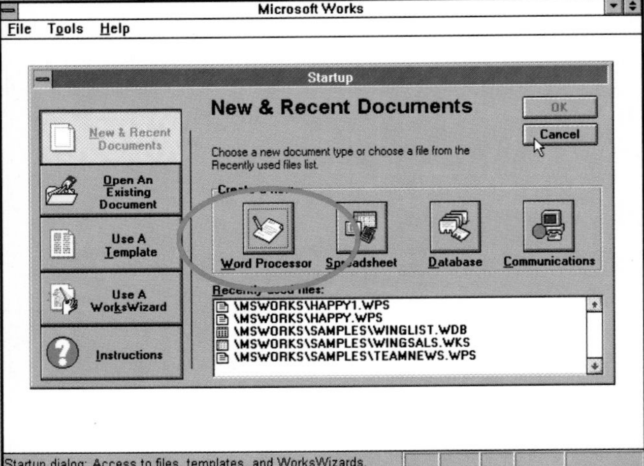

2 Click on the **Word Processor** button. This step opens a window in which you can type and edit a word processing document.

3 Start typing the first words in your document.

WHY WORRY?

Although useful, the Cue Cards window partially blocks your view of the document. To minimize the Cue Cards window, click the *Minimize button*—the down-arrow icon in the top right corner of the Cue Cards window. Double-click on the minimized window, at the bottom of the document window, to restore its size.

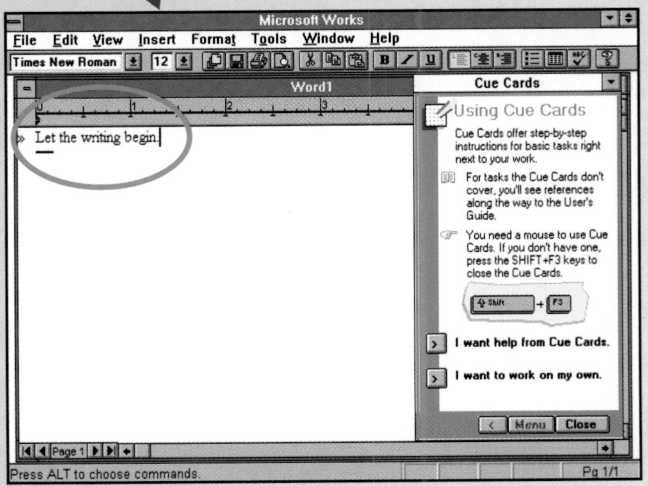

TASK 3

Using the Toolbar

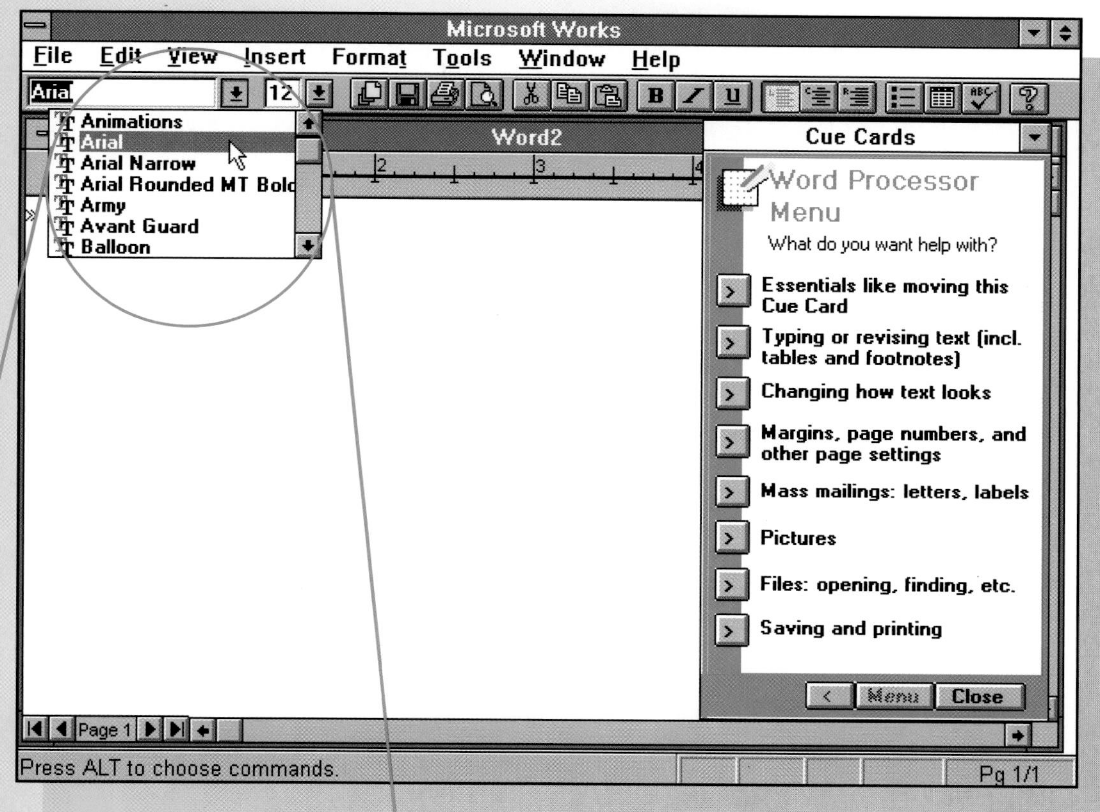

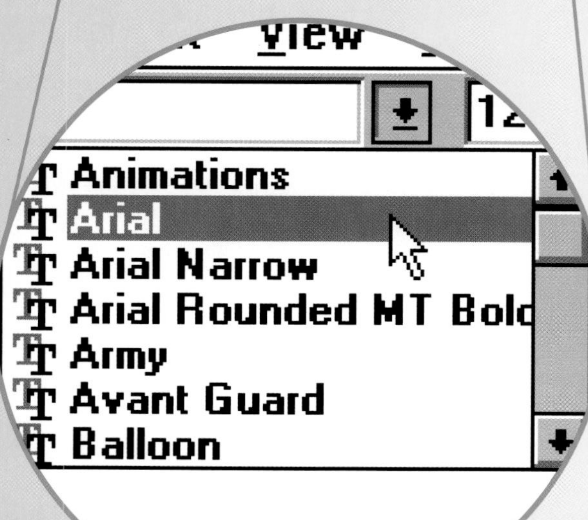

"Why would I do this?"

Each Works tool has a unique *toolbar* containing buttons that can speed your work. Rather than going through several steps of clicks and selections, you can click on a toolbar button to perform common tasks, such as saving your work or printing a document.

In this task, you'll explore the toolbar, display the Startup dialog box for New & Recent Documents, and return to the document window.

Task 3: Using the Toolbar

1 Click the **down-arrow** button to the right of the first box on the toolbar to open the Font Name drop-down list box. Works displays a list of all the fonts, or typefaces, installed for Windows.

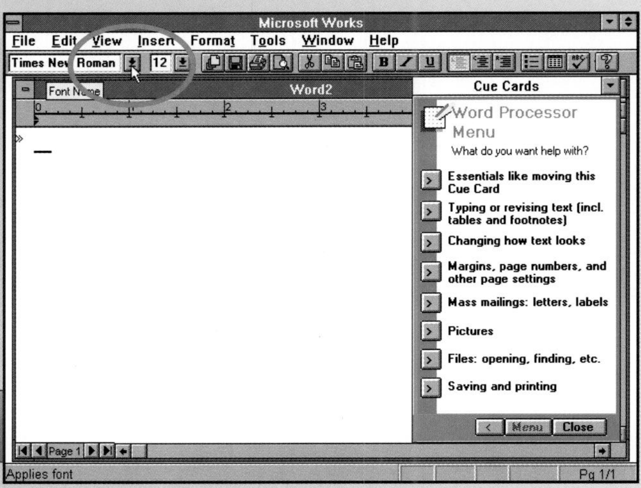

NOTE

When you move your mouse pointer to a button on the toolbar, Works displays a small yellow box that states the purpose of the button.

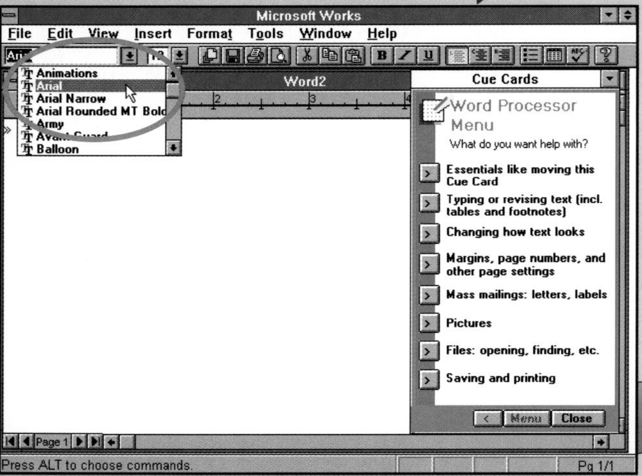

2 Click on **Arial.** When you select a new font, Works automatically changes to the new font and closes the drop-down list box.

WHY WORRY?

To close a drop-down list without making a selection, press Esc or click anywhere outside the list.

3 Click on the **Bold** button, which has a *B* on it. This step turns on boldface so that any text you type is bold. You can type some text to verify that it is bold.

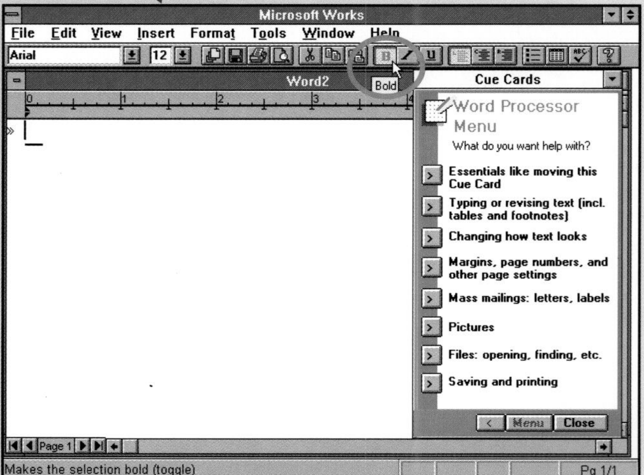

NOTE

After you click on the Bold button on the toolbar, it looks as though you have actually pressed it down. A "pressed down" button is an *active* button; clicking on it again makes it inactive, and it no longer looks pressed down.

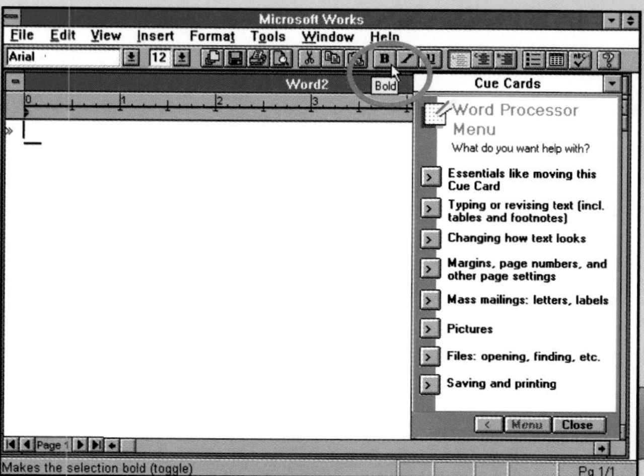

4 Click on the **Bold** button again to turn off boldface. Any text you type is normal (not bold, italicized, or underlined). You can type some more text to verify that it is not bold.

5 Click on the **Startup Dialog** button on the toolbar. Works displays the Startup dialog box for New & Recent Documents, but the document window stays open underneath.

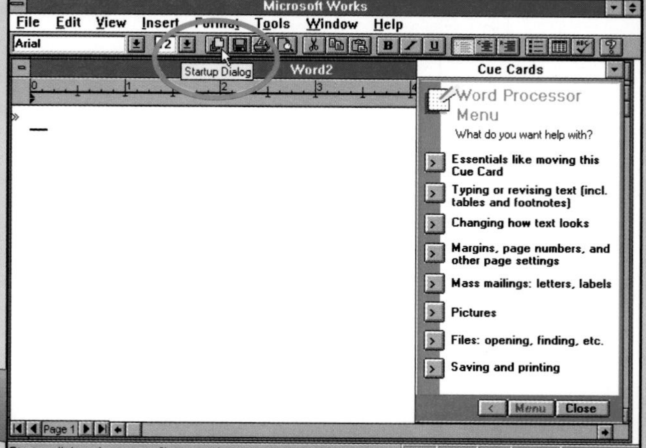

NOTE

One of the most important reasons for using Works is that you can work with multiple tools at once. The Startup Dialog toolbar button allows you to open another tool from the Startup dialog box for New & Recent Documents, yet the tool in which you have been working stays open.

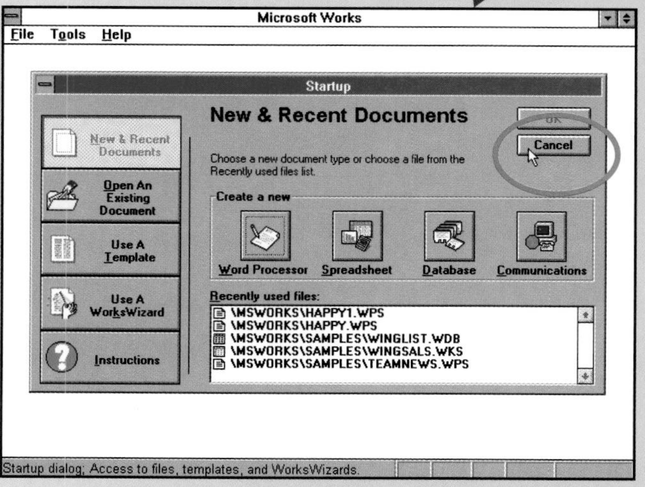

6 Click on the **Cancel** button. Clicking on the Cancel button closes a dialog box without saving any changes you made to it. Works returns to the document window.

TASK 4

Using Menus and Dialog Boxes

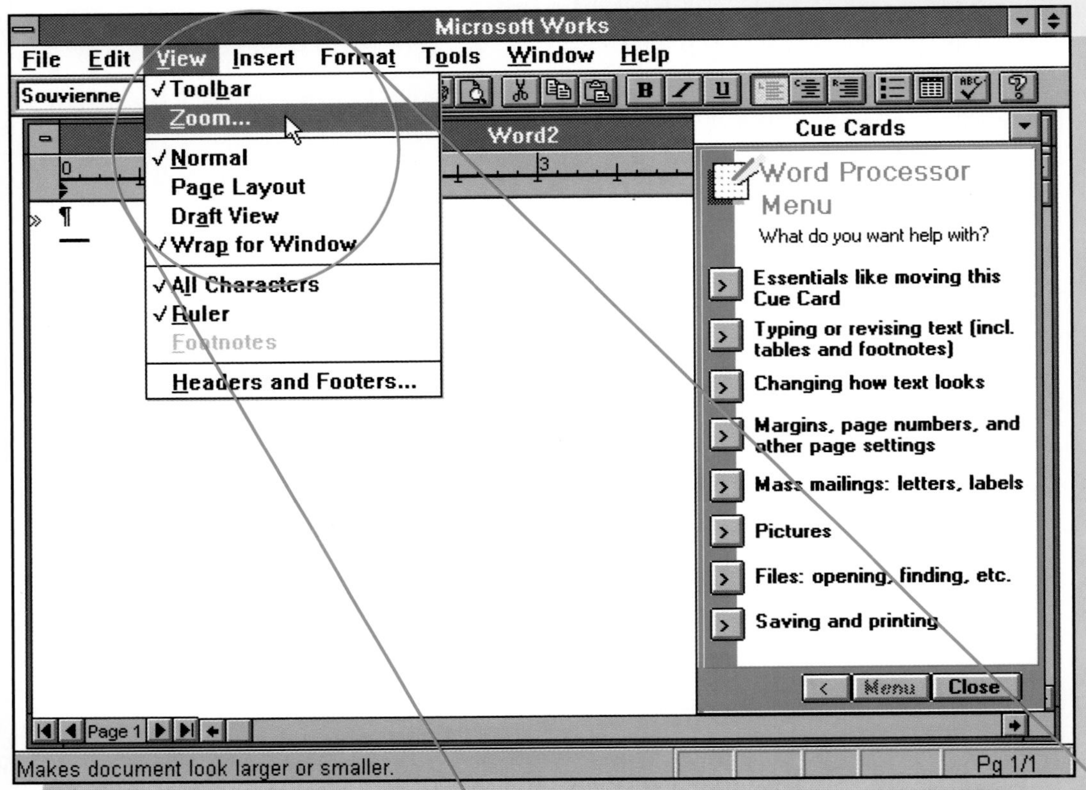

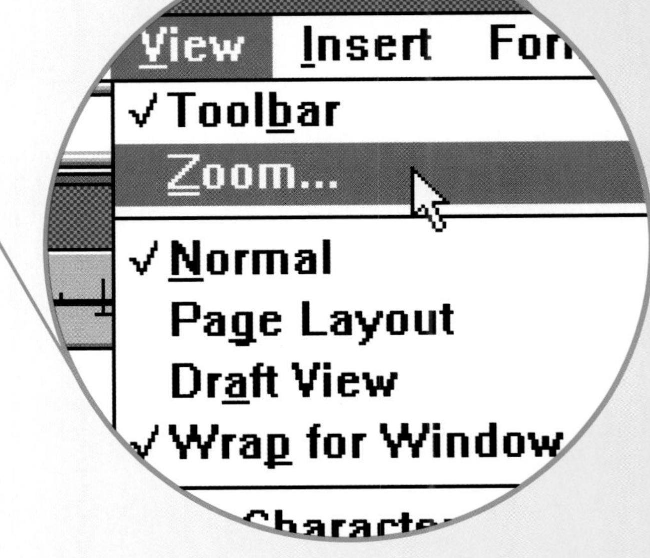

"Why would I do this?"

The building blocks in any Windows program are menus and dialog boxes, which provide commands and options for creating and editing documents. In this task, you use a special command and dialog box to shrink the size of the document on-screen.

This task assumes that the Word Processor document window appears on your screen.

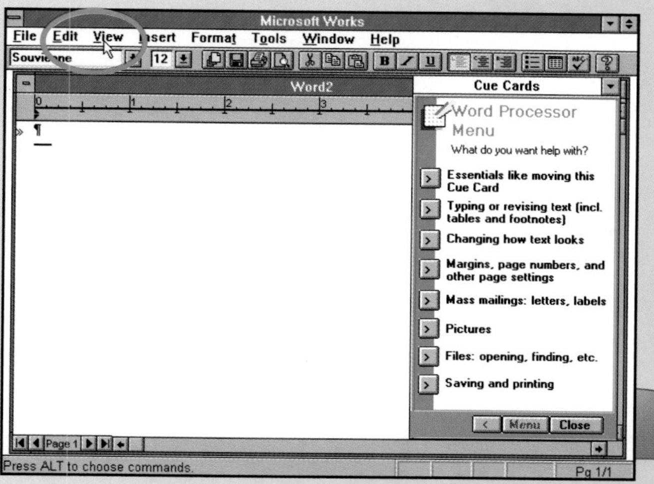

1 Click on **View** in the menu bar. This action opens the View menu, which contains commands that allow you to view the contents of a document in one of several ways and to display or hide elements at the top of the screen.

WHY WORRY?

To close a menu you don't want to use, click anywhere outside the menu or press Esc.

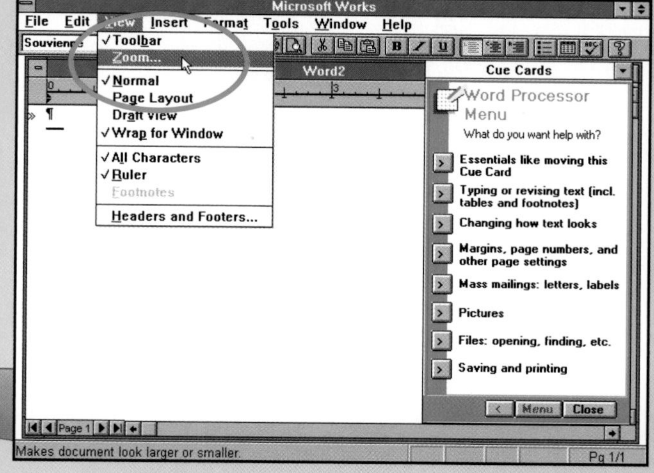

2 Click on **Zoom**. Works opens the Zoom dialog box. On any menu, a command followed by an ellipsis (...) indicates that choosing that command opens a dialog box.

NOTE

When a menu is open, the status bar displays a brief description of the highlighted command. Use the ↓ and ↑ keys to highlight a different command. To choose the highlighted command, press Enter.

3 Click on the circle next to **50**. To mark your selection, Works blackens the circle, or *option button*. You can select only one option button in a group. Selecting 50 means that you want to display the document window at 50 percent of its original size.

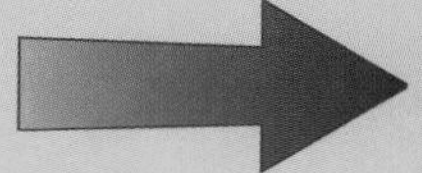

Task 4: Using Menus and Dialog Boxes

4 Click on **OK**. This step indicates that you are finished filling in the dialog box and want Works to implement your changes and close the dialog box.

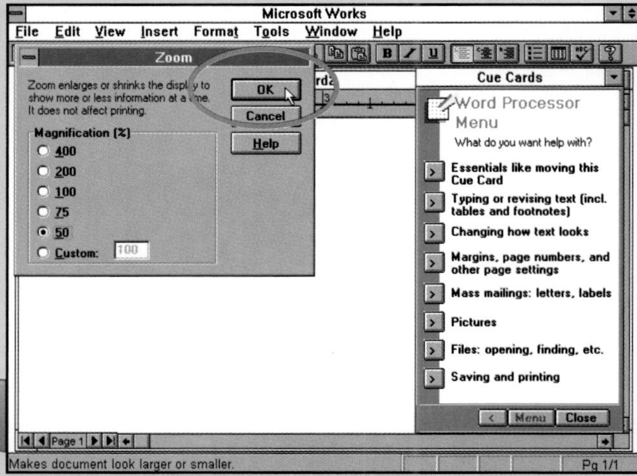

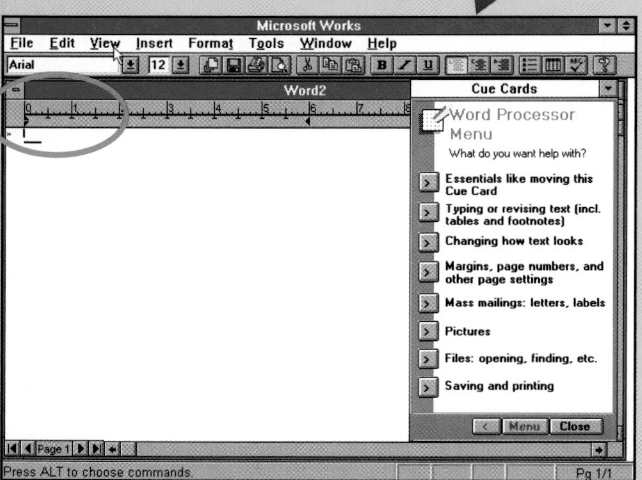

5 Notice that one inch on the ruler is about half the size shown on the 100% screen. To return the screen to 100% magnification, follow the preceding steps again, but select 100 in the Zoom dialog box.

NOTE

Zooming is viewing a document magnified (zoom in) so that you can see something close up, or reduced (zoom out) so that you can see an entire page on-screen.

TASK 5

Getting Help

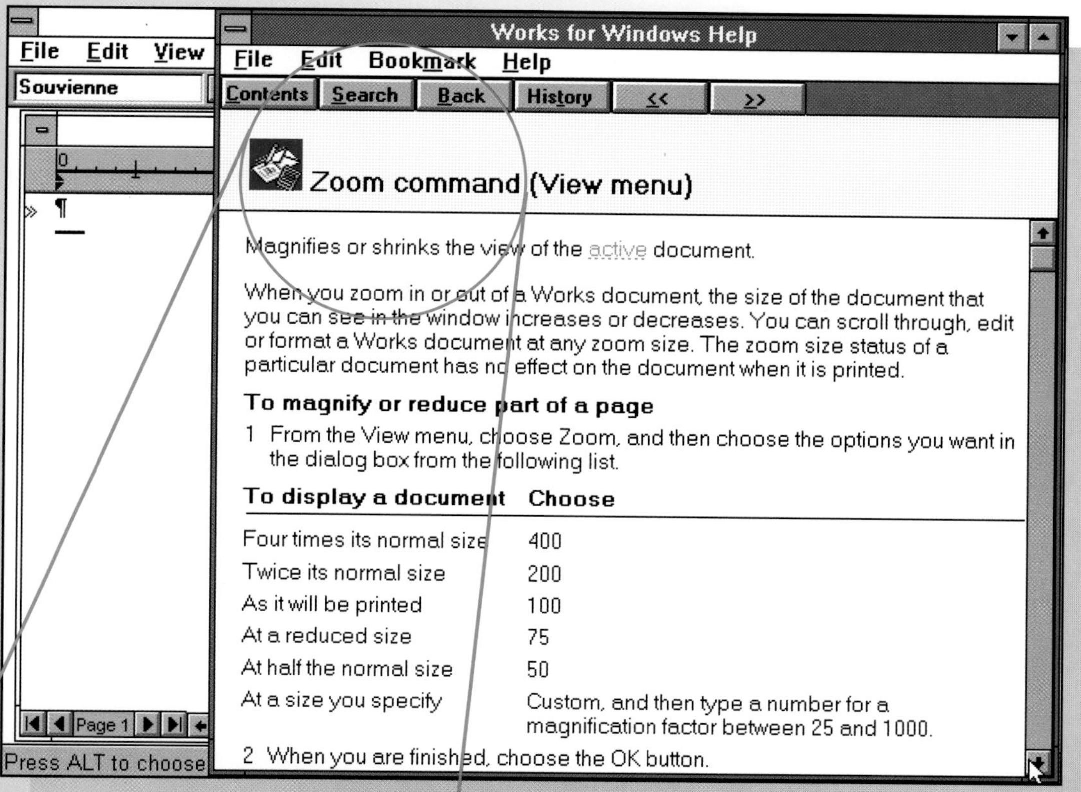

"Why would I do this?"

Microsoft Works provides several aids to getting your work done as easily and quickly as possible. You can rely on the Help menu commands, Cue Cards, AutoStart templates, and WorksWizards for the information you need. In this task, you learn how to search for and print a help topic from the Help menu.

This task assumes that the document window appears "unzoomed" (100%) on-screen and that your printer is turned on and ready to print.

Task 5: Getting Help

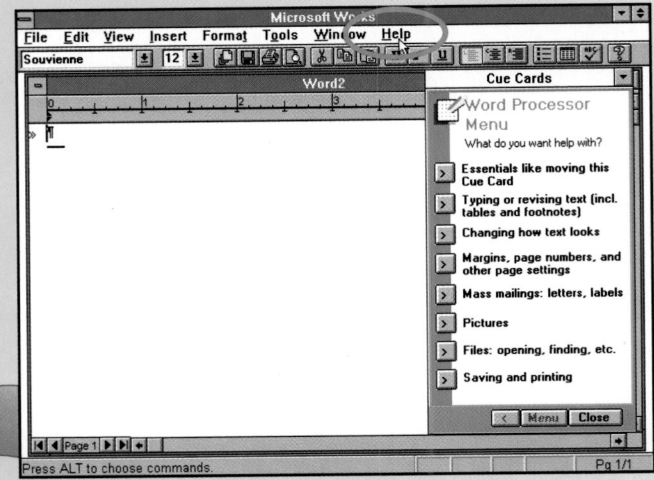

1 Click on **Help** in the menu bar. This step opens the Help menu to display its commands.

2 Click on **Search for Help on**. This command opens a dialog box with an alphabetical list of help topics.

3 Start typing **zooming** to get help with how to zoom in and out of a document. As you type, Works starts the search. For example, when you type *z*, Works highlights `zoom`. When you type *ing*, the highlight moves to `zooming a document`.

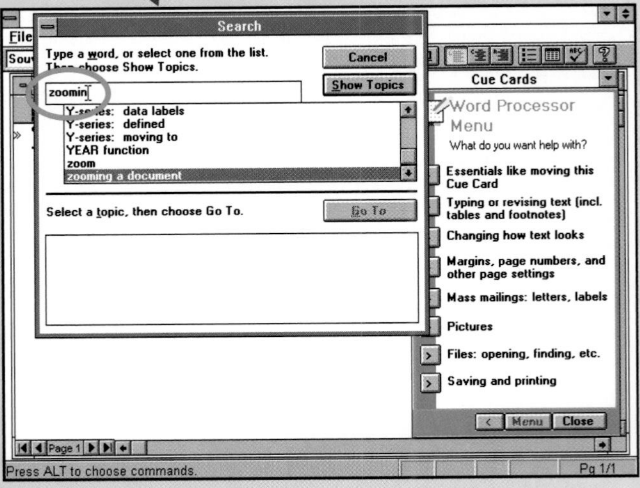

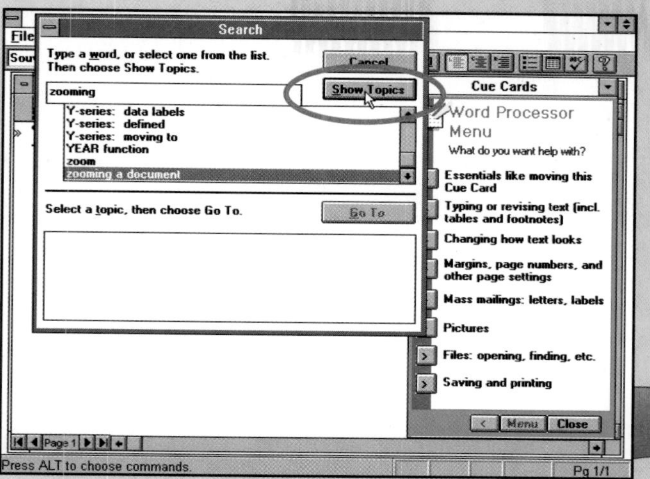

4 Click on **Show Topics**. Selecting this button shows you the list of help topics related to the word you typed. In this case, there is just one topic: `Zoom command (View menu)`.

NOTE

A command button with a thicker, darker border than other command buttons is the default button. To select the default button, you can either click on it or press Enter.

5 Click on **Go To**. This step displays the selected topic.

NOTE

If more than one help topic is displayed after you click on Show Topics, you must click on the topic you want to view before clicking on Go To.

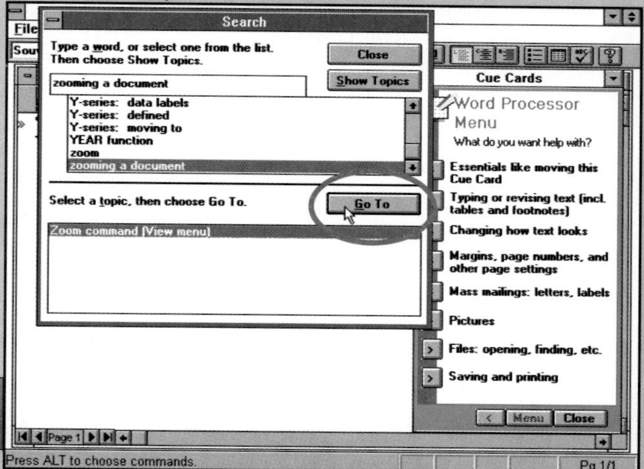

Works for Windows Help

File Edit Bookmark Help

Contents Search Back History << >>

Zoom command (View menu)

Magnifies or shrinks the view of the active document.

When you zoom in or out of a Works document, the size of the document that you can see in the window increases or decreases. You can scroll through, edit or format a Works document at any zoom size. The zoom size status of a particular document has no effect on the document when it is printed.

To magnify or reduce part of a page

1 From the View menu, choose Zoom, and then choose the options you want in the dialog box from the following list.

To display a document	Choose
Four times its normal size	400
Twice its normal size	200
As it will be printed	100
At a reduced size	75
At half the normal size	50
At a size you specify	Custom, and then type a number for a magnification factor between 25 and 1000.

2 When you are finished, choose the OK button.

6 After reading the displayed information, click on the **scroll arrow** at the bottom of the scroll bar to see the rest of the topic. This scrolls the topic down the screen.

7 Move the mouse pointer to **Toolbar shortcuts** at the very bottom of the topic. When the mouse pointer changes to a hand, click the left mouse button. This opens the topic *Toolbar shortcuts*.

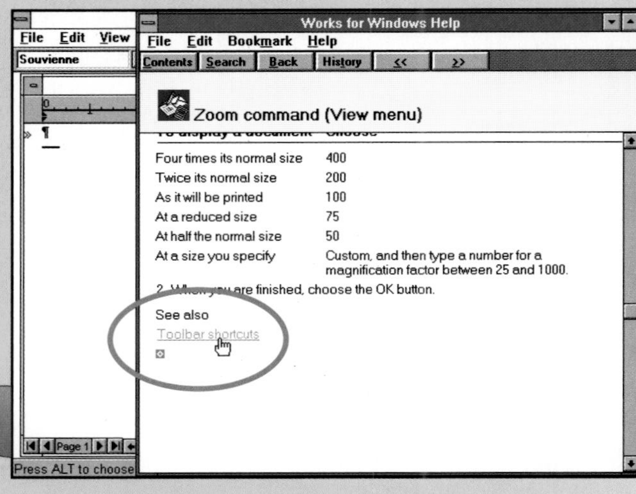

NOTE

Green, solidly underlined text within a help topic is known as *jump text*. When you click on jump text, you "jump" to another topic. To return to the previous help screen, click the Back button under the menu bar.

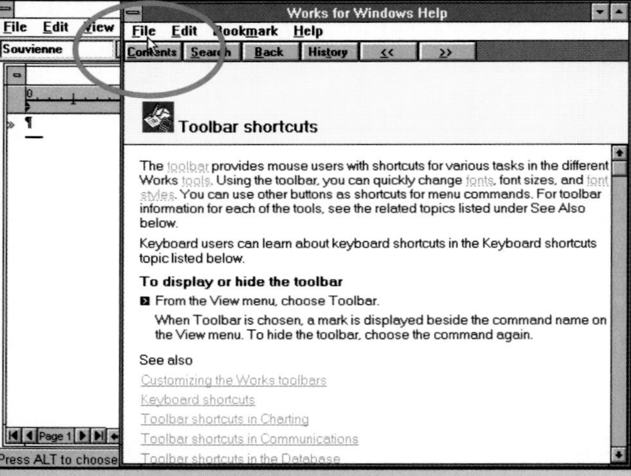

8 Click on **File** in the help window's menu bar. This opens a short File menu.

WHY WORRY?

If you accidentally click on File in the document window, the help window disappears and the Word Processor's File menu opens. To redisplay the help window, press Ctrl+Esc and double-click on Works for Windows Help in the task list.

9 Click on **Print Topic**. This step prints the topic displayed in the help window.

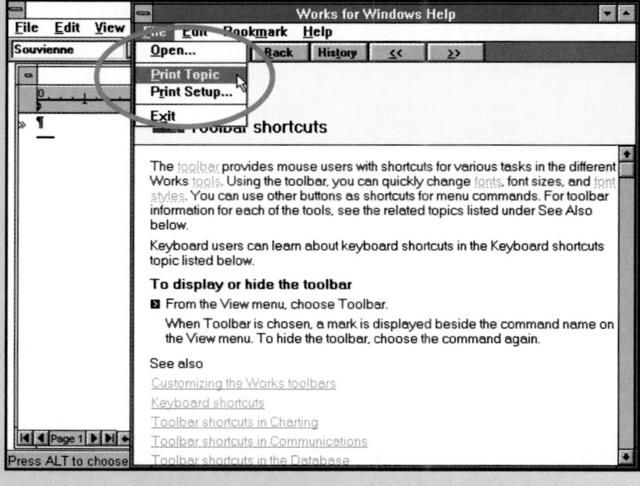

WHY WORRY?

If you start printing a help topic and decide that you'd prefer not to, you can click on the Cancel button in the dialog box that Works displays right before it prints. If you aren't quick enough and the printing begins, don't worry; help topics normally aren't longer than one or two pages.

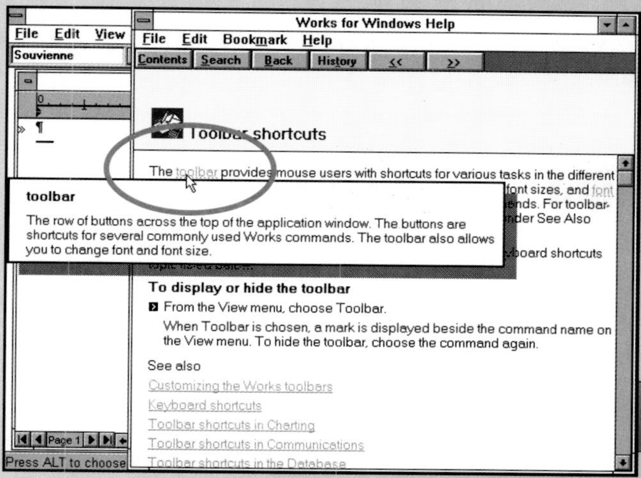

10 Click on **toolbar**, the green word with a dashed underline in the first line of the help text. This displays a short description of the word.

NOTE

Within a help topic, green text underlined in dashes indicates that there is a short definition associated with the text. Click on the text to display a small box containing the definition.

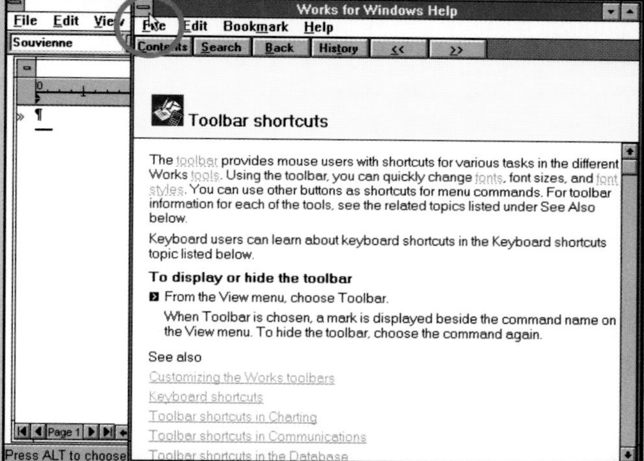

11 Double-click on the **Control menu** button at the top left corner of the help window. The help window closes and you return to the document window.

WHY WORRY?

If the topic for which you are searching has no help topics, first check for spelling or typing mistakes. Then try typing a synonym. You can also choose Contents from the Help menu to see whether one of the items in the Contents window leads to the topic you want.

TASK 6

Using Cue Cards

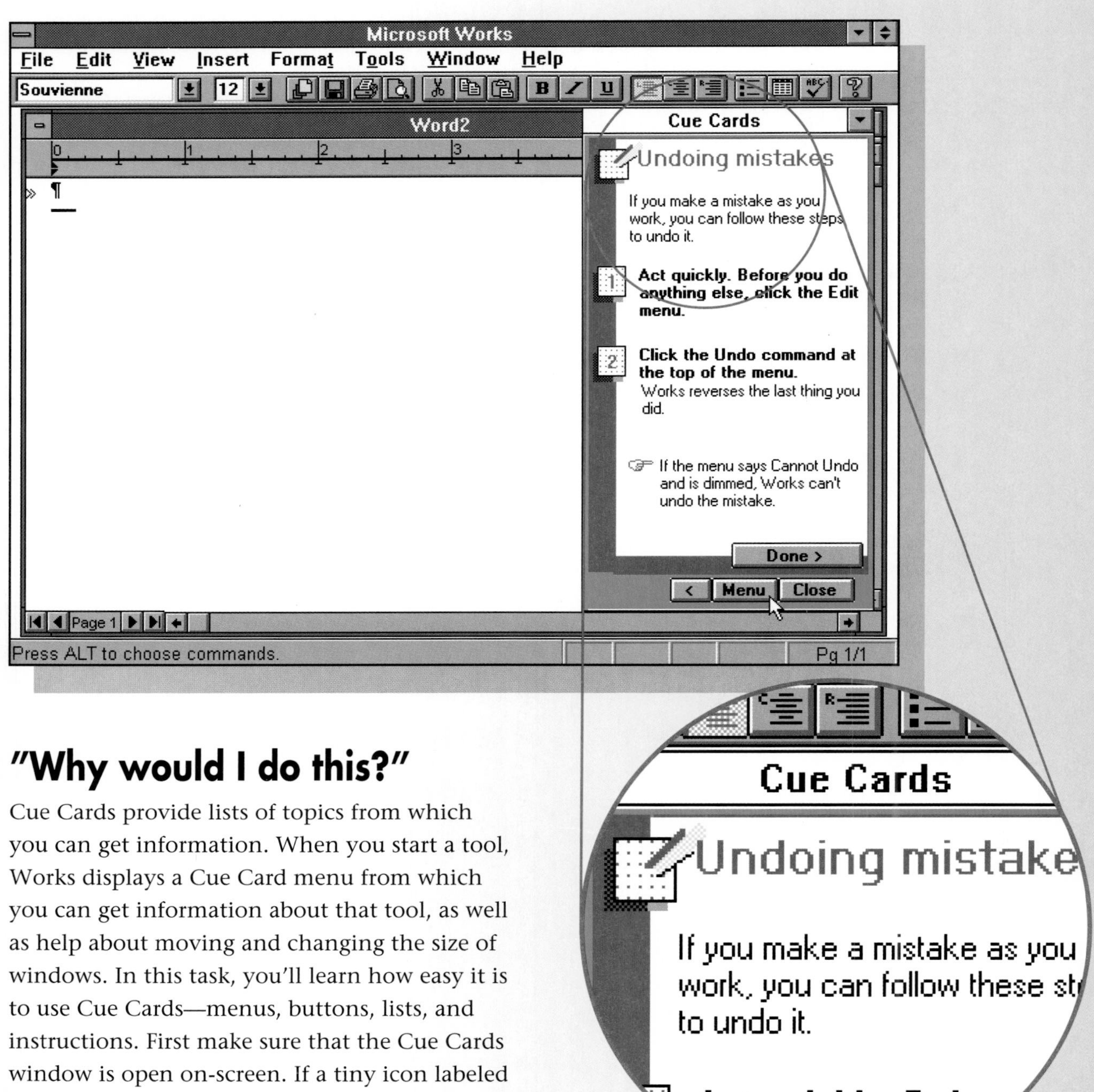

"Why would I do this?"

Cue Cards provide lists of topics from which you can get information. When you start a tool, Works displays a Cue Card menu from which you can get information about that tool, as well as help about moving and changing the size of windows. In this task, you'll learn how easy it is to use Cue Cards—menus, buttons, lists, and instructions. First make sure that the Cue Cards window is open on-screen. If a tiny icon labeled *Cue Cards* appears at the bottom of your screen, double-click on it to open the Cue Cards window.

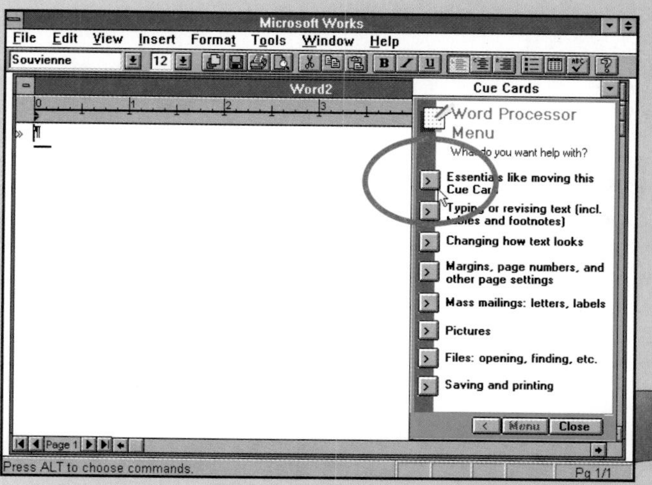

1 Click on the button next to **Essentials like moving this Cue Card**. This step displays the Essentials Menu screen. Buttons marked with right-pointing arrowheads indicate topics on which you can click.

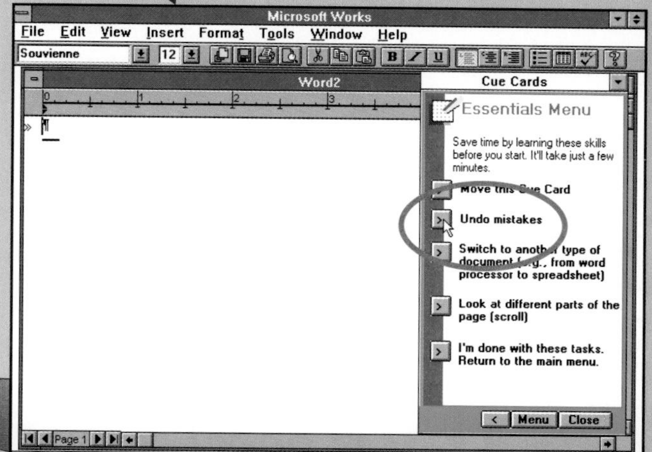

2 Click on the button to the left of **Undo mistakes**. Works displays the Undoing mistakes screen. Boxes containing numbers indicate items you should read.

WHY WORRY?

Clicking on the Close button at the bottom of any Cue Cards window closes the Cue Cards—not a good idea when you are a beginner. If you inadvertently close the Cue Cards, you can get them back by opening the Help menu and choosing the Cue Cards command.

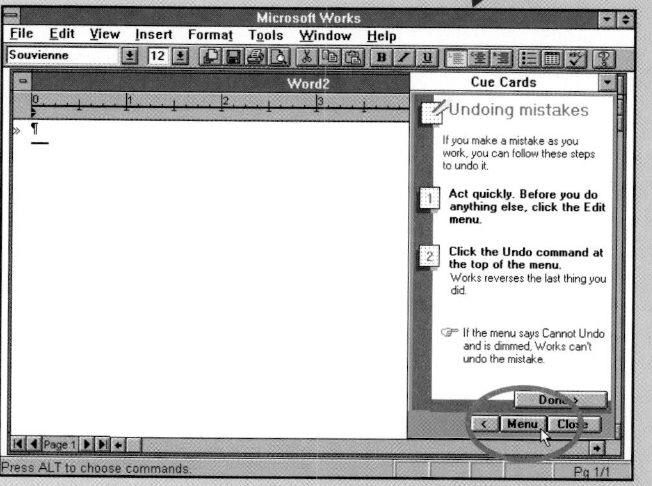

3 Click on the **Menu** button. This step returns you to the main Cue Cards menu for the tool you are presently using.

If you click on the Done button in a Cue Card window, you return to the menu from which you started. Using this task as an example, clicking on Done would return you to the Essentials Menu screen.

TASK 7

Creating a New File with an AutoStart Template

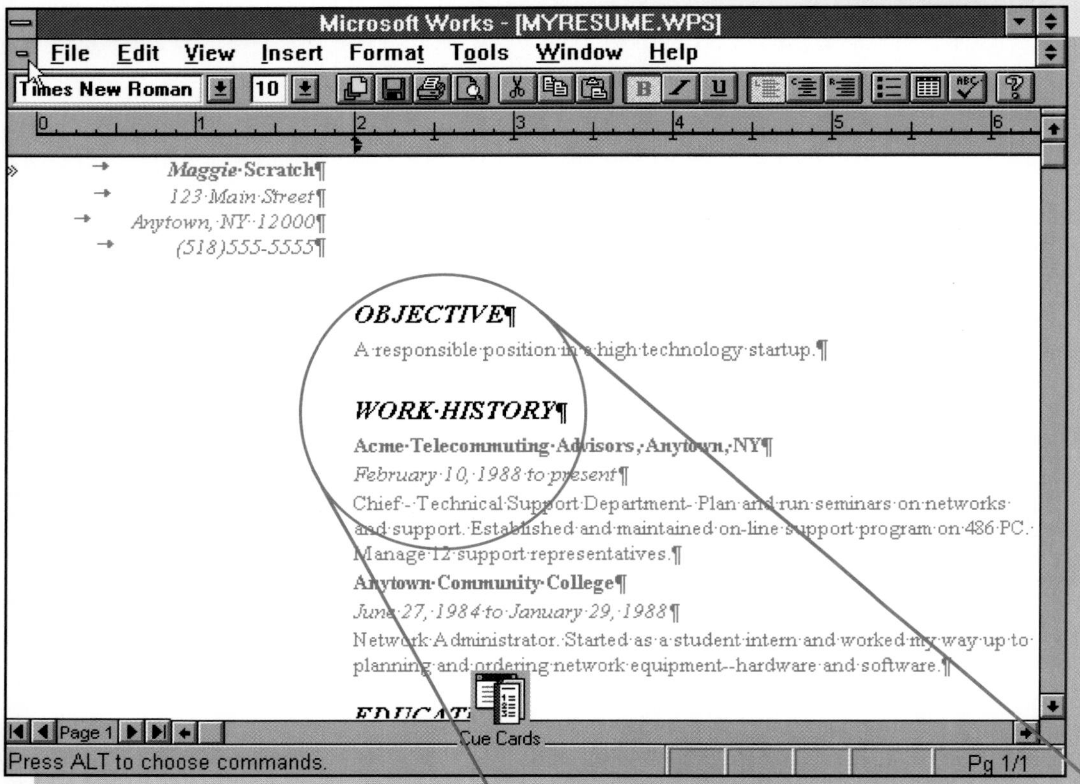

"Why would I do this?"

Works offers *AutoStart templates,* which allow you to work with files that are formatted and filled in. All you need to do with an AutoStart template is open it and replace its information with your own—a real time-saver. In this task, you will work on a resume.

This task assumes that the Word Processor tool is active and that the document window is empty.

Task 7: Creating a New File with an AutoStart Template

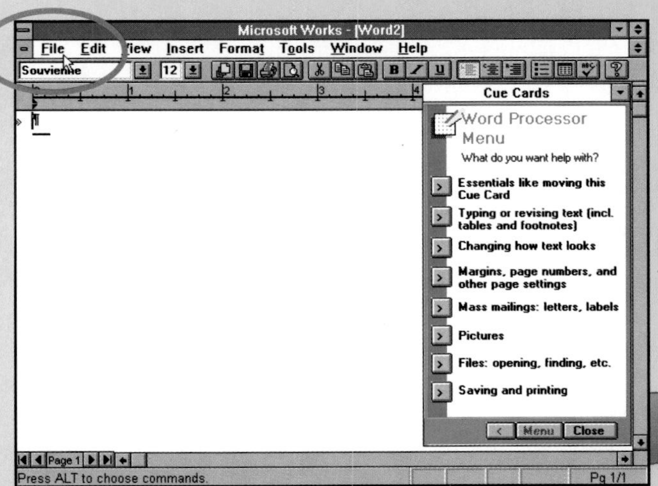

1 Click on **File** in the menu bar. This step opens the File menu.

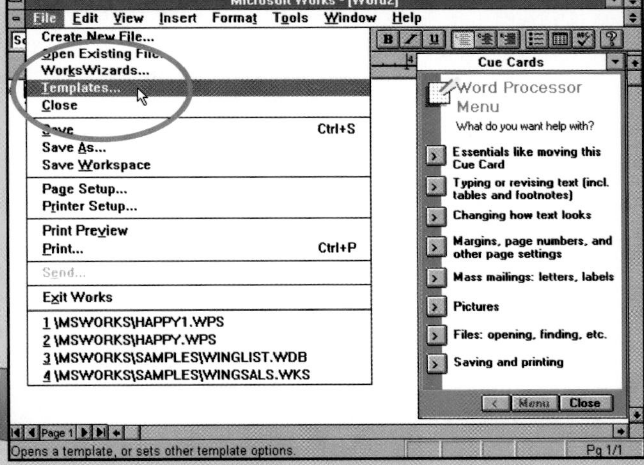

2 Click on **Templates**. Works opens the Use A Template Startup dialog box.

NOTE

If you are starting at the Startup dialog box for New & Recent Documents, click on the Use A Template button to open the Use A Template Startup dialog box.

3 Open the **Choose a template group** drop-down list box and click on the **AutoStart Personal** template group.

NOTE

To open a drop-down list box, click on the down-arrow button to the right of the box. To close a drop-down list box, make a selection, press Esc, or click on the down-arrow button again.

Task 7: Creating a New File with an AutoStart Template

4 Click on **Documents** in the Choose a category list box. In the Choose a template list, Works displays *Résumé*, the only template in the Documents category.

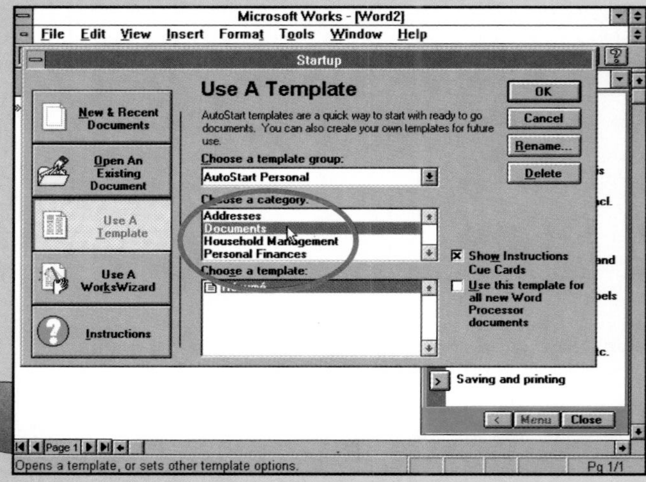

5 Double-click on **Résumé** in the Choose a template list box. Double-clicking is a shortcut for selecting an option (clicking once) and then clicking on OK. This step opens the resume template and the related Cue Cards screen.

6 Replace all the red text with your own information.

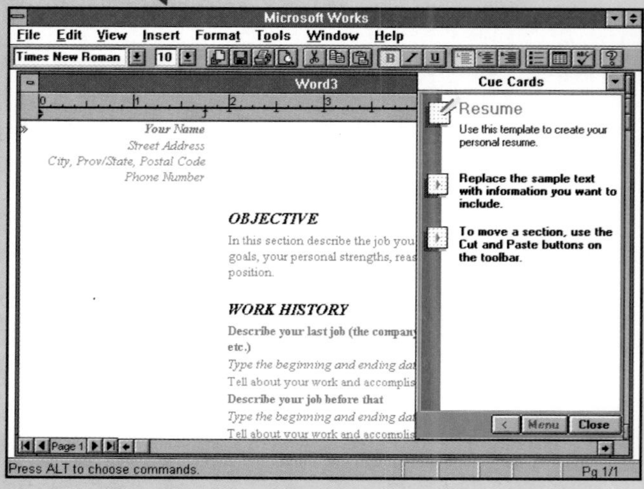

Creating a New File with a WorksWizard

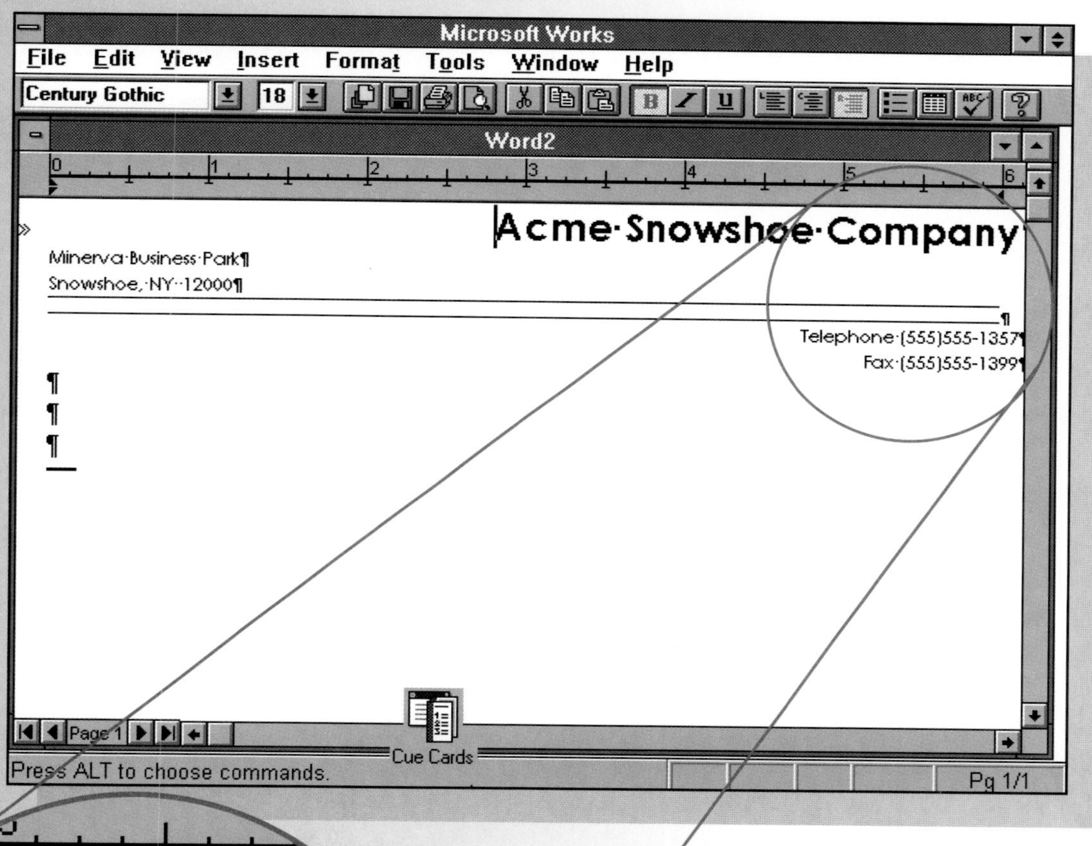

"Why would I do this?"

WorksWizards allow you to create files by answering a few simple questions on-screen. Then you click on one button, and Works creates a formatted document for you. All you have to do is add some information and save the file for later use. In this task, you will create a letterhead to use for all your correspondence.

This task assumes that the Startup dialog box for New & Recent Documents is open in the Word Processor tool.

Task 8: Creating a New File with a WorksWizard

1 Click on the **Use A WorksWizard** button. This step opens the Use A WorksWizard Startup dialog box.

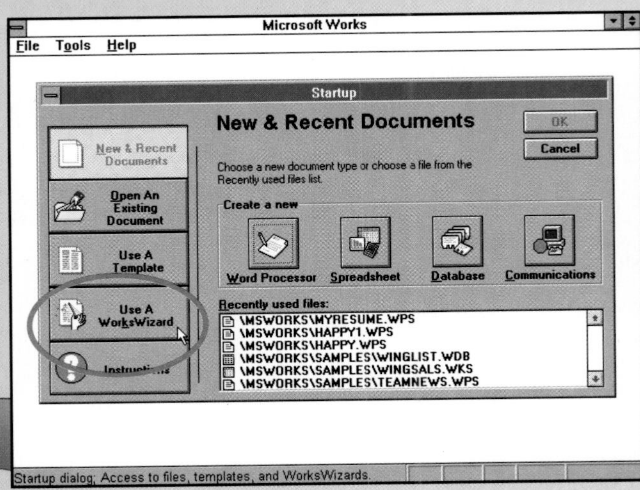

NOTE

If you are in a blank document window rather than the New & Recent Documents dialog box, open the File menu and choose the WorksWizards command to open the Use A WorksWizards dialog box.

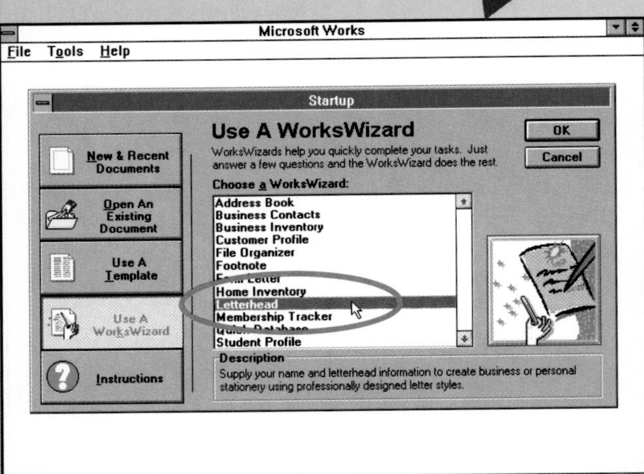

2 Double-click on **Letterhead** in the Choose a WorksWizard list box. Double-clicking is a shortcut for selecting Letterhead and clicking the OK button. You see a Welcome message.

NOTE

When you click once on an option in the list box, the Description box changes to describe the WorksWizard you selected.

3 After you read the Welcome message, click on the **Next** button to start creating your letterhead.

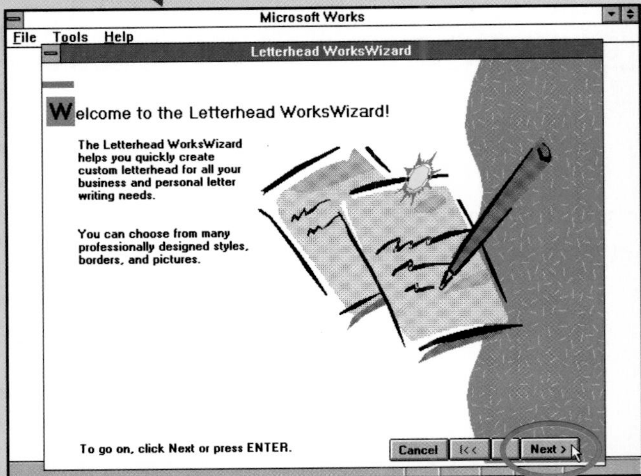

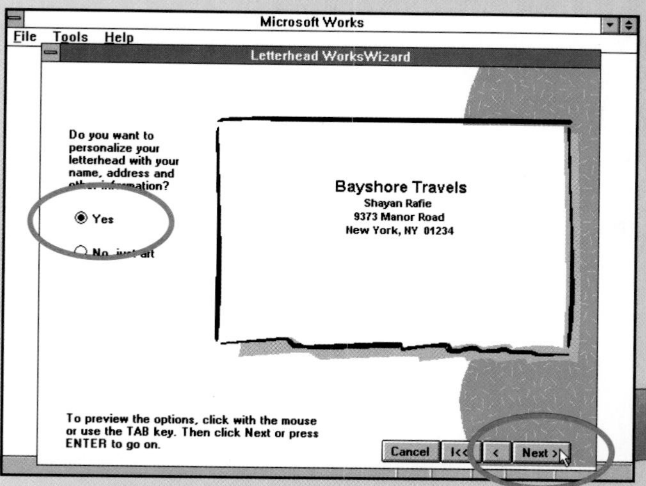

4 Click on the **Yes** option button and click on **Next**. Clicking Yes indicates that you want to create a simple letterhead with information such as your name, your company's name, address, and telephone numbers. The next screen appears.

5 Click on **My business name** and click on **Next**. Before you click on Next, the sample on the right side of the window illustrates how your option button choice will affect your letterhead. If you select *My initials only*, you can type your initials in the text box; otherwise, that text box isn't available.

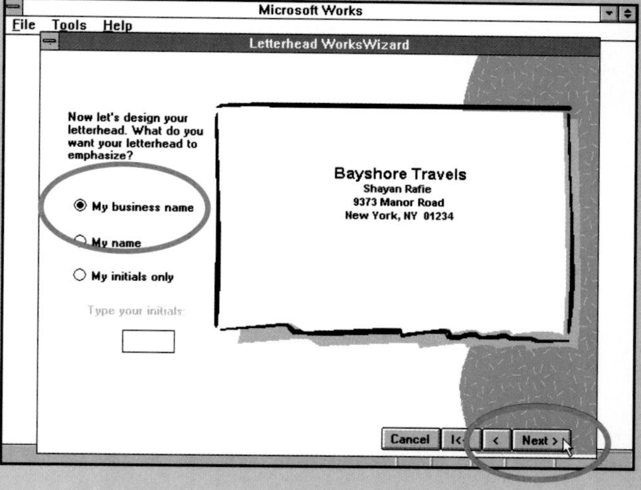

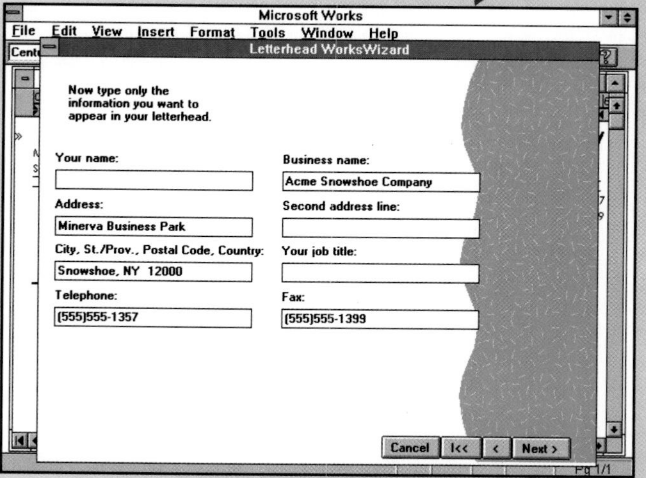

6 Type your address information in the text boxes. For example, type **Acme Snowshoe Company** in the Business Name text box, **Minerva Business Park** in Address, **Showshoe NY 12000** in City, **(555)555-1357** in Telephone, and **(555)555-1399** in the Fax text box. To move to the next text box, click in that box or press Tab. Press Shift+Tab to move to the previous text box.

Task 8: Creating a New File with a WorksWizard

7 Click on **Next**. This step moves you to the next screen of the Letterhead WorksWizard.

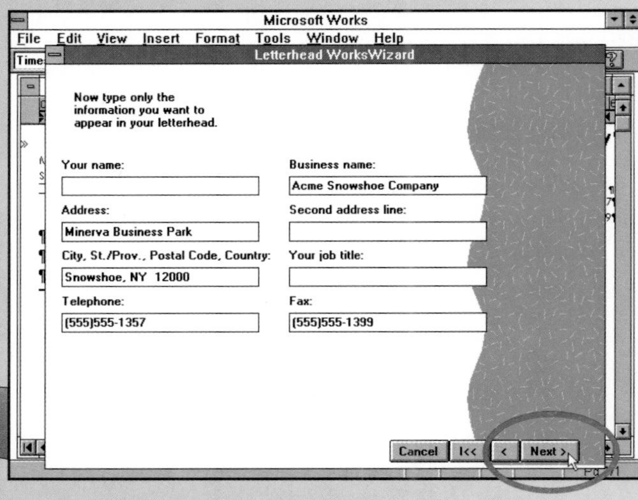

8 Click on **Prestige** and click on **Next**. Check the look of each Letterhead style by clicking on each option button in turn. On many WorksWizard screens, your choice determines the content of the next screen.

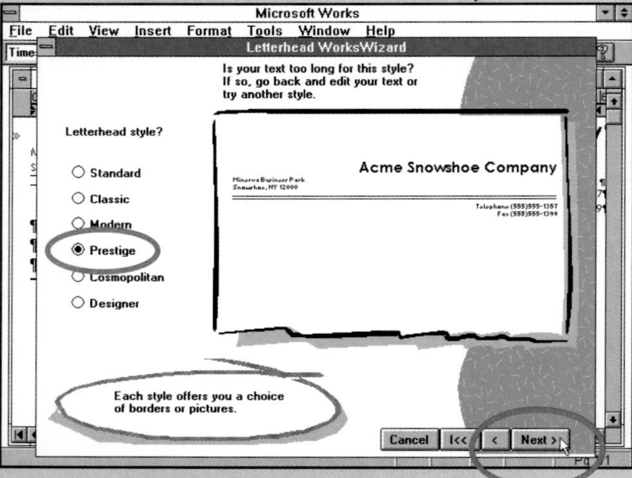

9 Click on the **third** option button and click on **Next**. This step selects a line design.

WHY WORRY?

If you don't like the way a WorksWizard document is turning out, you can start over or just go back to the previous screen. To return to the first Works-Wizard screen, click on the button to the right of Cancel (I<<). To return to the previous screen, click on the button to the left of Next (<).

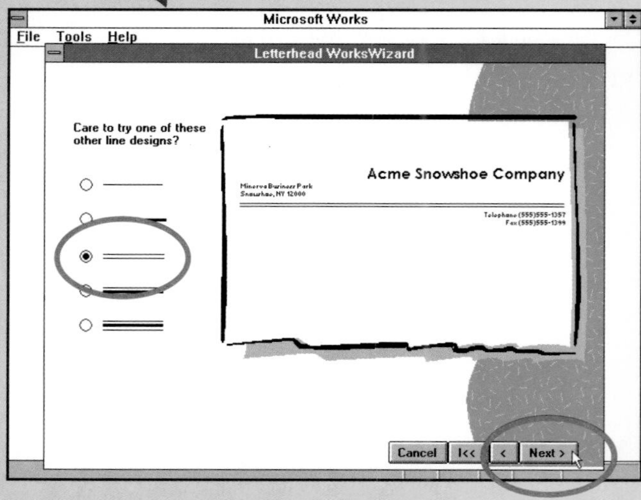

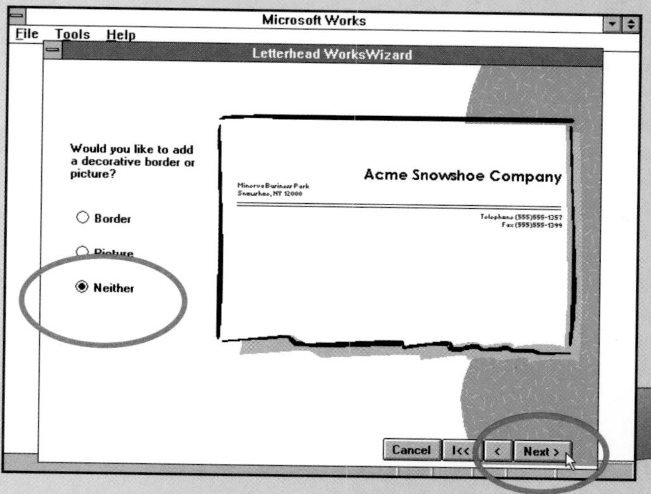

10 Click on **Neither** to skip adding a decorative border or picture. Then click on **Next**.

NOTE

When creating a letterhead or any other document, simplicity is your best bet.

WHY WORRY?

If you don't want to continue creating a document with the WorksWizard, you can click on the Cancel button in any screen.

11 Click on **Create** to let the WorksWizard turn all your choices into a letterhead. The WorksWizard goes through a series of steps that builds your letterhead and displays a "finishing line" screen.

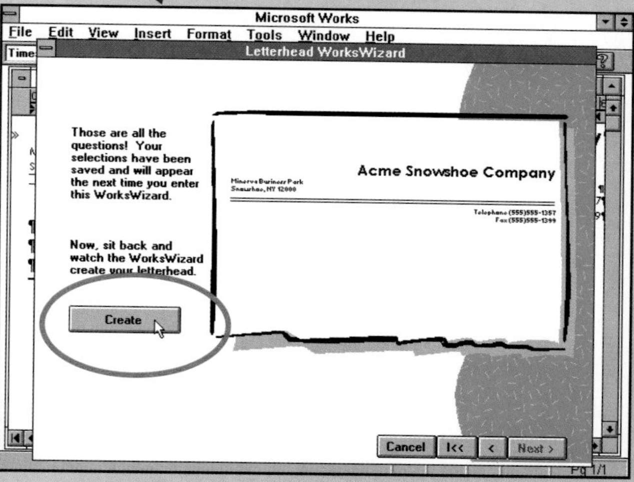

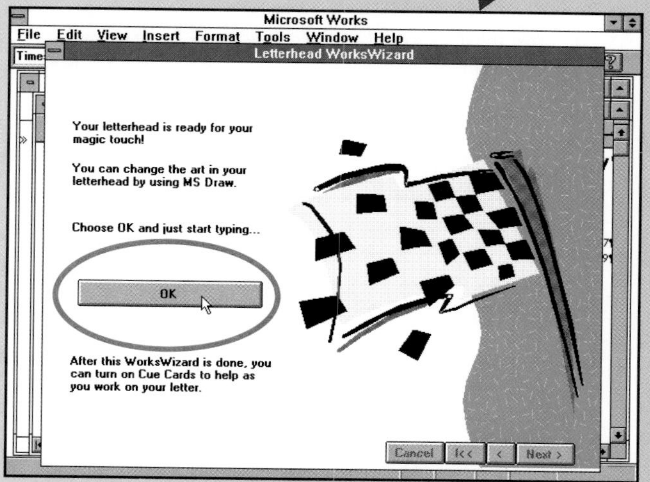

12 Click on **OK**. Your letterhead appears at the top of a document window.

NOTE

Minimize the Cue Cards window to reveal more of your letterhead.

TASK 9

Creating a New File from Scratch

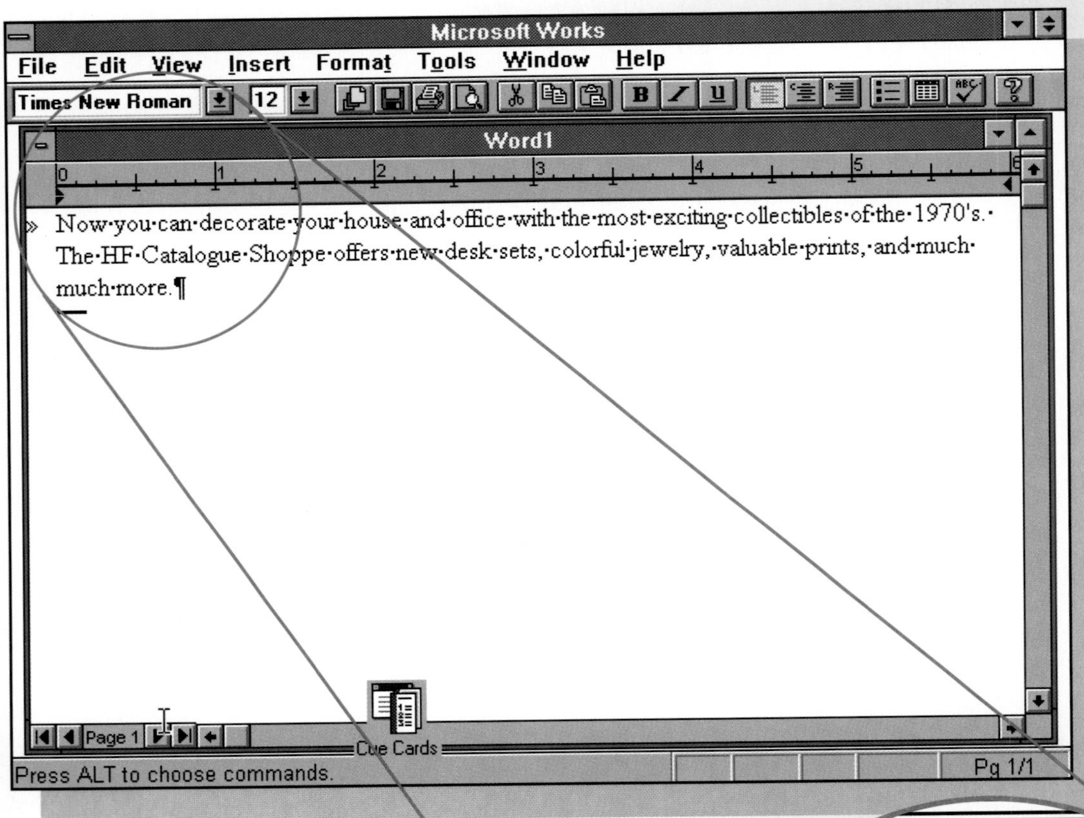

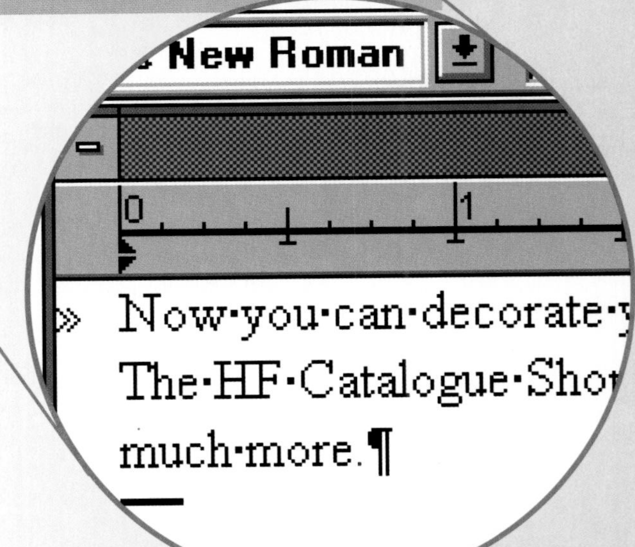

"Why would I do this?"

Many times you'll have to create a document, spreadsheet, or database from within an empty Works window. Whether you're writing a note to yourself, balancing your finances, or organizing your inventory, creating a new file in Works is easy. In this task, you start the Word Processor tool and create a document. This task assumes that you have started Works and that the New & Recent Documents Startup dialog box is on-screen.

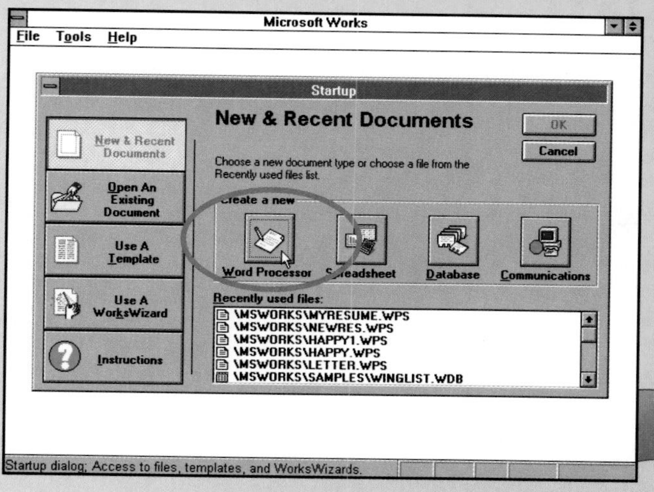

1 Click on the Word Processor, Spreadsheet, or Database button, depending on the type of file you want to create; for this example, click on the **Word Processor** button. (Because the New & Recent Documents button is active—that is, it looks "pressed down"—you don't need to click on it.) Works displays a document window and the Cue Cards window, which displays information about the Word Processor menu.

2 Click on the **Minimize** button in the Cue Cards window to provide typing room in the document window.

NOTE

This step is optional; however, minimizing the Cue Cards gives you more room to work on-screen.

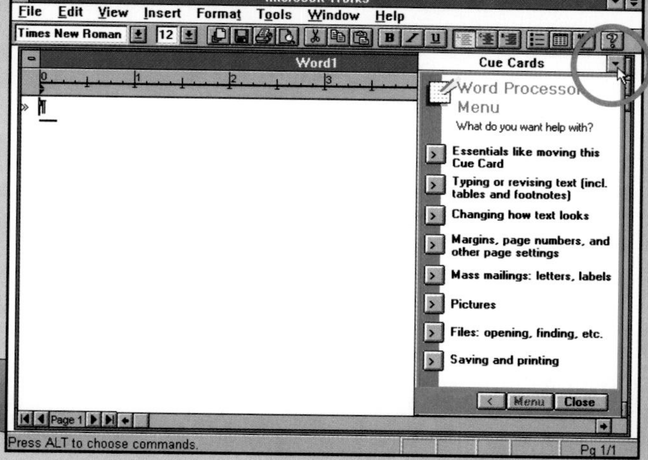

3 Now you can type your document, create your spreadsheet, or design your database.

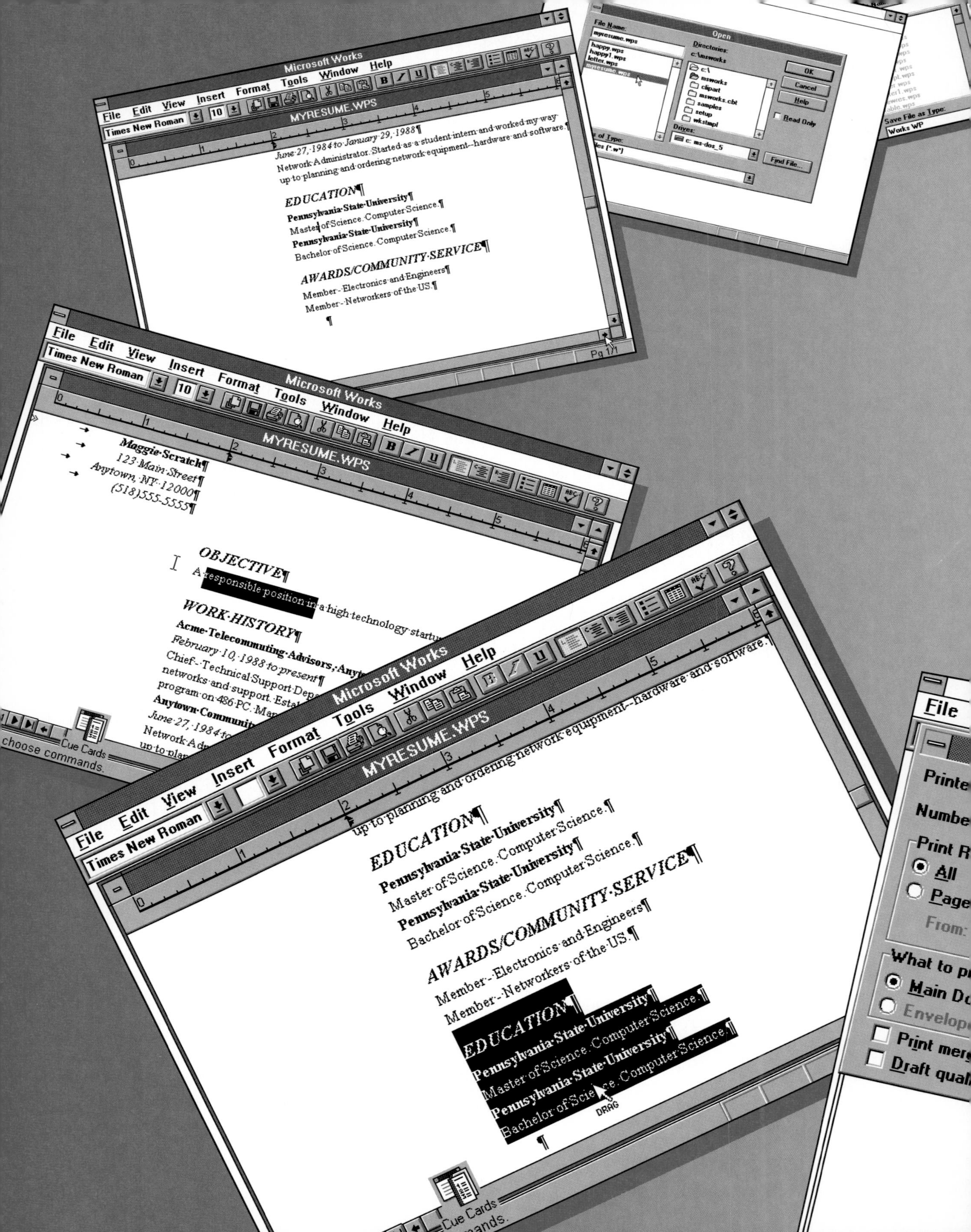

Microsoft Works
MYRESUME.WPS
Maggie Scratch
123 Main Street
Anytown, NY 12000
(518)555-5555
OBJECTIVE
A responsible position in a high technology startu
WORK HISTORY
EDUCATION
Pennsylvania State University
Master of Science. Computer Science.
Pennsylvania State University
Bachelor of Science. Computer Science.
AWARDS/COMMUNITY SERVICE
Member - Electronics and Engineers
Member - Networkers of the US.
DRAG
Cue Cards
Open

PART II

Working with Files

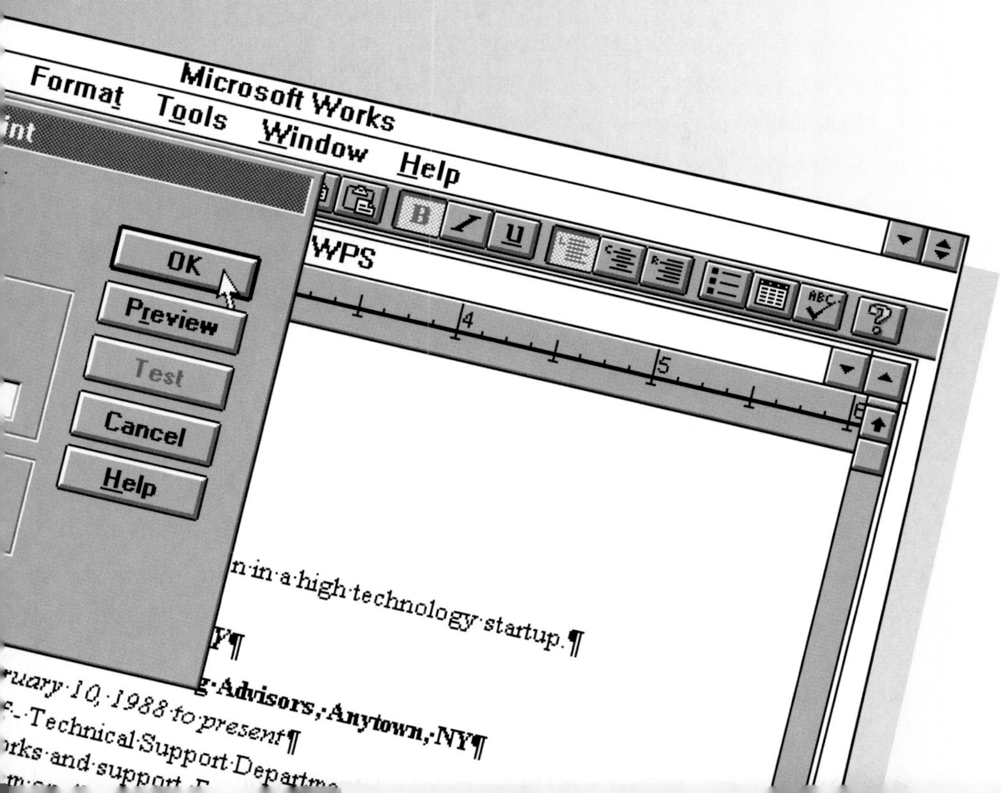

Part II: Working with Files

Part II of this book tells you everything you want to know about working with files. You'll find the information in this part useful for Works and other Windows applications.

In this part, you'll learn essential file management techniques—how to open a file, how to save it, how to close a file without saving, and how to print. Once you have mastered these techniques, you'll be able to use them in any Works tool.

Part II also introduces you to editing methods that are common to all Works tools. Before you can start modifying a file using Works Edit menu commands, you have to make a selection. Then you can copy, move, and even delete the selection.

With Works Undo command, you can cancel editing mistakes before they become permanent. For example, if you inadvertently delete several pages of information, choose Edit Undo (or press Ctrl+Z) to "undelete" your mistake.

Although you will learn how to print in Part II, each tool has its own printing options. Refer to your Works documentation for information about specific printing options for each tool.

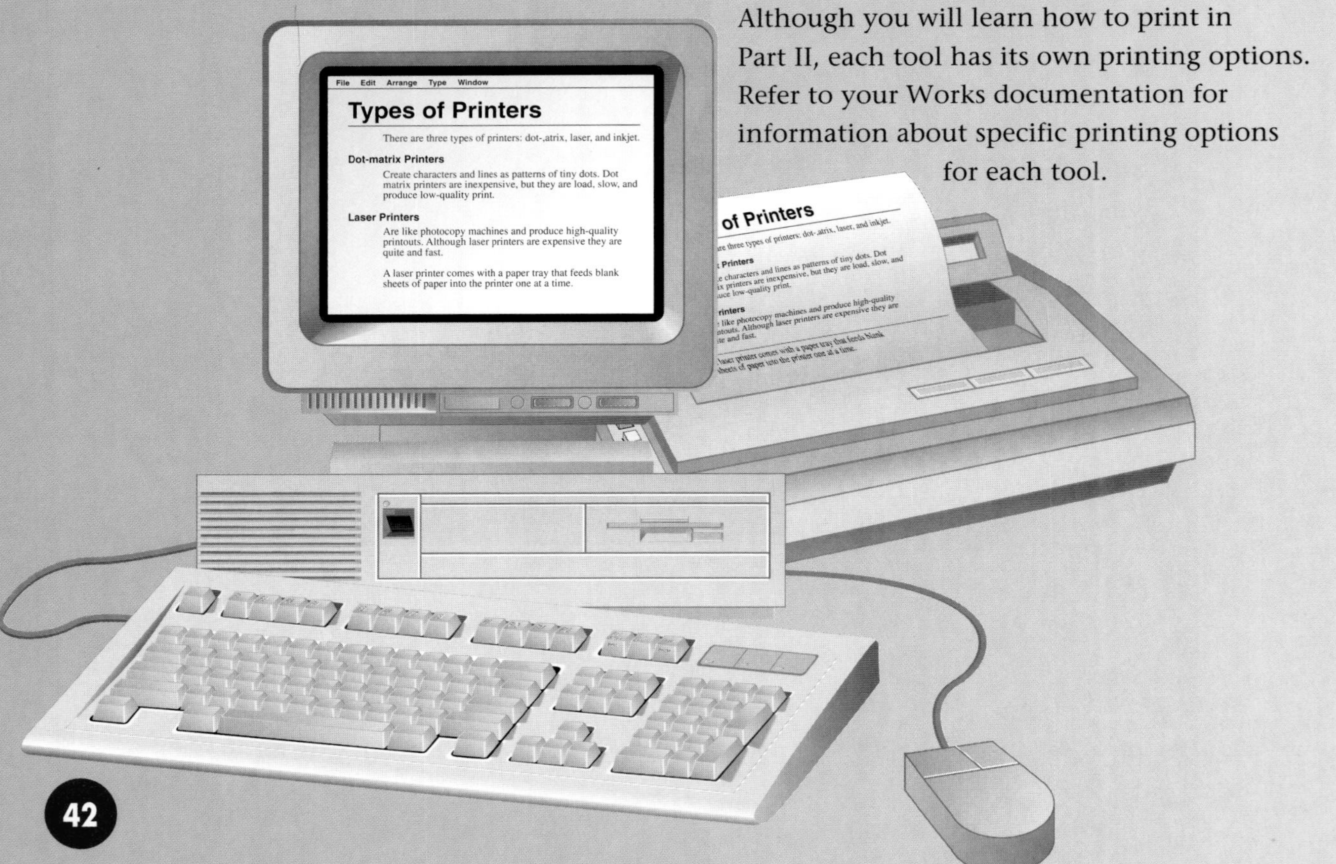

You can use the following shortcut keys and key combinations throughout Works:

Shortcut Key	Description
F1	Get help
F10	Activate the menu bar
Enter	Select the default command button
Esc	Close a dialog box or menu
Tab	Move to the next option in a dialog box
Shift+Tab	Move to the prior option in a dialog box
↓	Move to the next menu command
↑	Move to the prior menu command
Ctrl+Home	Move to the top of the file
Ctrl+End	Move to the bottom of the file
Ctrl+Z	Undo the last action
Ctrl+C	Copy the selection
Ctrl+X	Cut the selection
Ctrl+V	Paste the selection
Del	Delete the selection
Ctrl+P	Print a document
Ctrl+S	Save a document

The tasks in Part II cover common file-management techniques for all Works tools.

TASK 10

Saving and Closing a File

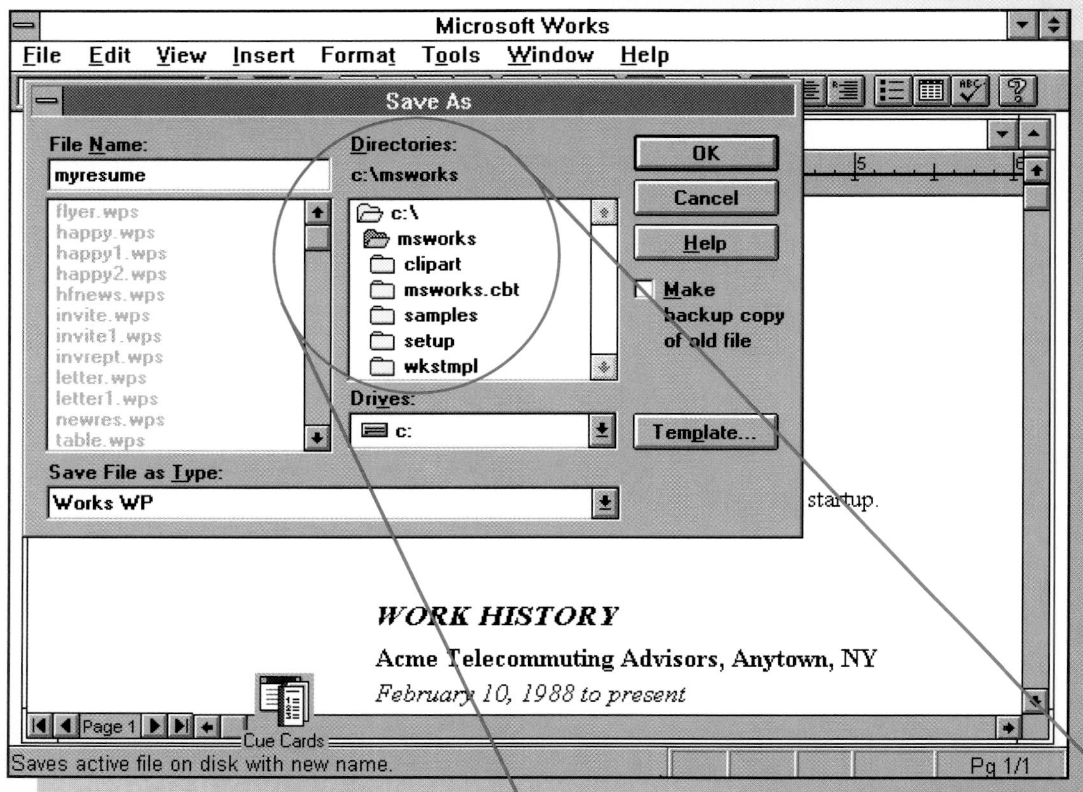

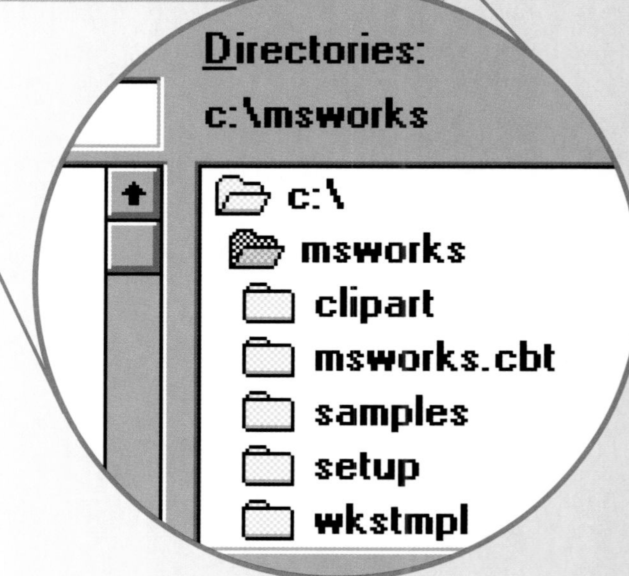

"Why would I do this?"

You should save files not only at the end of a work session, but every few minutes. When you save a file, you are actually creating a backup copy. Then, if there's ever a disk or power failure, you'll have a very recent version of your work. In this task, you will save a file, learn how to name files properly, and close a file.

This task assumes that a resume appears on-screen. You can use the Resume AutoStart Template to build a resume, or use a document of your own.

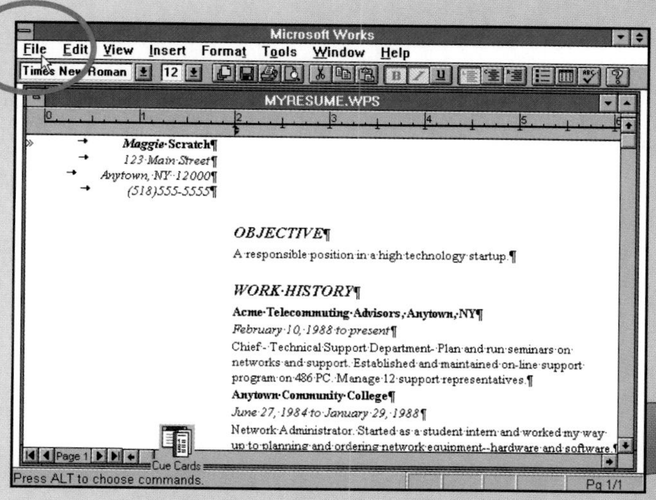

1 Click on **File** in the menu bar. This action opens the File menu.

2 Click on the **Save As** command. This step opens the Save As dialog box, regardless of whether you have already saved the file (and therefore named it).

NOTE

You can click the Save button on the toolbar to save a file. This shortcut is equivalent to choosing Save from the File menu. If you are saving the file for the first time, Works opens the Save As dialog box so that you can name the file.

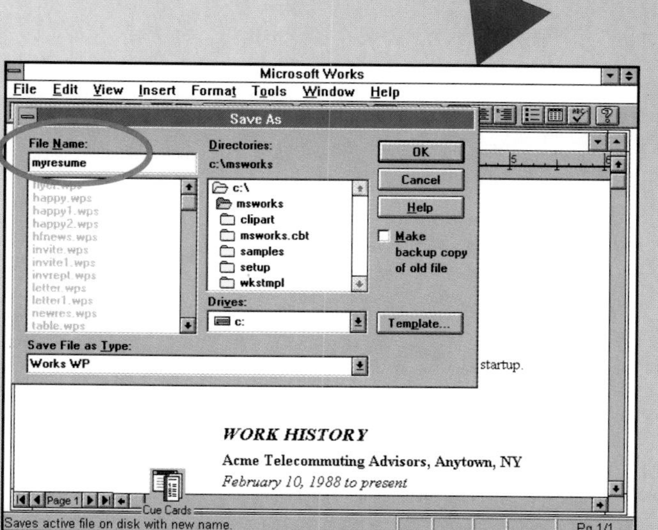

3 Type **myresume** in File Name text box in the Save As dialog box. This step specifies a name for your resume document.

Task 10: Saving and Closing a File

4 Click on **OK**. This saves the file with its new name and closes the dialog box.

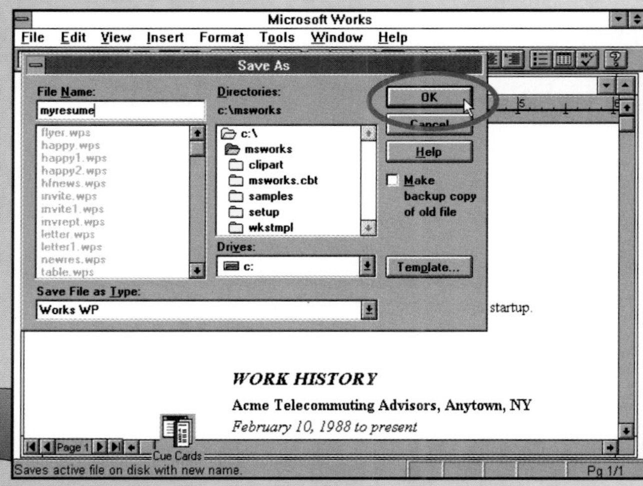

WHY WORRY?

One of the biggest worries for those working with computers is a sudden loss of electrical power. When the electricity fails, you lose all your unsaved work. Therefore, when creating or editing a document, save your work every few minutes by clicking on the Save button on the toolbar.

5 Click on **File** in the menu bar. This step opens the File menu.

6 Click on the **Close** command. This closes a file whether or not you have saved it. Works closes the document window and displays the New & Recent Documents Startup dialog box.

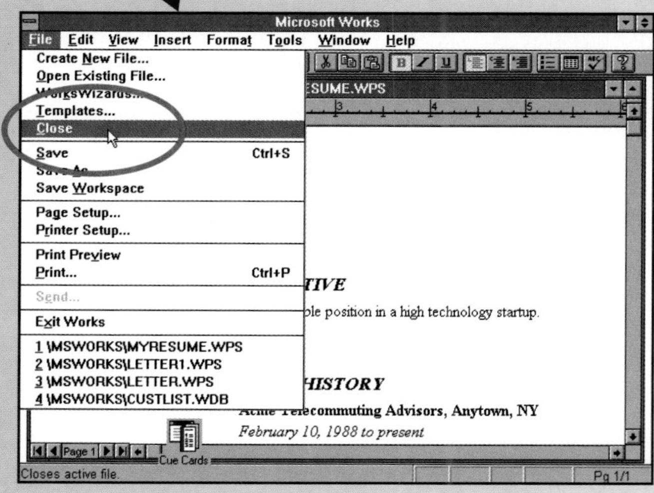

NOTE

If you change a file after saving it and then try to close the file, Works prompts you to save it. Click on Yes to save or on No to close without saving.

Opening a File

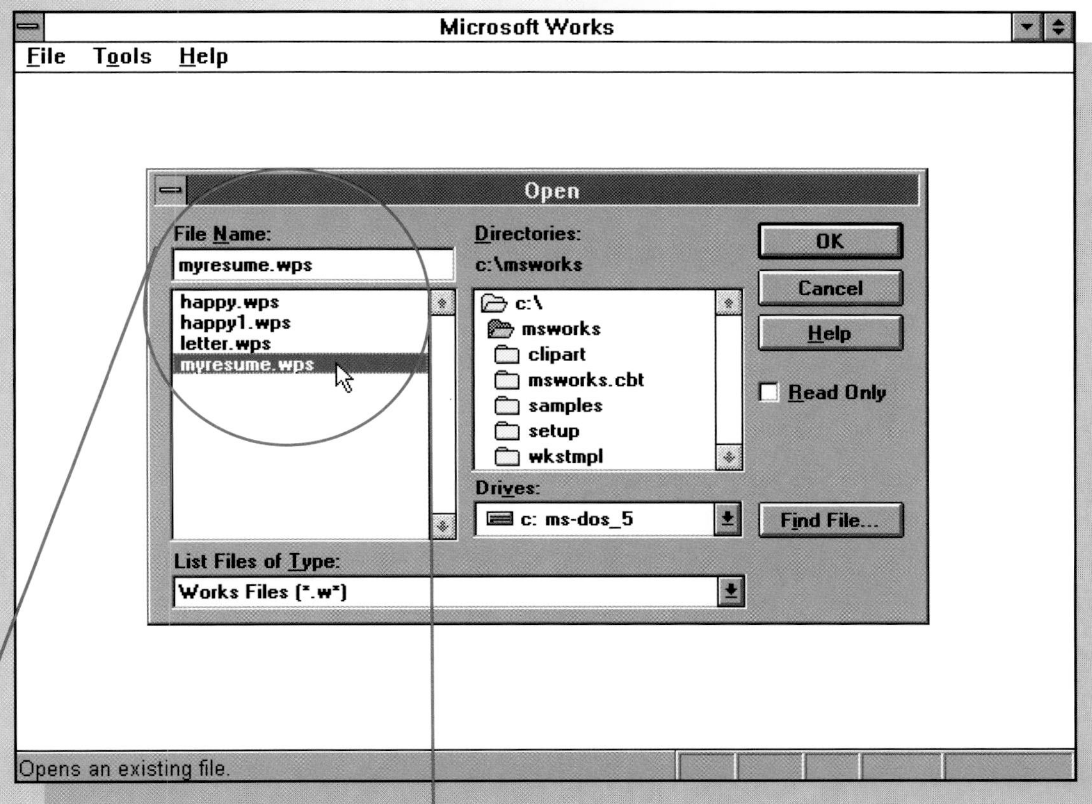

"Why would I do this?"

Since your computer and Works are not running 24 hours a day, you not only have to learn how to start your computer, Windows, and Works for Windows, but you also have to learn how to open a file that you created and saved in the past—whether an hour ago or a year ago. In this task, you will open the file you created in the previous task, but you can open any file you want.

This task assumes that you have opened the New & Recent Documents Startup dialog box in Works.

Task 11: Opening a File

1 Click on the **Open An Existing Document** button. This is the same as choosing the Open Existing File command from the File menu in the document window.

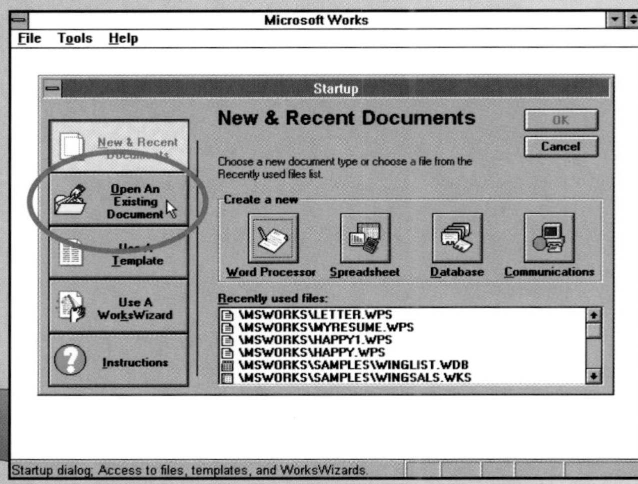

NOTE

If the document you want to open is a recently opened file, look for its name in the Recently used files list box at the bottom of the dialog box. If it's listed, double-click it to open it.

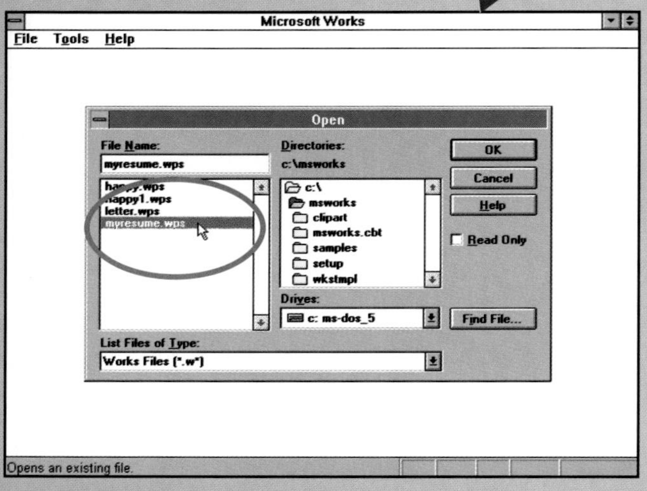

2 Double-click on **myresume** in the Open dialog box. Double-clicking is equivalent to selecting the file and clicking on OK. Works opens the file and displays a Cue Cards screen.

WHY WORRY?

If you don't see the file you want to open in the Open dialog box, it may have an extension other than .WPS. If so, open the List Files of Type drop-down list box and search for the appropriate extension. You can also type *.* in the File Name text box to display every file in the current directory.

TASK 12

Moving around the Screen

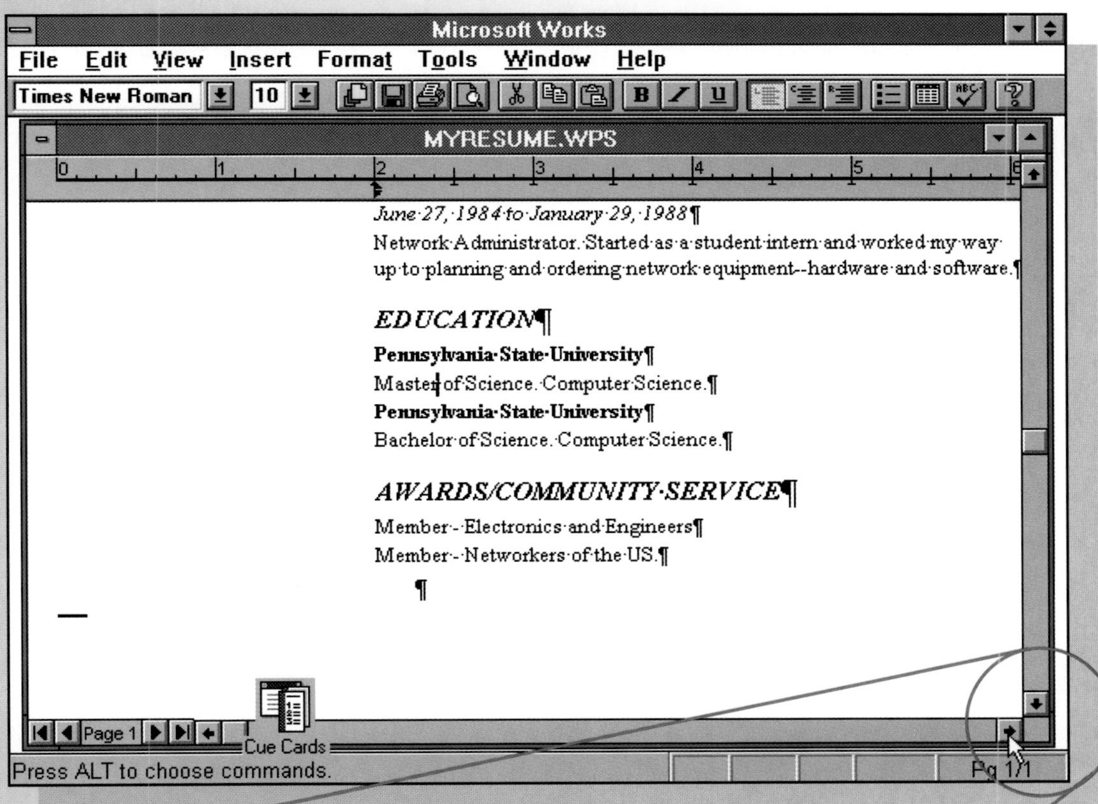

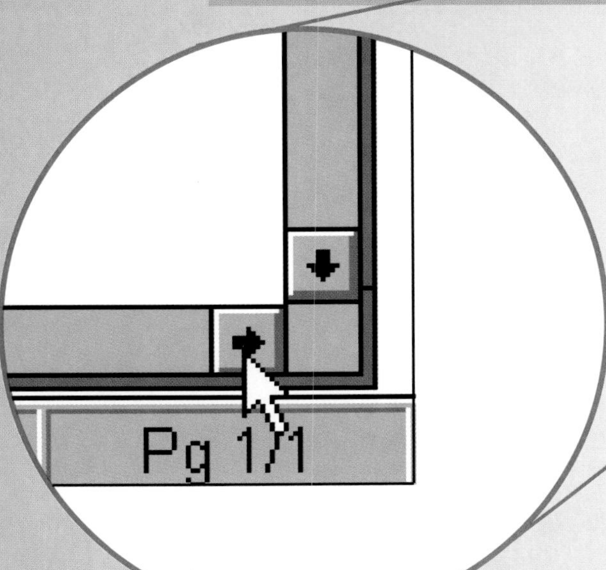

"Why would I do this?"

Before you can edit a file, you have to be able to move around within the file, within other Works files, and perhaps even within other Windows applications to get the information you need. In this task, you will move around within a document and Windows.

This task assumes that the resume is open and that you have minimized the Cue Cards window.

Task 12: Moving around the Screen

1 Point to the **down arrow** on the vertical scroll bar; then press and hold down the left mouse button. This step scrolls toward the bottom of the document. You can press ↓ or PgDn to move toward the bottom of a document, and you can press Ctrl+End to go to the very end of it.

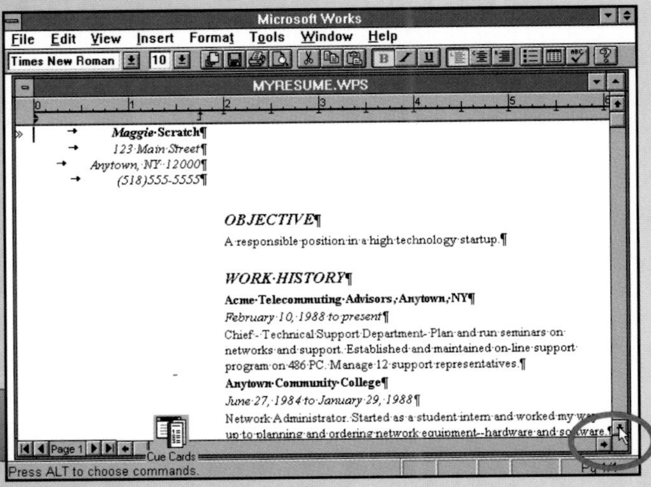

NOTE

To scroll slowly through a document, *click* on the scroll bar arrows rather than holding down the mouse button. Each click moves you up or down a line, or left or right about eight characters.

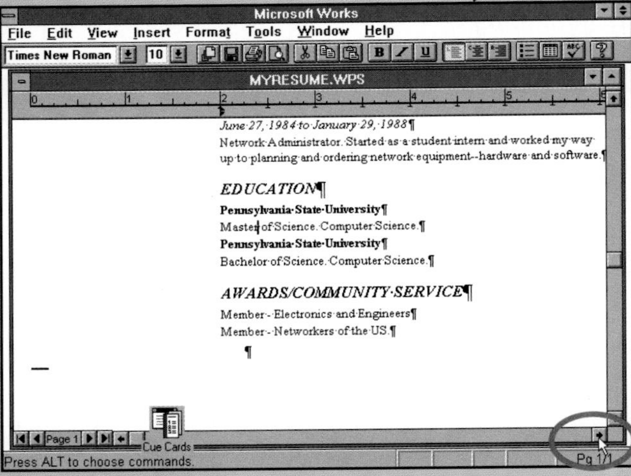

2 Point to the **right arrow** on the horizontal scroll bar; then press and hold down the left mouse button. This step scrolls toward the right side of the document. You can press → to move toward the right margin or press End to go to the right end of the line.

NOTE

Using the arrows at either end of the horizontal scroll bar is especially useful for moving around within a wide document, such as a spreadsheet.

3 Point to the **scroll box** in the vertical scroll bar, click and hold down the mouse button, and drag the scroll box down the scroll bar. This scrolls toward the bottom of the document. If you drag the scroll box to the very bottom of the scroll bar, all you'll see is the document's end mark.

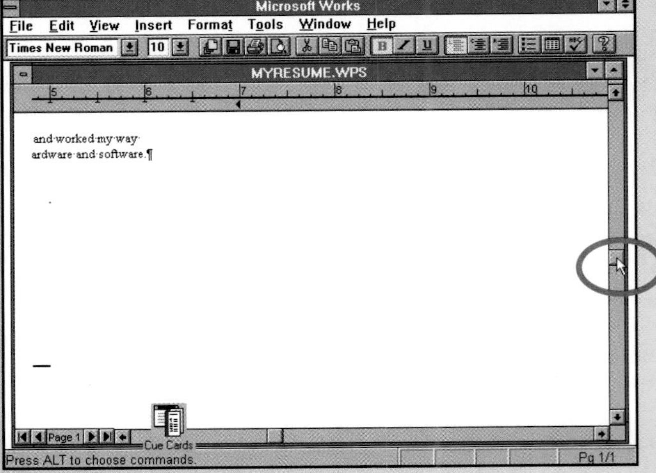

NOTE

If the Cue Cards icon is ever in your way, you can drag it to another location on-screen.

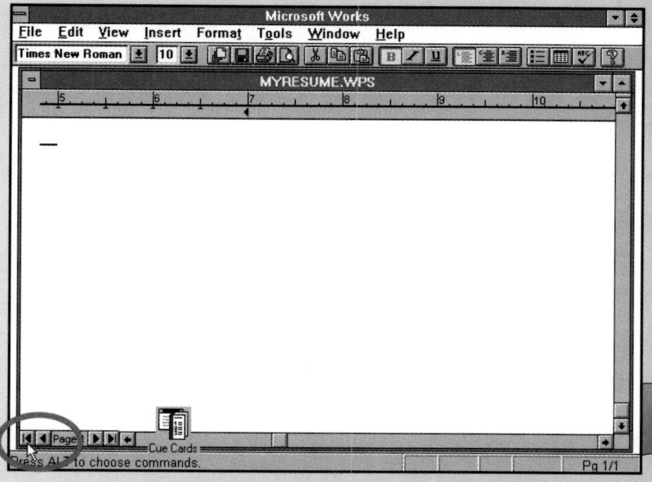

4 Click on the **left-arrow** icon in the bottom left corner of the screen. This step moves to the first character in the document. You can press ↑ or PgUp to move toward the top of a document, and you can press Ctrl+Home to go to the first character in a document.

NOTE

The other arrows at the bottom left side of the screen move you up a page, down a page, and to the bottom of the document, left to right, respectively.

5 Click on the **Restore** button in the top corner of the Works application window. This step reduces the size of the Works window so that you can see other windows on the Windows desktop.

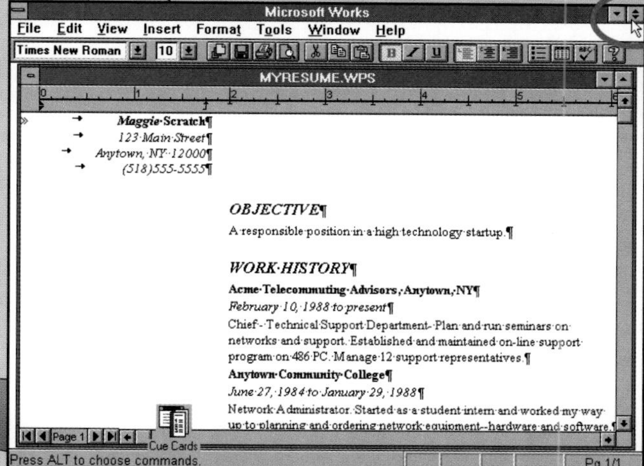

NOTE

If you see a Maximize button instead of a Restore button, the window is already restored. In that case, you can skip step 5.

6 Move the mouse pointer to the Program Manager window and click. This step brings the Program Manager window in front of the Works window. The Works window is still open, but it's underneath the Program Manager window.

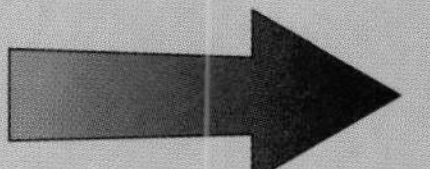

Task 12: Moving around the Screen

7 Press **Ctrl+Esc**. This step displays the Task List window, which lists each open application, so that you can quickly switch to the one you want to make active.

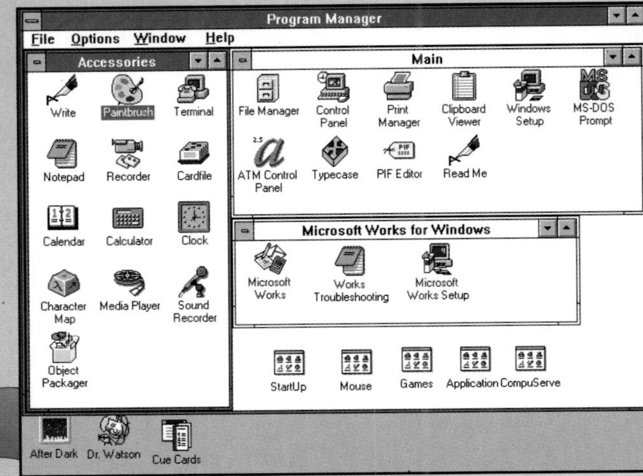

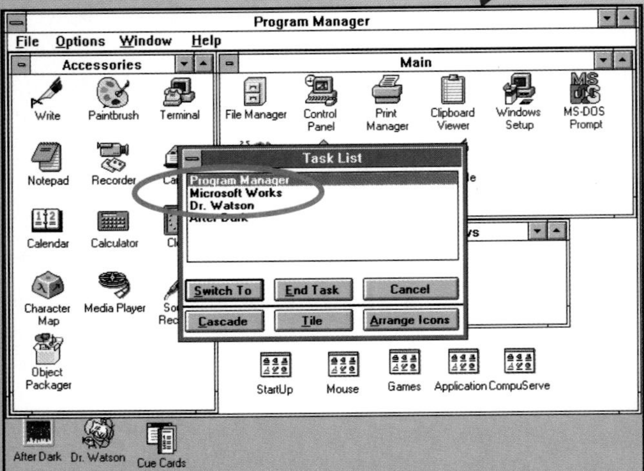

8 Double-click on **Microsoft Works** in the Task List window. Double-clicking is equivalent to selecting the name of the application you want to make active and then clicking on the Switch To button. The Works window appears.

9 Now you can edit the text in the file.

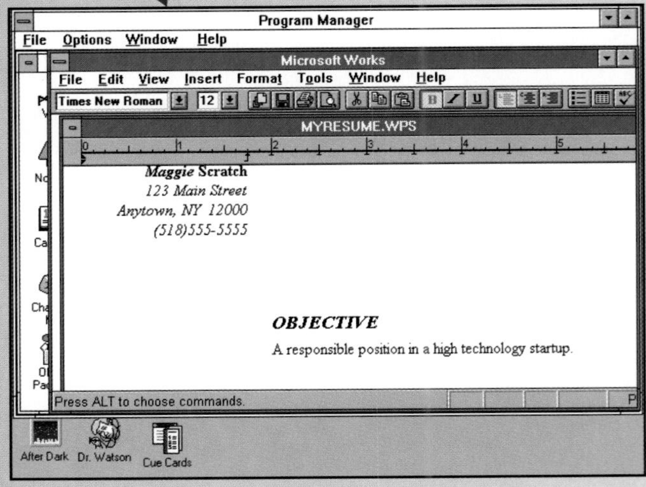

NOTE

Another way to switch to a different application that's running in Windows is to press Alt+Esc repeatedly until the desired application appears on your screen.

TASK 13

Making a Selection

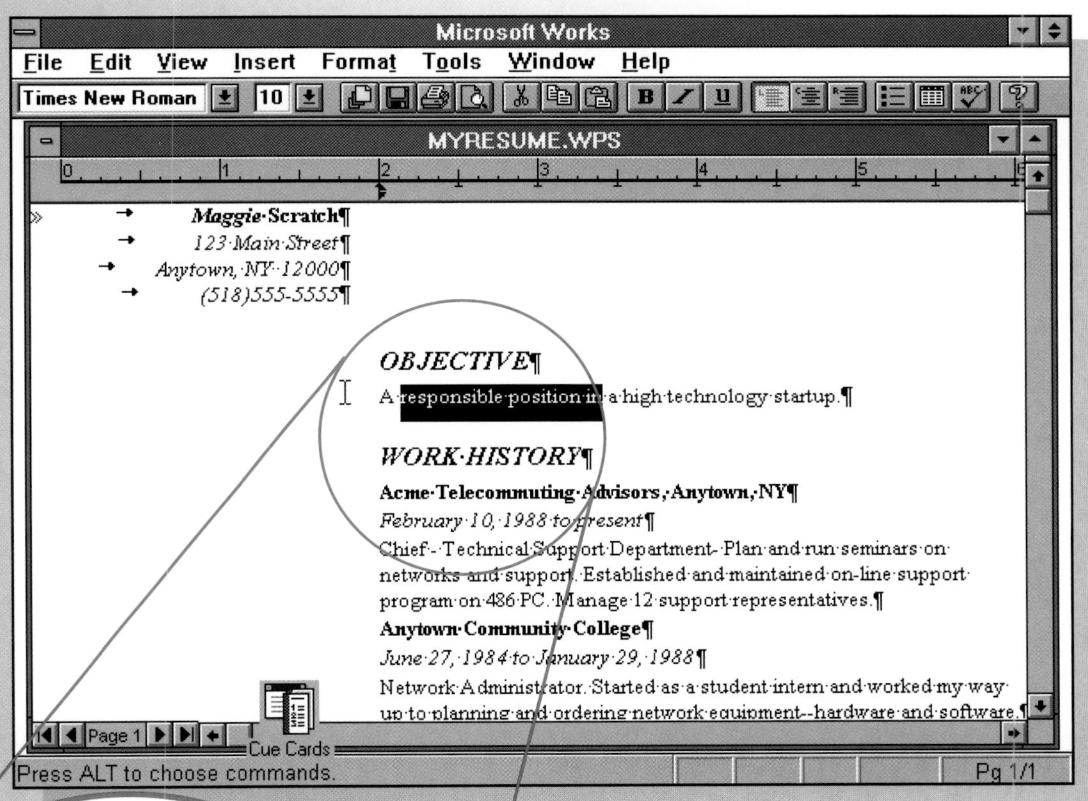

"Why would I do this?"

After navigating to find information, you'll have to do something with it. In most cases, you'll select all or part of the information to copy or move it or to enhance it in some way. In this task, you'll select words, sentences, and the entire document.

To work through the steps in this task, open a completed resume and minimize the Cue Cards window.

Task 13: Making a Selection

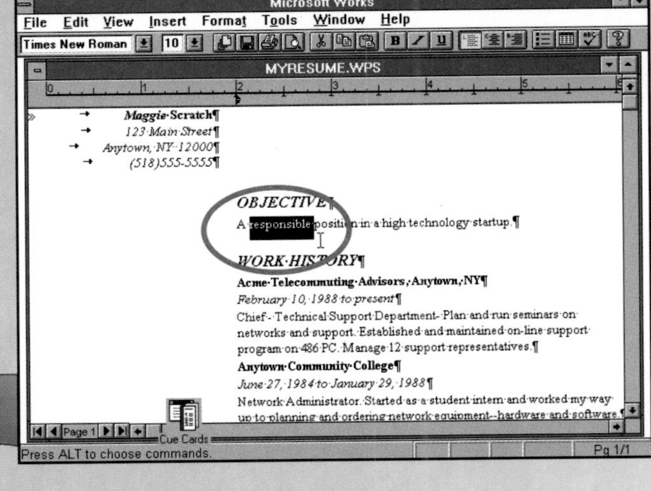

1 Move the pointer anywhere within the word you want to select, and double-click the left mouse button. This step selects the entire word plus the space immediately after it. Another way to select a word is to click on the left side of it and drag to the right until the entire word is highlighted.

2 Select more text by holding down the **Shift** key and repeatedly pressing →. You can also use the Shift key with ←, ↑, or ↓, in any combination.

3 Select an entire sentence by holding down the **Ctrl** key and clicking the left mouse button anywhere in the sentence.

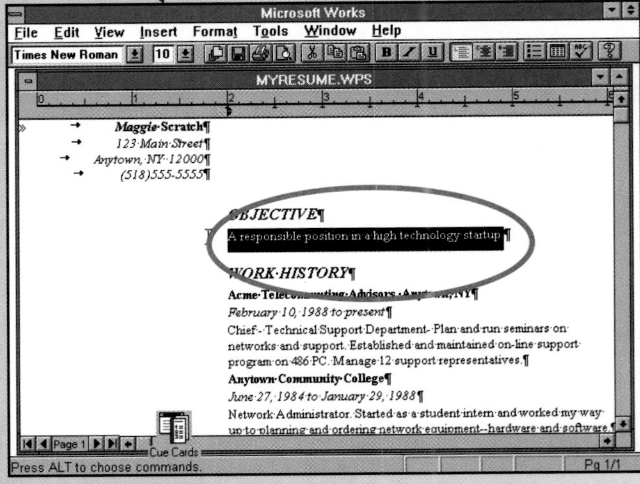

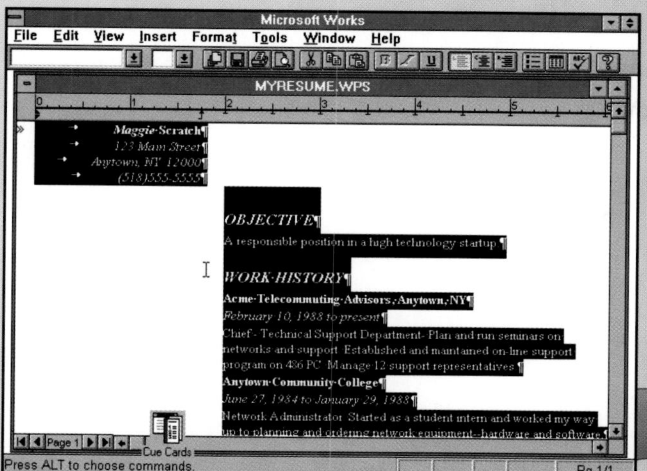

4 Select the entire document by opening the **Edit** menu and choosing the **Select All** command.

5 Remove the highlight from selected text by clicking the left mouse button anywhere on-screen.

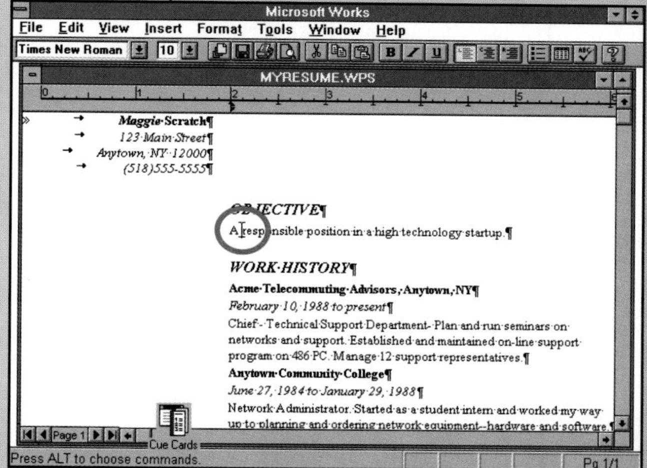

TASK 14

Deleting, Copying, Moving, and Undoing

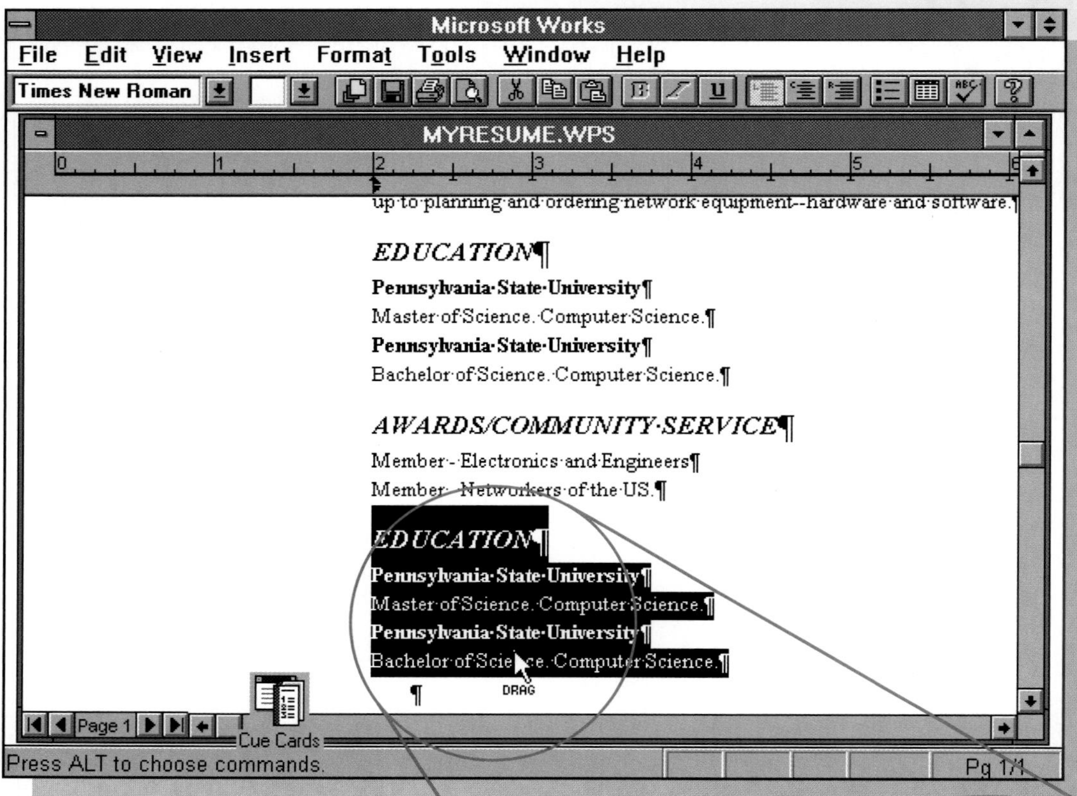

"Why would I do this?"

This task covers the functions you'll use most often when editing documents. You'll find that you have to cut old information, copy or move information to new locations, and undo any mistakes you might make along the way. In this task, you will copy text, delete the copy, undo the deletion, and move text. This task assumes that you have a completed resume open on-screen and have minimized the Cue Cards window.

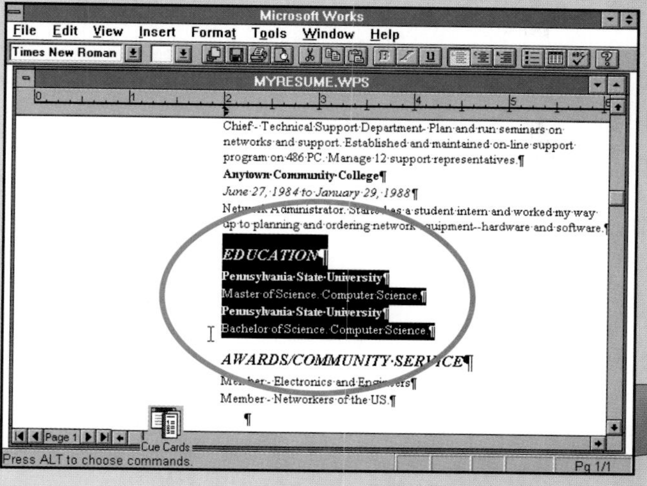

1 Select the EDUCATION section of the resume by clicking at the beginning of the section and dragging to the end of it. Before you can copy, delete, or move text, you must select it.

2 Click on the **Copy** button on the toolbar. This action is the equivalent of choosing the Edit Copy command or pressing Ctrl+C. When you copy text, Works places the copied text in the Windows Clipboard.

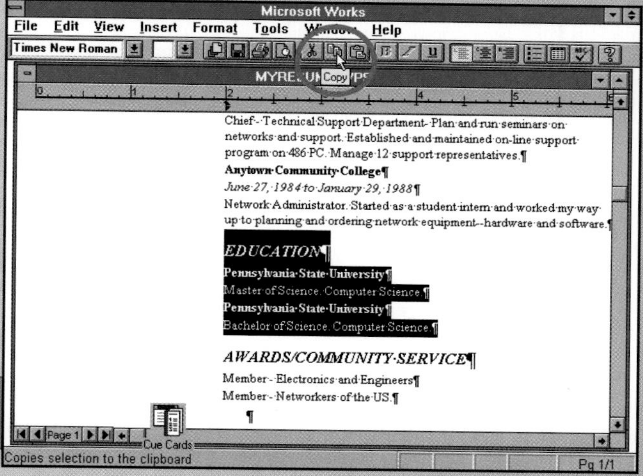

3 Click below the AWARDS/COMMUNITY SERVICE section of the document to move the insertion point there. This is the location to which the copied text will go.

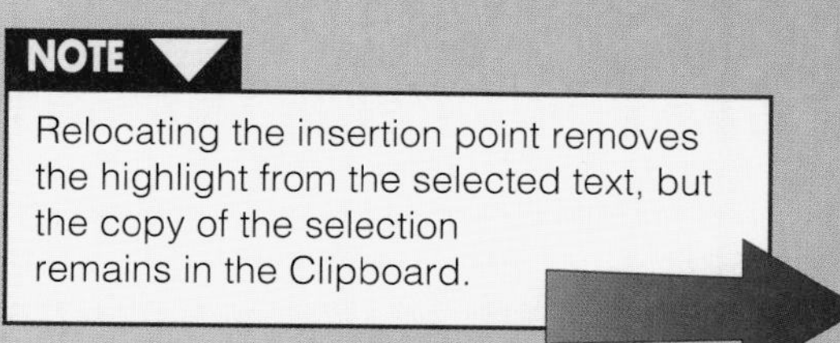

NOTE

Relocating the insertion point removes the highlight from the selected text, but the copy of the selection remains in the Clipboard.

4 Click on the **Paste** button on the toolbar. This action is the equivalent of choosing the Edit Paste command or pressing Ctrl+V. When you paste, you place the copied text in its new location, but a copy remains in the Windows Clipboard.

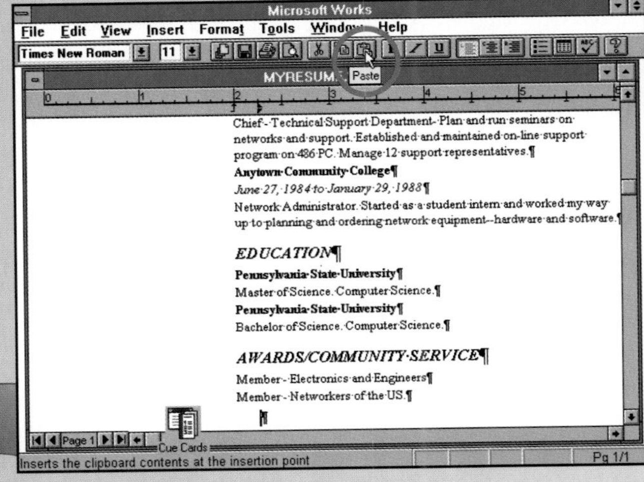

5 Select the pasted text.

6 Click on **Edit** in the menu bar. This step opens the Edit menu.

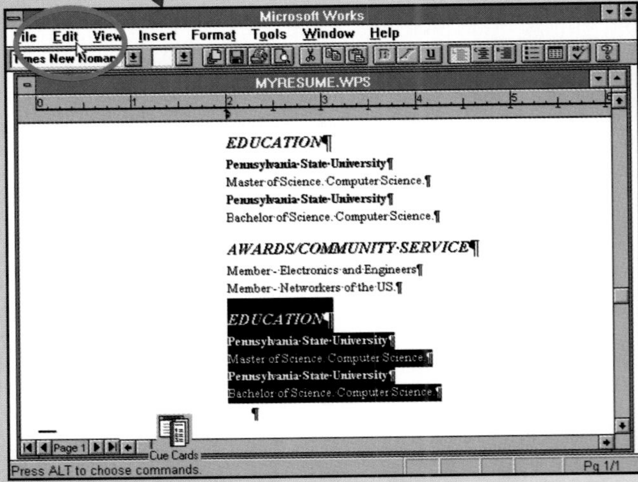

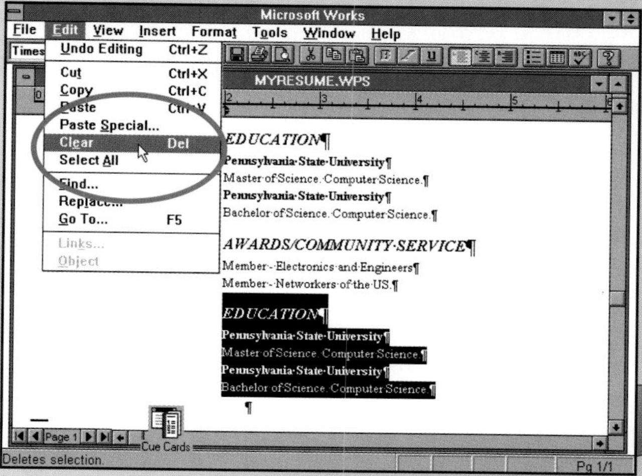

7 Click on the **Clear** command. This action deletes, or clears, the selection.

> **NOTE**
>
> On a Works menu, the keys listed next to some of the commands are shortcut keys. Press a shortcut key to perform the related command.

8 Press **Ctrl+Z**. This is the same as performing the Edit Undo command. This action returns the deleted text to the document.

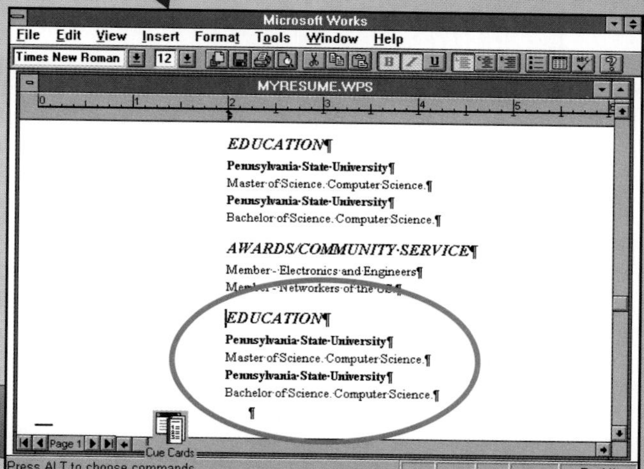

> **NOTE**
>
> Once you choose Edit Clear, the only way to get back the text you deleted is to choose the Edit Undo command or press Ctrl+Z. However, if you perform any actions after deleting, the Undo command cannot help you; the deleted text is gone forever. Once you have performed Edit Undo, the Undo command changes to the Redo command.

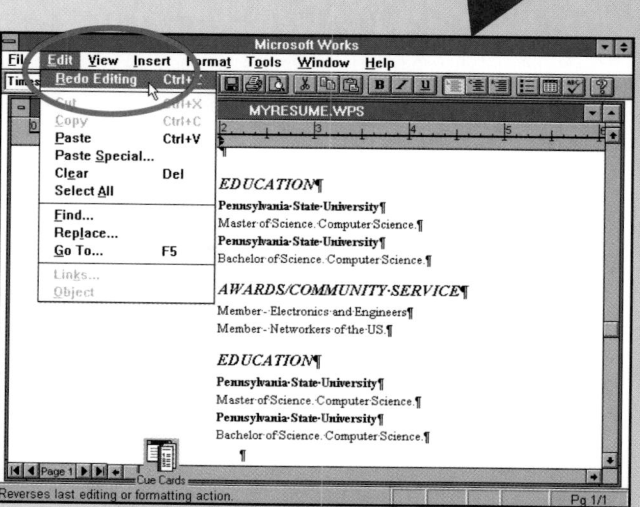

9 Click on **Edit** in the menu bar and click on **Redo Editing** to undo the undo. Works removes the extra EDUCATION section from the screen. Ctrl+Z is also the shortcut key for Edit Redo.

10 Select the first EDUCATION section again.

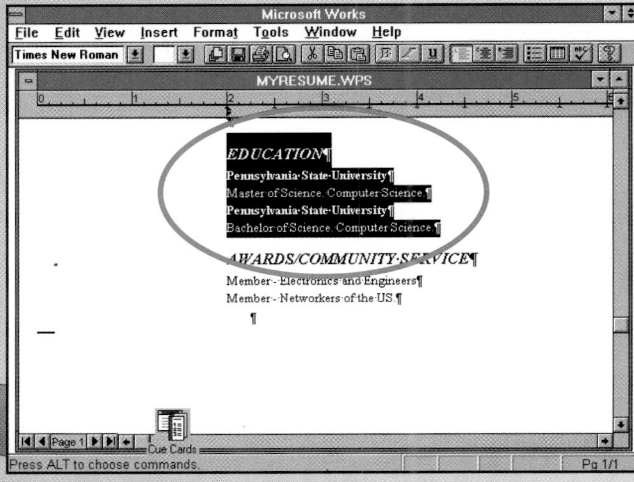

11 Move the mouse pointer inside the highlighted area.

NOTE

When the mouse pointer displays **DRAG** on its tail, you can drag the text to another location in the document window.

12 Drag the pointer toward the bottom of the AWARDS/COMMUNITY SERVICE section. Notice that the message on the mouse pointer tail now reads `MOVE`.

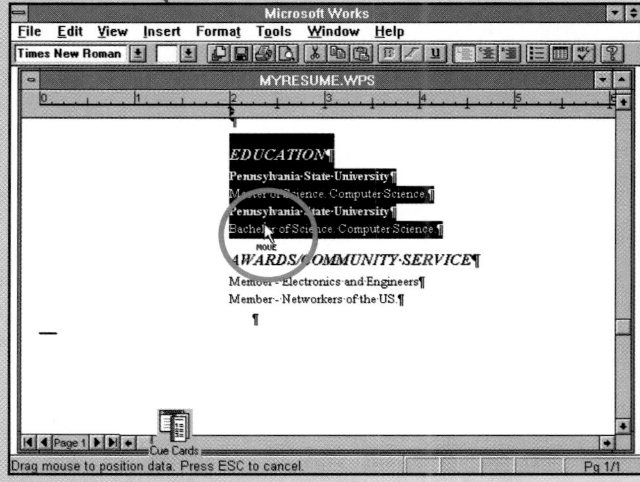

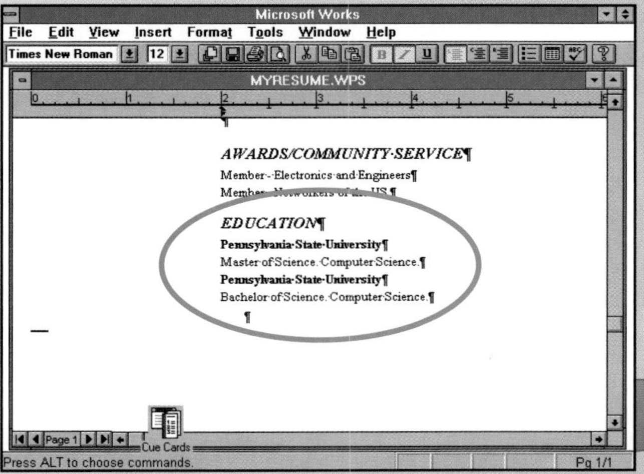

13 Release the mouse button after you have positioned the pointer where you want to move the selected text. Works places the text in its new location and removes the highlight.

14 Move the EDUCATION section back to its original location, above the AWARDS/COMMUNITY SERVICE section.

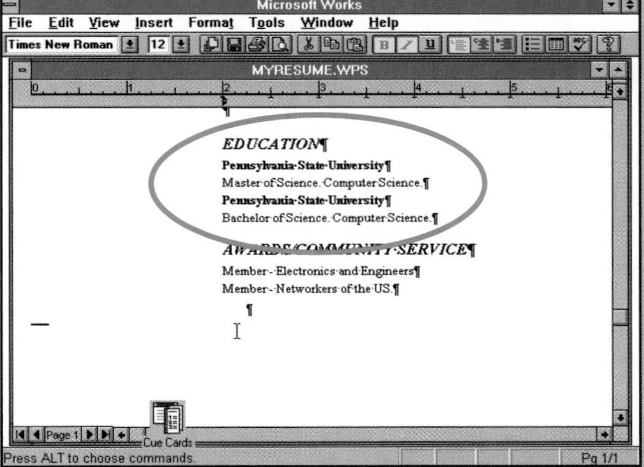

TASK 15

Printing a File

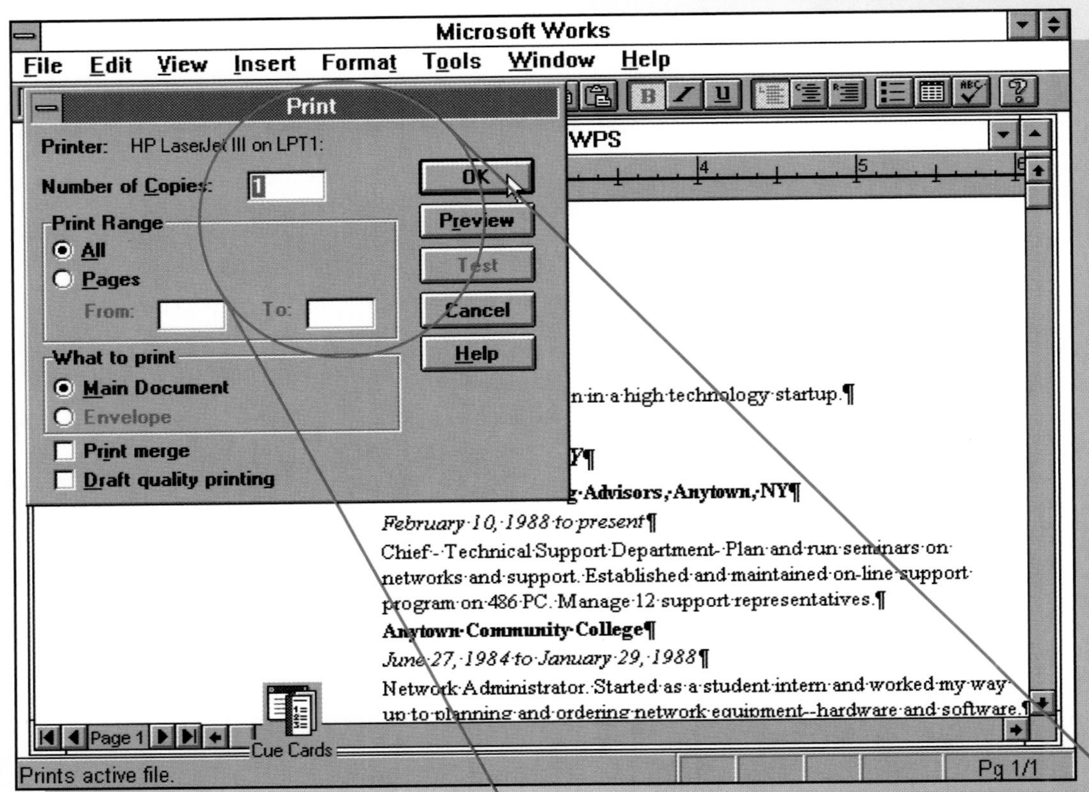

"Why would I do this?"

Printing a file enables you to pass it to someone else. Although we are supposedly heading for a paperless society, we have a long way to go. Printing and distributing documents are the end result of creating them. In this task, you will print a resume without changing the printing defaults.

This task assumes that you have a completed resume open on-screen and have minimized the Cue Cards window.

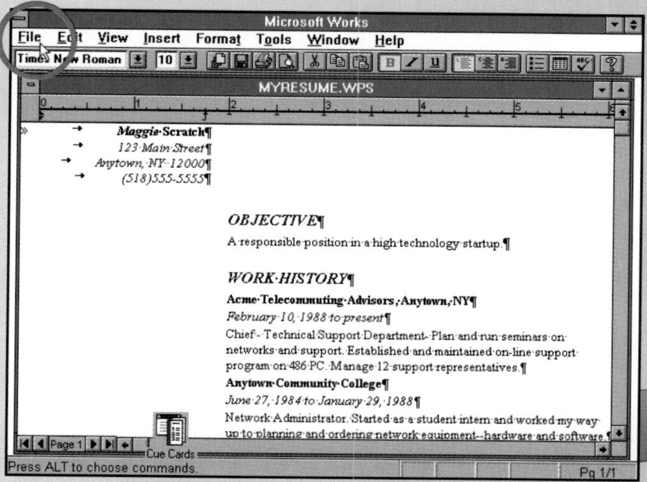

1 Click on **File** in the menu bar. This action opens the File menu.

2 Click on **Print**. Works opens the Print dialog box, which enables you to indicate the number of copies and range of pages to print.

NOTE

To see how your document looks before you print, click on the Preview button in the Print dialog box. Works displays your document one page at a time in the Print Preview window. To magnify the page, click with the ZOOM mouse pointer. To close the Print Preview window, click on Cancel or press Esc.

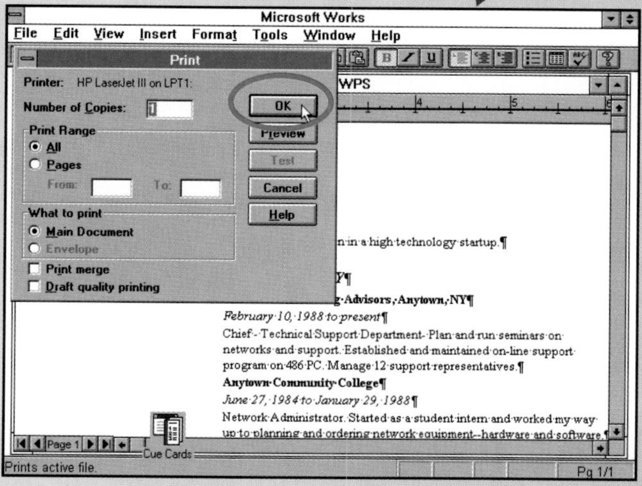

3 Click on **OK**. Works displays an information box that tells you about the print job.

NOTE

To quickly print only one copy of your entire document, you can click on the Print button on the toolbar, which bypasses the Print dialog box. Another shortcut is to press Ctrl+P, which opens the Print dialog box so that you can select options before printing.

PART III

Using the Word Processor

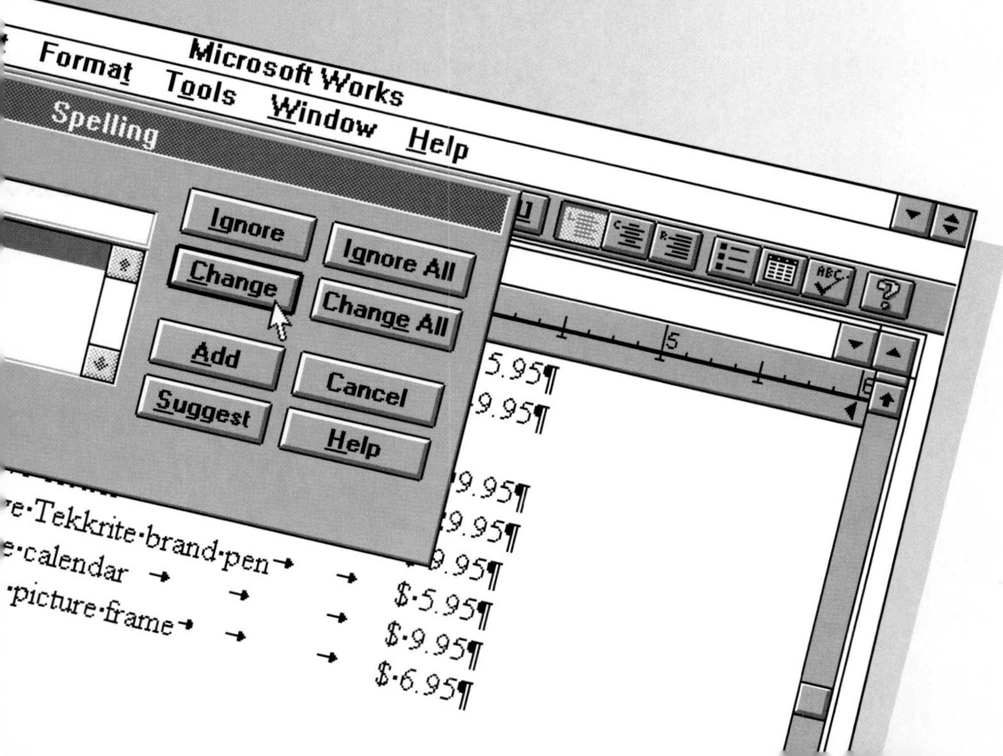

Part III: Using the Word Processor

Part III introduces you to your first Works tool: the Word Processor. Although you have used the Word Processor to explore the basic elements of Works, now you'll find out its capabilities.

In this part, you'll learn about Works' two typing modes, how to insert a tab, how to break a page, and how to go to a specific page. Finally, you'll discover how to use Works' spelling checker and thesaurus to fine-tune your work.

One of the advantages of working with a word processor rather than a typewriter is that you can add chunks of text in any location. Rather than starting at the beginning and ending at the end, you can create the body of a document first and then later write the introduction and summary, based on the contents of the middle of the document. Creating a document simply involves starting the Word Processor and typing on the blank screen. There are no other preparations.

Correcting a Word Processor document is also much simpler than using correction fluids and crumpling endless pieces of paper. Either insert the text you want to add or overtype the text you want to delete.

You can let the Word Processor format a document for you. Rather than listening for a bell to signal the approach of the right margin, you can relax and keep on typing. The Word Processor automatically wraps your text to the next line.

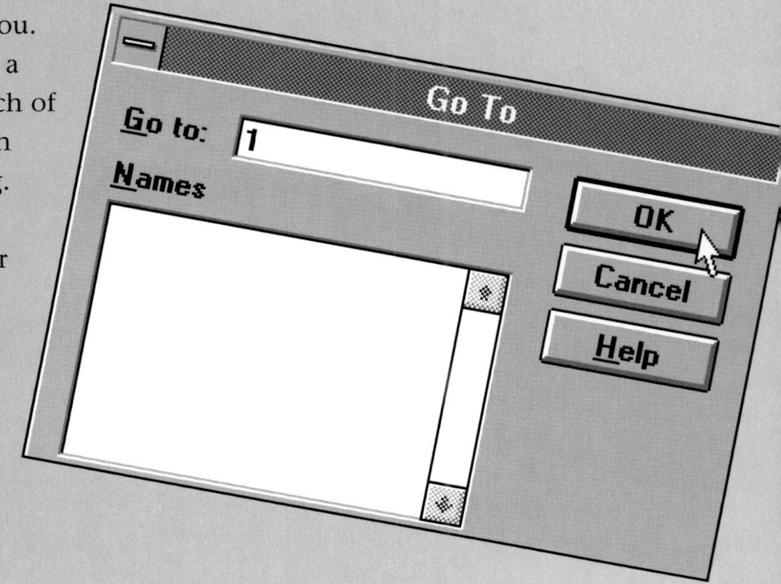

When you reach the end of a page, the Word Processor inserts a page break and moves you to the top of the next page; however, if you feel like inserting a page break yourself, you can choose a command that inserts the break.

The Word Processor's spelling checker helps you get a document ready for others to see. The spelling checker uses a dictionary of over 100,000 words to check your spelling and locate repeated words, such as *the the*. Works allows you to add words to its dictionary; for example, if you regularly use industry jargon or company names, you can add those words to prevent the spelling checker from flagging them as misspellings.

Works' 200,000-word thesaurus helps you find substitute words for those that you use too often. It also aids in finding a better word than the one you are currently using.

The tasks in this section provide basic information to help you get up and running with the Word Processor.

Beautiful

Lovely

Pretty

Exquisite

Gorge o us

TASK 16

Inserting and Overtyping Text and Inserting a Tab

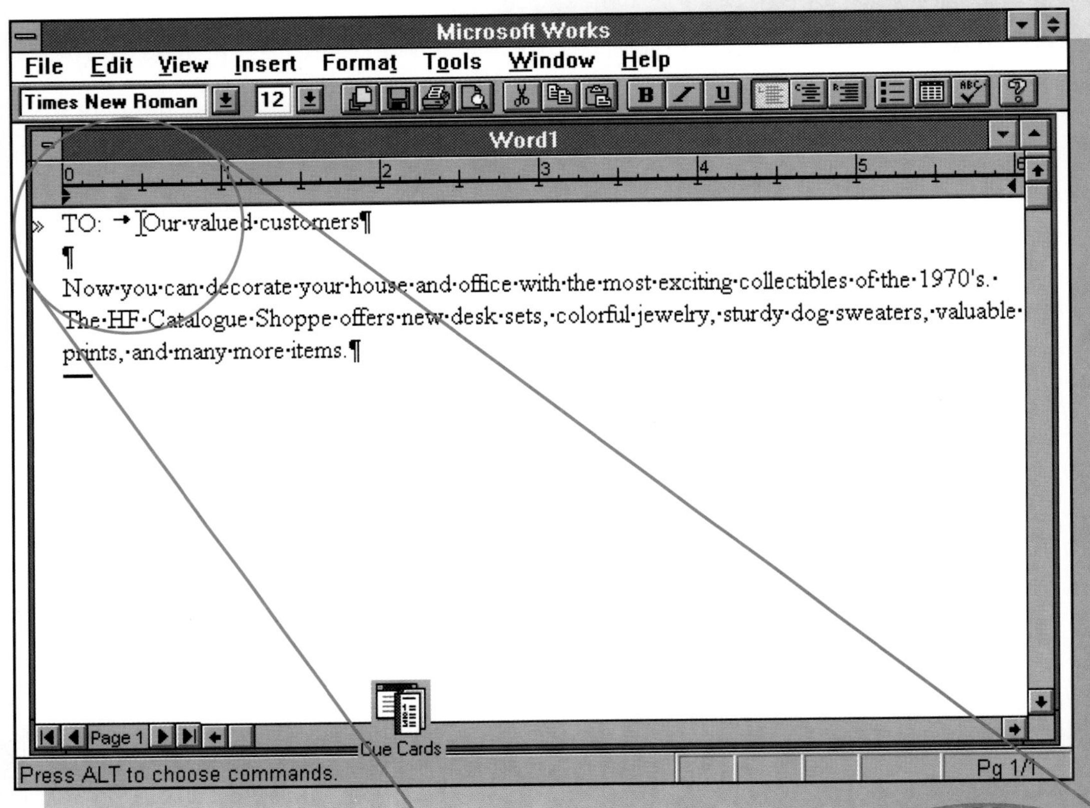

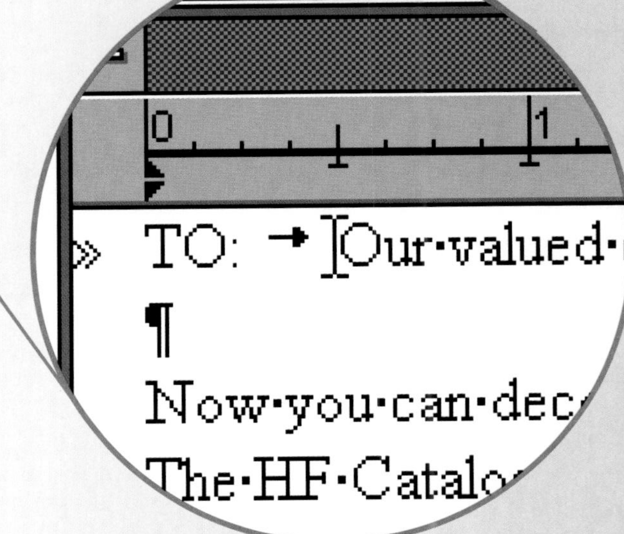

"Why would I do this?"

In the Word Processor, you can add, change, or delete words in a variety of ways. In this task, you will learn how to insert text into an existing document. You'll work in both Insert and Overtype modes, and you'll insert a tab.

This task assumes that the Word Processor tool is active and displaying a specific document on-screen, but you can use any text you want.

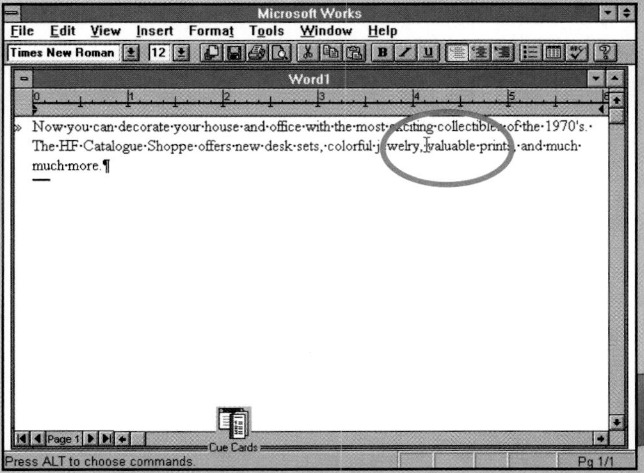

1 Click before the word *valuable.* To add text to a particular place in a document, you must first move the insertion point to that place. To relocate the insertion point, either click on the new location or press the arrow keys until the insertion point is where you want it.

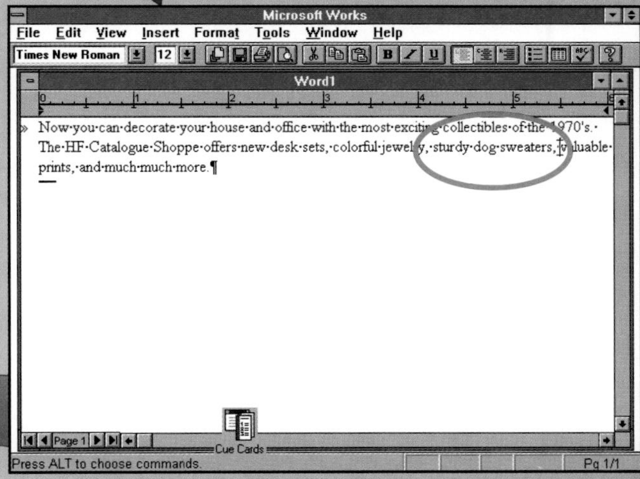

2 Type **sturdy dog sweaters**, followed by a comma and a space. As you type, notice that the new characters seem to push the text that's in front of them, without erasing any existing characters. The screen is in *Insert mode.* In Insert mode, every character or space you enter pushes the existing text to the right and down the document.

3 Press the **Insert** key. Pressing the Insert key changes the screen from Insert mode to *Overtype mode.* In Overtype mode, every character or space you type replaces an existing character or space. Works displays the OVR indicator in the status bar.

4 Move the insertion point in front of the word *much.* Whether the screen is in Insert or Overtype mode, to add new text to a particular place in a document, you must first move the insertion point to that place.

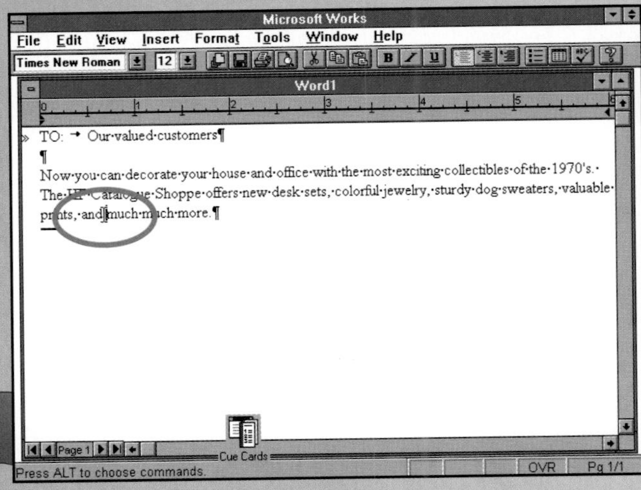

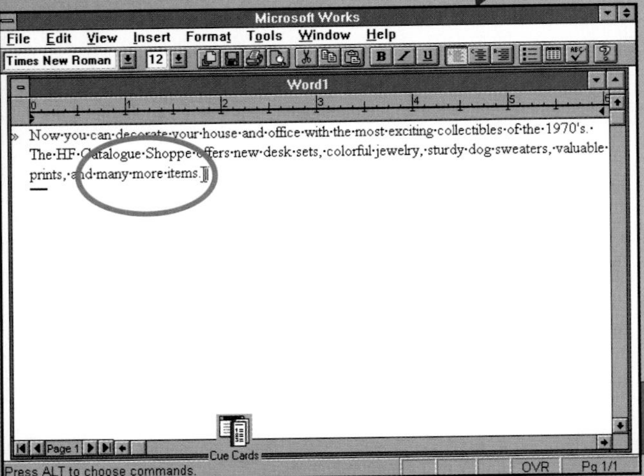

5 Type **many more items**, followed by a period to end the sentence. Notice that the words *much much more* disappear, one character at a time, as you type.

WHY WORRY?

To prevent erasing text by mistake, you should always work in Insert mode.

6 Press the **Insert** key again. Works removes the OVR indicator and returns to Insert mode.

NOTE

Any key that enables you to switch back and forth between two modes is known as a *toggle key*.

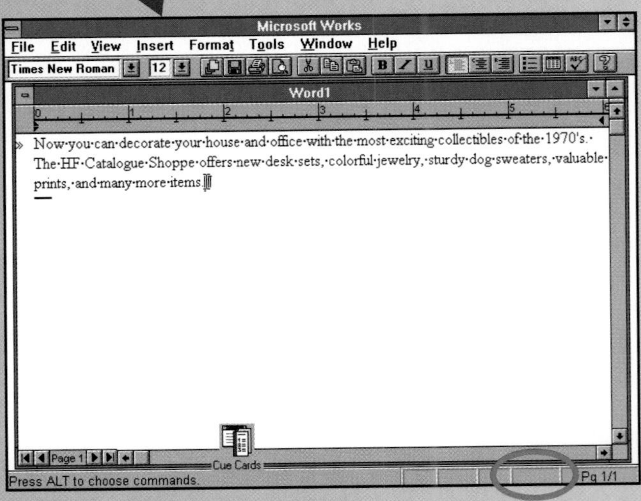

Task 16: Inserting and Overtyping Text and Inserting a Tab

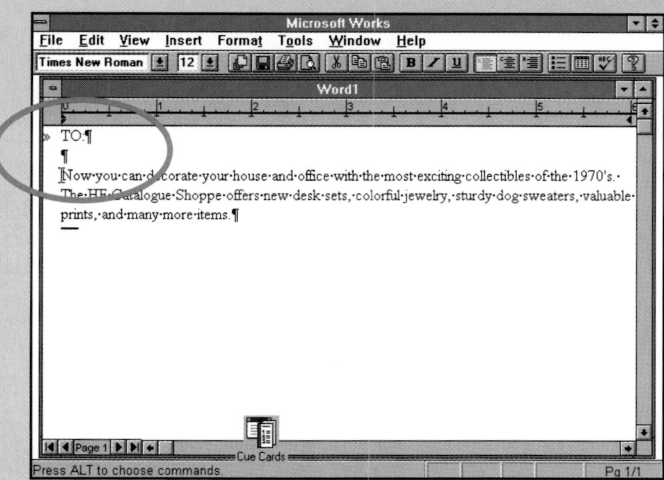

7 Move the insertion point before the word *Now,* type **TO:**, and press **Enter twice.**

8 Click after *TO:* and type **Our valued customers**. Because you're going to place a tab between TO: and the new text, you don't need to insert a space.

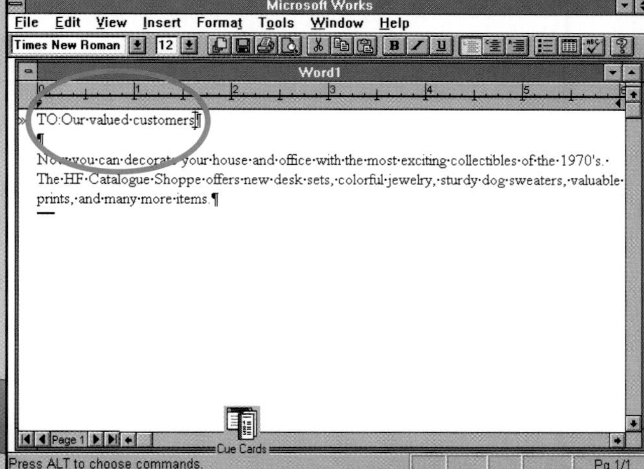

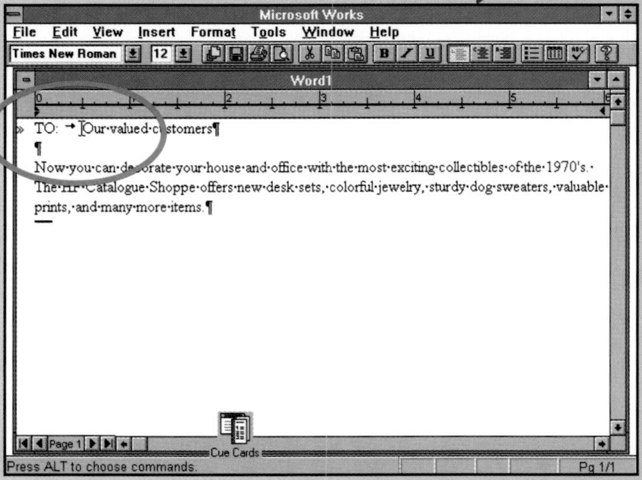

9 Move the insertion point after *TO:* and press **Tab**. Pressing the Tab key inserts a tab symbol and moves the insertion point to the next tab stop. Works sets tab stops every half inch.

WHY WORRY?

To remove a tab that you just entered, press the Backspace key.

TASK 17

Inserting a Page Break and Going to a Page

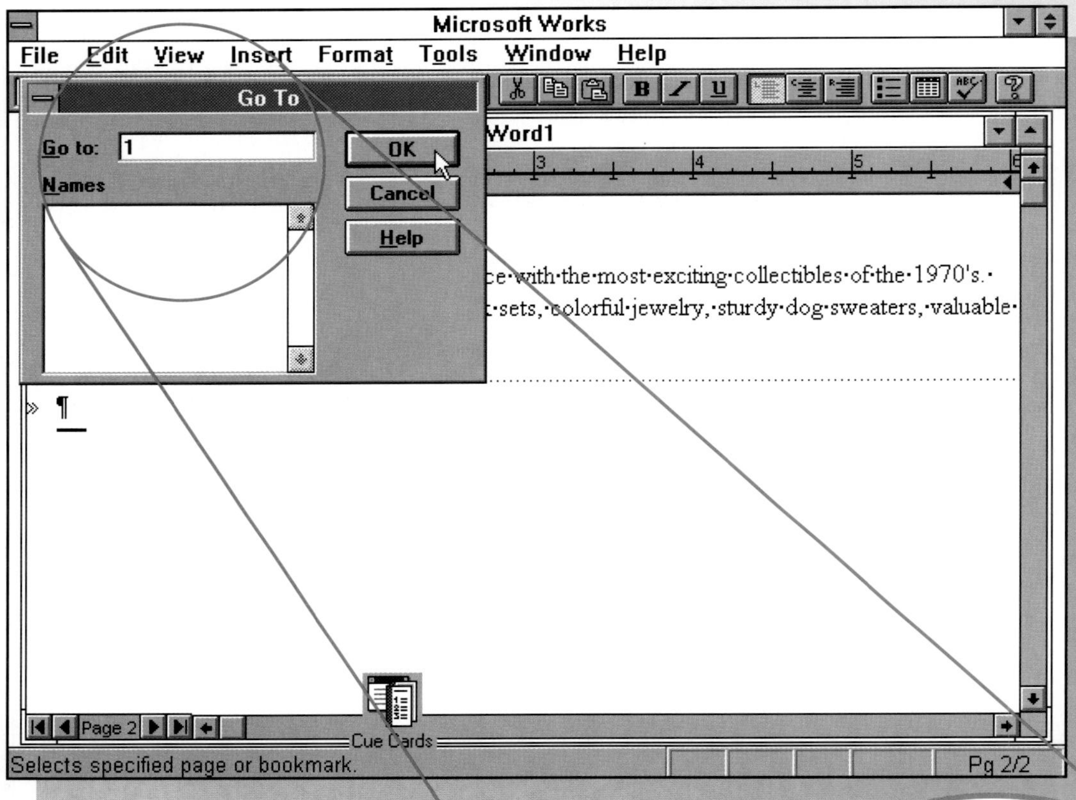

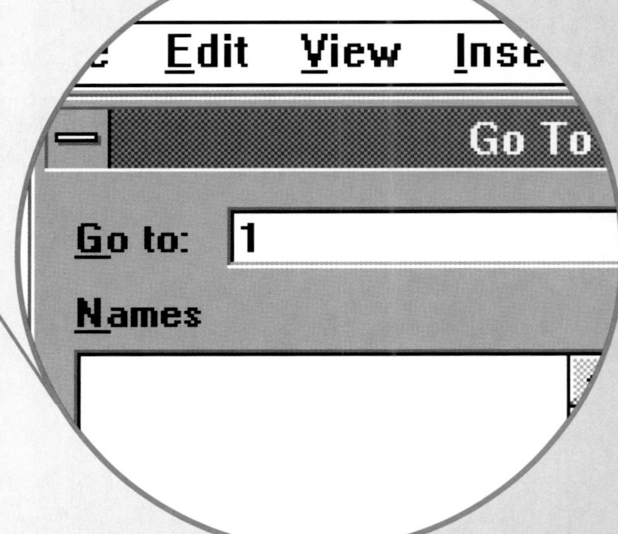

"Why would I do this?"

Although the Word Processor inserts page breaks for you, you can insert your own breaks. In this task, you will insert a page break between introductory text and a list of items. You'll also learn how to use the Go To command.

This task assumes that the Word Processor tool is active and displaying the document you used in the last task, but you can use any text you want.

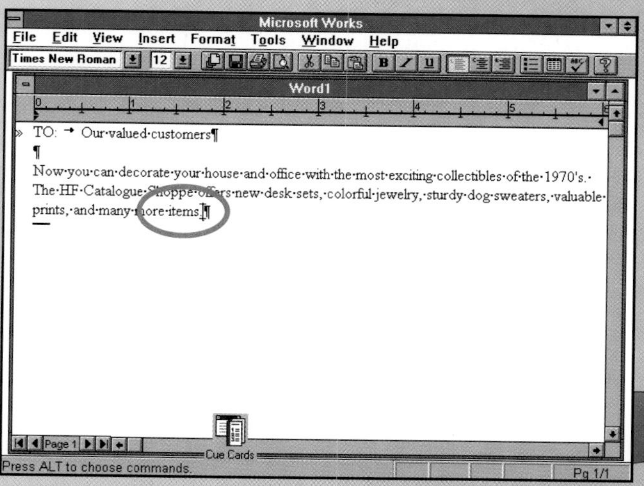

1 Click after the word *items* or wherever you want a page break. This moves the insertion point to the location where you will insert a page break.

2 Click on **Insert** in the menu bar. This step opens the Insert menu. You can choose from the list of commands.

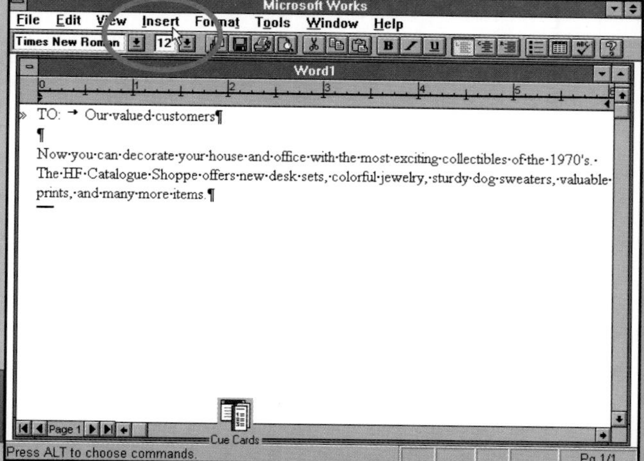

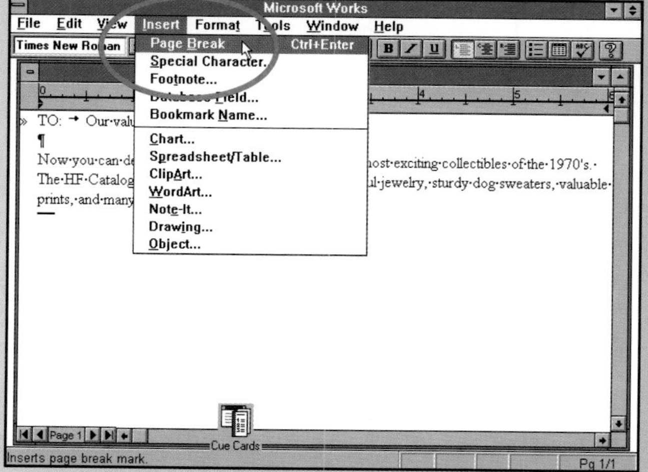

3 Click on **Page Break**. Works adds a dotted line to indicate the page break.

To quickly insert a page break at the insertion point, press Ctrl+Enter.

Task 17: Inserting a Page Break and Going to a Page

4 Click on **Edit** in the menu bar. This step opens the Edit menu.

WHY WORRY?

To delete a page break, either position the insertion point right after the page break and press Backspace, or position the insertion point on the page break line and press Delete.

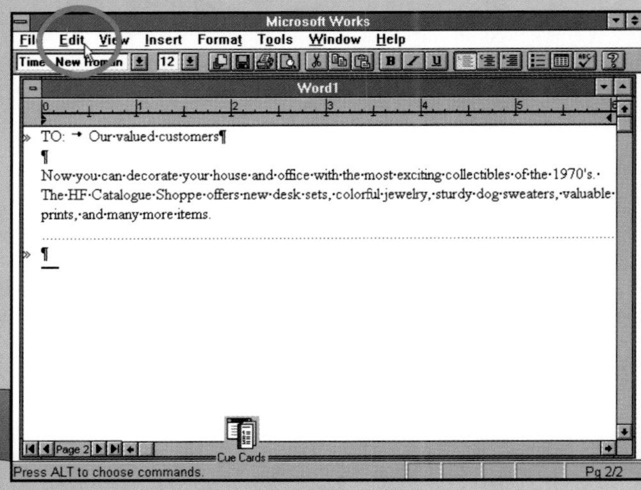

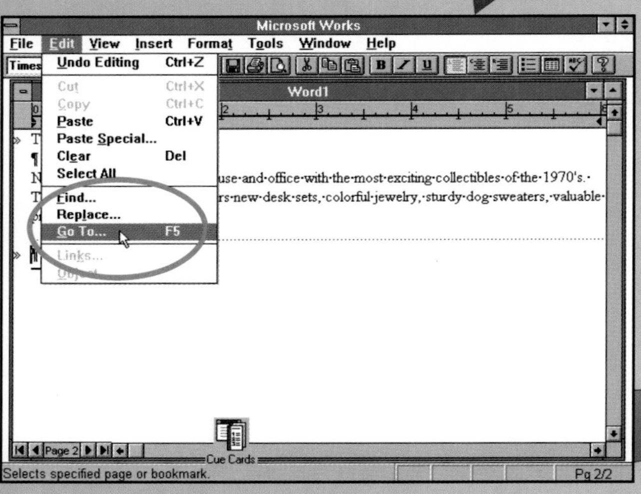

5 Click on **Go To**. Works opens the Go To dialog box. The insertion point is flashing inside the Go To text box.

NOTE

As a shortcut, you can press F5 to open the Go To dialog box, bypassing the menus.

6 Type **1** and click on **OK**. When the dialog box closes, Works moves the insertion point to the top of page 1. If the document contains many pages, the scroll box moves to the top of the vertical scroll bar.

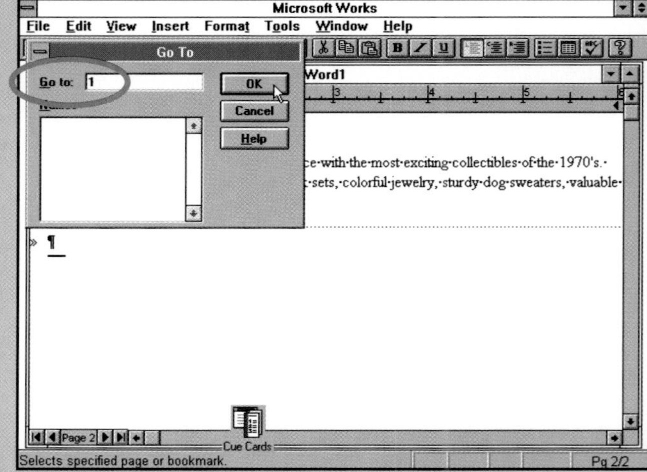

TASK 18

Checking Spelling and Words

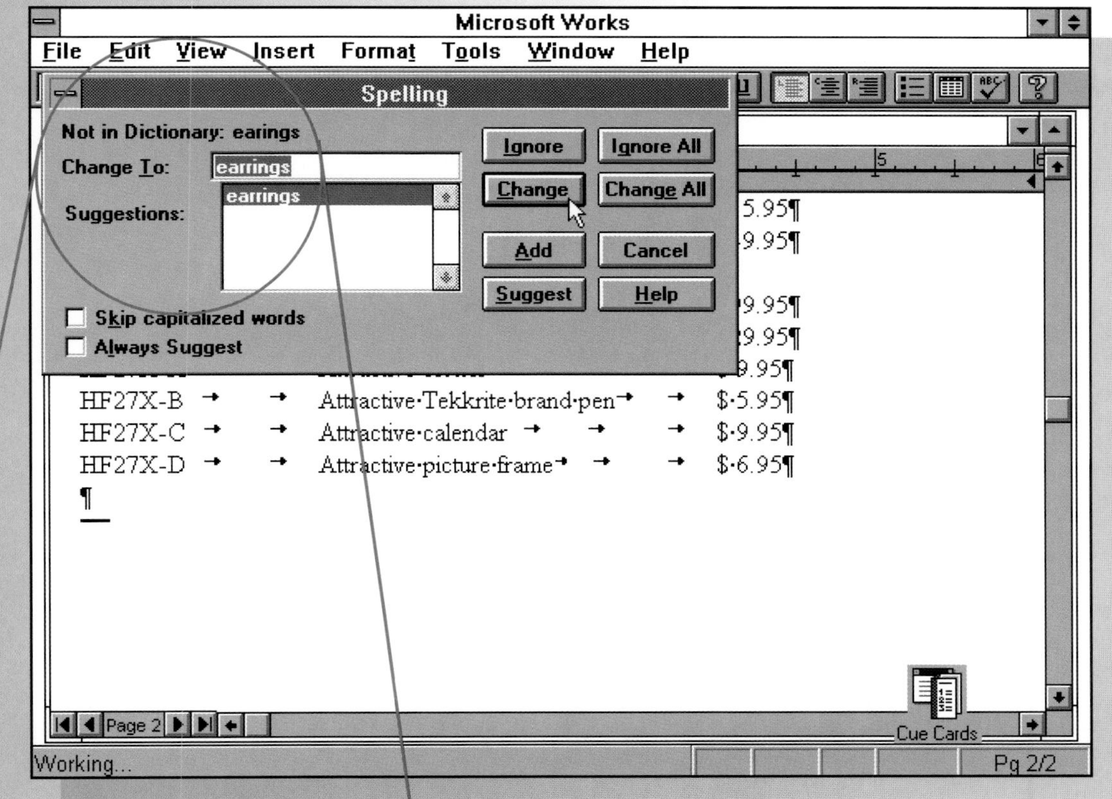

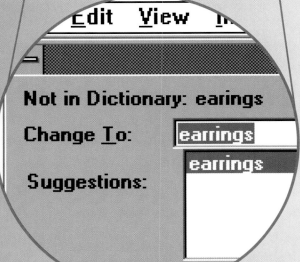

"Why would I do this?"

Works' spelling checker helps you present an accurate document to all those who see it. To provide extra polish to a document, use the thesaurus to find synonyms for words you use too often or inaccurately. In this task, you will practice using these features.

This task assumes that the Word Processor tool is active and displaying the document you used in the last task, but you can use any text you want, preferably containing misspellings.

Task 18: Checking Spelling and Words

1 Click on **Tools** in the menu bar. This step opens the Tools menu.

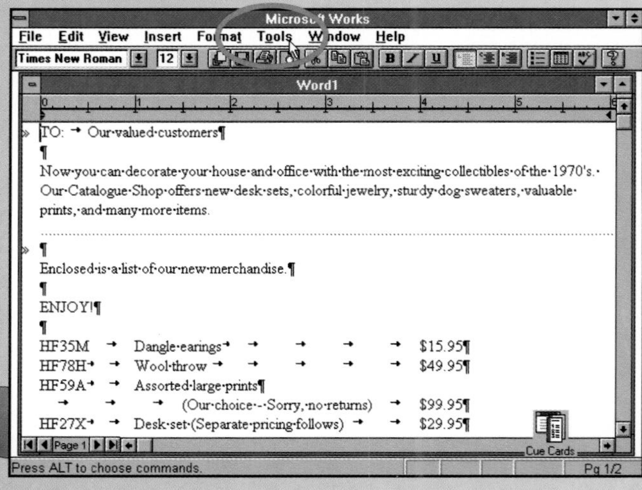

2 Click on **Spelling**. Works begins checking the document for misspelled and repeated words.

WHY WORRY?

To stop the spelling check at any time, click on Cancel in the Spelling dialog box.

3 When it finds a spelling error such as *earings,* Works opens the Spelling dialog box. In this dialog box, you can change the spelling by typing in the text box or accepting a suggestion, add the word to a custom dictionary, or ignore the word and move to the next misspelling. Click on **Suggest**. This step suggests the correct spelling in the Suggestions scroll box.

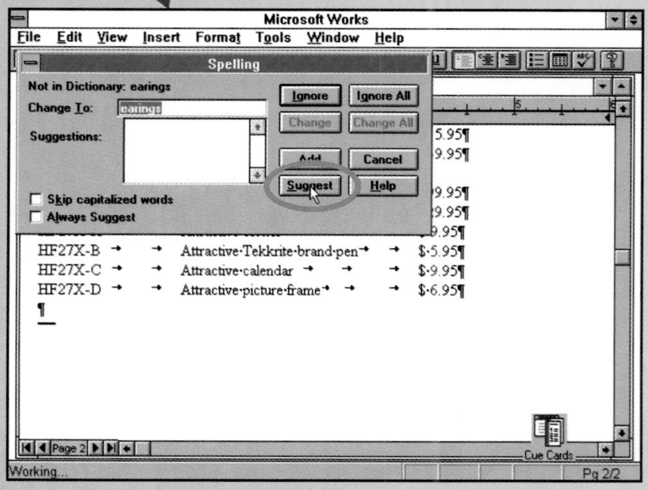

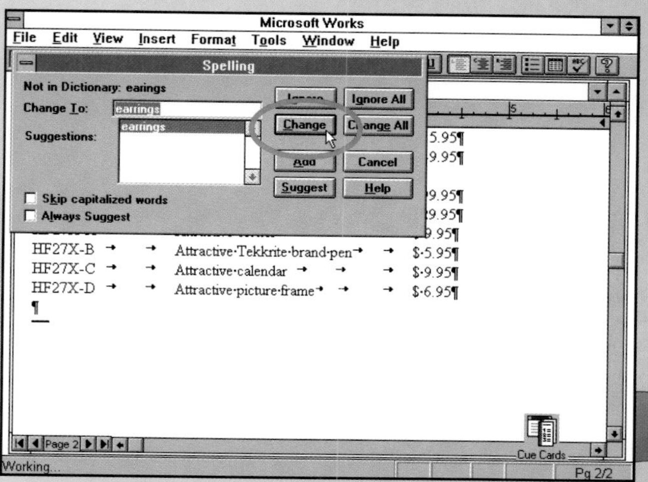

4 Click on **Change**. This changes the spelling of this occurrence of the word; Works continues checking. If you click on Change All rather than Change, Works will change all occurrences of this word.

5 Click on **Add**. Clicking on the Add button adds the highlighted word—in this case, *Tekkrite,* a brand name—to your own dictionary. If you don't want to add or change the word, click on Ignore instead of Add.

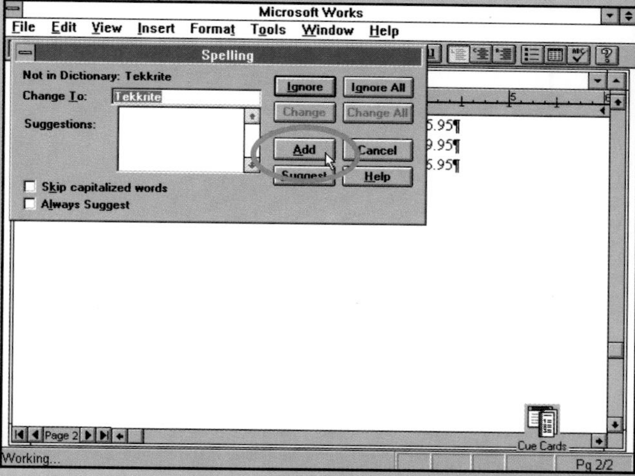

6 When Works displays a message saying that the spelling check is complete, click on **OK**.

Task 18: Checking Spelling and Words

7 Click to the left of any word for which you want to find a synonym. Several occurrences of the same word in a small area of a document—such as the word *Attractive* in this illustration—is never a good idea.

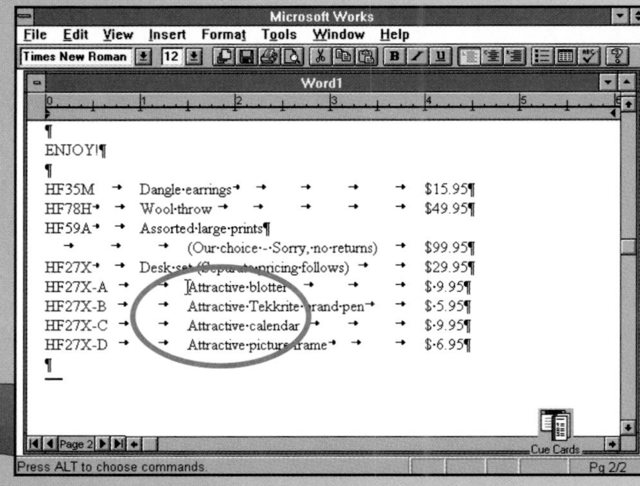

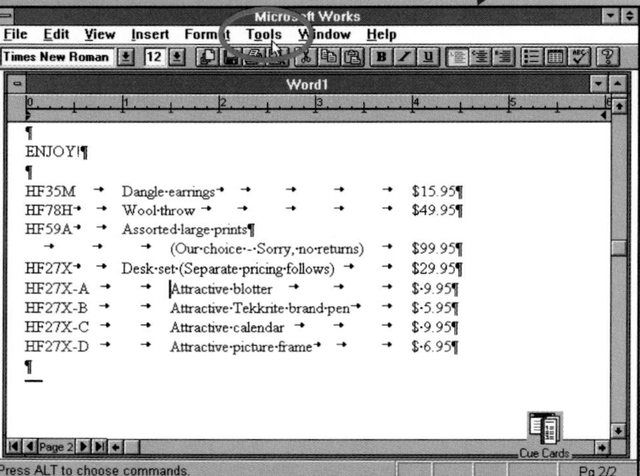

8 Click on **Tools** in the menu bar. This step opens the Tools menu.

9 Click on **Thesaurus**. Works displays the Thesaurus dialog box, which lists the synonyms for the word you indicated in step 7.

WHY WORRY?

To quit using the thesaurus at any time, click on Cancel in the Thesaurus dialog box.

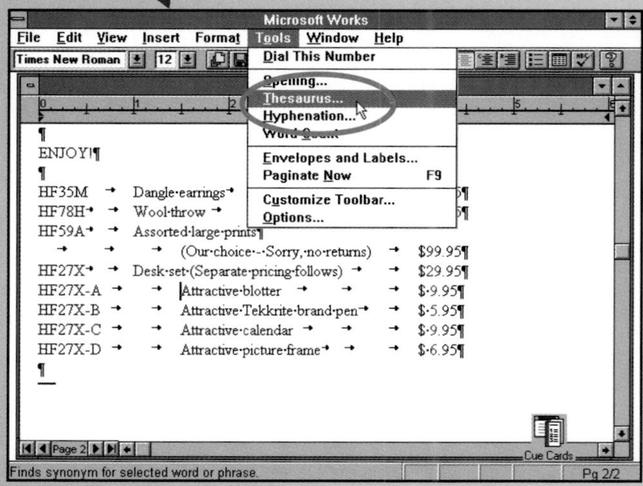

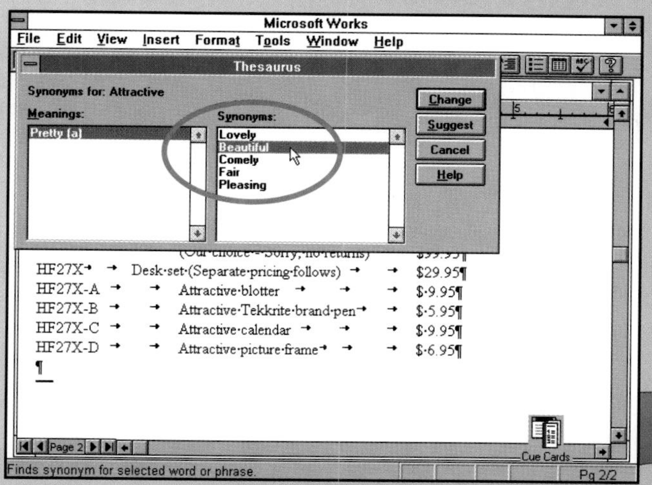

10 Click on the synonym you like best in the Synonyms list. For example, if you want a synonym for *Attractive*, you might click on *Beautiful* in the Synonyms list.

NOTE

To count the number of words in a selection of text or in an entire document, open the Tools menu and choose the Word Count command. Works displays the word count in a message box.

11 Click on the **Suggest** button. Works displays a list of synonyms for the word you selected in step 10.

NOTE

To return to the word you selected originally, such as *Attractive*, click on the Suggest button again.

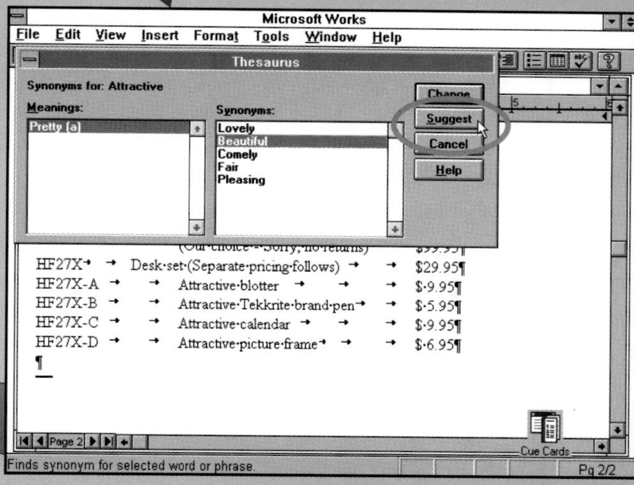

12 Select the synonym you like best in the Synonyms list and click on the **Change** button. Works inserts the selected synonym, such as *Gorgeous*, in place of the word you indicated in step 7.

Microsoft Works
File Edit View Insert Format Tools Window Help
Times New Roman 12
Word1
On·Hand¶
Equipment
Executive·Desks → 11¶
Computer·Tables → 24¶
Office·Chairs → 28¶
Guest·Chairs → 31¶
CPU 486 Rm. 12
CPU 486 Rm. 13
CPU 386 Rm. 15
CPU 486 Rm. 16
CPU 386 Rm. 18
Cue Cards
Pg 1/1
HAPPY2.WPS
Our·valued·customers¶
Cue Cards
Pg 1/2
Microsoft Works
File Edit View Insert Format Tools Window Help
Times New Roman 12
INVREPT.WPS
Monthly Inventory Report
Page - *page*
1/30/95
choose commands.
Microsoft Works
File Edit View Insert Format Tools Window Help
Arial 10
Italic
INVREPT.WPS
Monthly Inventory Report
Page - *page*
1/30/95
Item ID
Item
On Hand
Min.
Ordered
ItemPrice
HF35M Dangle earrings 24 5 50 $15.95
HF78H Wool throw (lg) 132 10 100 $49.95
HF59A Prints 45 10 10 $99.95
HF59B Prints 39 10 20 $99.95
HF59C Prints 81 10 25 $99.95
HF59D Prints 91 10 25 $99.95
HF59E Prints 83 10 25 $99.95
HF59F Prints 35 10 - $99.95
HF27X Desk set 29 10 20 $29.95
HF27X-A Blotter 23 50 - $ 9.95
HF27X-B Tekkrite brand pen 56 10 100 $ 5.95
HF27X-C Calendar 350 50 - $ 9.95
HF27X-D Picture frame 120 100 50
Cue Cards
(toggle)
File
Times
gloves,

PART IV

Formatting a Document

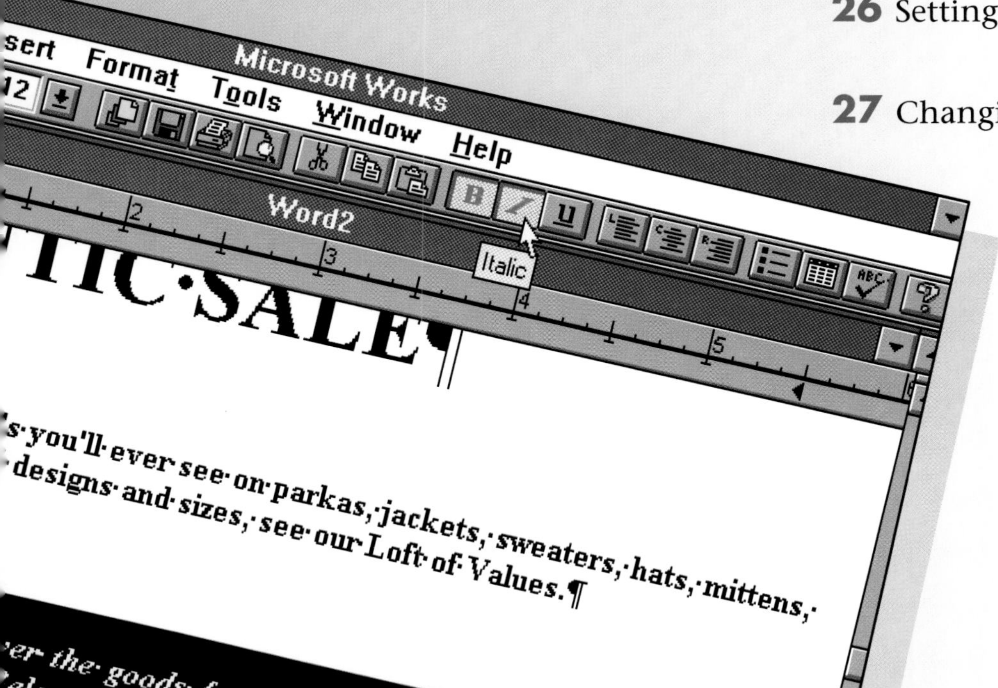

Part IV introduces you to the many ways that you can change a document from a bland "before" version to a stunning "after" version. In this part, you'll find out how to search for text—either to find it or to replace it. Searching and replacing enables you to automate the process of keeping your documents up-to-date. For example, if you need to update a name or address, it's much easier to give a command and see the changes occur automatically. In fact, you can use search and replace as a text-entry shortcut. Type a two- or three-character substitute for a technical term or company name in your document—one that's easy to type—and then find it and replace it with one command. Just be sure that your short substitute is an uncommon combination, such as *tyh* or *u89*.

Part IV also shows you how to create and remove bulleted lists, an important part of many documents. You'll also find out how to create two types of tables—one with a border and one without.

Headers and footers provide information at the top and bottom of pages. Using headers and footers, you can display information on every page, and you'll only have to type that information once. You'll also learn about page numbering, an automatic feature of the Word Processor's footers.

The major emphasis in this part is on teaching you about formatting characters, paragraphs, and even the entire document. You'll enhance text by using boldface, italics, and underlines. You'll learn about paragraph formatting, such as aligning text between the left and right margins, indenting text, and changing the spacing between lines and paragraphs. You'll find out about setting tab stops and changing margins. Because formatting features play such a big role in the Word Processor, Works provides many toolbar buttons and keyboard shortcuts to help.

Bold

Italic

Underline

Character formats are based on *fonts*—families of characters, numbers, and symbols based on the same design. A font includes sets of characters in several point sizes, from very small to very large. A *point,* the measurement from the top of a character to the bottom, is 1/72 inch high. A character that is 36 points is therefore approximately 1/2 inch high, depending on its design. A font typically contains sets of normal, bold, italic, and bold-italic characters.

You can select and format a Works document with these formatting shortcut keys and key combinations:

Shortcut Key	Description
Ctrl+B	Apply or remove boldface
Ctrl+I	Apply or remove italics
Ctrl+U	Apply or remove underlining
Ctrl+E	Center the selection
Ctrl+L	Left-align the selection
Ctrl+R	Right-align the selection
Ctrl+J	Justify the selection
Ctrl+H	Create a hanging indent for a paragraph
Ctrl+G	Undo a hanging indent
Ctrl+N	Indent within an indent
Ctrl+O	Insert space before a paragraph
Ctrl+0 (zero)	Remove space before a paragraph
Ctrl+1	Apply single-spacing
Ctrl+5	Apply one-and-one-half spacing
Ctrl+2	Apply double-spacing

The tasks in this part instruct you in the fundamentals of character, paragraph, and document-wide formatting.

TASK 19

Searching for and Replacing Text

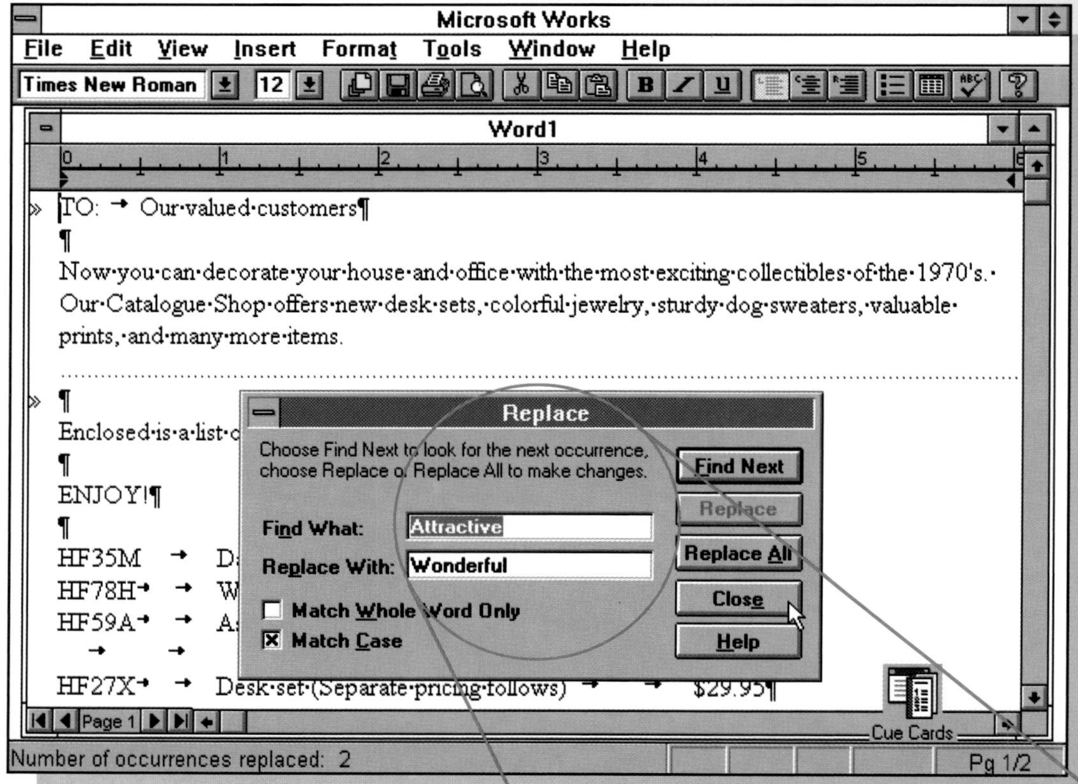

"Why would I do this?"

The Word Processor's search and replace feature allows you to automate the replacement of text in a document. Rather than searching through a document page-by-page, you can replace all occurrences of a word by selecting a command, filling in a dialog box, and clicking on command buttons. In this task, you will search for a word and use two techniques to replace it. This task assumes that the Word Processor tool is active and that a document is open on-screen.

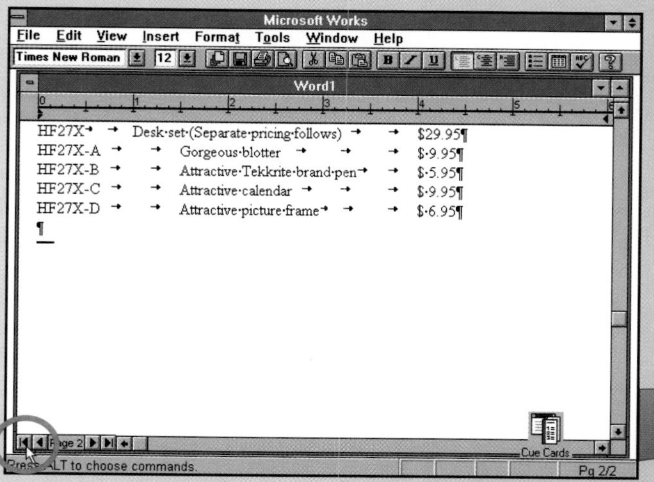

1 Click on the **leftmost arrow** to the left of the horizontal scroll bar. This action moves the insertion point to the top of the document. You will want to start most searches at the beginning of the document, since the Find command works from the current position of the insertion point toward the end of the document.

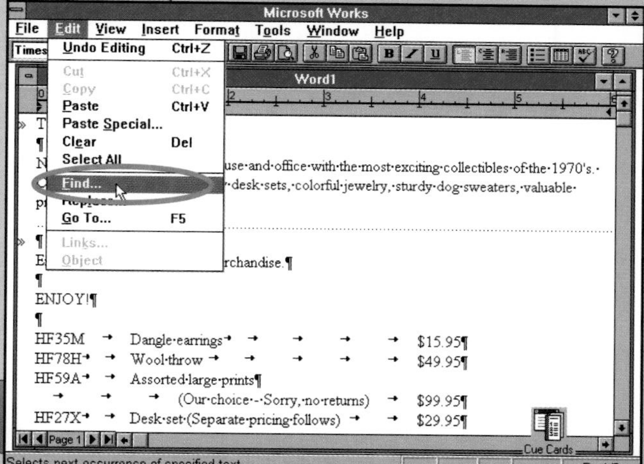

2 Click on **Edit** in the menu bar and click on the **Find** command. This step displays the Find dialog box.

NOTE

Pressing Ctrl+Home is another way to go to the top of a document.

3 In the Find What text box, type the word you want to find, such as **Attractive**. This word is called the *search string*. When the Match Case check box is selected, Works searches for only those words whose uppercase and lowercase characters exactly match the word in the Find What text box.

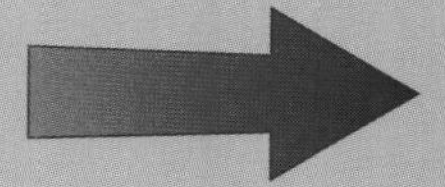

4 Click on **Find Next**. This step starts the search for the word you want to find, such as *Attractive*. When Works find the word in the document, it highlights it.

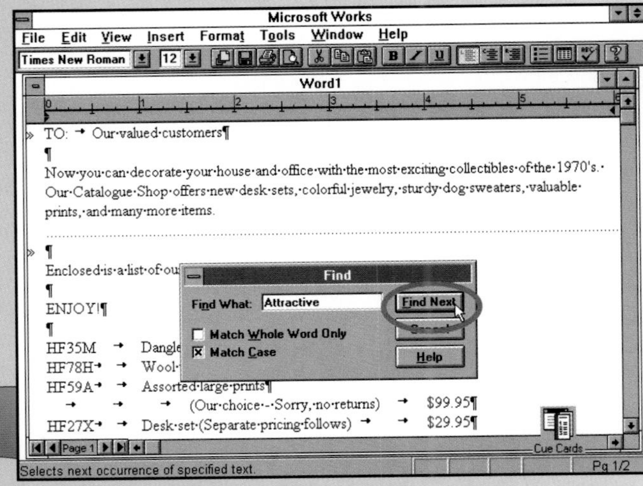

5 Click on **Find Next** again. As long as Works finds the word in the document, the search continues. When the search reaches the end of the document, Works displays an information box.

6 Click on **OK**. The information box closes.

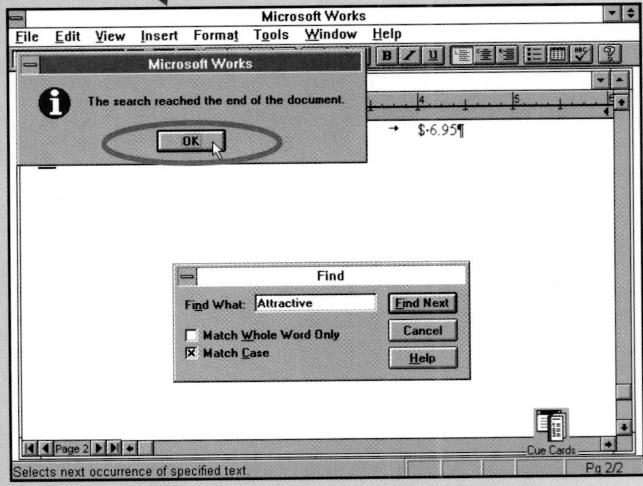

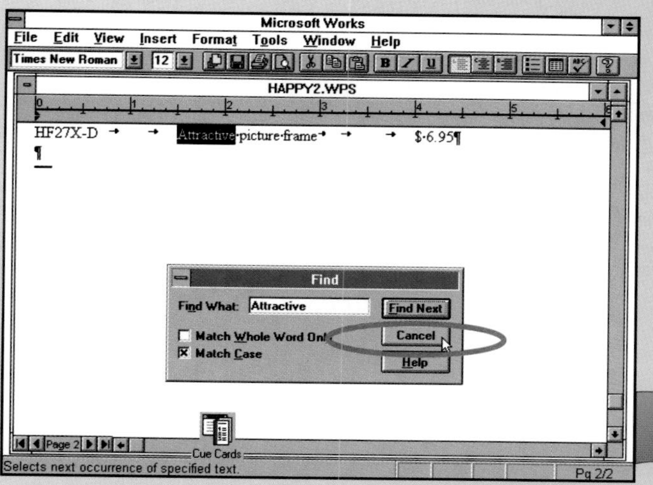

7 When you are finished searching, click on **Cancel**. The Find dialog box closes. The last occurrence of the word remains highlighted.

WHY WORRY?

If Works doesn't find the word you typed in the Find dialog box, it displays an information box telling you that no match was found. Click on OK to close this box. Before you give up, make sure that you spelled the search string correctly.

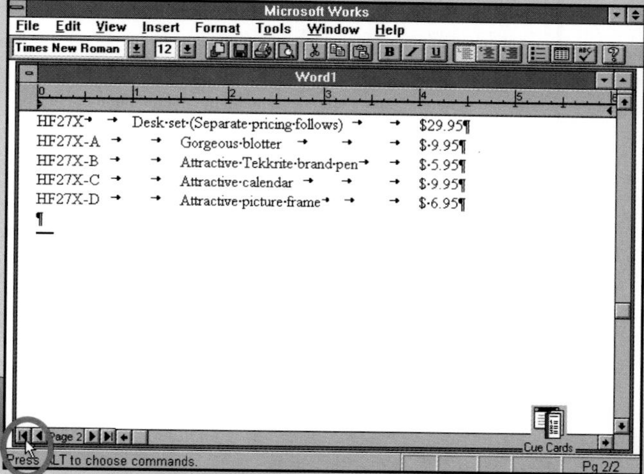

8 Click on the **leftmost arrow** to the left of the horizontal scroll bar. This action moves the insertion point to the top of the document. You can also press Ctrl+Home to go to the top of a document.

9 Click on **Edit** in the menu bar and click on **Replace**. Works opens the Replace dialog box, in which you type a search string and the text that should replace it, called the *replace string*.

Task 19: Searching for and Replacing Text

10 If needed, type a search string, such as **Attractive**, in the Find What text box.

NOTE

If you have already performed a search, the Replace dialog box contains your previous search string. If you want to replace that text, half the dialog box is already filled in for you.

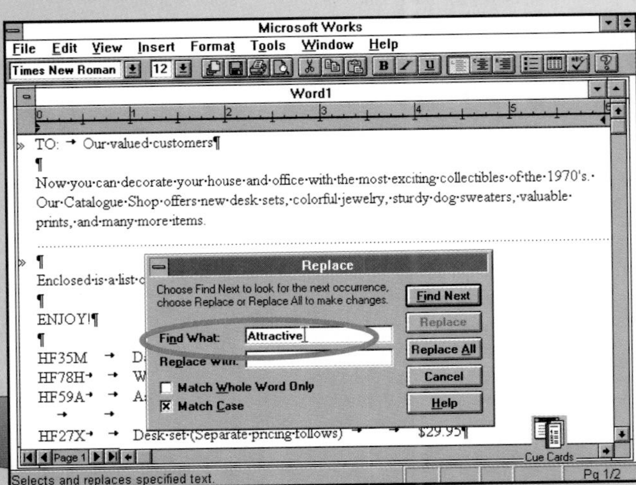

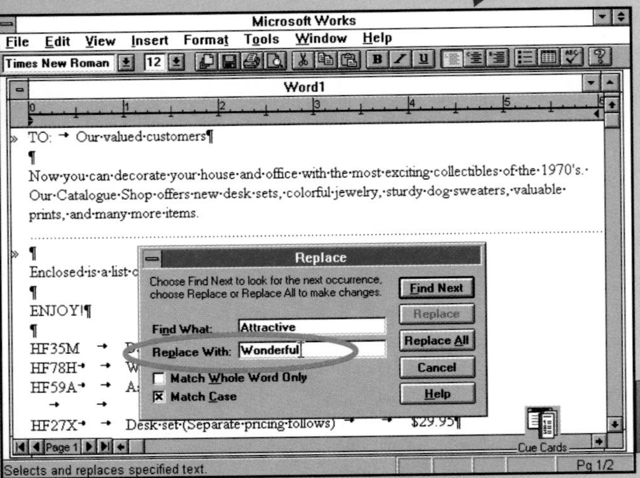

11 Type a replace string, such as **Wonderful**, in the Replace With text box. In this example, Works will look for *Attractive* and, if you choose, will replace it with *Wonderful*.

12 Click on **Find Next**. This step tells Works to look for the search string. In this example, Works finds and highlights the first occurrence of *Attractive*.

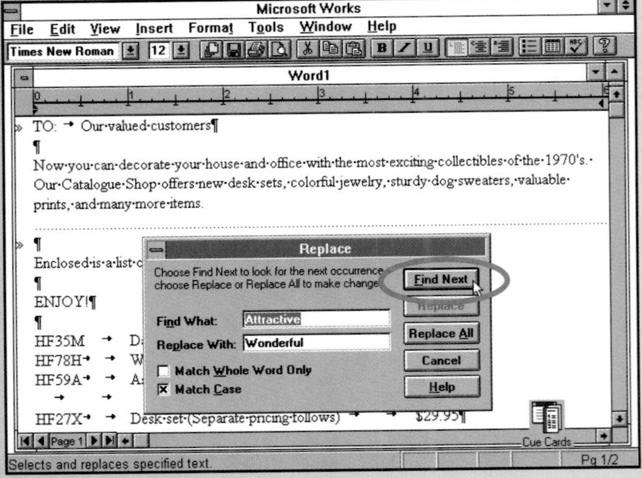

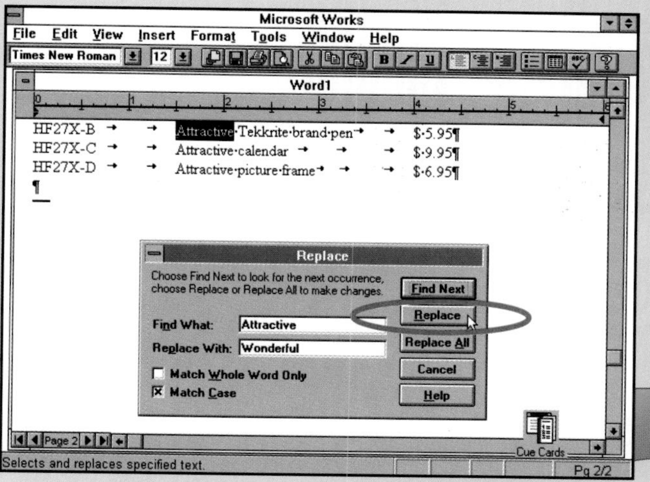

13 If you want to replace this occurrence of the word, click on the **Replace** button. Clicking on Replace gives Works the go-ahead to replace the highlighted search string with the replace string. In this example, Works replaces *Attractive* with *Wonderful* and finds the next occurrence of *Attractive.* If you want to skip the replacement and continue the search, click on Find Next rather than Replace.

14 If you want Works to replace every occurrence of the search string, click on **Replace All**. In this example, Works finds every occurrence of *Attractive,* from the insertion point down, and automatically replaces it with *Wonderful.* When you use this button, Works does not prompt you to confirm each replacement; instead, it displays a message in the status bar to tell you how many replacements were made.

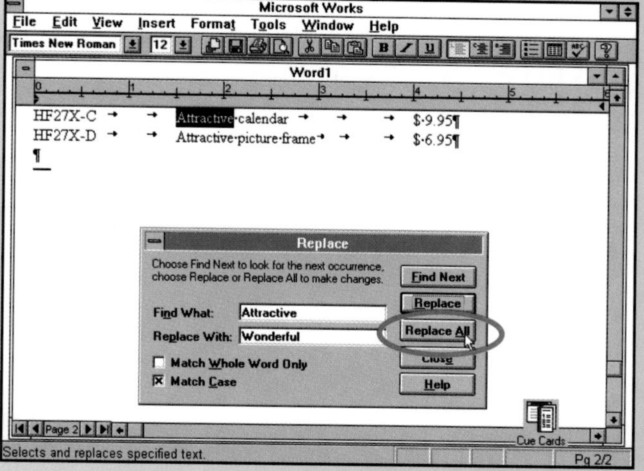

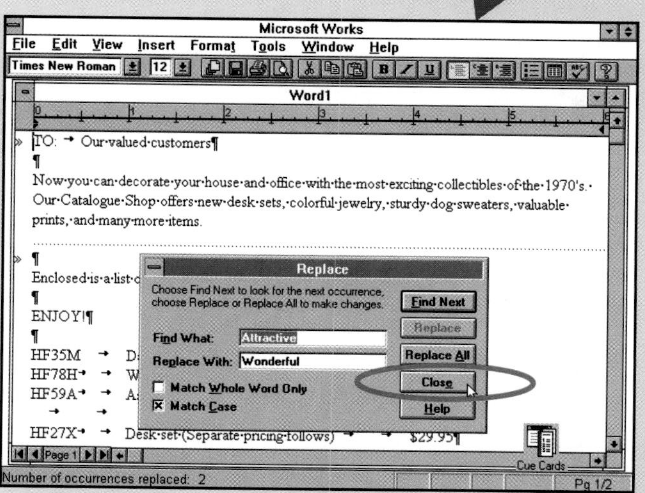

15 Click on **Close** when you are finished with your replacements. The dialog box closes.

WHY WORRY?

If Works doesn't find any occurrence of the search string, it displays an information box telling you that no match was found. After reading the information in the box, click on OK to close it. Make sure that the search string isn't misspelled.

TASK 20

Creating Bulleted and Numbered Lists

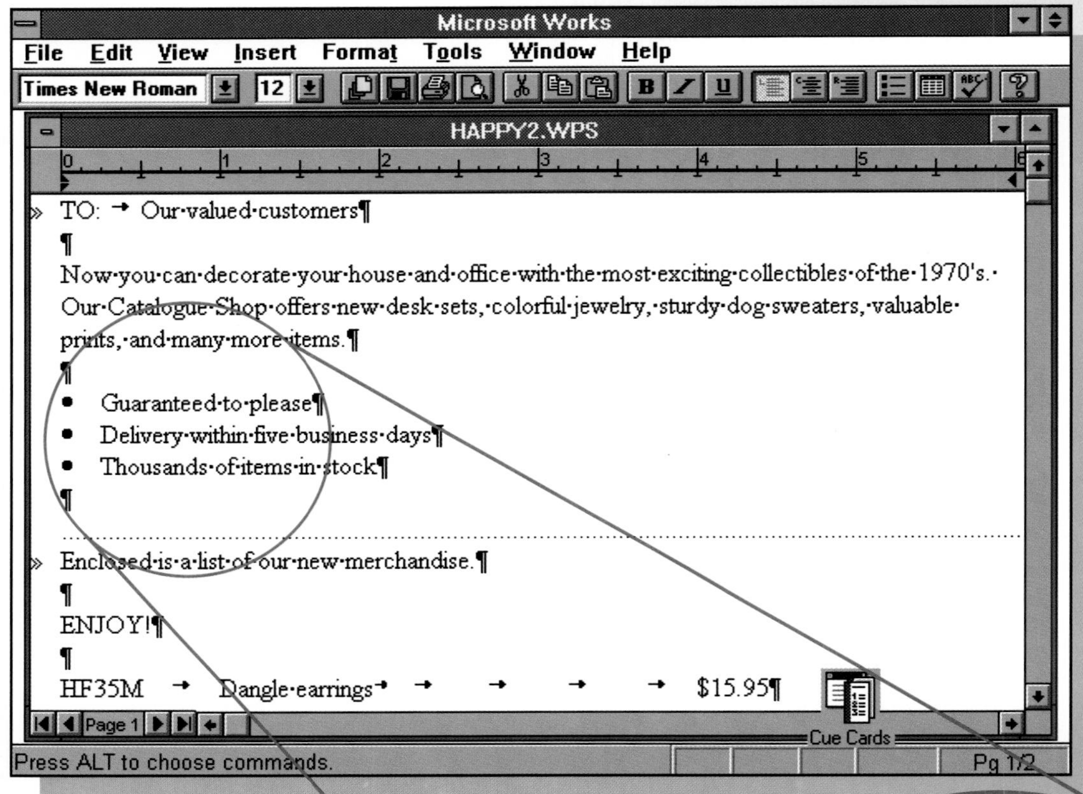

"Why would I do this?"

Bulleted and numbered lists allow you to emphasize lists that would otherwise be hidden in your document, providing a way to point out important phrases or sentences in a document. In this task, you will create a bulleted list and then remove the bullets.

This task assumes that the Word Processor tool is active and that you have a document open on-screen.

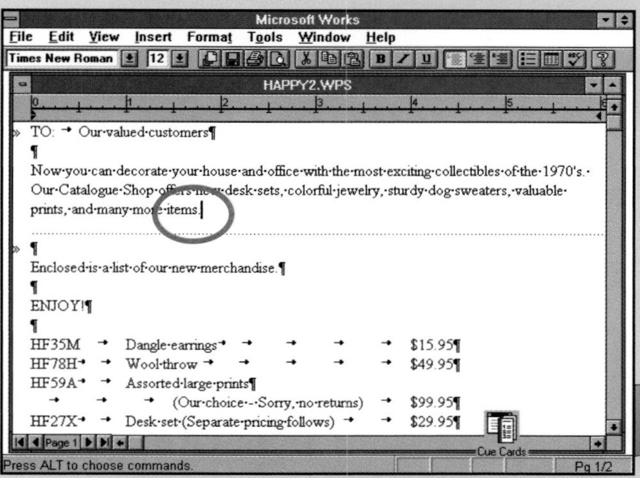

1 Move the insertion point where you want the bulleted list, in this case, after the word *items*.

2 Press **Enter twice**. This step inserts a blank line, creating an area in which you can type a list.

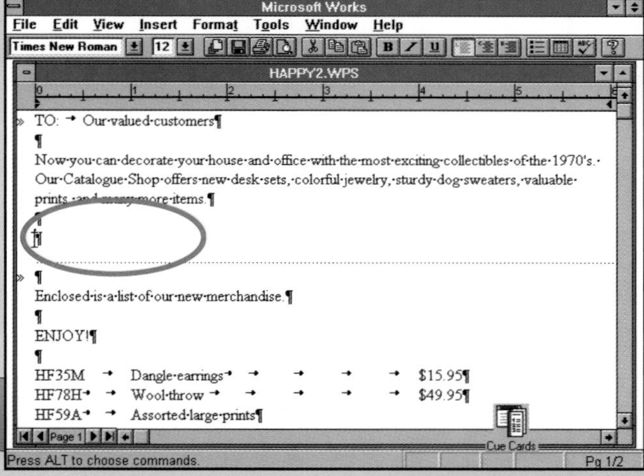

3 Type the items you want in your bulleted list, one item per line, and press Enter at the end of each line. For this example, type **Guaranteed to please** and press **Enter**; type **Delivery within five business days** and press **Enter**; and type **Thousands of items in stock** and press **Enter**.

4 Select the lines you want to make into a bulleted list. You must select a paragraph before you can add a bullet to it.

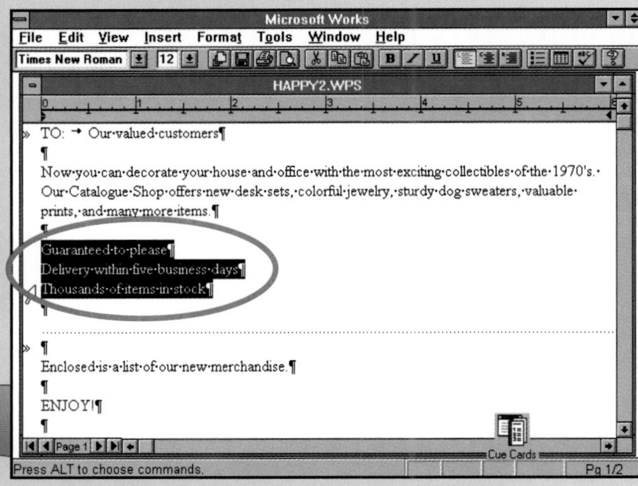

5 Click on the **Bullets** button on the toolbar. Works adds bullets to the selected paragraphs.

NOTE

To remove the highlight from selected text, click anywhere on the screen.

6 Click on **Format** in the menu bar. This step opens the Format menu.

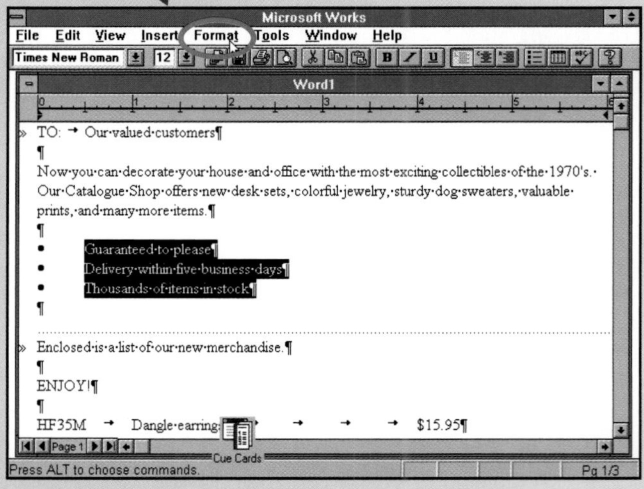

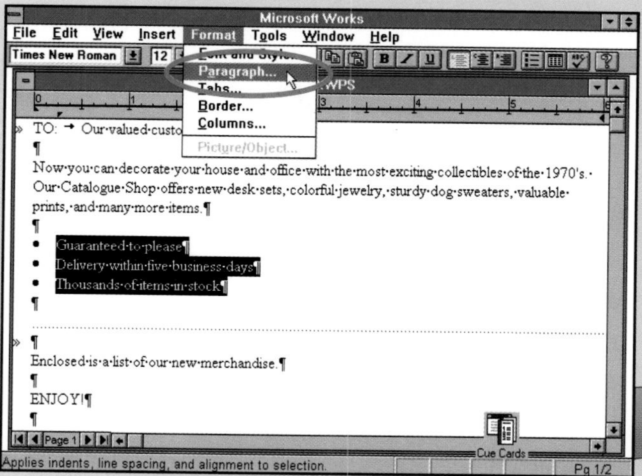

7 Click on the **Paragraph** command. Works displays the Paragraph dialog box.

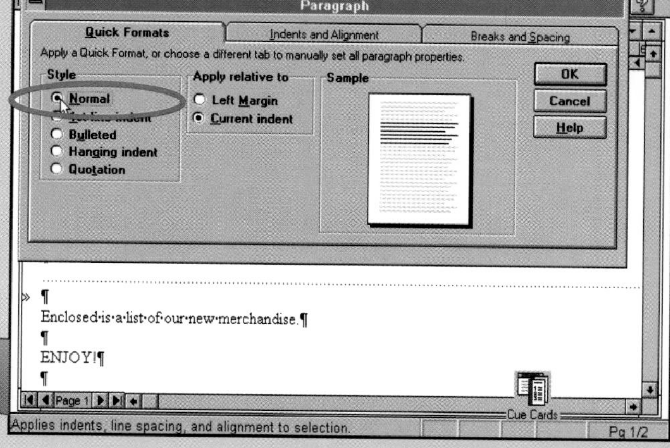

8 Click on the **Normal** option button. This option tells Works to change the style of the selected text back to normal, removing any bullets and aligning the text with the left margin.

NOTE

The Paragraph dialog box has three *tabs* you can click to display its various options. Clicking on the Quick Formats tab, for example, displays options that allow you to apply paragraph formats instantly.

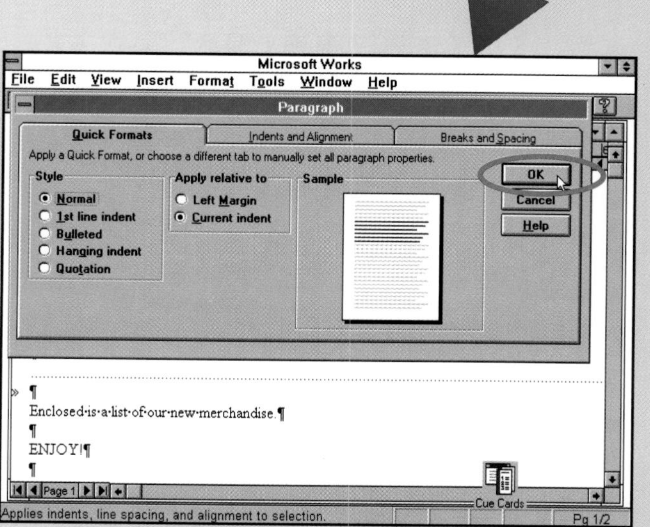

9 Click on **OK**. Works closes the dialog box and removes the bullets from the selected paragraphs.

NOTE

To create a numbered list, select the paragraphs and choose the Format Paragraph command. In the Quick Formats part of the Paragraph dialog box, click on the Hanging Indent option button and click on OK. In front of each paragraph, type the appropriate number and press Tab.

TASK 21

Working with Tables

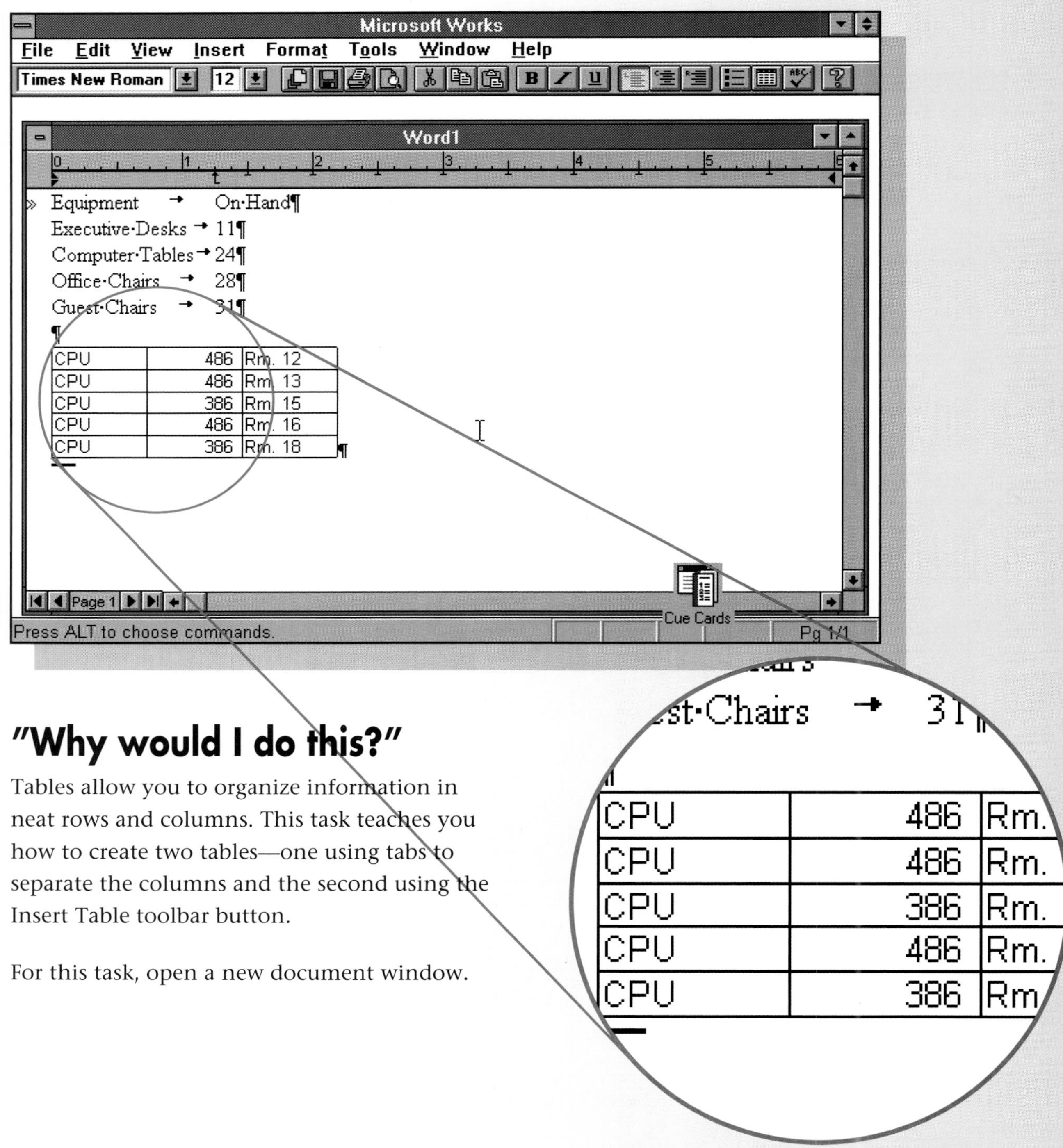

"Why would I do this?"

Tables allow you to organize information in neat rows and columns. This task teaches you how to create two tables—one using tabs to separate the columns and the second using the Insert Table toolbar button.

For this task, open a new document window.

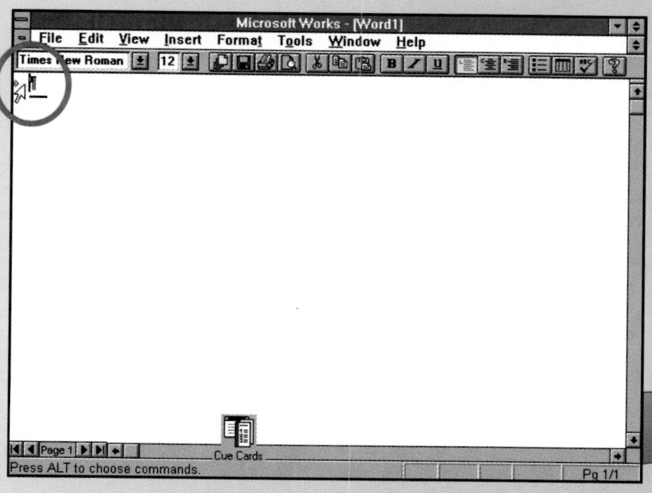

1 Move the insertion point to the area in which you want the table.

2 Follow these instructions to enter the text for your two-column table, or substitute your own information: (1) Type **Equipment**, press **Tab**, type **On Hand**, and press **Enter.** (2) Type **Executive Desks**, press **Tab**, type **11**, and press **Enter**. (3) Type **Computer Tables**, press **Tab**, type **24**, and press **Enter**. (4) Type **Office Chairs**, press **Tab**, type **28**, and press **Enter**. (5) Type **Guest Chairs**, press **Tab**, and type **31**.

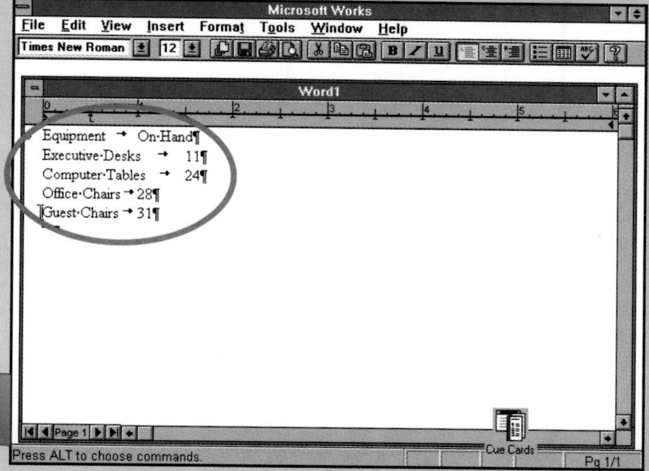

3 Select the entire table. (Press and hold down the left mouse button; then drag from the beginning of the first line to the end of the last line so that the entire table is highlighted.) This step gets the table ready for column alignment.

Task 21: Working with Tables

4 Move the mouse pointer to the ruler and drag the first tab stop from the 1/2-inch mark to the 1 1/4-inch mark.

NOTE

When setting tab marks, look for the longest item in a table and set a tab slightly to the right of the last character in that item.

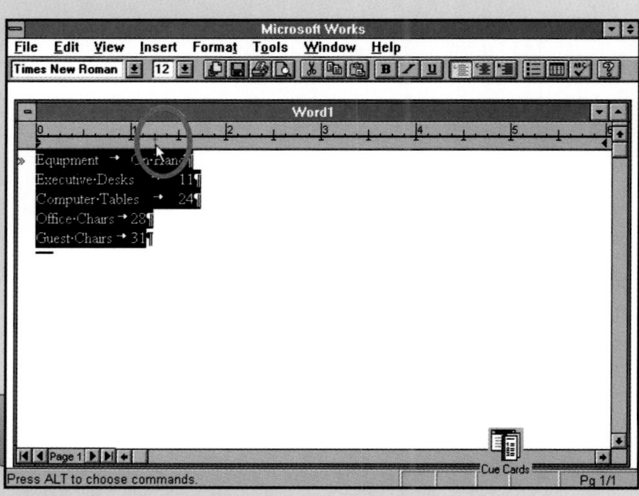

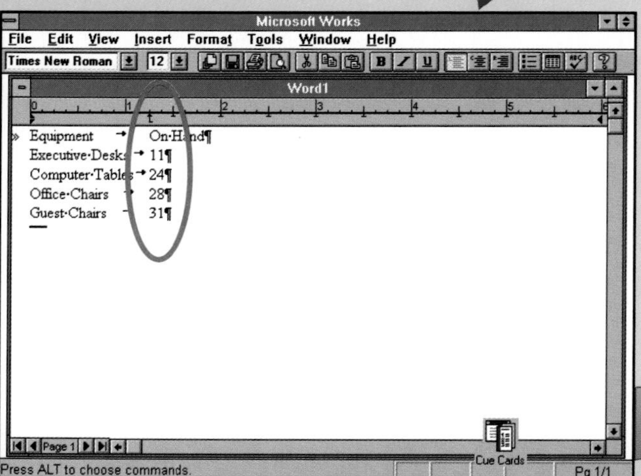

5 Release the mouse button. Works aligns the items in the second column.

NOTE

To make further adjustments to table columns, highlight the appropriate lines and adjust the tabs. For example, in the table, you could select the lines that contain numbers and drag the tab to the 1 1/2-inch mark.

6 Move the mouse pointer after *31* and press **Enter twice**. This inserts a blank line between the table you just created (by using tabs to separate the columns) and the table you will create next (by using the Insert Table button).

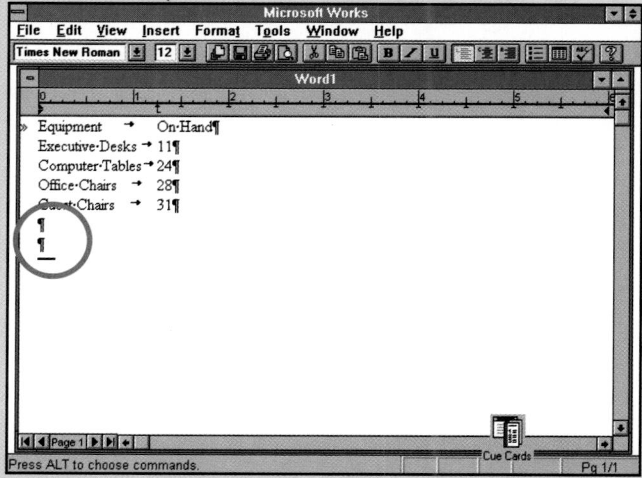

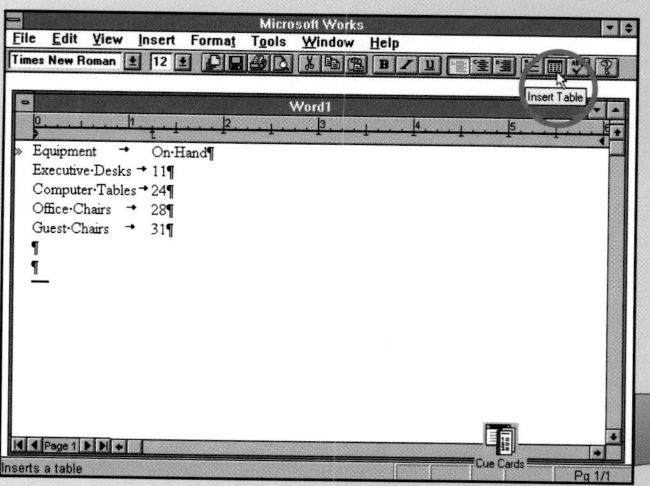

7 Click on the **Insert Table** button on the toolbar. Works opens the Spreadsheet/Table dialog box. Clicking on the toolbar button is the same as opening the Insert menu and choosing the Spreadsheet/Table command.

WHY WORRY?

To prevent the top of a table from being hidden at the top of a page, press Enter two or three times to move the insertion point down; then insert the table.

8 Click on **New Table**. This option lets you start with blank columns and rows. The other option button—Use Existing Spreadsheet Range—enables you to link to an existing spreadsheet.

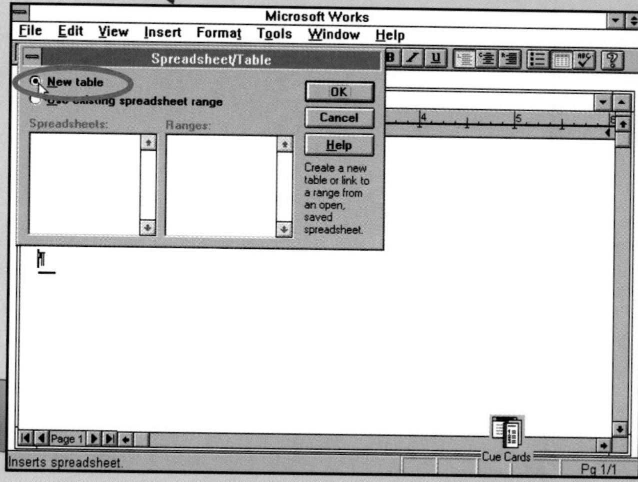

9 Click on **OK**. Works opens a small table showing three columns and five rows. You can use the scroll bar to display table cells not currently on-screen.

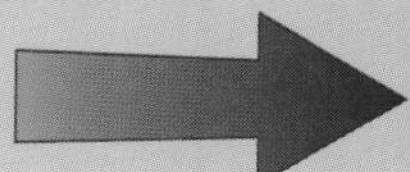

10 Click on the **first cell** in the table. A *cell,* a small box in a spreadsheet, holds data or formulas. This step makes the cell active and ready for you to type text. An active cell is surrounded by a boldface border.

NOTE

This type of table is actually a small spreadsheet. For information about spreadsheet formatting and editing, see the spreadsheet tasks.

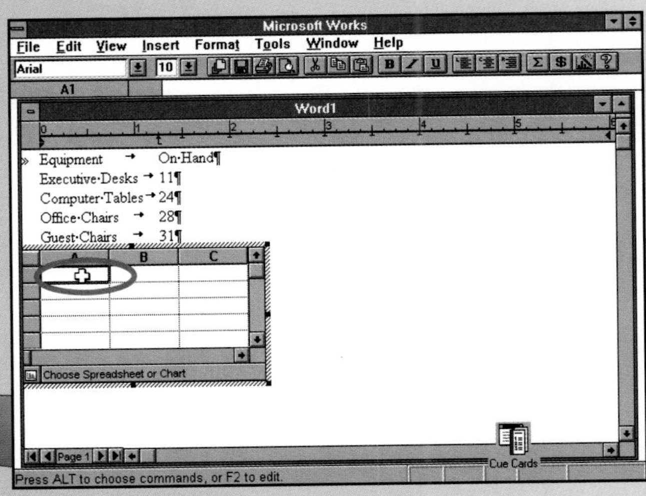

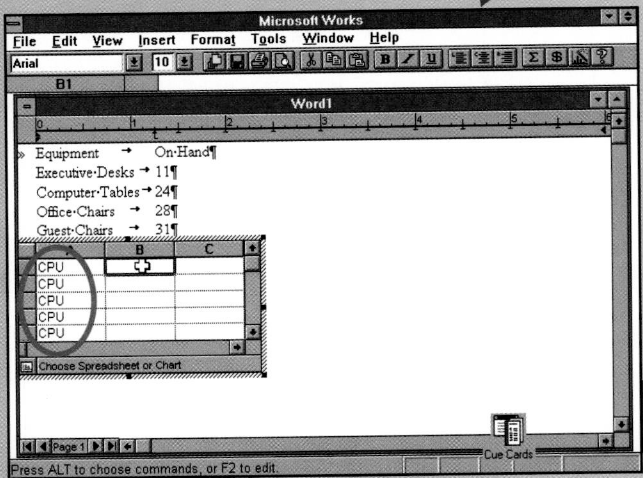

11 Type **CPU** in every cell in the first column of the table. To move from cell to cell down a column, press ↓ or click in the cell to which you want to move.

12 Fill in the remaining cells from top to bottom as follows: In column B, type **486**, **486**, **386**, **486**, and **386**. In column A, type **Rm. 12**, **Rm. 13**, **Rm. 15**, **Rm. 16**, and **Rm. 18**. Other keys you can press to move from cell to cell are ↑, ←, →, Tab, and Shift+Tab.

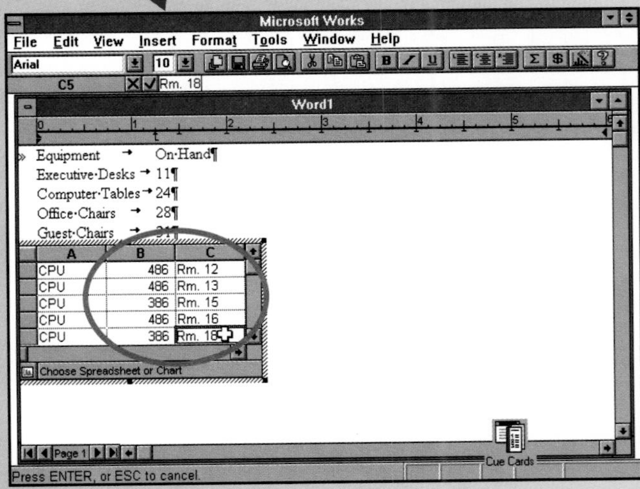

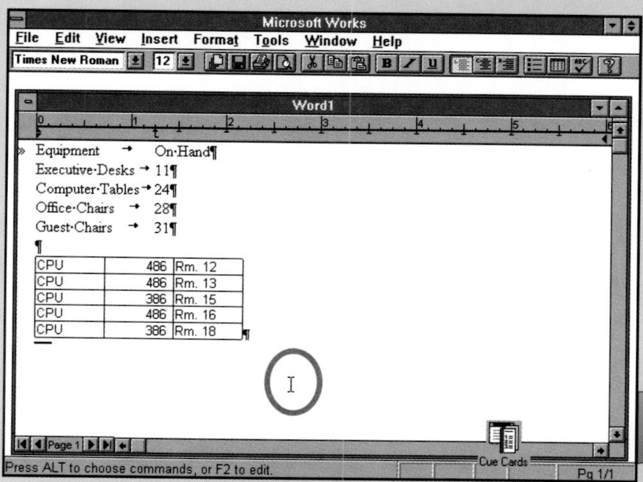

13 Click outside the boundaries of the table to return to your document.

WHY WORRY?

If clicking outside the table shows an empty space where the table should be, click once more to display the table.

14 Double-click in the table to return to the table. The only time you can edit a spreadsheet table is when it has a thick border and two scroll bars.

NOTE

To change the size of the table, drag any of the table's *handles*—the small black squares at the corners and sides of the table—to make the table longer, wider, or both. When you return to the document, the table maintains its new dimensions.

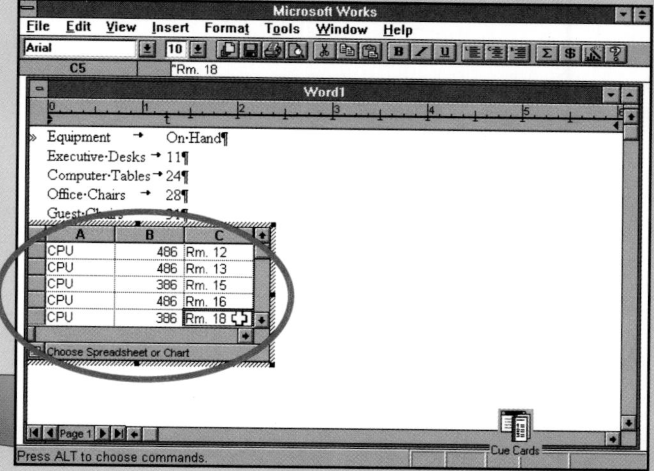

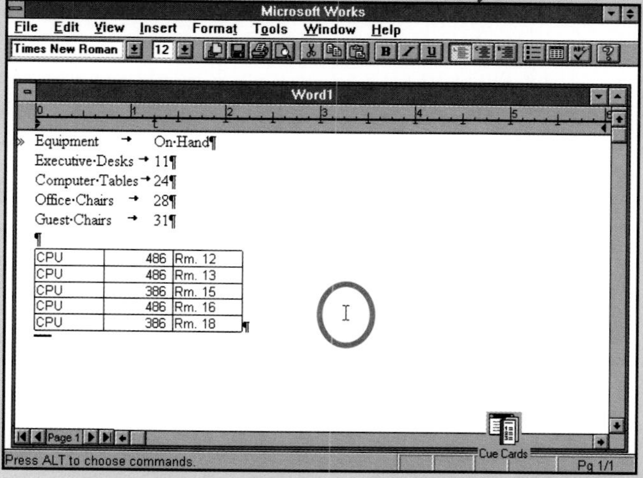

15 Click outside the boundaries of the table to return to your document.

TASK 22

Adding Headers, Footers, and Page Numbers

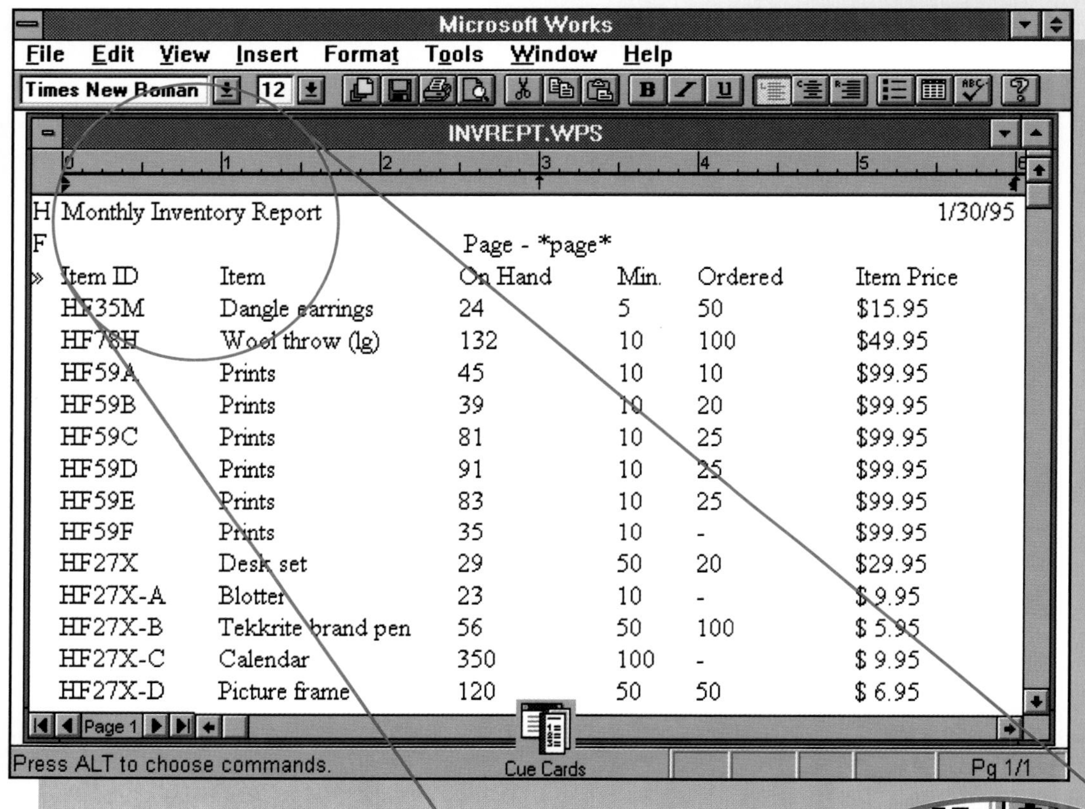

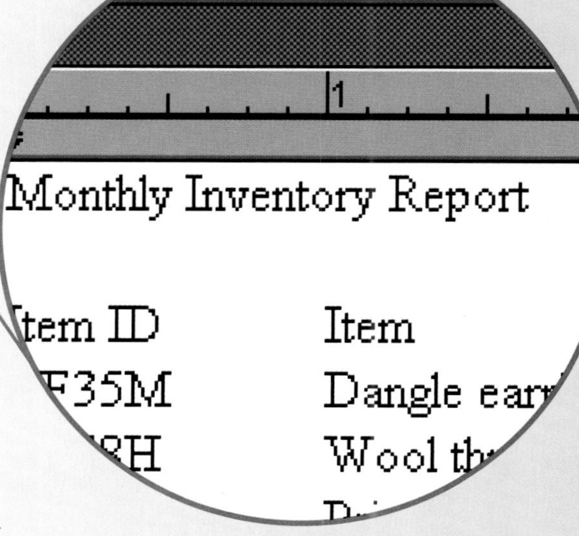

"Why would I do this?"

Headers and footers add a professional look to a document. Headers are common for long documents, in which it's important to stamp each page with text such as the page number, file name, author's name, title, or today's date. In this task, you will add a header and footer (with a page number) to a document.

This task assumes that the Word Processor tool is active and that a document is open on-screen.

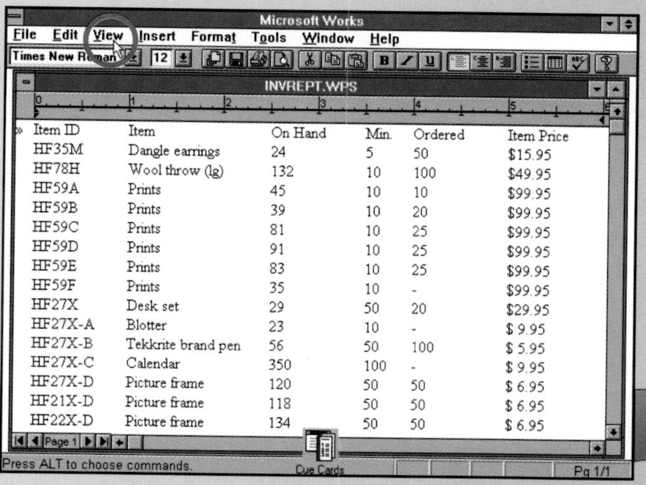

1 Click on **View** in the menu bar. This step opens the View menu.

2 Click on the **Headers and Footers** command. Works opens the Headers and Footers dialog box. The insertion point is in the Header text box.

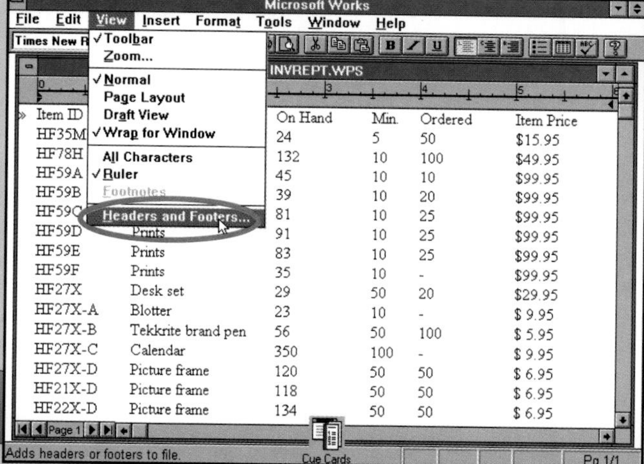

3 Click on the **Use header and footer paragraphs** check box and click on **OK**. Selecting this option allows you to have multiple-line headers and footers.

WHY WORRY?

Although a footer paragraph appears at the top of the page on-screen, it will appear at the bottom of the page when you print.

Task 22: Adding Headers, Footers, and Page Numbers

4 Click to the right of H and type your header text, such as **Monthly Inventory Report**. Press **Tab twice** to move to the header's right zone, and press **Ctrl+;** to insert your computer system date.

NOTE

Headers and footers contain three zones: the left zone for left-aligned text, the middle for centered text, and the right for right-aligned text. The footer's middle zone has a page number placeholder, which you can delete.

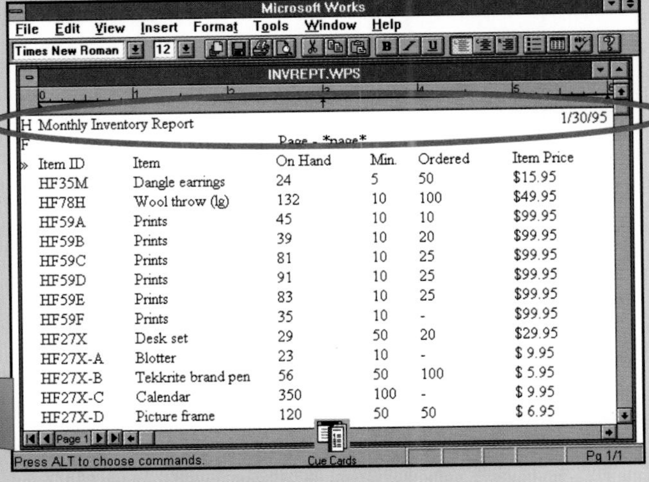

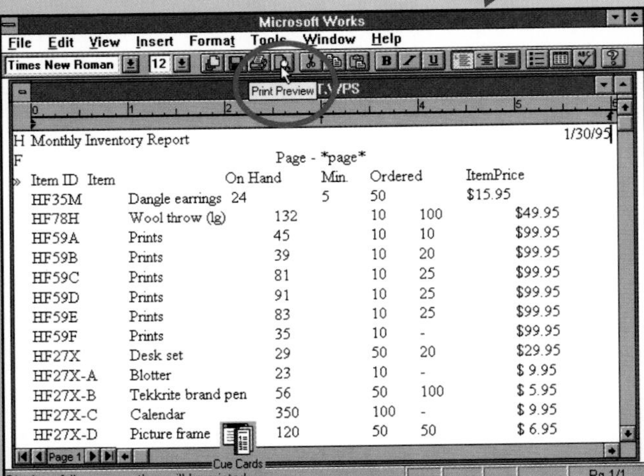

5 Click on the **Print Preview** button on the toolbar. Clicking this button is equivalent to choosing File Print Preview. Works switches the screen to Print Preview, which is the only way to see header and footer paragraphs before you print.

6 View the page to make sure that the headers and footers look the way you want. Use the magnifying glass pointer, if necessary, to increase the size of the text. Click on Cancel when you're done.

NOTE

To use a starting page number other than 1, choose File Page Setup, click the Other Options tab, type a number in the 1st Page Number text box, and click on OK.

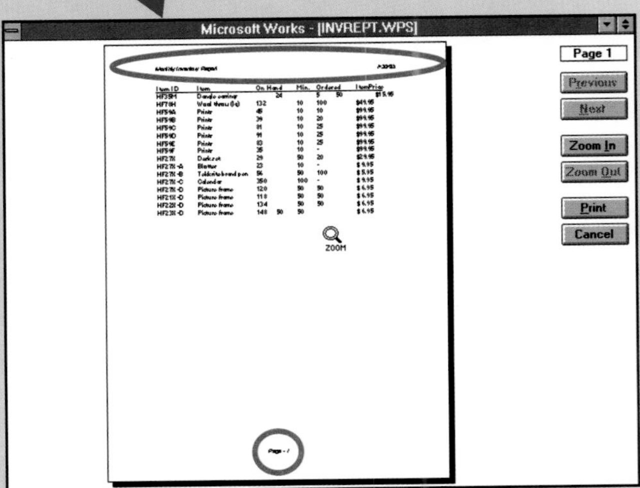

TASK 23

Formatting Text

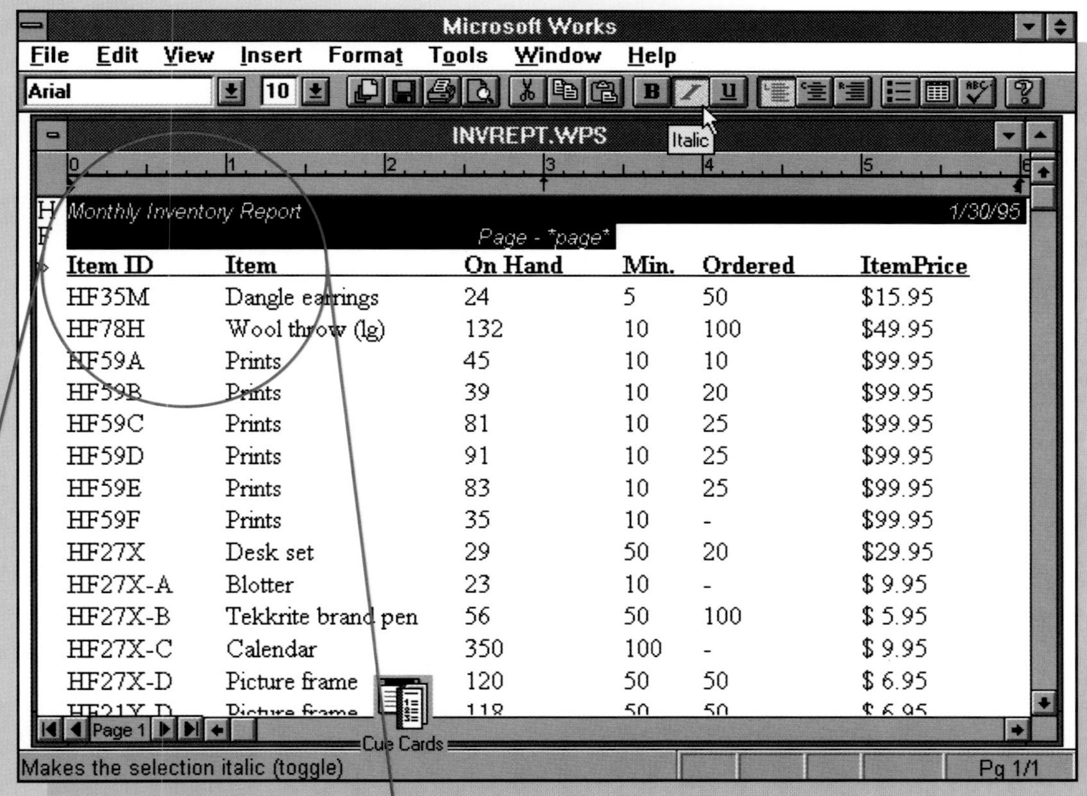

"Why would I do this?"

Character or text formatting spells the difference between a run-of-the-mill document and one that impresses its audience. In this task, you'll format and enhance text by applying boldface, italics, and underlines and by changing the font and font size.

This task assumes that the Word Processor tool is active and that you have a document open on-screen.

Task 23: Formatting Text

1 Select a line of text to format as boldface and underlined. In this example, select the line that contains the table's column headings.

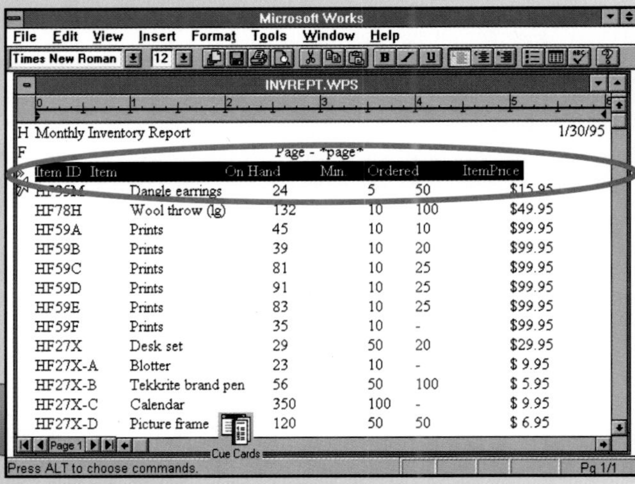

NOTE

A one-step way to select a line of text is to move the mouse pointer toward the left margin. When the insertion point changes to an arrow that points up and toward the right, point to the line you want to select and click the left mouse button.

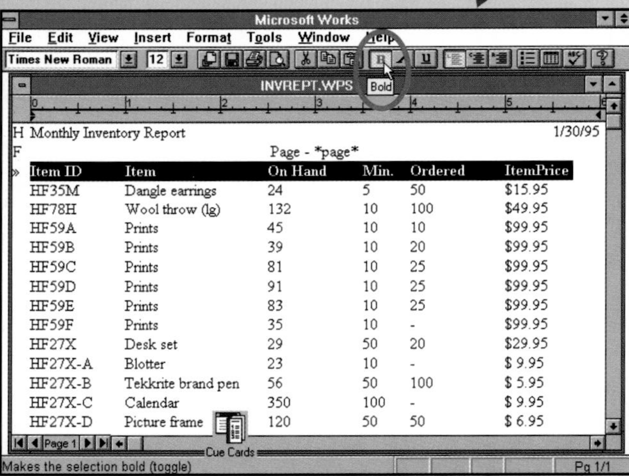

2 Click on the **Bold** button on the toolbar. The highlighted text changes to boldface and the Bold button looks pressed. You can also apply and remove boldface by pressing Ctrl+B.

3 Click on the **Underline** button on the toolbar. Works underlines the highlighted text, and the Underline button looks pressed. Notice that the selected text remains bold and that the Bold button still looks pressed. You can also apply and remove underlines by pressing Ctrl+U.

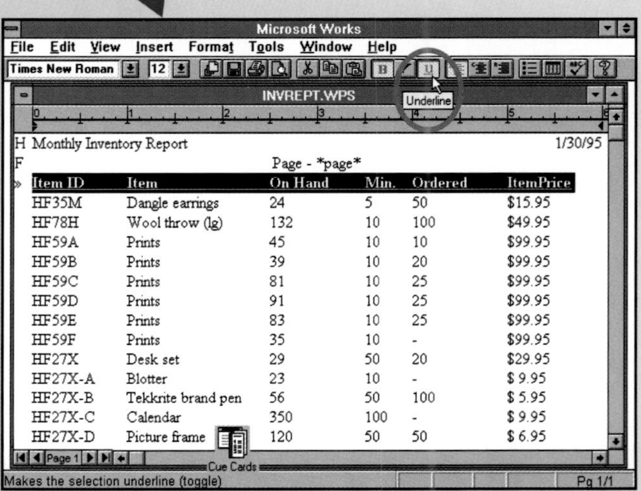

NOTE

To return text to normal, select it and press Ctrl+Spacebar.

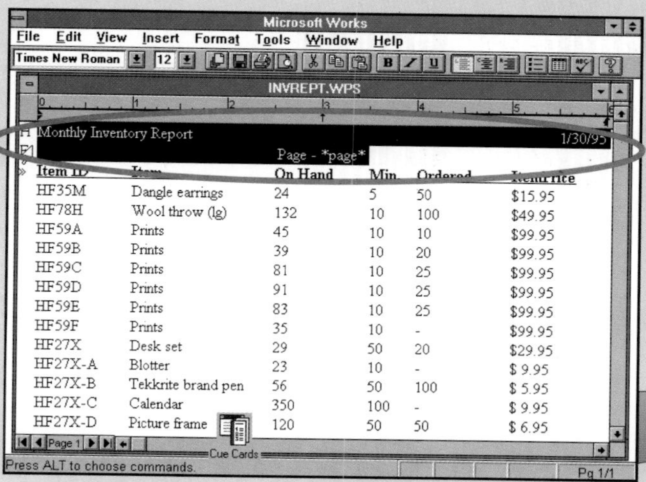

4 Select any text of which you want to change the font and font size. For this example, select the document header and footer.

5 Click on the **down-arrow** button to the right of the Font Name drop-down list box on the toolbar. This opens the drop-down list box so that you can choose a different font for the selected text.

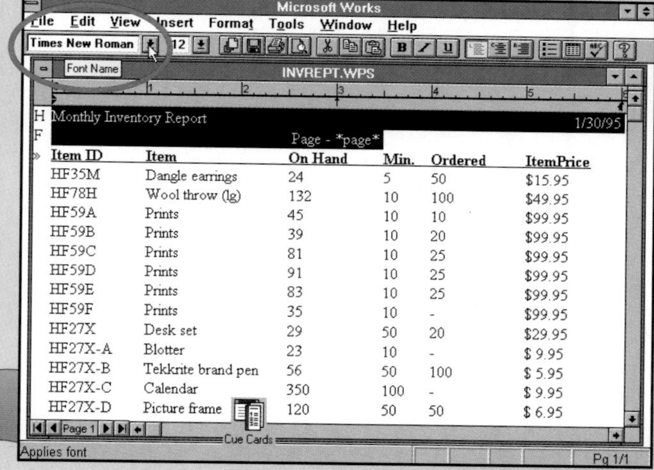

6 Click on the name of the font you want to apply to the selected text; for example, click on **Arial**. You might have to scroll through the list to find the name of the font you want. Works changes the font of the selected text.

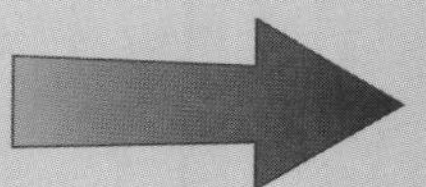

Task 23: Formatting Text

7 Click on the **down-arrow** button to the right of the Font Size drop-down list box on the toolbar. This opens the drop-down list box so that you can choose a different point size for the selected text.

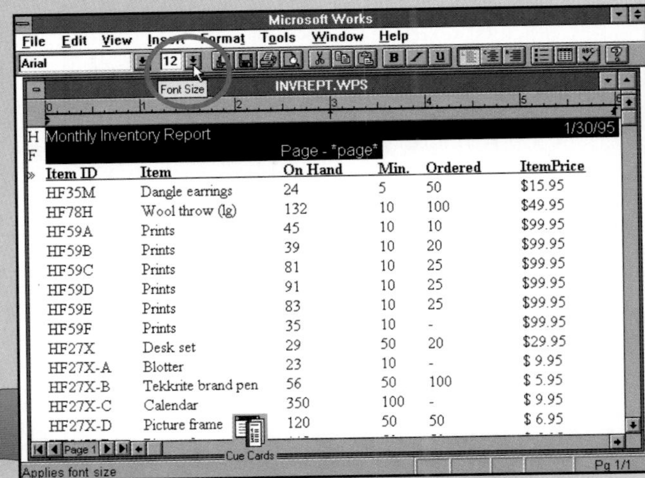

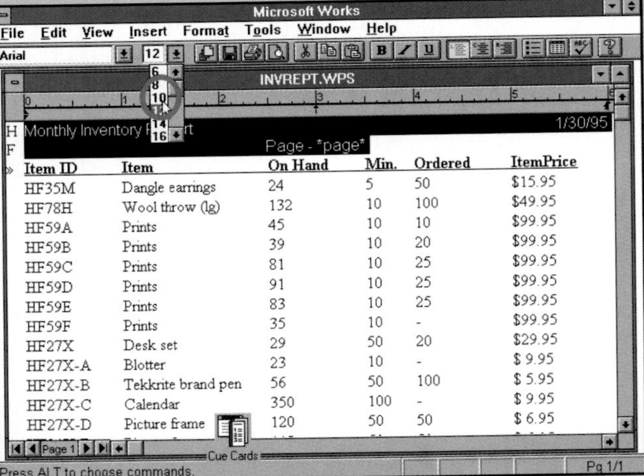

8 Click on the font size you want to apply to the selected text, such as **10**. Works changes the selected text's size. In this example, the selected text becomes smaller than the text in the body of the report, which is 12.

9 Click on the **Italic** button on the toolbar. Works italicizes the selected text, and the Italic button looks pressed. You can also apply and remove italics by pressing Ctrl+I.

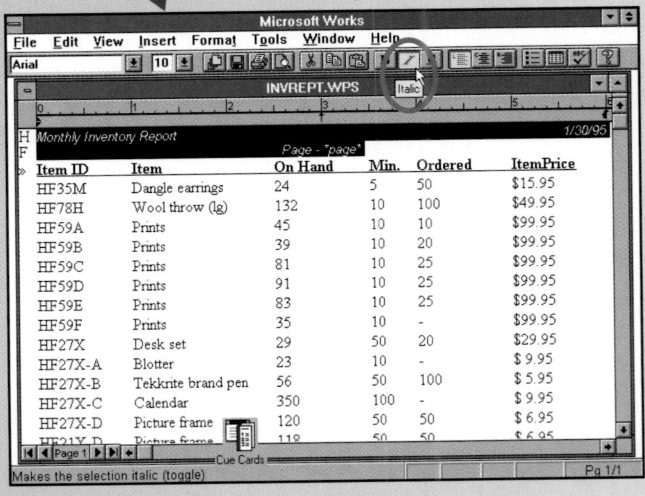

NOTE

You can also format text by choosing the Font and Style command from the Format menu. In the Font and Style dialog box, you can change all sorts of text characteristics.

TASK 24

Changing Paragraph Alignment

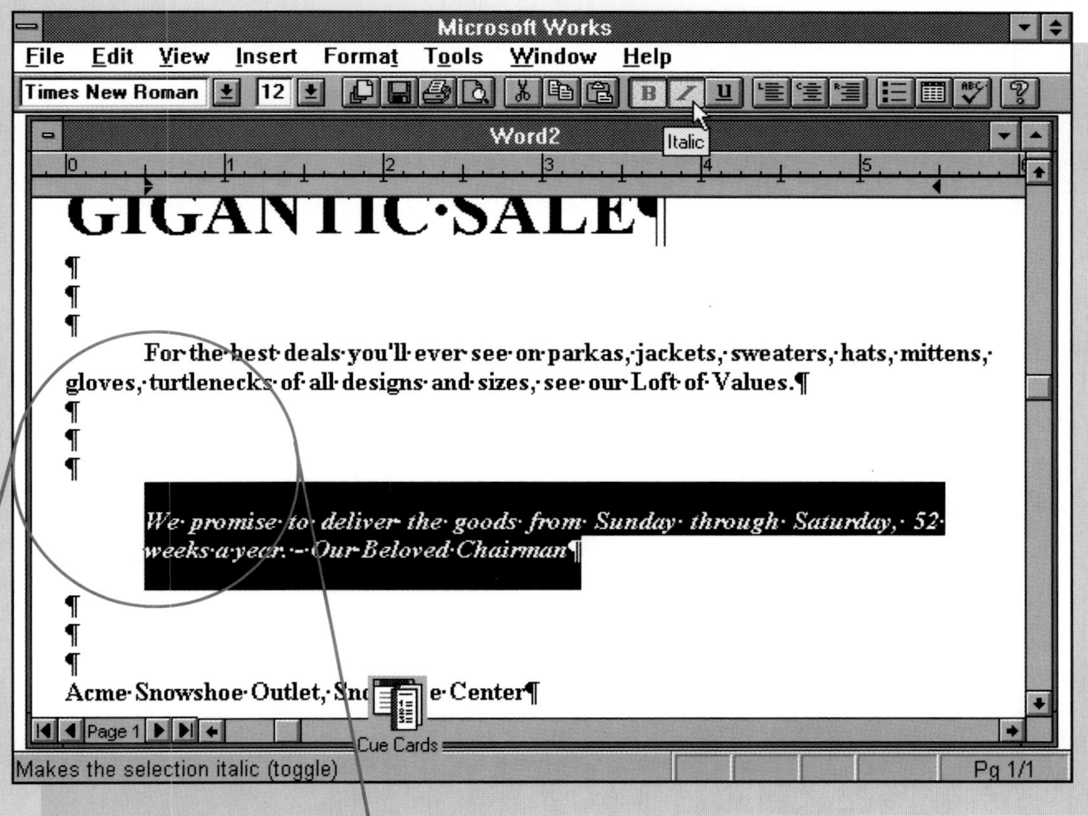

"Why would I do this?"

Paragraph alignment allows you to adjust lines of a paragraph between the left and right margins. You can show the importance of a quotation by justifying and indenting it. In this task, you will create a simple sales flyer and align and indent selected paragraphs.

This task assumes that the Word Processor tool is active, with a blank document open on-screen.

Task 24: Changing Paragraph Alignment

1 Click on **View** in the menu bar and click on the **Page Layout** command. This command allows you to view the page on-screen as it will print.

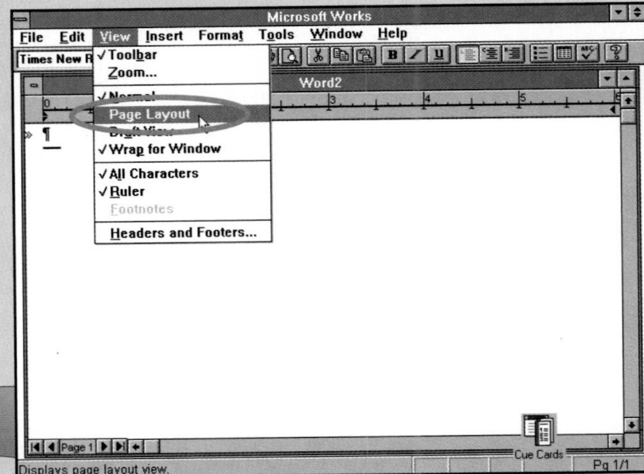

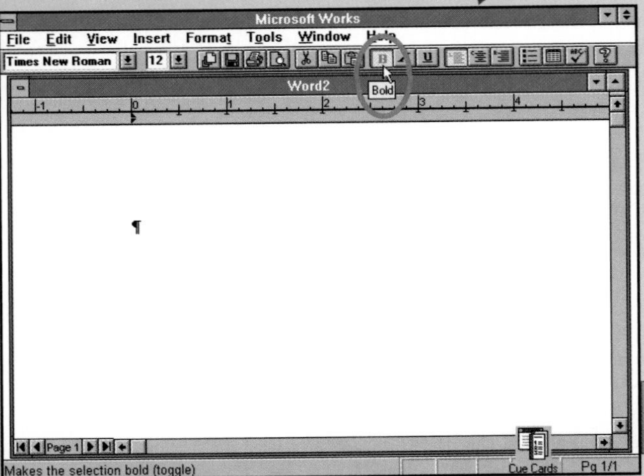

2 Click on the **Bold** button on the toolbar. This step enables you to add emphasis to any text you type.

3 Type **GIGANTIC SALE** and press **Enter twice**; then repeat this process two more times. Press **Enter 11 times** and type **Acme Snowshoe Outlet, Snowshoe Center**.

NOTE

To see tab marks and paragraph marks on-screen, choose View All Characters. Even though you can see tab marks and paragraph marks on-screen, they will not print.

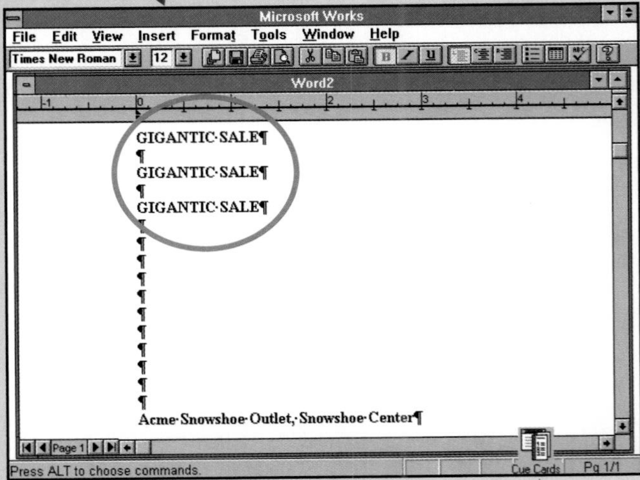

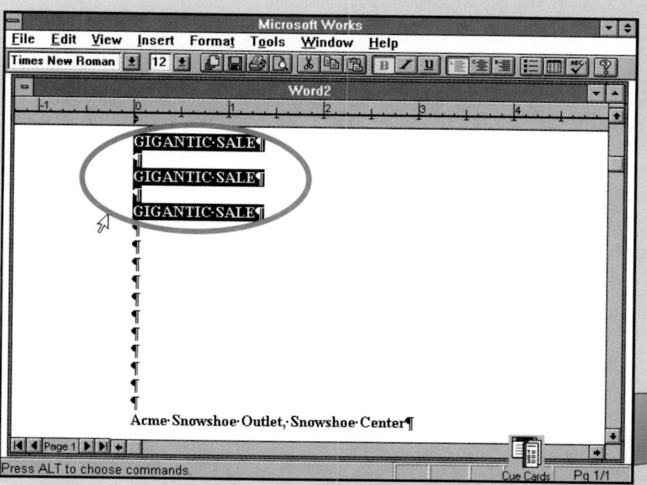

4 Select the three lines that say GIGANTIC SALE. This step prepares for a change in font size for the selected text.

5 Click on the **down-arrow** button to the right of the Font Size drop-down list box on the toolbar, and click on **32**. This step specifies a different point size for the selected text, making it large enough to get some attention.

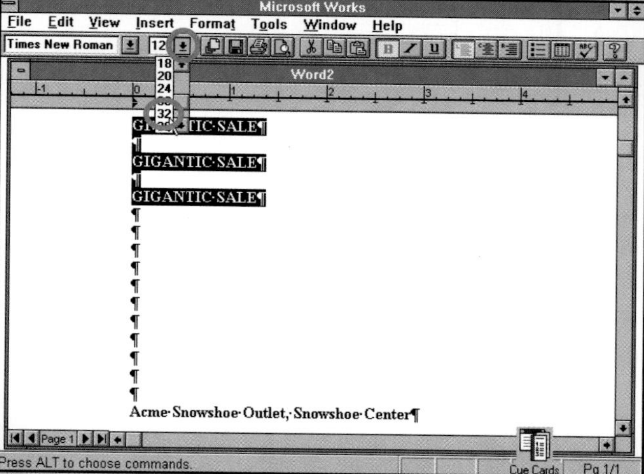

6 Select the first line of text in the document. This step prepares for a change in alignment for the selected line.

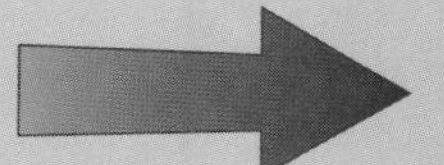

Task 24: Changing Paragraph Alignment

7 Click on the **Right Align** button on the toolbar. This aligns the selected text with the right margin. You can also right-align text by pressing Ctrl+R.

NOTE

By default, Works text is *left-aligned* — that is, the beginning of each line is lined up with the left margin and end of each line is *ragged* (not aligned). You can left-align text by pressing Ctrl+L.

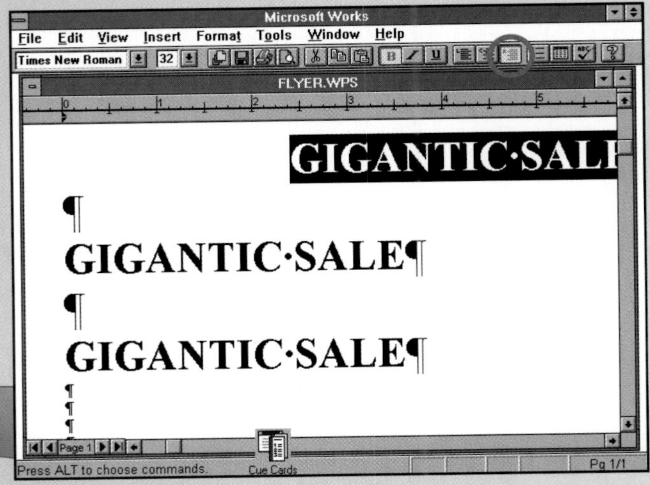

8 Select the second line of text in the document. This step prepares for a change in alignment for the selected line.

9 Click on the **Center Align** button. This centers the selected text between the left and right margins. You can also center-align text by pressing Ctrl+E.

NOTE

Another way to set paragraph alignment is to choose Format Paragraph, click on the Indents and Alignment tab, and click on the appropriate option button in the Alignment group.

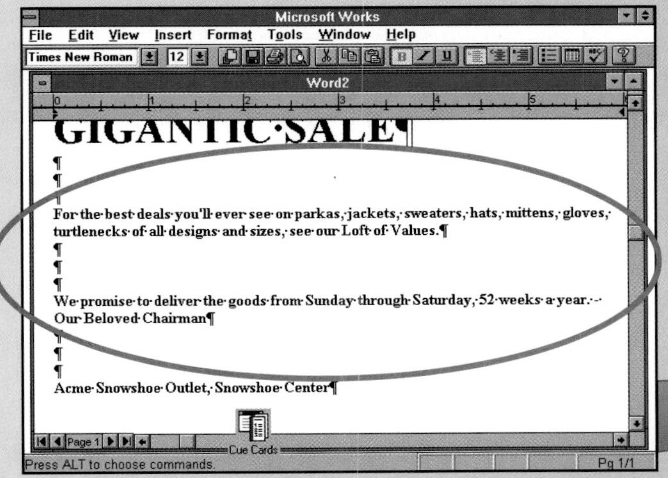

10 Move the insertion point down six lines and type: **For the best deals you'll ever see on parkas, jackets, sweaters, hats, mittens, gloves, turtlenecks of all designs and sizes, see our Loft of Values.**

Move the insertion point down four lines and type: **We promise to deliver the goods from Sunday through Saturday, 52 weeks a year. - Our Beloved Chairman.**

11 Select the first of the paragraphs you just typed. This step prepares for a change in indentation for the selected paragraph.

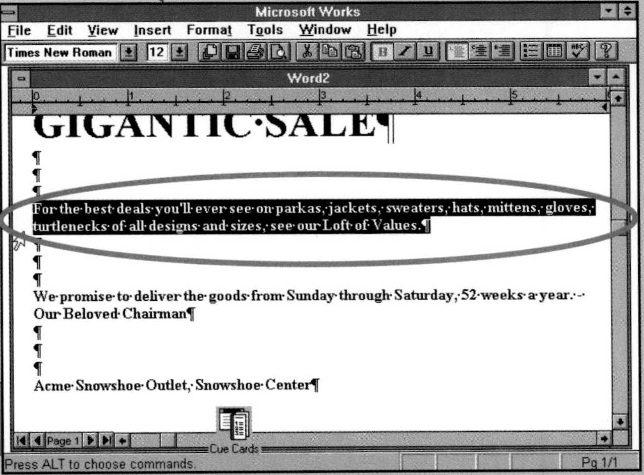

12 Click on **Format** in the menu bar and click on **Paragraph**. This step opens the Paragraph dialog box. If necessary, click on the Quick Formats tab to bring that part of the dialog box forward.

Task 24: Changing Paragraph Alignment

13 Click on the **1st line indent** option button. This option indents the first line of the selected paragraph; all other lines in the selected paragraph remain aligned with the left margin.

NOTE

When you click on an option button in the Style group in the Paragraph dialog box, the Sample box illustrates what the paragraph will look like. This allows you to view all the styles until you find the best one.

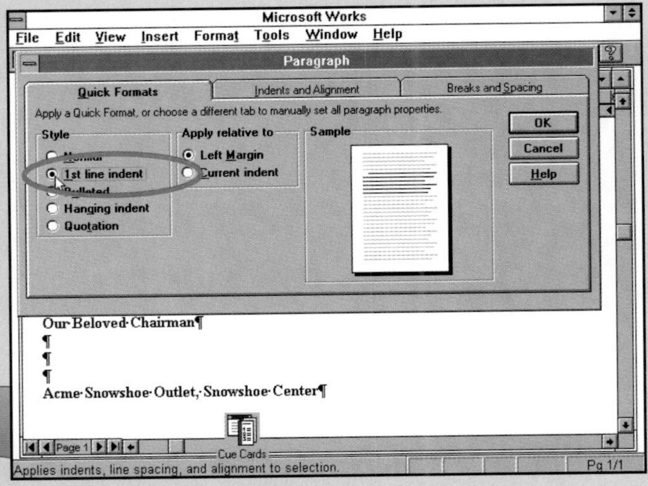

14 Click on **OK**. This closes the dialog box and applies the first-line indent style to the selected paragraph.

NOTE

To apply indents to a paragraph, you also can choose File Paragraph, click on the Indents and Alignment tab in the Paragraph dialog box, and change the values in the Indents group. If you have selected a Quick Format, Works displays the values in the Left, Right, and First Line text boxes.

15 Highlight the second paragraph you typed in step 10. This step prepares for a change in indentation for the selected paragraph.

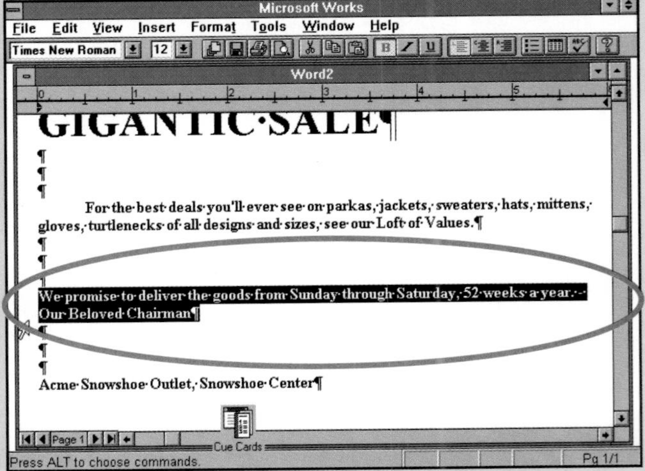

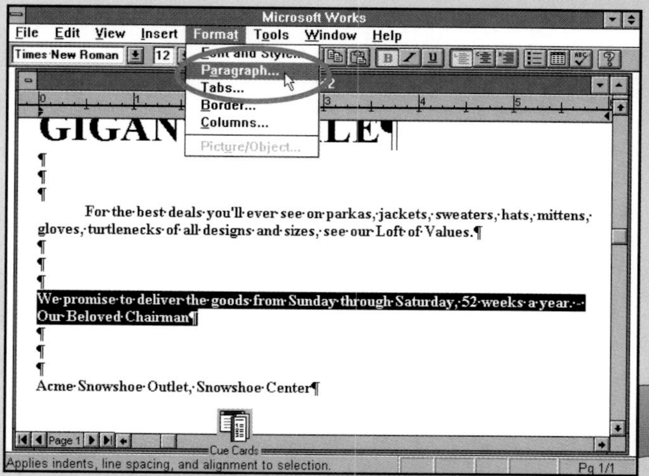

16 Click on **Format** in the menu bar and click on **Paragraph**. This step opens the Paragraph dialog box. If necessary, click on the Quick Formats tab to bring that part of the dialog box forward.

17 Click on the **Quotation** option button and click on **OK**. The Quotation option indents every line of a selected paragraph from both the left and right margins. This step closes the dialog box and applies the quotation indent style to the selected paragraph.

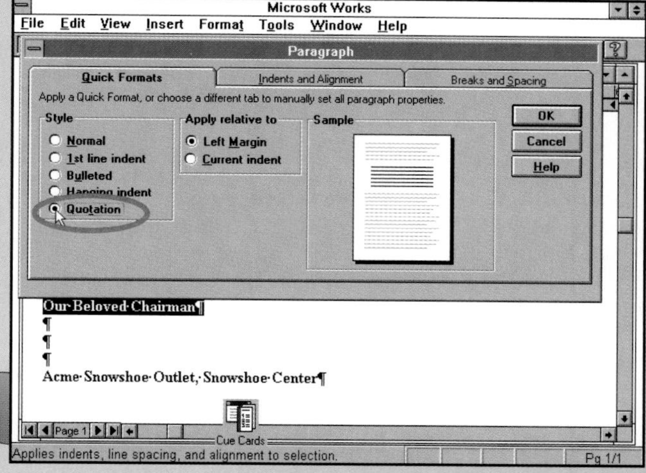

18 Click on the **Italic** button on the toolbar. This step italicizes the quotation.

TASK 25

Changing Line and Paragraph Spacing

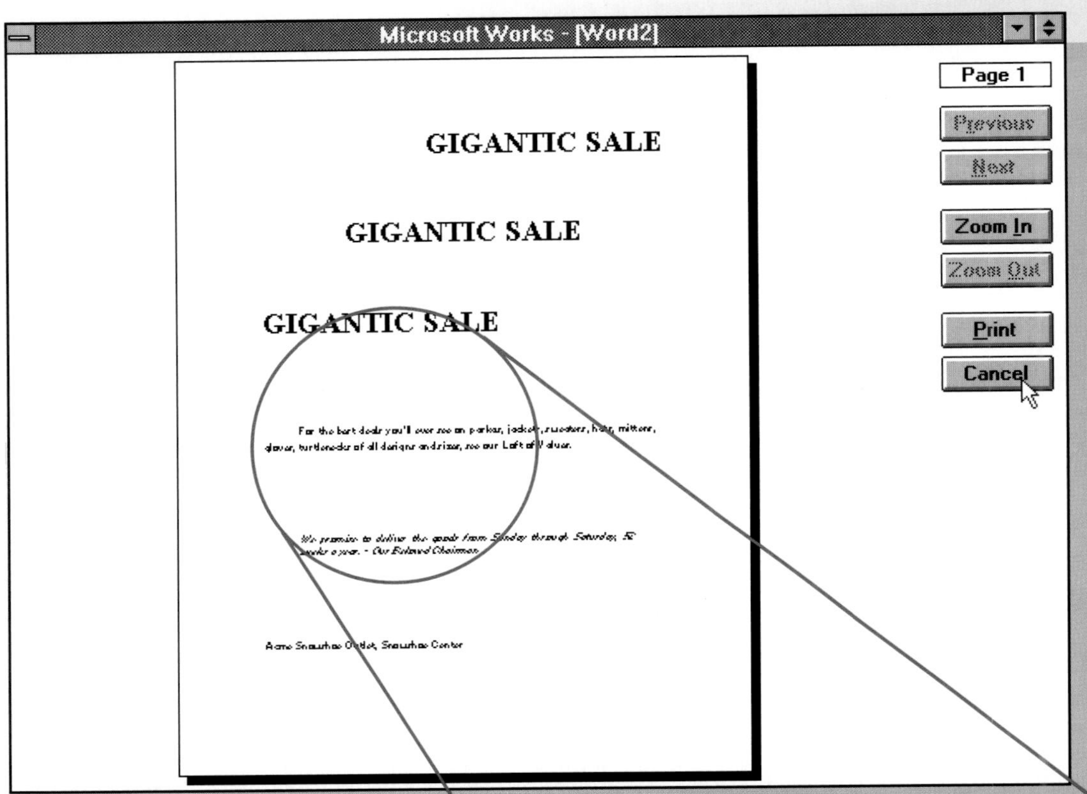

"Why would I do this?"

Spacing between lines and paragraphs helps you conform to a standard. Business letters are usually single-spaced, whereas documents with left-aligned or justified paragraphs usually look better with space between the paragraphs. In this task, you'll change line and paragraph spacing. This task assumes that the Word Processor tool is active and displaying a document such as the flyer created in the previous task.

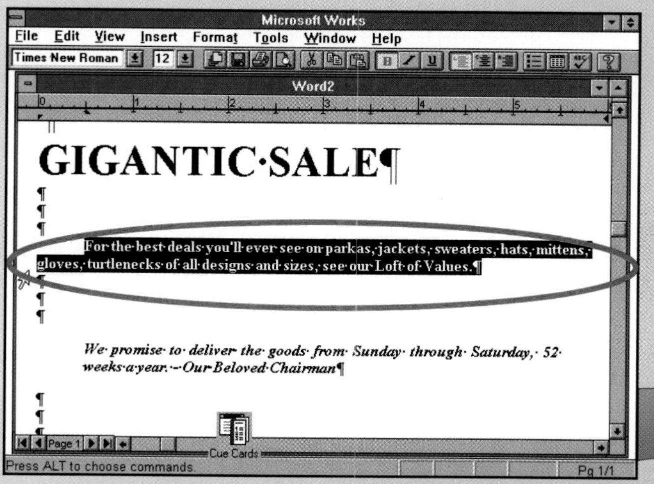

1 Select the paragraph for which you want to increase the line spacing; for this example, select the paragraph that begins *For the best deals ....*

2 Press **Ctrl+5**. This increases the space between lines to one-and-one-half lines. Other shortcut keys are Ctrl+1 for single-spacing and Ctrl+2 for double-spacing.

NOTE

Another way to set line spacing is to choose Format Paragraph. In the Paragraph dialog box, click on the Breaks and Spacing tab. Then type a number in the Between Lines text box.

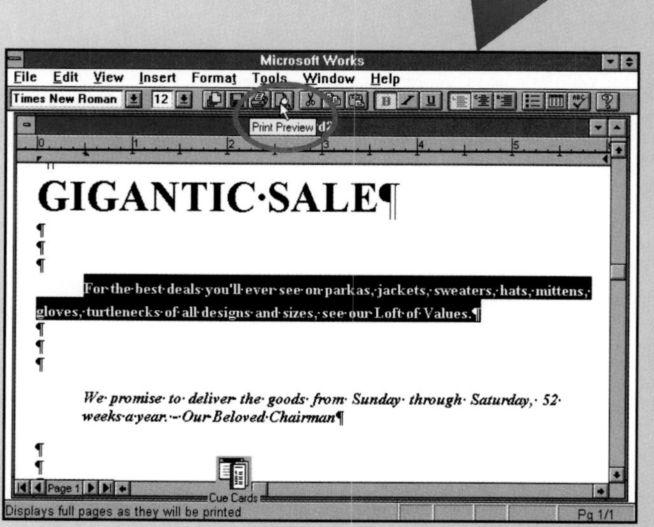

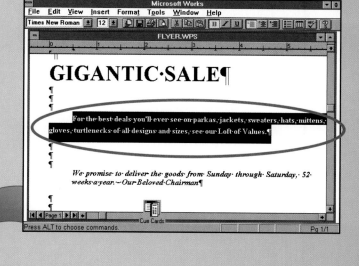

3 Click on the **Print Preview** button on the toolbar. This step shows you how your document will look when printed and provides a good way to see how the lines fit on the page.

4 Click on **Cancel**. This returns you to the document so that you can increase the spacing between paragraphs.

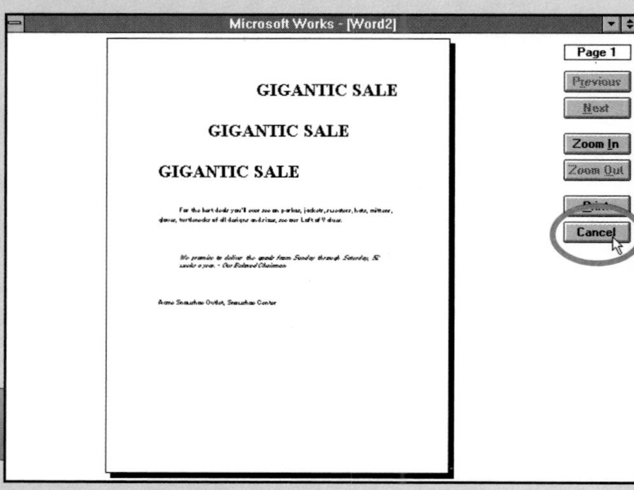

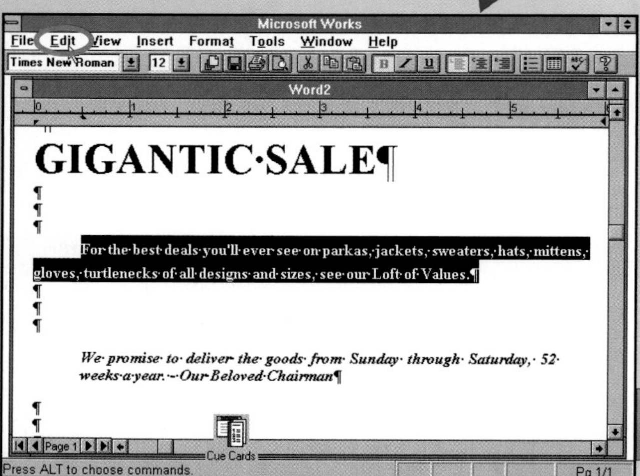

5 Click on **Edit** in the menu bar. This opens the Edit menu.

6 Choose **Select All**. This command selects the entire document.

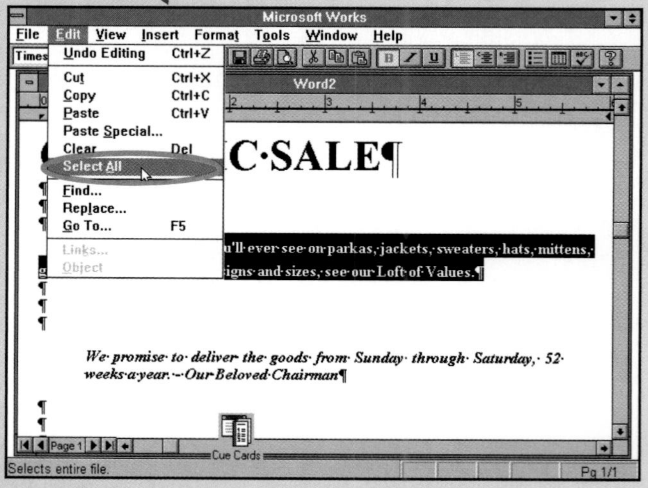

WHY WORRY?

When you select an entire document and change formats universally, there is a chance that some individual paragraph or character formats that you have applied will be erased by the new formats. For this reason, before you change an entire document, save your document so that you have a backup version.

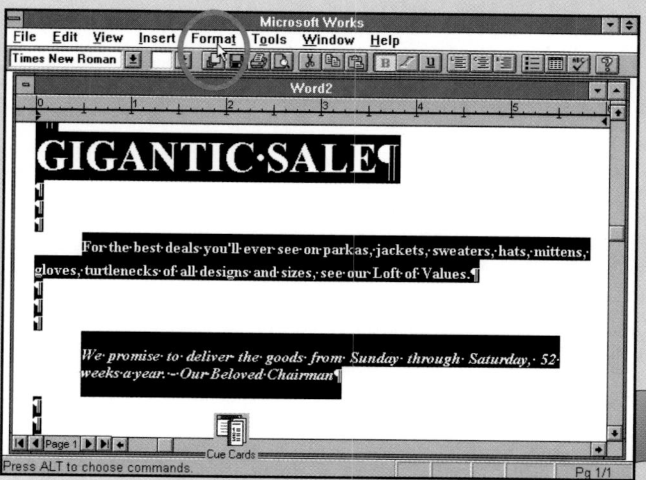

7 Click on **Format** in the menu bar. This opens the Format menu.

8 Click on **Paragraph**. This step opens the Paragraph dialog box. If necessary, click on the Breaks and Spacing tab to display that part of the dialog box.

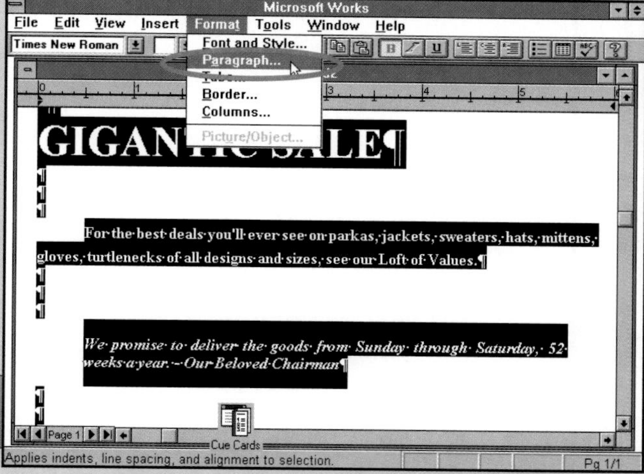

9 Type **1** in the After Paragraphs text box and click on **OK**. This indicates how many lines you want after each selected paragraph; the default setting is 0. Works closes the dialog box and adds the spacing. Use Print Preview to see the change.

NOTE

The shading in the check boxes in this dialog box indicates that a combination of settings exists in this document.

TASK 26

Setting Tab Stops

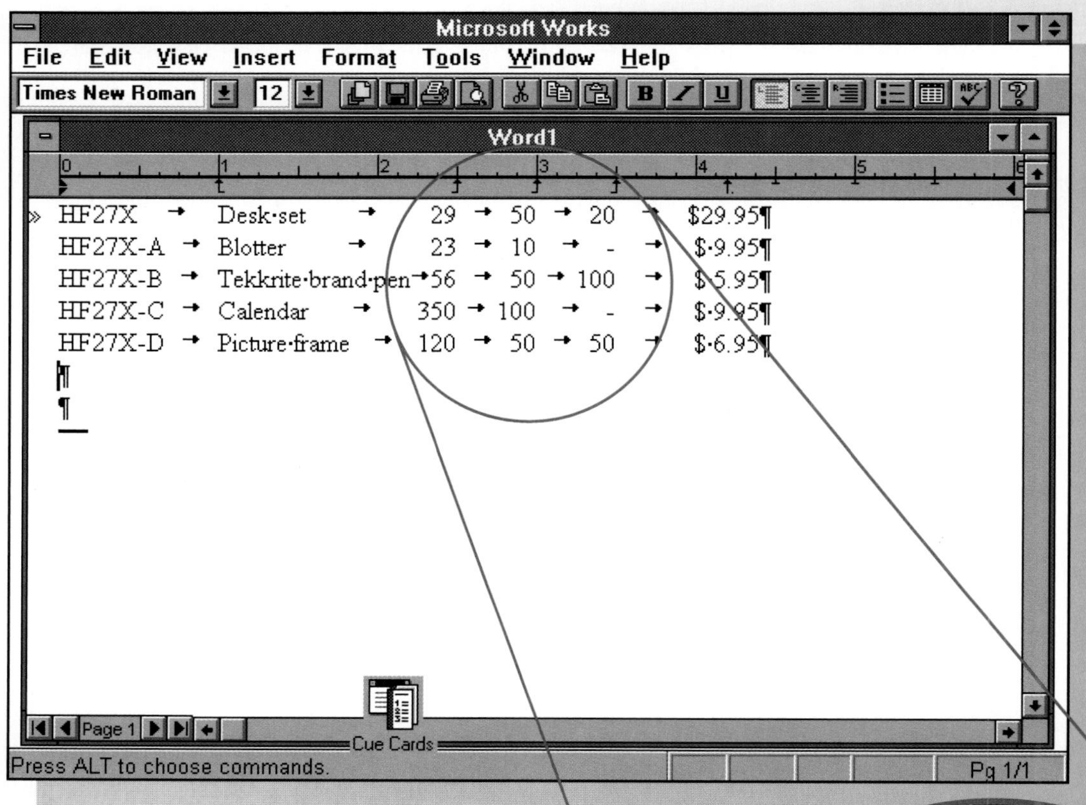

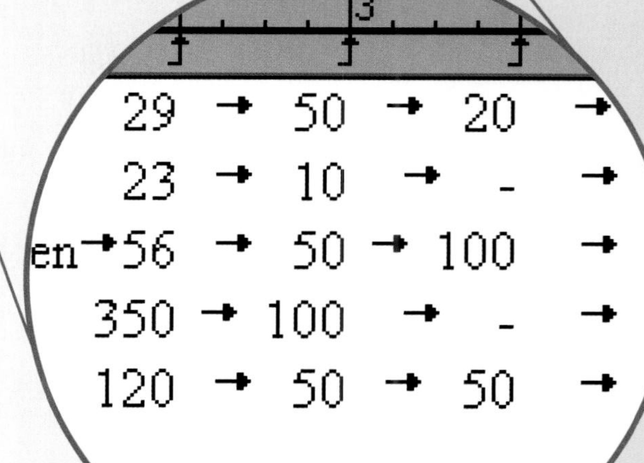

"Why would I do this?"

Tabs allow you to set spacing between words or columns of text. In a memo, for example, you can line up the words after TO:, FROM:, and SUBJECT; in a table, you can left-, center-, or right-align columns, or you can align them by decimal point. In this task, you'll set tab stops for a few lines of an inventory report, starting at the left column and working across.

This task assumes that the Word Processor tool is active, with a new document window open.

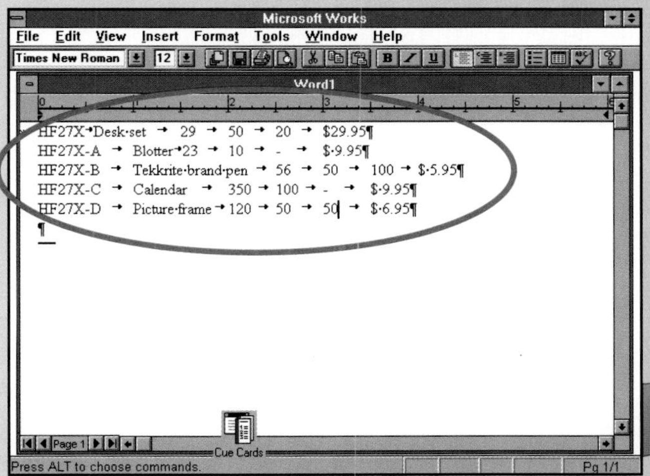

1 Enter the text of your choice for a six-column, five-row table, pressing **Tab** to separate each column and **Enter** to end each row. For this example, you can use the text shown in the illustration.

2 Select the entire table.

3 Click on **Format** in the menu bar. This step opens the Format menu.

4 Click on the **Tabs** command. Works opens the Tabs dialog box.

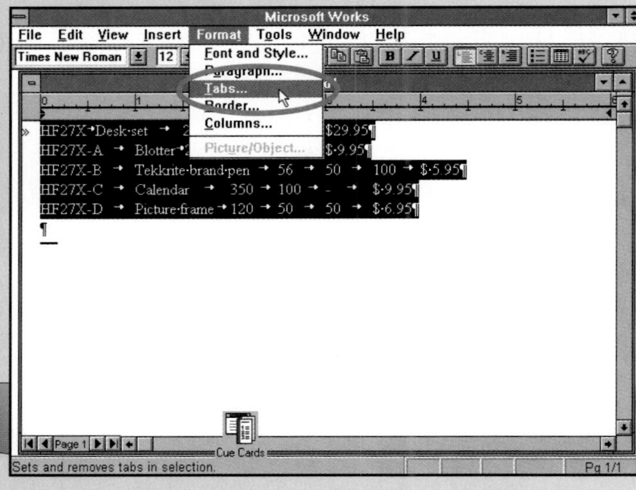

5 Drag the dialog box down the screen so that you can see the table. (Position the mouse pointer in the title bar, press and hold down the left mouse button, and drag the dialog box toward the bottom of the screen.)

NOTE

Works' default unit of measure is inches. You can look at the ruler to guess the best location for tabs.

6 Type **1** and click on the **Insert** button. This step sets the first tab at 1 inch, keeps the default left alignment, and adds no leader characters. (*Leaders* are the dots between items and page numbers in tables of contents.)

NOTE

Judge the length of the longest item in a column before you set the tabs. Allow for a few spaces between columns.

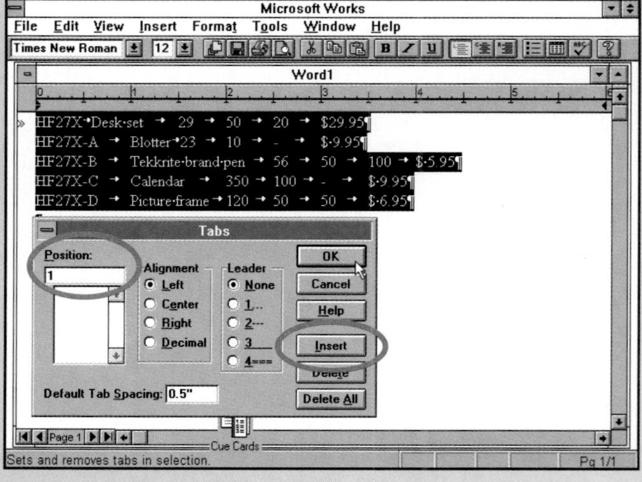

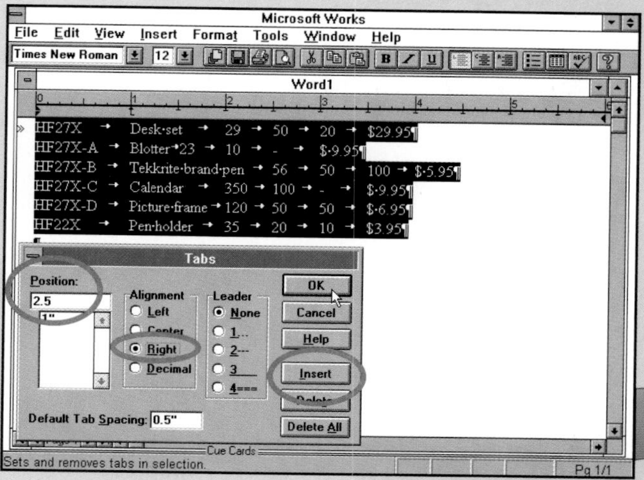

7 Type **2.5**, click on the **Right** option button if you're aligning numbers, and click on **Insert**. This step sets the second tab at 2.5 inches, right-aligns it, and adds no leader characters.

NOTE

You can adjust a tab setting by dragging it to a new position on the ruler. Works changes that value in the Tabs dialog box. You can delete a tab stop by dragging it off the ruler.

8 Type **3**, click on **Right** if you're aligning numbers, and click on **Insert**. This sets the third tab at 3 inches and right-aligns it with no leader characters.

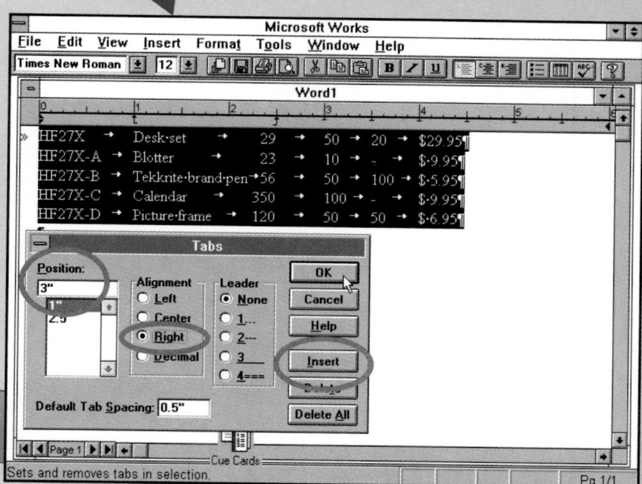

9 Type **3.5**, click on **Right** if you're aligning numbers, and click on **Insert**. This sets the fourth tab at 3.5 inches and right-aligns it with no leader characters.

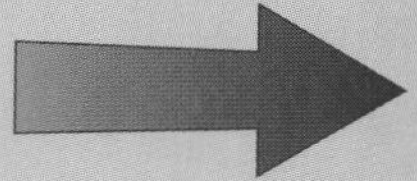

10 Type **4.2**, click on **Decimal** if you want to align numbers at the decimal point, and click on **OK**. This sets the fifth tab at 4.2 inches, aligns it at the decimal point, and adds no leader characters.

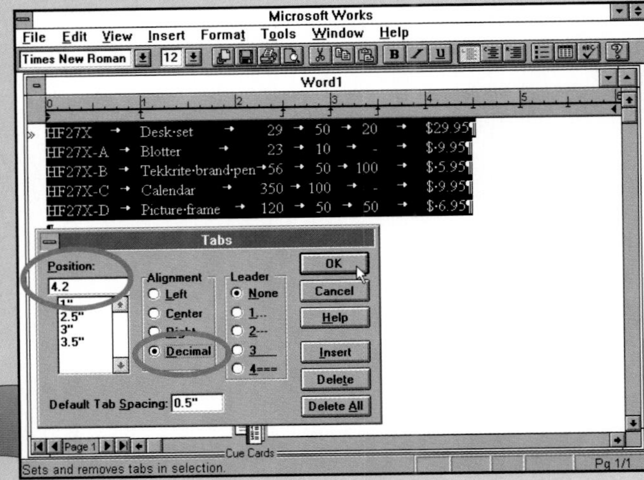

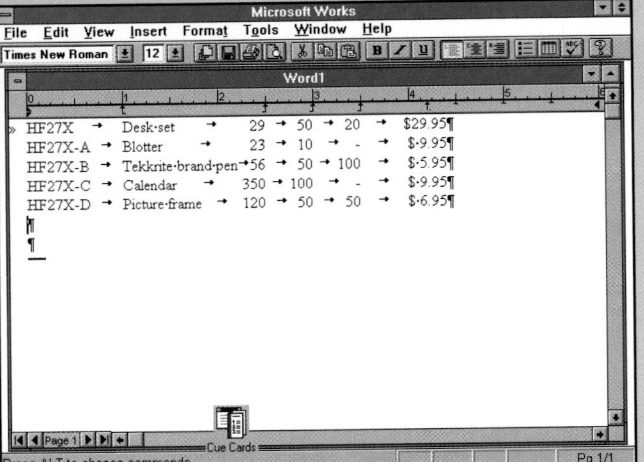

11 Evaluate the table. To change a tab stop, drag it left or right on the ruler, making sure to adjust all the tabs affected by the change.

NOTE

If you make a mistake entering tabs or selecting options in the Tab dialog box, click on the incorrect value in the Position list box. Works displays that value in the text box. Either edit the tab setting by changing the options and clicking on OK, or remove it completely by clicking on the Delete button and clicking on OK.

TASK 27

Changing Margins

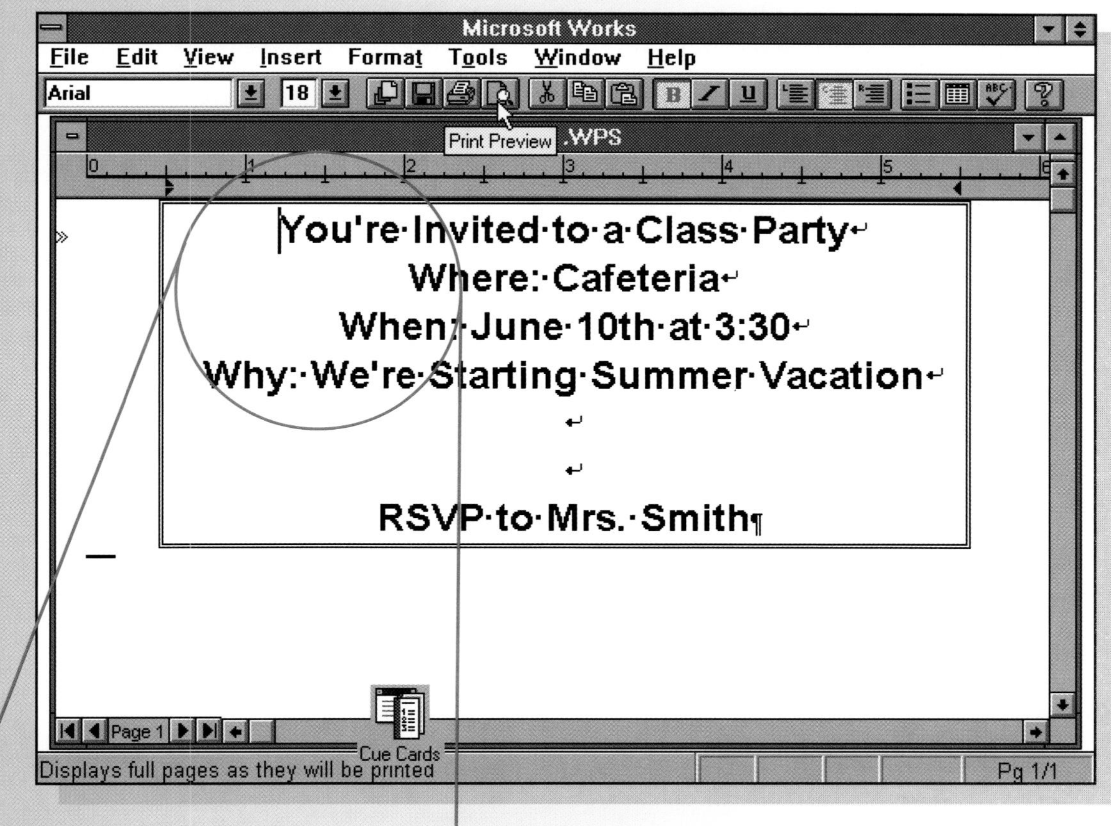

"Why would I do this?"

Every document has margins, whether they are the default margins or are user-defined. You can use margins to center a small document on a single page or to squeeze more lines on a one-page document. You can even increase the margin measurements to reduce the text on a page to reach a minimum page count. In this task, you will create and format an invitation.

This task assumes that the Word Processor tool is active and displaying an empty document window.

Task 27: Changing Margins

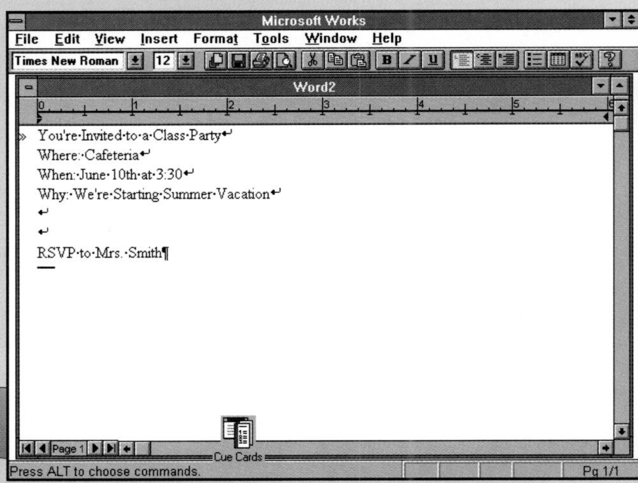

1 In a new document, enter text for a party invitation, as follows: Type **You're Invited to a Class Party** and press **Shift+Enter**. Type **Where: Cafeteria** and press **Shift+Enter**. Type **When: June 10th at 3:30** and press **Shift+Enter**. Type **Why: We're Starting Summer Vacation** and press **Shift+Enter three times**. Finally, type **RSVP to Mrs. Smith**.

2 Select all the text in the document. This step prepares for a change in formats for the selection.

3 Open the **Font Name** drop-down list box and select **Arial**. This changes the font of the selected text. If you don't see the font name when you open the drop-down list box, use the scroll bar to scroll to your choice.

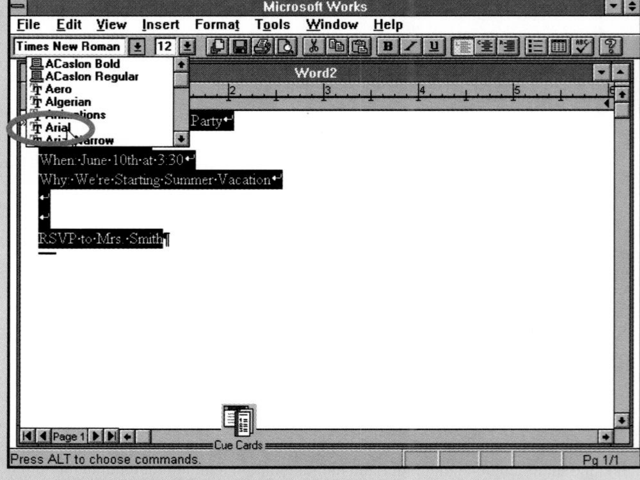

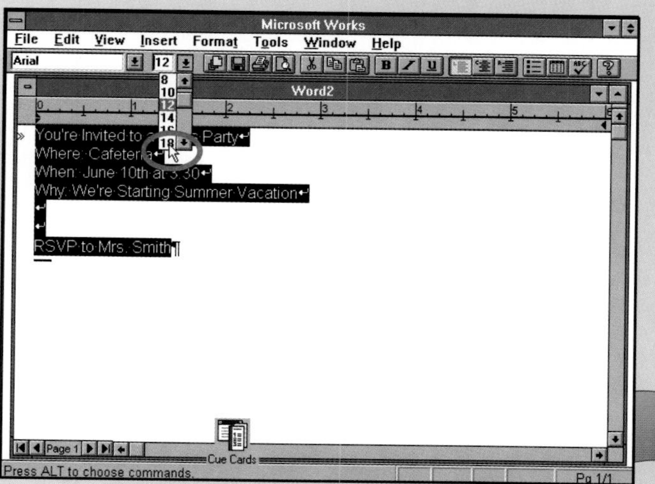

4 Open the **Font Size** drop-down list box and select **18**. This changes the font size of the selected text. If you don't see the font size you want in the drop-down list box, use the scroll bar to scroll to your choice.

5 Click on the **Bold** button on the toolbar. This button applies boldface to the selection.

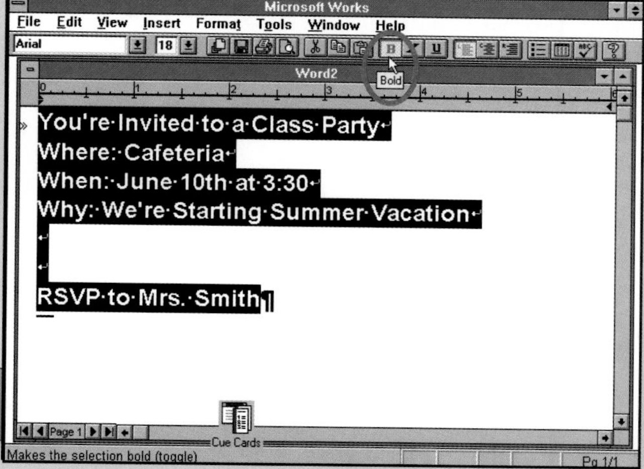

6 Click on **Format** in the menu bar and click on **Border**. This step opens the Border dialog box.

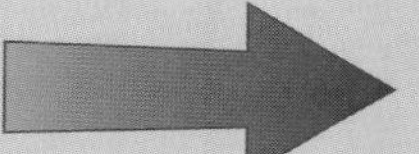

7 Click on **Outline**, click on **Double,** and click on **OK**. This creates an outline around the selection.

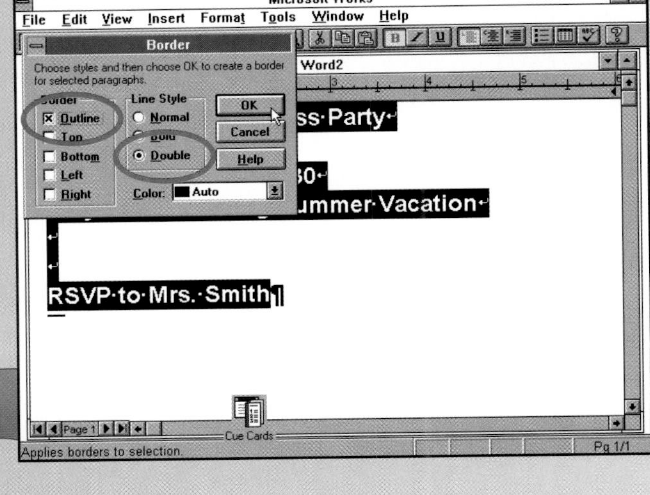

NOTE

If you had pressed Enter rather than Shift+Enter when you typed the text, each line would have its own border. Pressing Shift+Enter starts a new line without adding a paragraph mark.

8 Click on the **Center Align** button on the toolbar. This action centers the selected text between the margin markers so that you can see how wide the left and right margins should be.

NOTE

Margin markers are the black triangles on either end of the ruler. Both the left and right margin markers point toward the center of the ruler.

9 Drag the left margin marker to the 1/2-inch mark. This steps moves the border closer to the text on the left side. This step is equivalent to choosing File Page Setup, clicking on the Margins tab, entering a value in the Left margin text box, and clicking on OK.

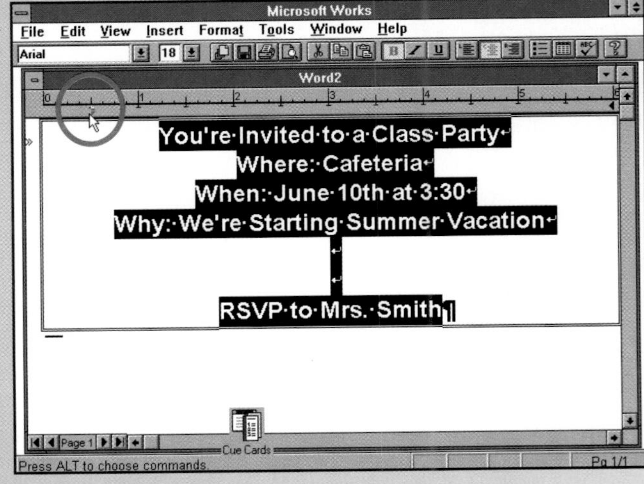

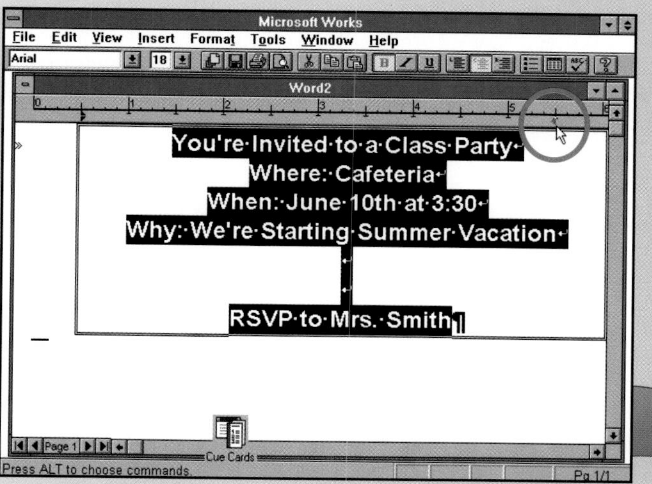

10 Drag the **right margin marker** to the 5 1/2-inch mark. This step moves the border closer to the text on the right side. This step is equivalent to choosing File Page Setup, clicking on the Margins tab, entering a value in the Right margin text box, and clicking on OK.

11 Click on **File** in the menu bar and click on **Page Setup**. This step opens the Page Setup dialog box. If necessary, click on the Margins tab to display that part of the dialog box.

> **NOTE**
>
> In the Margins part of the Page Setup dialog box, Works displays a sample page that shows you how your margin changes will alter the look of the page.

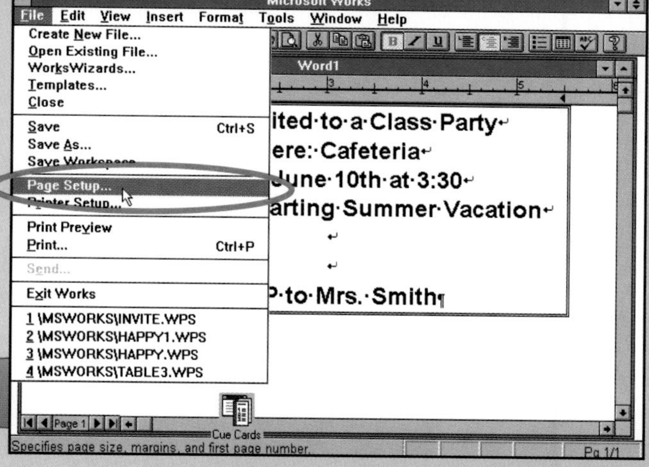

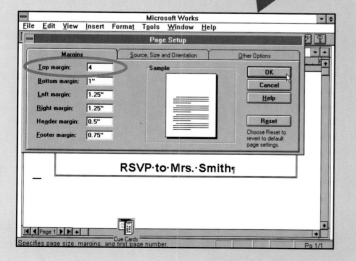

12 Type **4** in the Top Margin text box and click on **OK**. This increases the size of the top margin to 4 inches. The document moves down the page.

> **NOTE**
>
> Click on the Print Preview button on the toolbar. Works shows you how the document will look when you print it.

Microsoft Works
File Edit View Insert Format Tools Window Help
INCOME.WKS
Row Height
Height: 12
Best Fit
OK
Cancel
Help
Income
January
February
March
April
May
June
Jewelry
Throws
Desk Sets
Calendars
Prints
Dog Sweaters
Catalog Total
Average
Retail Total
Cue Cards
1,800
1,600
1,400
1,200
1,000
800
600
400
200
0
January

PART V

Using the Spreadsheet

The Spreadsheet tool helps you control and organize your finances. With spreadsheets, you can analyze your household budget item-by-item to see when you pay your bills and how much you pay. You can also keep track of your credit card purchases and mortgage or rent payments. Then you can predict future spending and income.

In Part V, you'll find out how the Spreadsheet tool works. You'll create a spreadsheet; enter text, numbers, and formulas; and edit and format the spreadsheet. Although this book doesn't cover the AutoFormat feature, you can use it to automatically format your spreadsheet. Finally, you'll create a chart based on the data in your spreadsheet.

Spreadsheets are made up of rows, which run horizontally, and columns, which run vertically. A *cell* is the place at which a row and column meet. A cell holds one piece of information. The Spreadsheet tool labels its columns and rows. At the top border of a spreadsheet are column labels: *A, B, C,..., Z,* then *AA, AB,..., IV* (the 256th column). Row labels, on the left border of the spreadsheet start at 1 and continue well beyond 10,000.

Works formulas include numbers, cell addresses, cell ranges, and mathematical operators. In the order in which Works calculates them, valid operators are:

Operator	Description
( )	Contains parts of the formula that you want to calculate first
+ and –	Positive and negative signs (numbers not preceded by a minus sign are regarded as positive numbers)
^	Exponentiation
* and /	Multiplication and division
+ and –	Addition and subtraction
= and < >	Equal and not equal
< and >	Less than and greater than
<= and >=	Less than or equal to and greater than or equal to
#NOT#	Logical NOT
#OR# and #AND#	Logical OR and logical AND

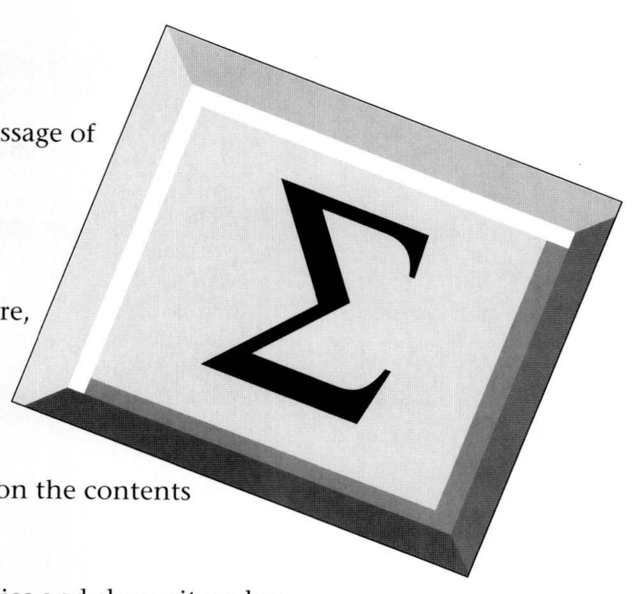

Works charts consist of the following elements:

- *X-axis.* The horizontal axis, which shows the passage of time or areas, such as sales regions.
- *X-axis title.* The title that you give to the x-axis.
- *Y-axis.* The vertical axis, used for units of measure, such as currency.
- *Y-axis title.* The title that you give to the y-axis.
- *Plot.* The bars, lines, areas, or slices of pie based on the contents of spreadsheet rows and columns.
- *Legend.* The chart's key, which lists each data series and shows its color and/or pattern.
- *Tick mark.* A short line, which shows a value on an axis.
- *Gridline.* A line that extends a tick mark across or down the chart.
- *Title.* The optional heading for the chart.
- *Subtitle.* The chart's optional subheading.

The Spreadsheet tool provides these chart types: Area, Bar, Line, Pie, Stacked Line, XY (Scatter), Radar, Combination, 3-D Area, 3-D Bar, 3-D Line, and 3-D Pie.

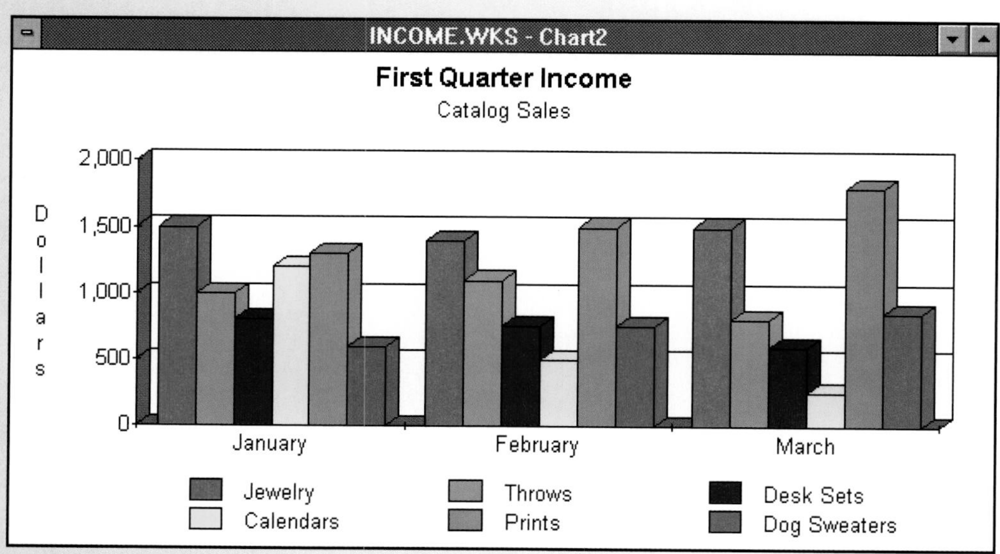

TASK 28

Entering Text and Numbers

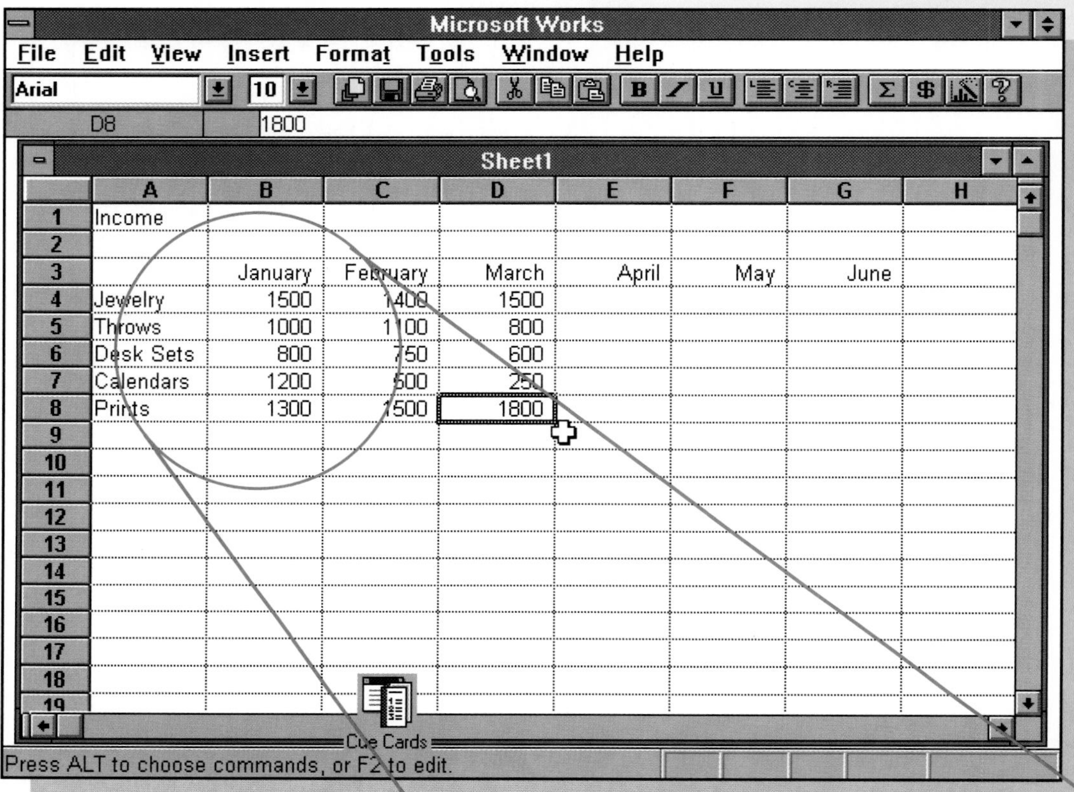

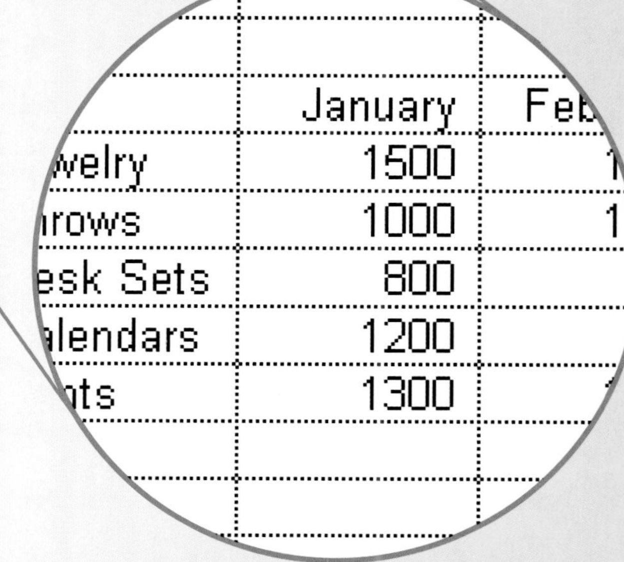

"Why would I do this?"

Spreadsheets hold both numerical data and text. Although you enter both the same way, Works interprets and displays them differently. In this task, you'll enter both text and numbers and learn how Works identifies and displays them.

This task assumes that you have started the Spreadsheet tool and have a blank spreadsheet open on-screen.

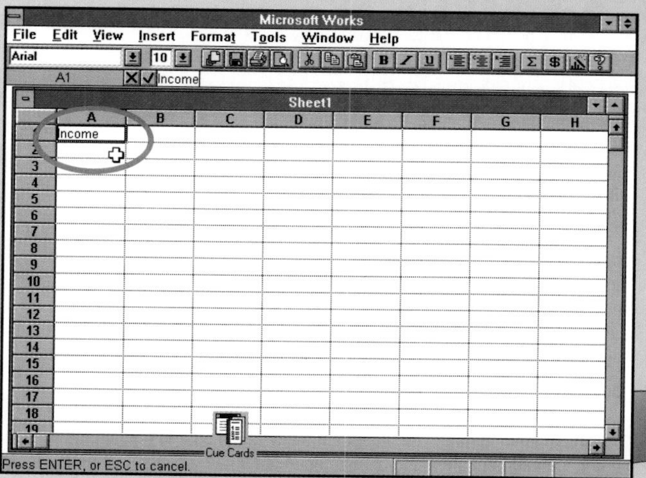

1 Type **Income.** As you type, Works enters the word *Income* in the formula bar, which is right under the toolbar.

WHY WORRY?

If you make a typing mistake, you can press Backspace to erase the value preceding the insertion point.

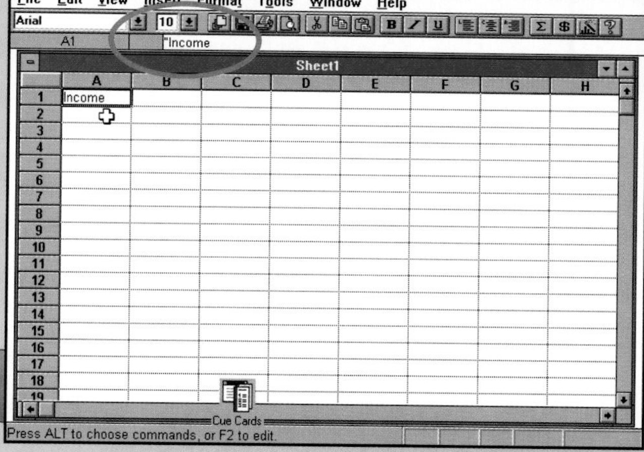

2 Press **Enter**. This instructs Works to enter the word *Income* in cell A1. In the formula bar, the quotation mark in front of *Income* indicates that Works interprets this entry as text. In cell A1, *Income* is left-aligned, another indicator that the word is text.

NOTE

Instead of pressing Enter, you can press Tab or → to move right one cell, Shift+Tab or ← to move left one cell, ↓ to move down one cell, or ↑ to move up one cell.

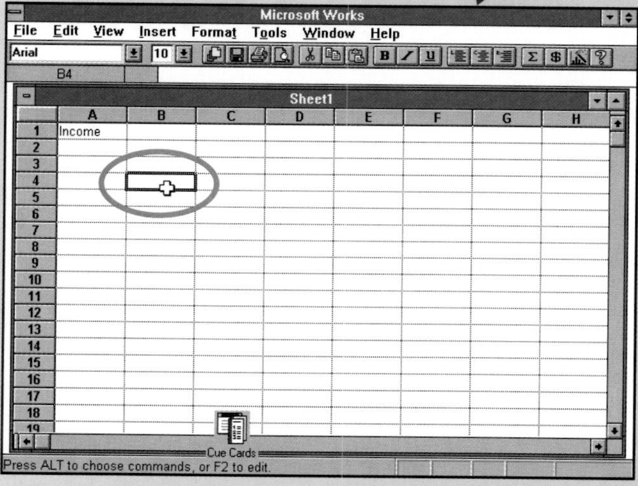

3 Click on cell **B4**. This step makes cell B4 the active cell. Works displays B4 in the cell reference area, which is to the left of the formula bar.

4 Type **1500**. The number 1500 appears in the formula bar.

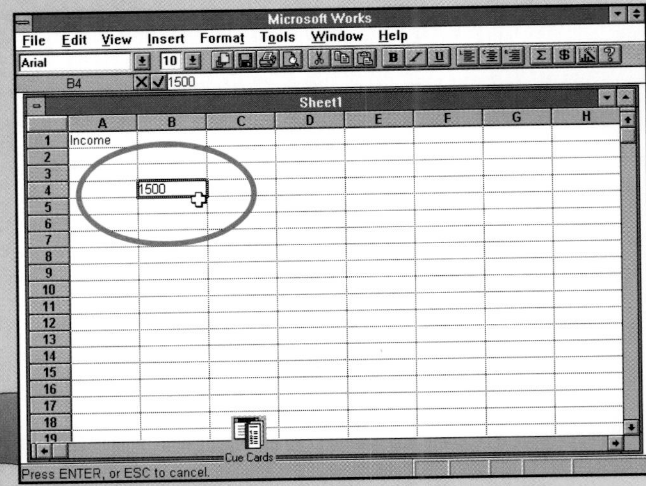

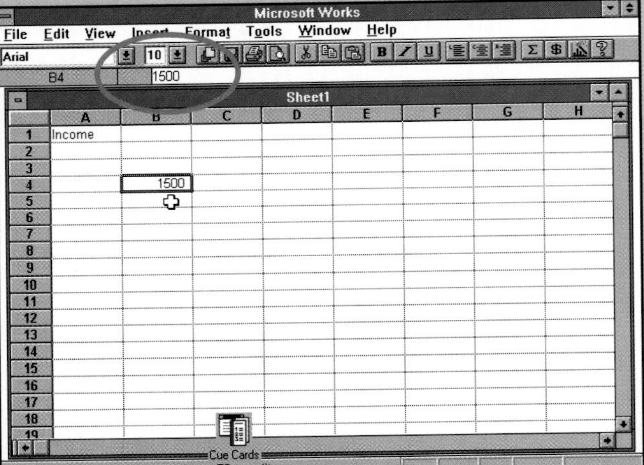

5 Press **Enter**. In the formula bar, there is no quotation mark in front of 1500. Works has intexrpreted the contents of B4 as a number and right-aligns it in the cell. Notice that Works has not added a decimal point, comma, or dollar sign. Unless you select a specific number format, numbers are displayed without these symbols.

6 Click on cell **B5**. This makes cell B5 the active cell.

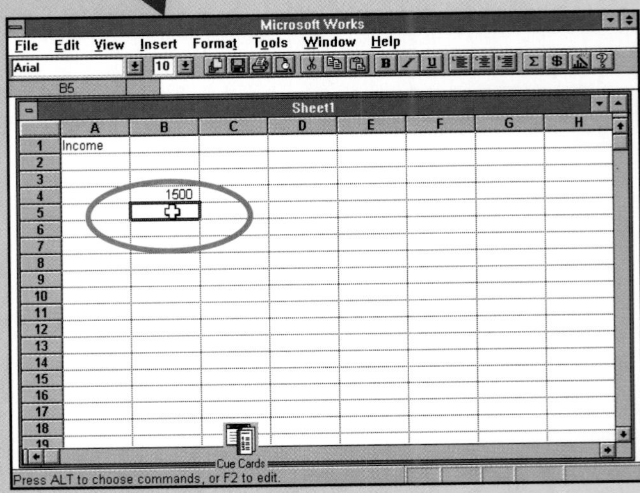

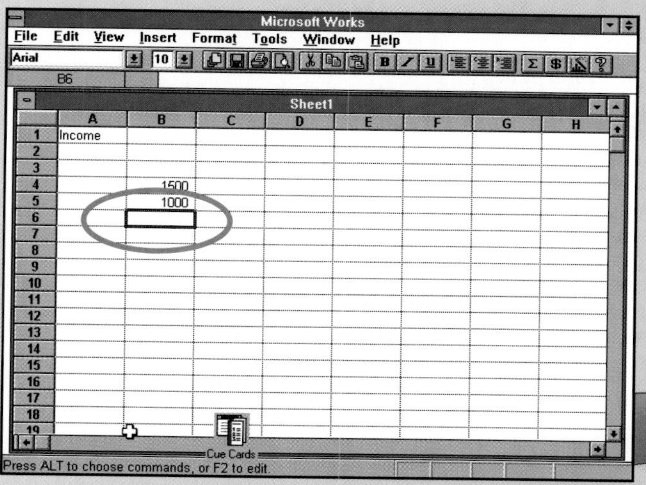

7 Type **1000** and press ↓. Pressing ↓ closes cell B5 and makes cell B6 the active cell, both in one step.

8 Type **800**, press ↓, type **1200**, press ↓, type **1300**, and press **Enter**. This fills in the rest of column B.

NOTE

To enter a negative number, type a minus sign before typing the number.

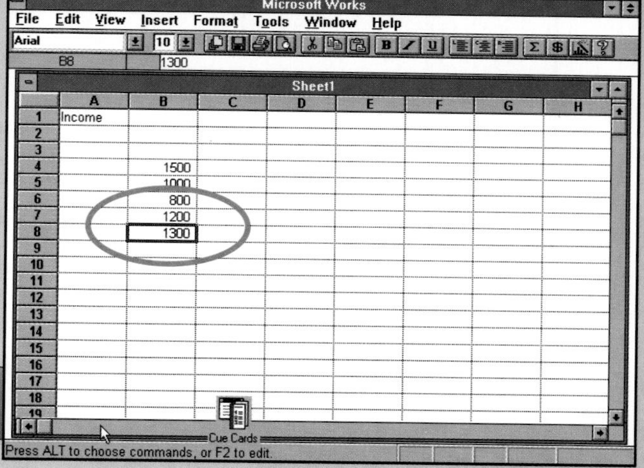

9 Click on cell **B3,** type **January**, and press **Enter**.

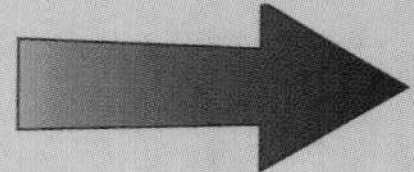

10 Click and hold down the left mouse button in cell **B3** and drag to cell **G3**. This selects the range of cells from B3 to G3. Notice that the cell reference area specifies `B3:G3`. The colon is a shorthand way of indicating "all cells from B3 to G3."

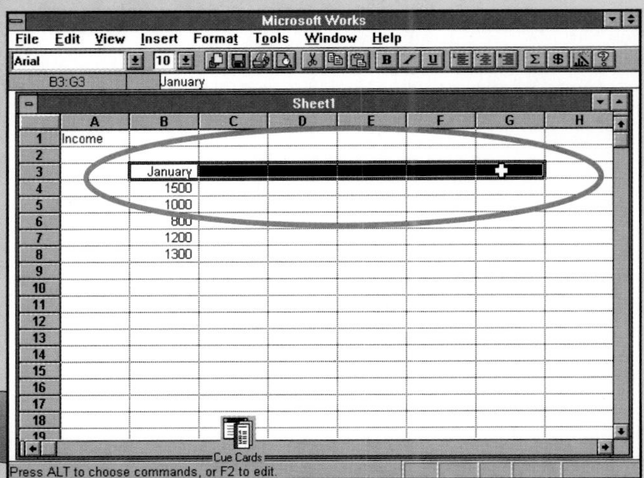

NOTE

Another way to select a range is to click on the cell in one corner of the range, press and hold down Shift, and click on the cell at the opposite corner of the range.

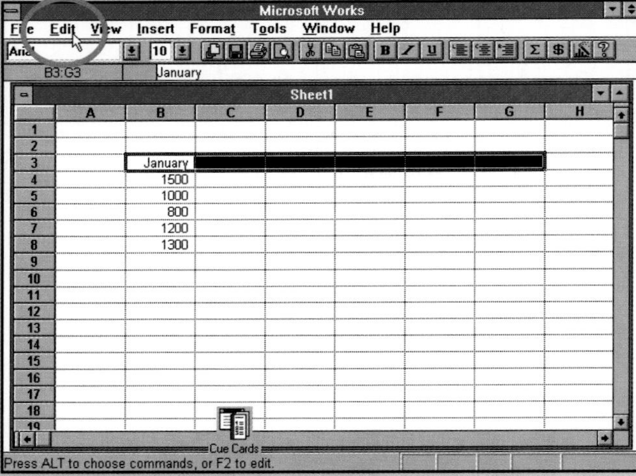

11 Click on **Edit** in the menu bar. This opens the Edit menu.

12 Click on **Fill Series**. This opens the Fill Series dialog box, where you select the type of value with which to fill the selected cells.

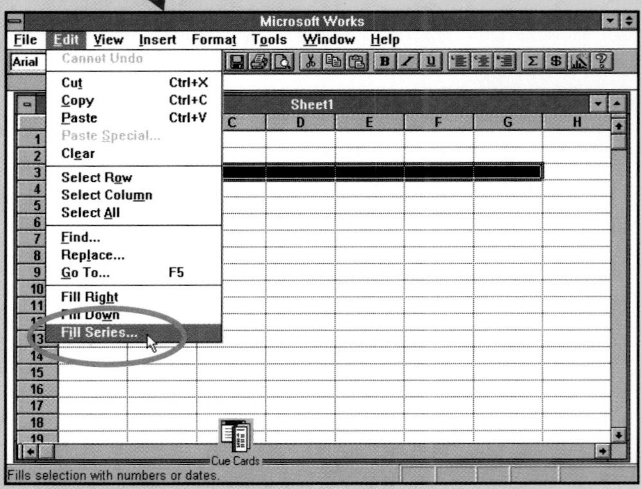

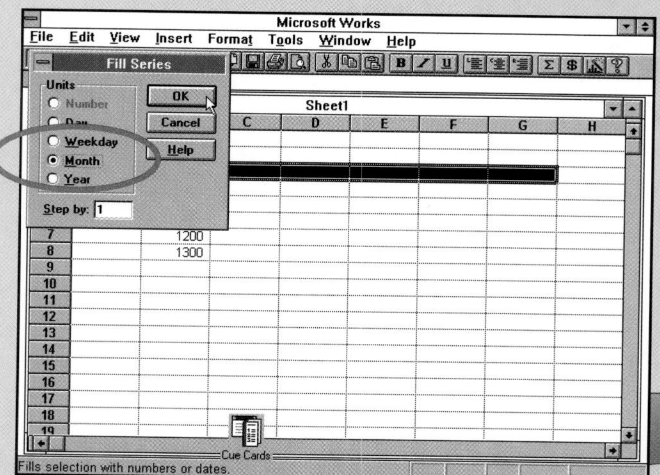

13 Click on **Month** and click on **OK**. Works fills in the selected cells with the months *February, March, April, May,* and *June*. Because you selected the cell containing *January,* Works fills in the selected cells beginning with *February*.

NOTE

Other series that Works places in selected ranges of cells are numbers, days, weekdays, and years.

14 Click on cell **A4**, type **Jewelry**, and press ↓. Fill in the next four cells in the column with **Throws**, **Desk Sets**, **Calendars**, and **Prints**. Notice that Works left-aligns all these text items. These values are called *row labels,* because they label the contents of their rows; likewise, *January, February, March,* and so on are *column labels.*

NOTE

To save your spreadsheet, choose File Save As, specify a file name, and click on OK.

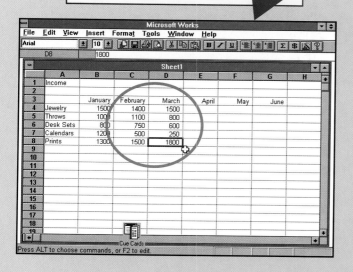

15 Fill in the February and March columns:

February	March
1400	1500
1100	800
750	600
500	250
1500	1800

TASK 29

Selecting and Naming Ranges

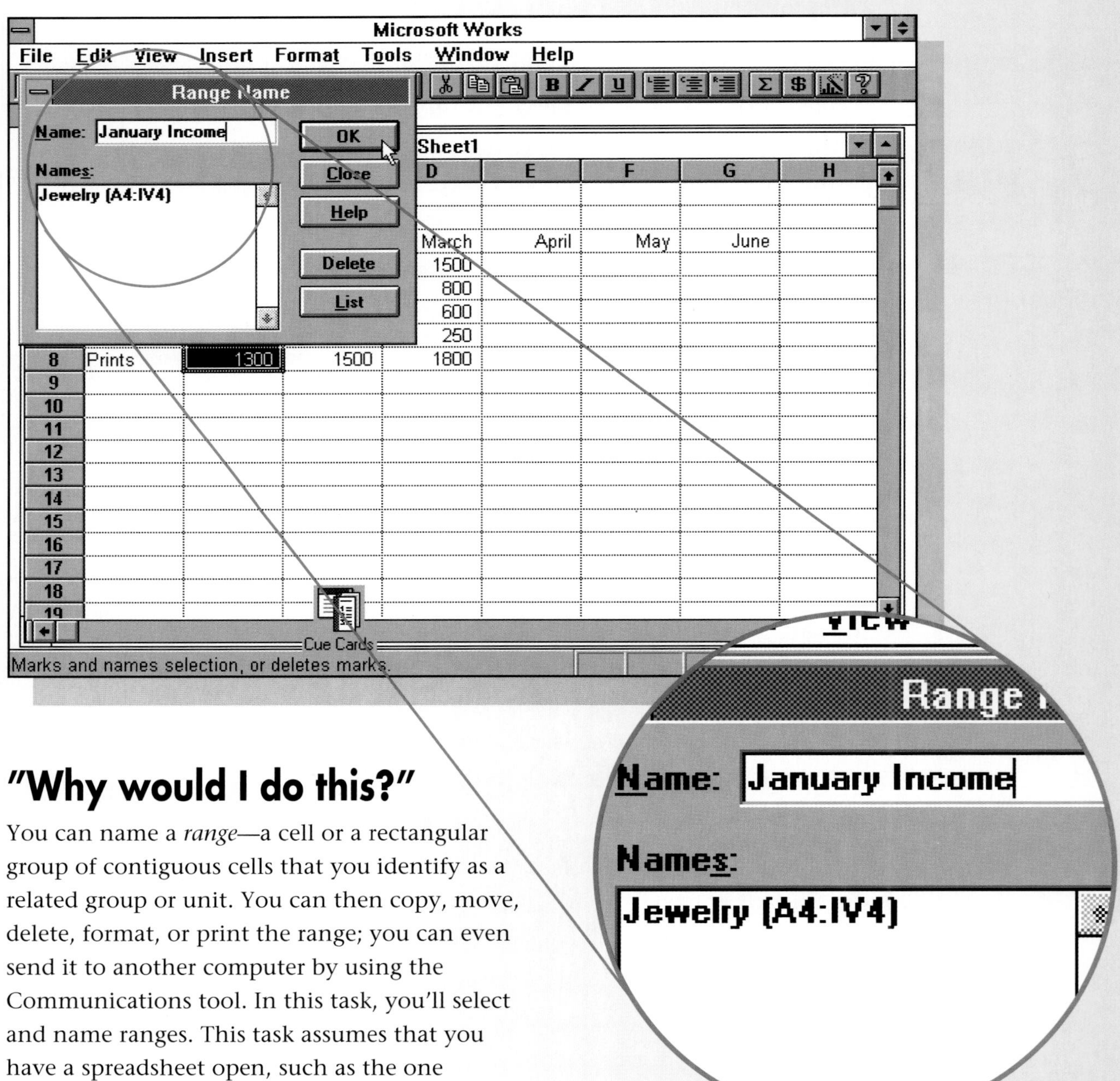

"Why would I do this?"

You can name a *range*—a cell or a rectangular group of contiguous cells that you identify as a related group or unit. You can then copy, move, delete, format, or print the range; you can even send it to another computer by using the Communications tool. In this task, you'll select and name ranges. This task assumes that you have a spreadsheet open, such as the one created in the last task.

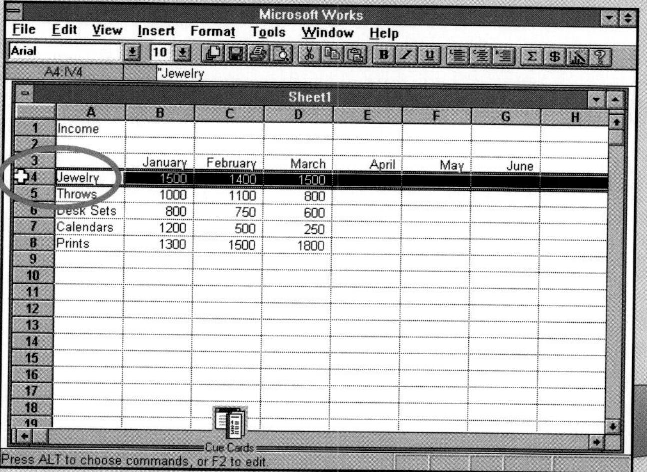

1 Click on **4** at the left side of the spreadsheet. Works highlights the entire row, including empty cells. Notice that `A4:IV4` appears in the cell reference area and that in the formula bar, Works displays the contents of the first cell in the range. You will assign a name to this range of selected cells.

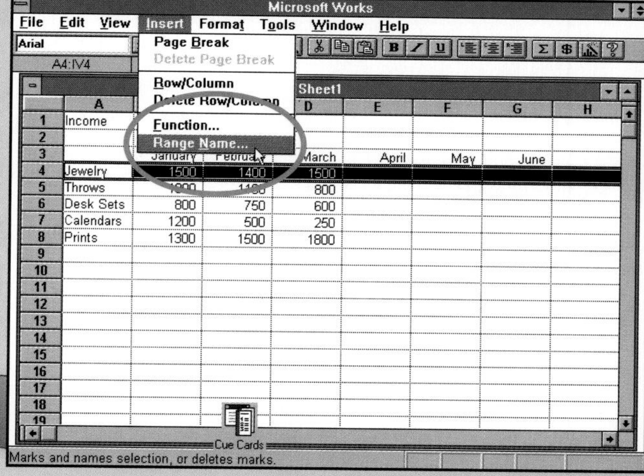

2 Click on **Insert** in the menu bar and click on **Range Name**. This step opens the Range Name dialog box, in which you specify a name for the range of selected cells.

3 Click on **OK** to accept the name that Works suggests for the range name—*Jewelry* in this example.

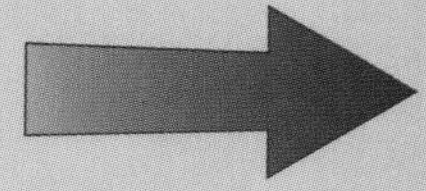

Task 29: Selecting and Naming Ranges

4 Select the next range of cells you want to name; for this example, select cells **B4** to **B8**. Works highlights all five cells in the range.

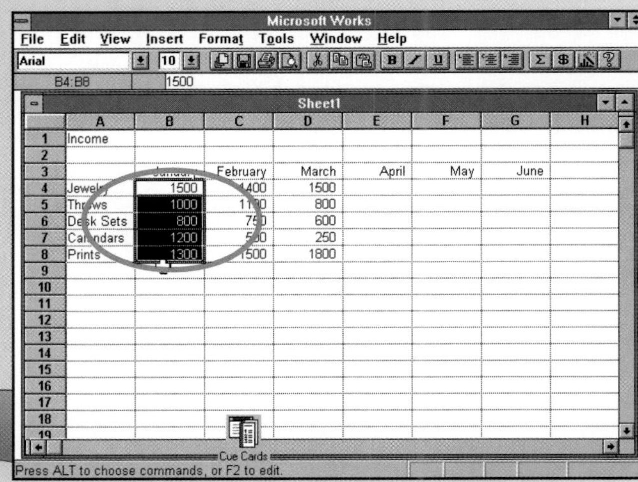

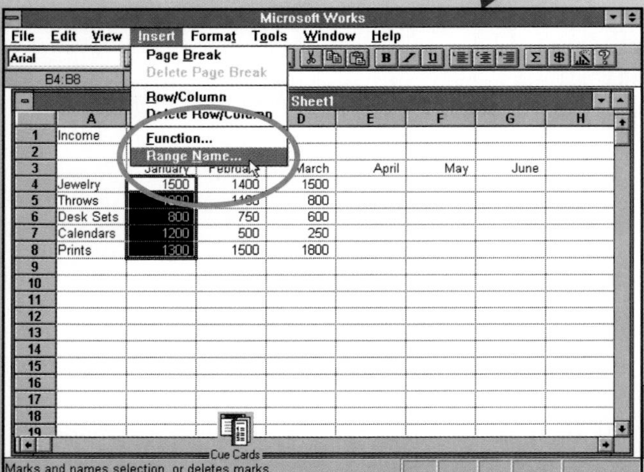

5 Click on **Insert** in the menu bar and click on **Range Name**. This step opens the Range Name dialog box.

NOTE

Works doesn't suggest a range name if the selected cells contain only numbers. It does suggest a name if the selected range begins with a text item.

6 In the Name text box, type a name for the range, such as **January Income**, and click on **OK**. Works names the range, closes the dialog box, and returns to the spreadsheet.

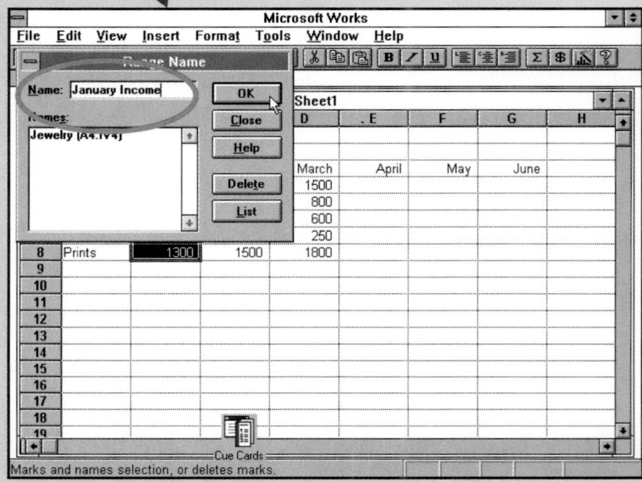

TASK 30

Entering Formulas

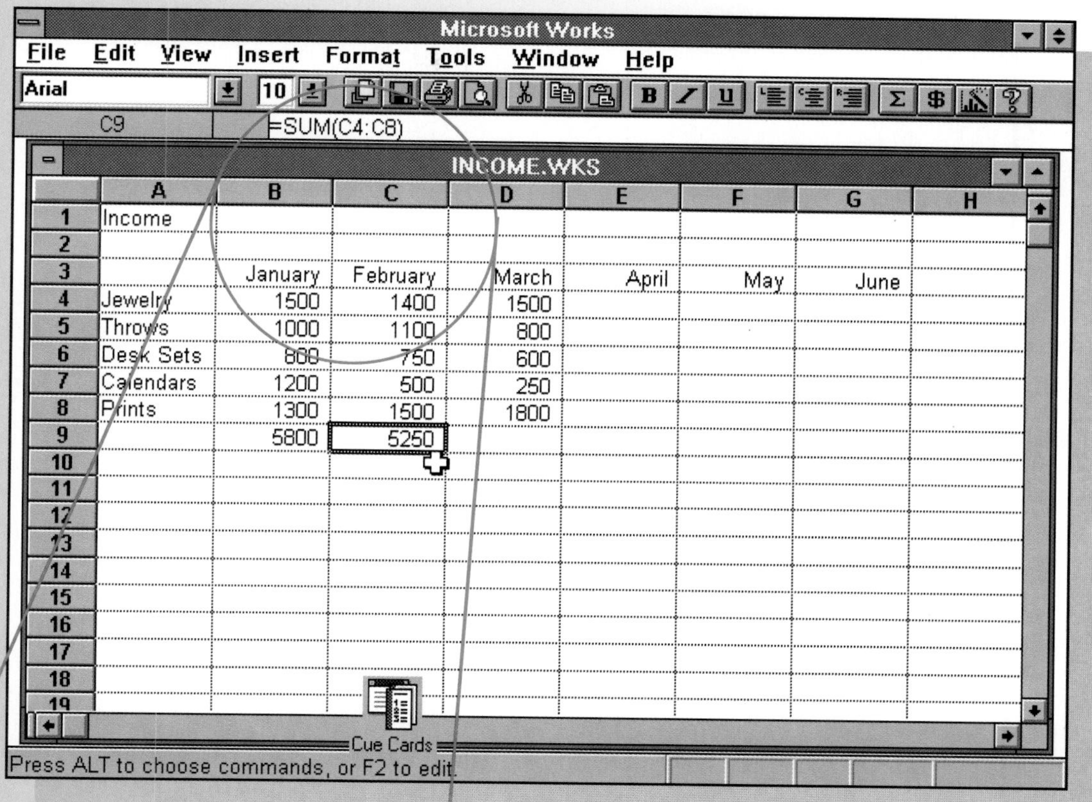

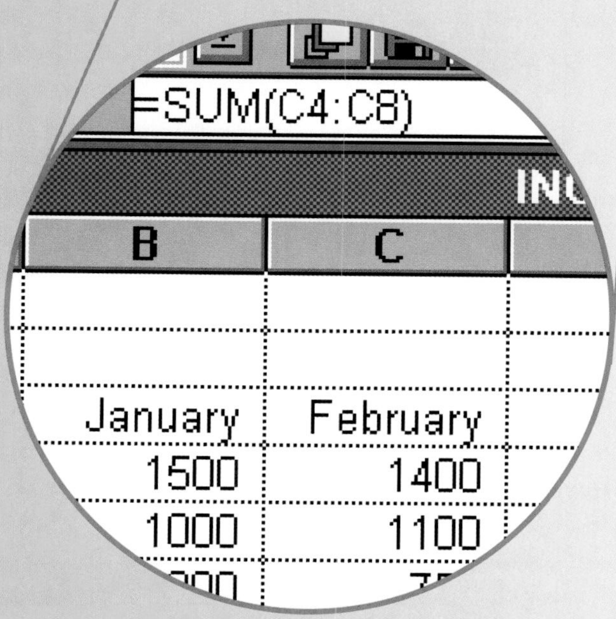

"Why would I do this?"

Perhaps the most important factor in using an electronic spreadsheet program rather than keeping written worksheets is that you can keep your data up to date—as you enter it. Thanks to formulas, you can change a number or two and see the changes immediately. In this task, you'll learn how formulas work and how to enter them in a spreadsheet.

This task assumes that you have a spreadsheet open that contains data and named ranges, such as the spreadsheet you worked on in the last task.

Task 30: Entering Formulas

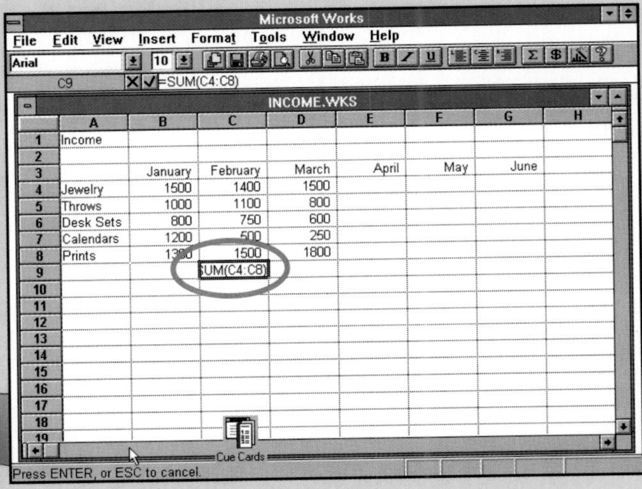

1 Click on cell **C9** and type the formula **=SUM(C4:C8)**. Works displays the formula in cell C9 and in the formula bar. This formula totals the values in the range C4:C8.

NOTE

An equal sign at the beginning of an entry indicates that you have entered a formula. Otherwise, Works interprets the entry as a number (if you type a number first) or text (if you type an alphabetic character first).

2 Press **Enter**. Works calculates the formula and displays the total in cell C9; however, notice that the formula bar continues to display the formula.

NOTE

SUM is a *function*—a built-in formula—you can use rather than typing a long formula such as =C4+C5+C6+C7+C8. You also can select a cell and click on the Autosum button (left of the dollar sign on the toolbar) to add the numbers above or to the left of that cell.

3 Click on cell **B9** to make it the active cell, and click on the **Autosum** toolbar button. This step totals the cells above B9. Works highlights the range B4 to B8 (the cells above B9) and highlights part of the formula in the formula bar. The selected part of the formula is the range name *January Income*. When you have named a range, Works substitutes the range name for the range of cells.

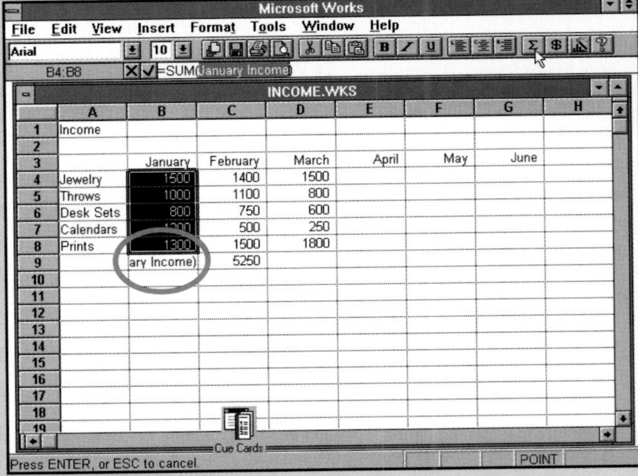

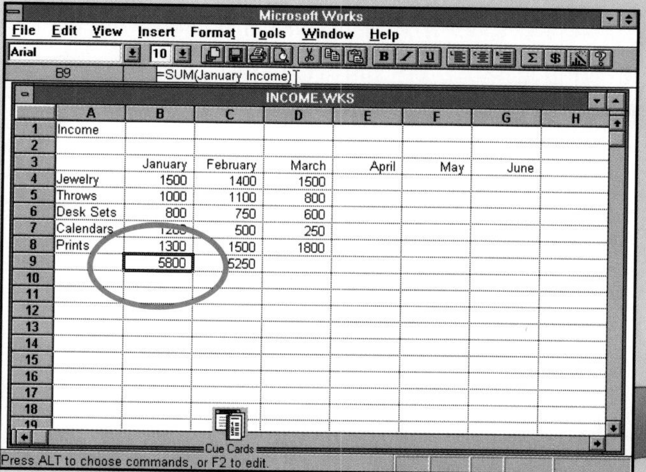

4 Press **Enter**. In cell B9, Works enters the formula that sums the range and then calculates the formula. Works displays the total in cell B9, but continues to display the formula in the formula bar.

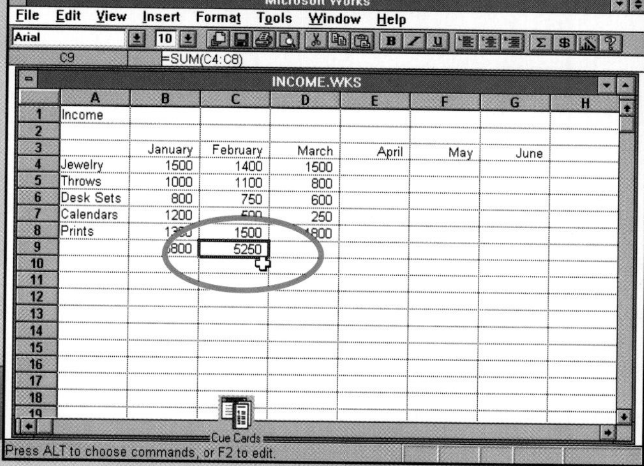

5 Click on cell **C9**. This makes cell C9 the active cell. You will copy its contents to the Clipboard.

NOTE

The Clipboard is a temporary storage area for text or graphics that you copy or cut to paste elsewhere later.

6 Click on the **Copy** toolbar button. This step copies the contents of C9 to the Clipboard. Since the selected cell contains a formula rather than a value, Works copies the formula to the Clipboard.

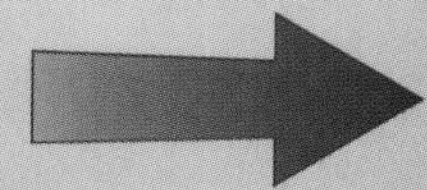

Task 30: Entering Formulas

7 Click on cell **D9**. This action makes cell D9 the active cell.

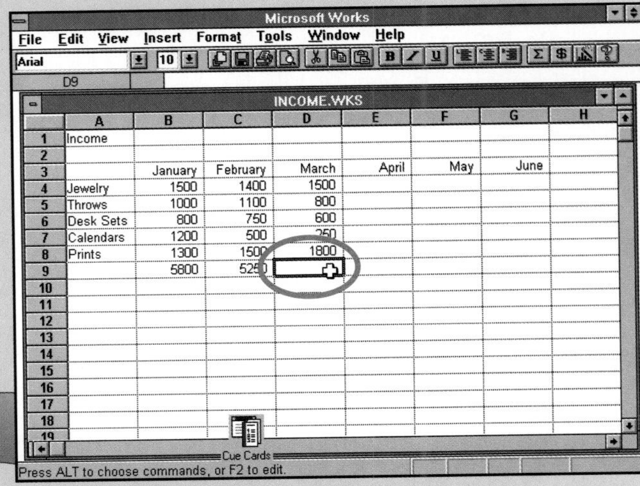

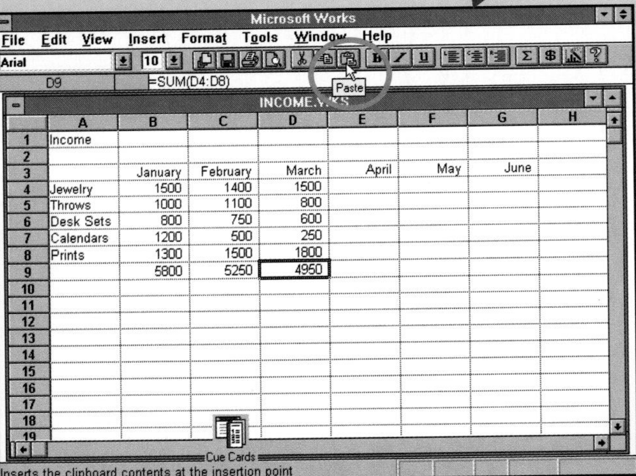

8 Click on the **Paste** toolbar button. Works copies the formula into cell D9 and calculates the result, based on the formula in the formula bar.

NOTE

When you copy a formula to another cell, Works doesn't copy the formula's exact cell addresses, but instead copies its cell references—known as *relative references*. Works also can use *absolute references*, when you want to use an exact unchangeable cell address in a formula.

9 Click in cell **A9**, type **Total**, and press **Enter**. Works inserts the word *Total* in cell A9. Notice the quotation mark in the formula bar. Remember, this means that *Total* is a text entry.

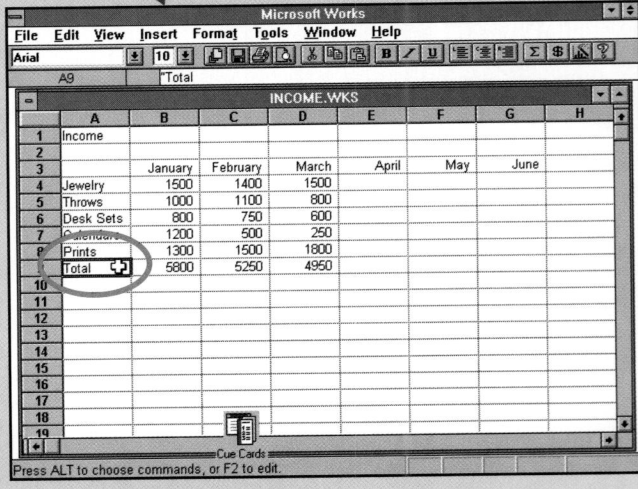

TASK 31

Using Functions in Formulas

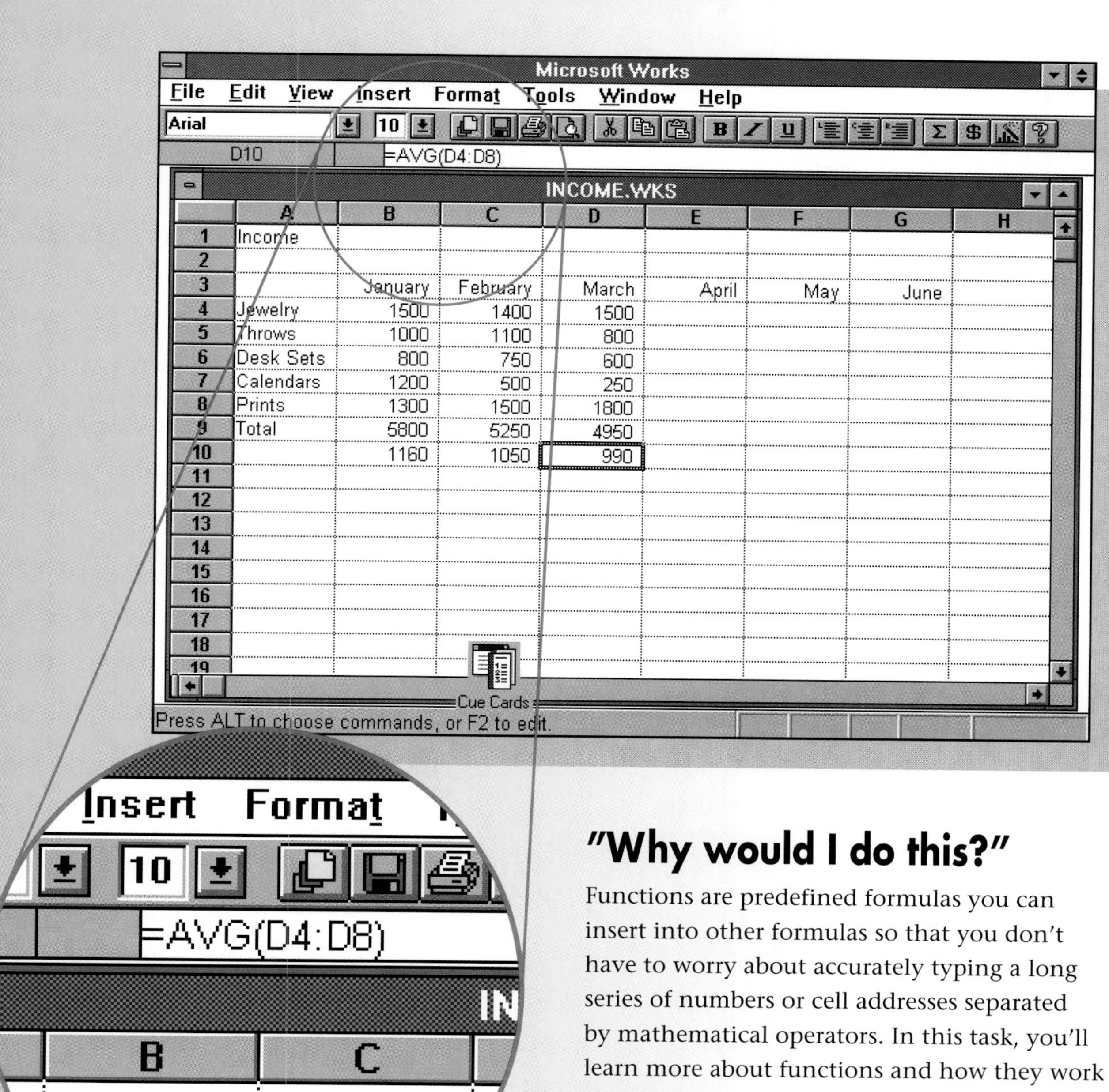

"Why would I do this?"

Functions are predefined formulas you can insert into other formulas so that you don't have to worry about accurately typing a long series of numbers or cell addresses separated by mathematical operators. In this task, you'll learn more about functions and how they work in formulas.

This task assumes that a spreadsheet, such as the one you used in the last task, appears on-screen.

Task 31: Using Functions in Formulas

1 Click on cell **B10**. This makes cell B10 the active cell. You will insert a function in this cell.

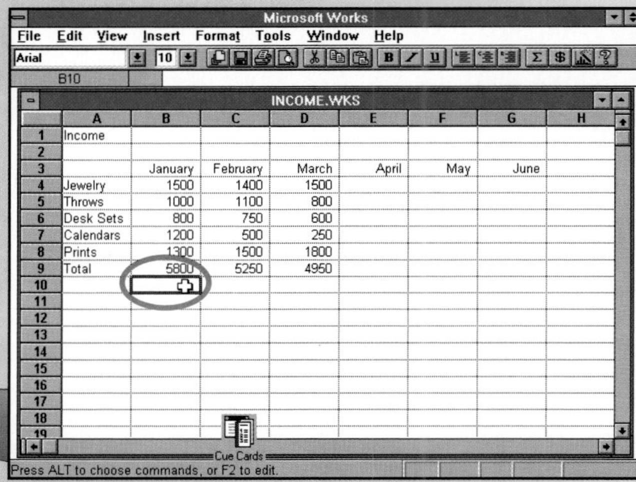

2 Click on **Insert** in the menu bar and click on **Function**. Works opens the Insert Function dialog box.

NOTE

If you don't know the specific name of the function you want to use, click on a Category option to narrow your choices. To find a date function, for example, click on Date and Time. Works lists all date and time functions. Click on a function to display a description of it.

3 In the Functions list, double-click on **AVG**. Works closes the dialog box and inserts the function, showing its proper format.

NOTE

The highlighted part of the AVG function is an *argument*, which provides required information to the function so that it can calculate successfully. Two examples of arguments are: cells or ranges containing numbers, and text that the function uses in its calculations.

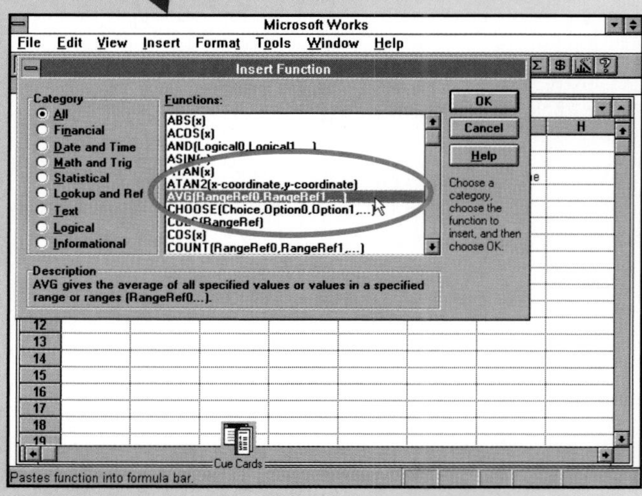

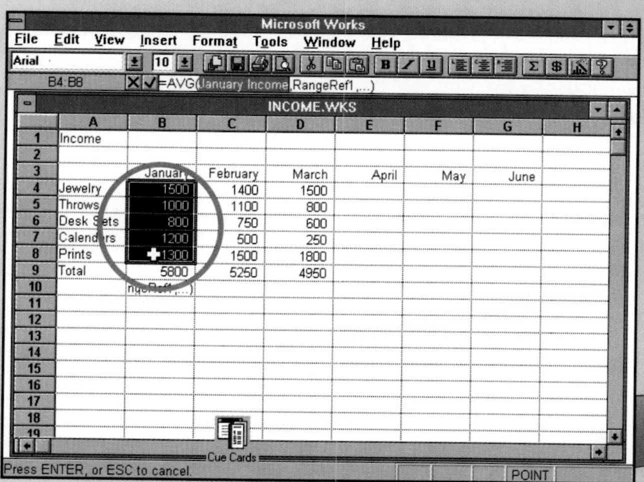

4 Drag the mouse pointer from cell B4 to B8. In the formula bar, Works replaces the first argument in the formula with *January Income,* the name of the range B4:B8.

5 Place the insertion point in the formula bar, highlight **,RangeRef1,...**, press **Delete**, and press **Enter**. Don't forget to remove the comma and the ellipsis (...). This step removes the selected text from the formula and makes cell B10 the active cell. *January Income* is the only argument that the formula requires.

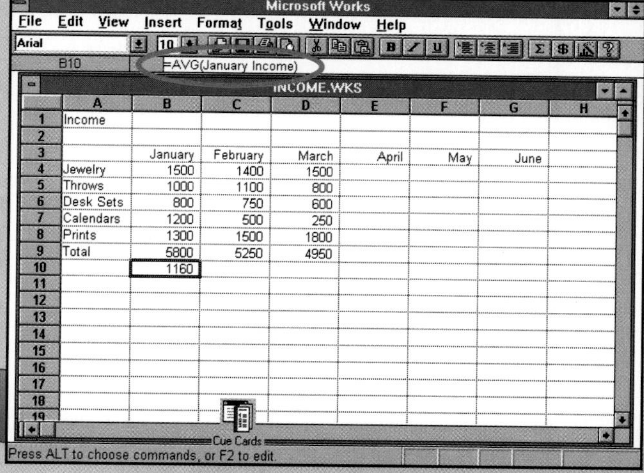

6 Click on the **Copy** toolbar button. This step copies the formula in cell B10, the active cell, to the Clipboard.

7 Click on cell **C10**, hold down the mouse button, and drag to cell **D10**. This action selects cells C10 and D10.

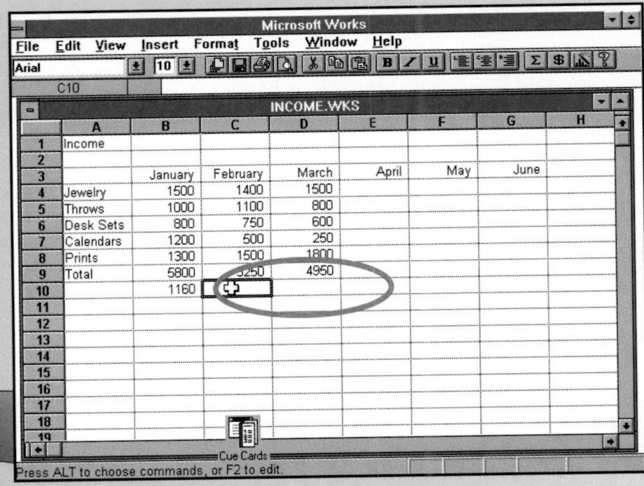

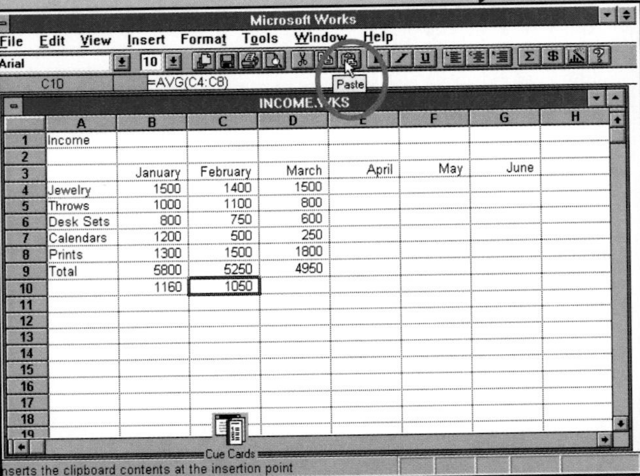

8 Click on the **Paste** toolbar button. Works copies the formula into cells C10 and D10 and changes the formula to fit columns C and D. Remember that the only column assigned a range name is column B; therefore, the formula includes the range of cell addresses.

9 Click on cell **A10**, type **Average**, and press **Enter**. This inserts a row label, *Average*.

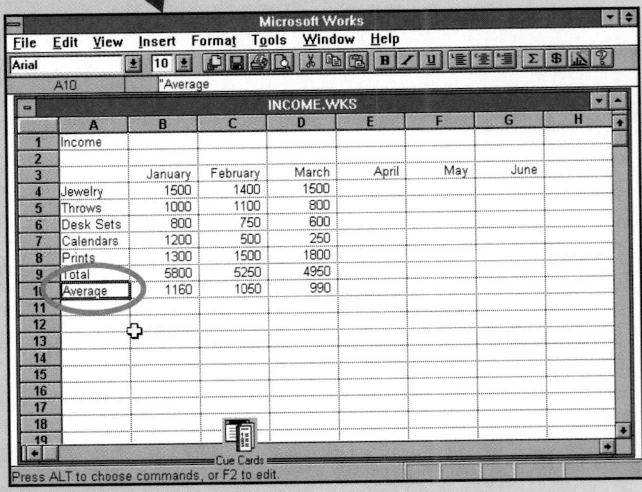

NOTE

For help on Works functions, choose Help Contents from the menu. Scroll to the bottom of the Contents window and click on the button that looks like a spreadsheet. In the Functions window, click on any of the green text to see functions by category. Click on a specific function to view information about that function.

TASK 32

Copying and Moving Data

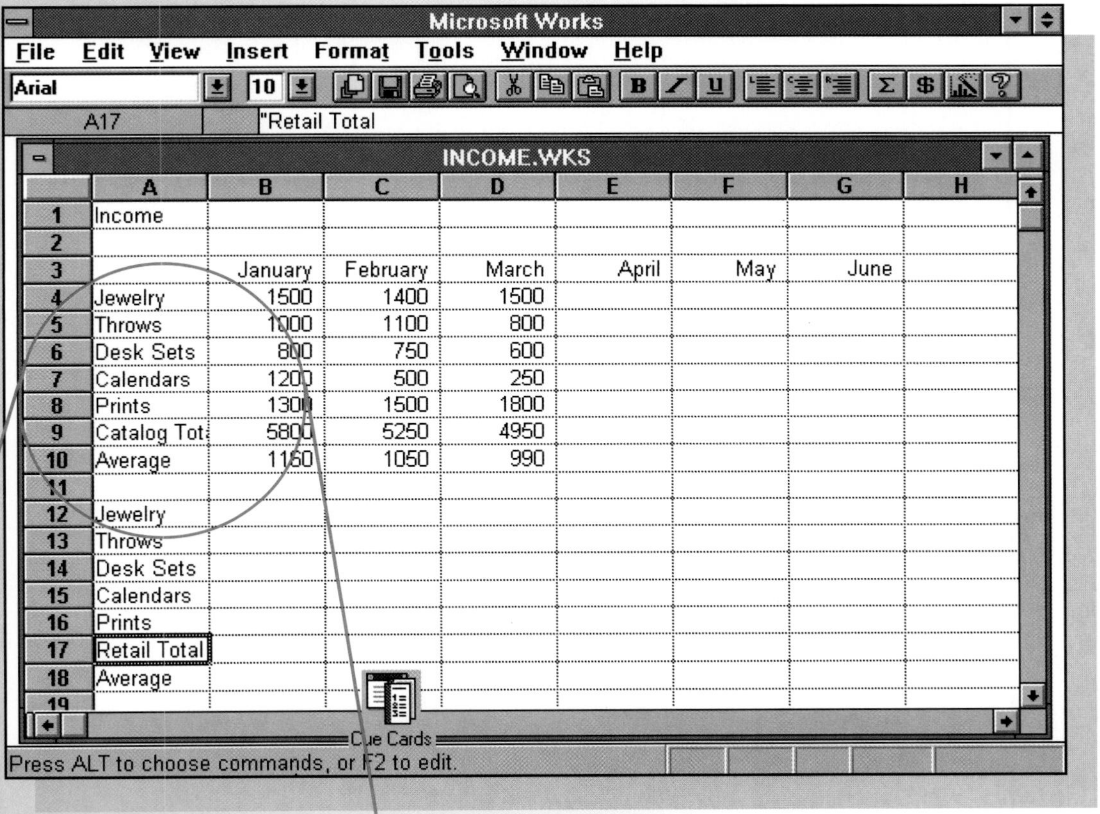

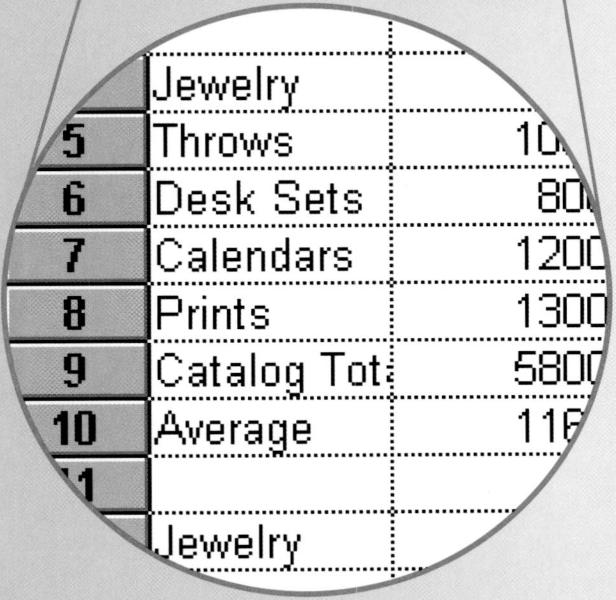

"Why would I do this?"

Copying information is easier than retyping it. You can copy items to build a new part of the spreadsheet or to serve as a template for another spreadsheet that contains similar information. To make room in a spreadsheet for an extra row of titles or totals, you can either insert a row or drag the contents of selected cells to a new location. In this task, you'll learn how to copy and move spreadsheet data.

This task assumes that a spreadsheet, such as the one you used in the last task, appears on-screen.

Task 32: Copying and Moving Data

1 Select the range of cells you want to copy to a new location; for this example, select the cells from **A4** to **A10**. Works highlights the selected cells.

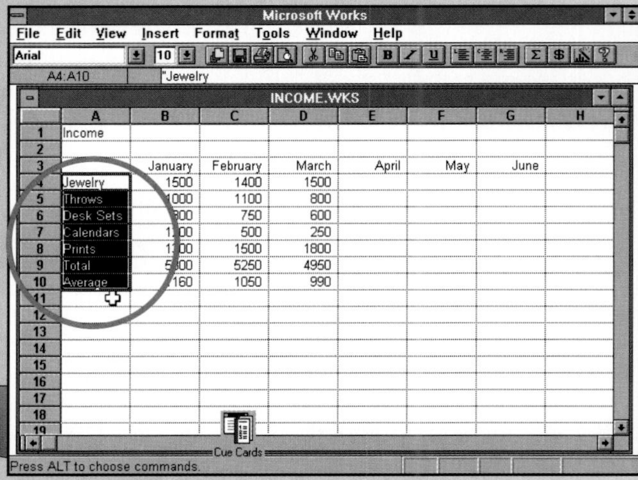

2 Click on the **Copy** toolbar button. Works copies the contents of the selected cells into the Windows Clipboard. In this case, Works copies the column labels into the Clipboard.

3 Click on the cell into which you want to paste the copied range; for this example, click on cell **A11**. Works makes cell A11 the active cell.

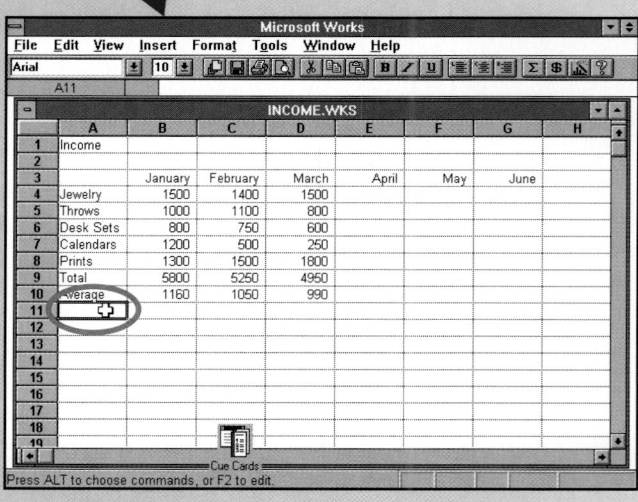

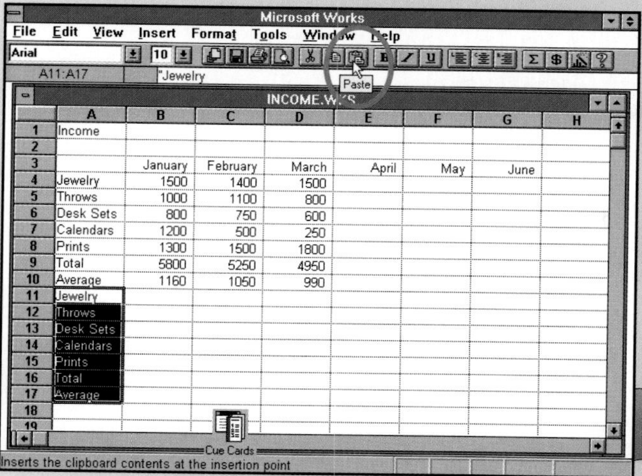

4 Click on the **Paste** toolbar button. Works pastes the contents of the Clipboard into the selected cell and down the column until every copied label appears.

WHY WORRY?

If you paste a value into a cell that already contains text, numbers, or a formula, Works replaces the current contents. To return to the previous value, press Ctrl+Z or choose Edit Undo from the menu to undo your error.

5 Move the mouse pointer to the border surrounding the highlighted cells until the pointer turns into an arrow with a tail that displays `DRAG`. You will move the selected range of cells down one row by dragging it.

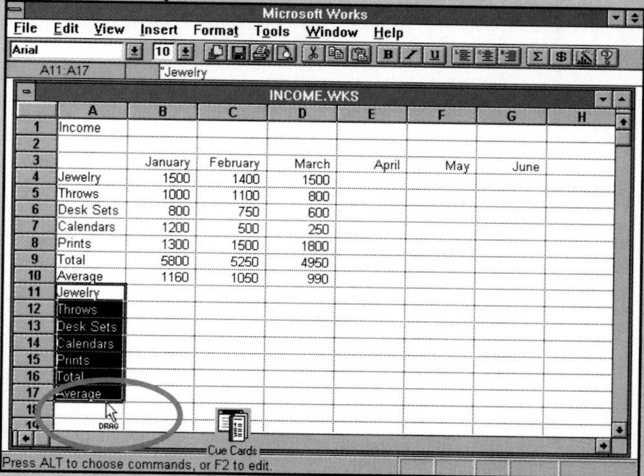

6 Drag the pointer down to the next cell—cell **A18** in this example. Notice that the mouse tail now says `MOVE`.

Task 32: Copying and Moving Data

7 Release the mouse button. Works moves the selection down one cell.

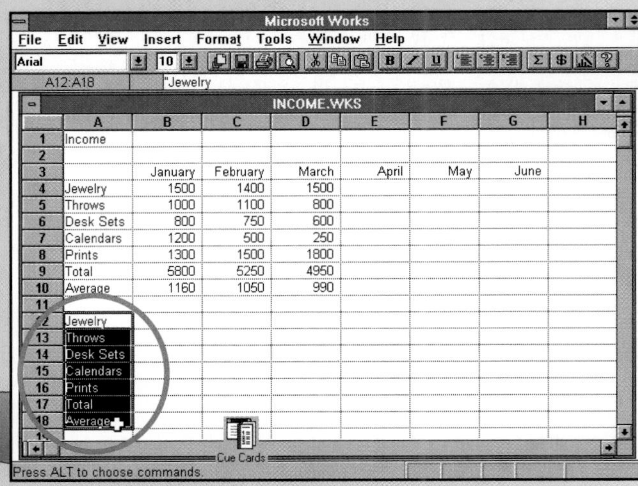

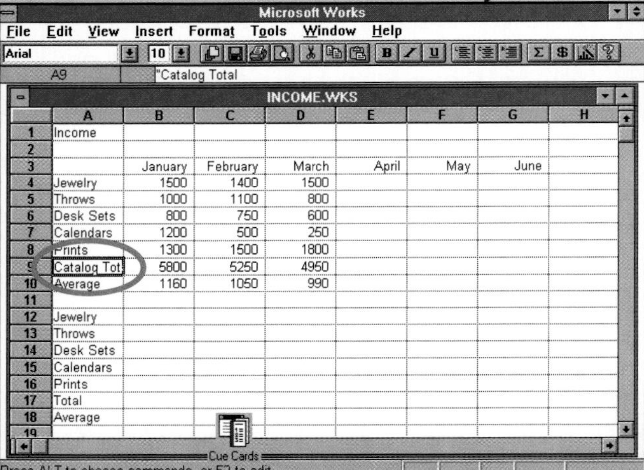

8 Click on cell **A9**, type **Catalog Total**, and press **Enter**. This action changes the column label. (Because the column label is too wide to fit in the column, you cannot see its last two characters.)

9 Click on cell **A17**, type **Retail Total**, and press **Enter**. This action changes the column label.

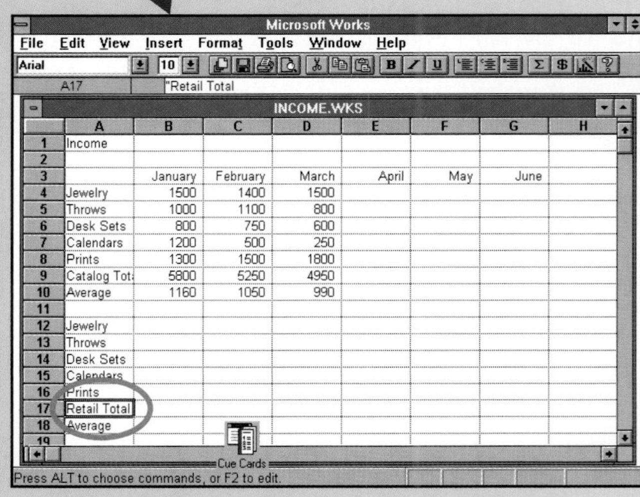

TASK 33

Choosing a New Number Format

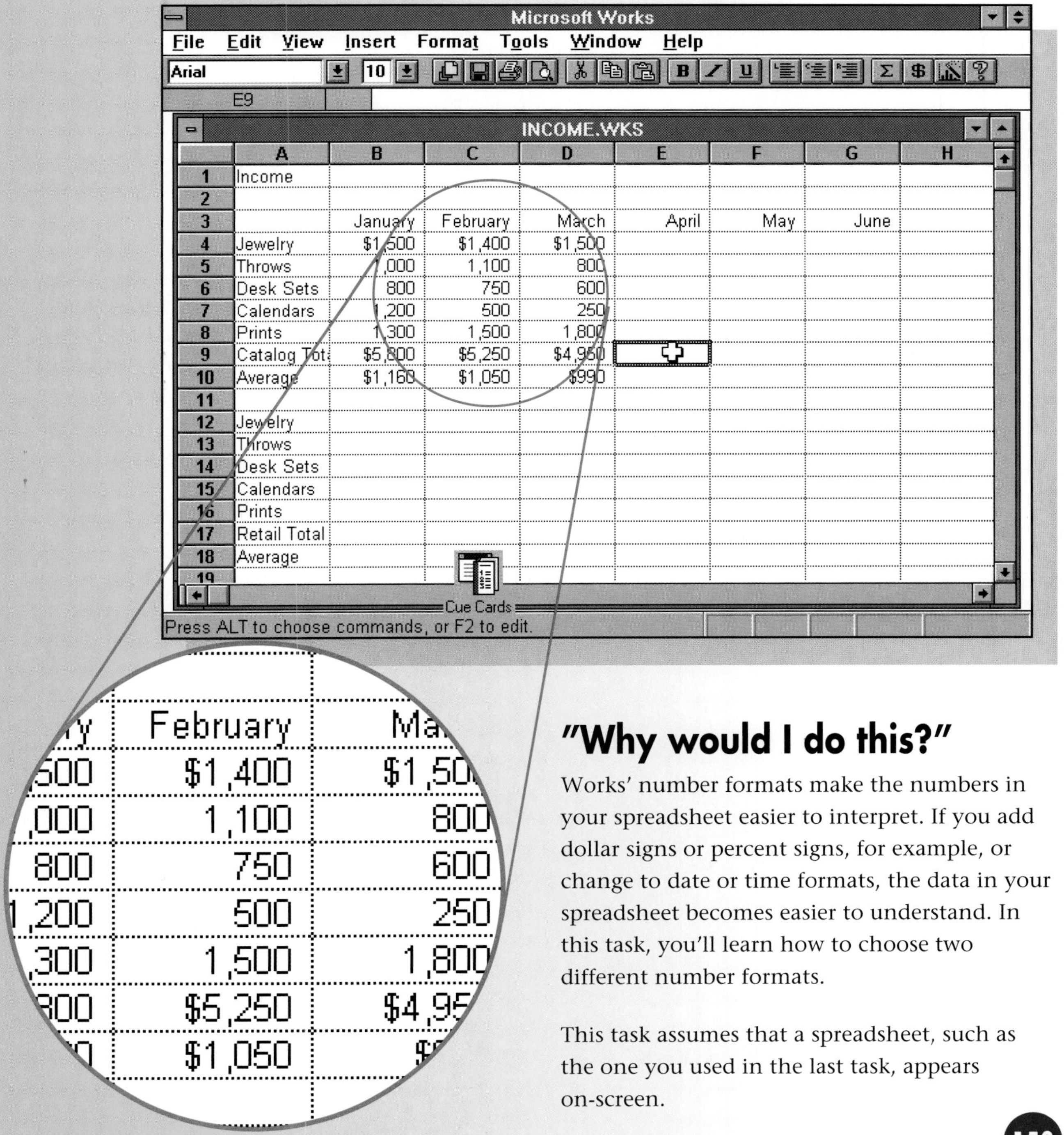

"Why would I do this?"

Works' number formats make the numbers in your spreadsheet easier to interpret. If you add dollar signs or percent signs, for example, or change to date or time formats, the data in your spreadsheet becomes easier to understand. In this task, you'll learn how to choose two different number formats.

This task assumes that a spreadsheet, such as the one you used in the last task, appears on-screen.

Task 33: Choosing a New Number Format

1 Select the range of cells containing the numbers you want to format; for this example, select from cell **B4** down to cell **B10** and over to cell **D10**. Works highlights the block of cells.

> **NOTE**
>
> Another way to select a range is to click on the cell in one corner of the range, press and hold down Shift, and click on the cell at the opposite corner of the range.

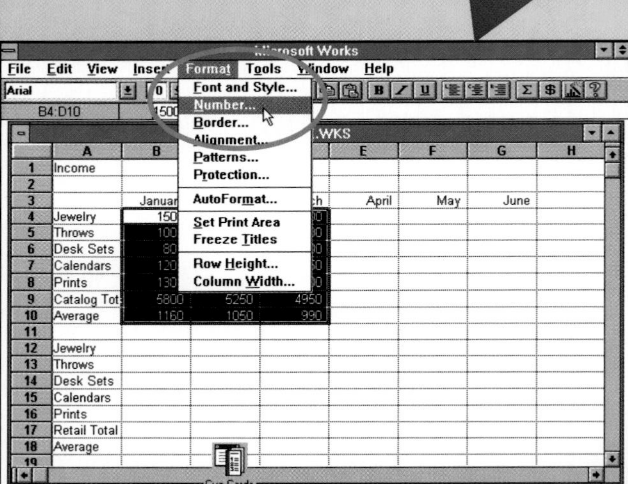

2 Click on **Format** in the menu bar and click on the **Number** command. This opens the Number dialog box, which lists, explains, and shows a sample of the selected format.

3 Click on **Currency**. This action selects the number format for money. Works adds some options to the dialog box and displays a sample of the format in the Sample box.

> **NOTE**
>
> The Currency format adds a dollar sign to numbers and inserts commas to separate thousands. You can also specify the number of digits you want after a decimal point.

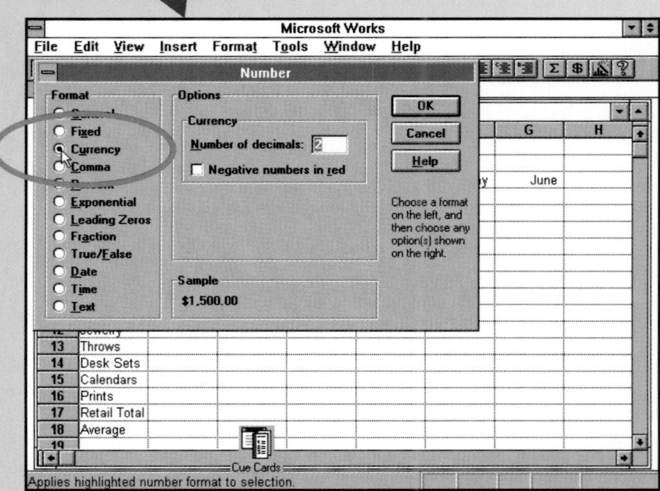

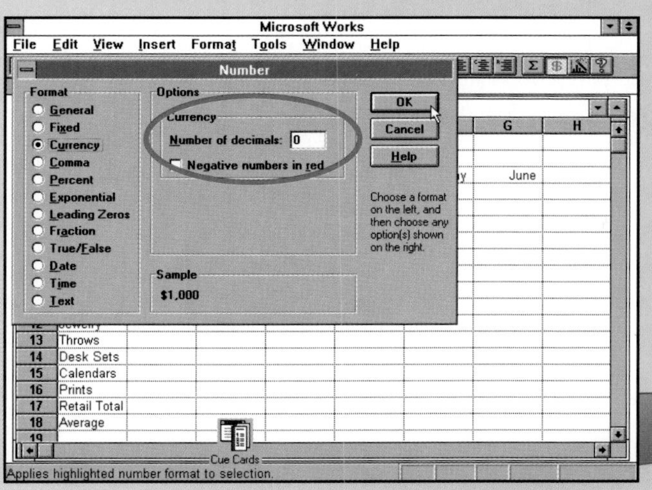

4 Type **0** in the Number of Decimals text box. (Since there are no numbers with decimal points in the spreadsheet, it's not necessary to define any decimal places.) Click on **OK**. Works adds dollar signs to each of the numbers in the selection.

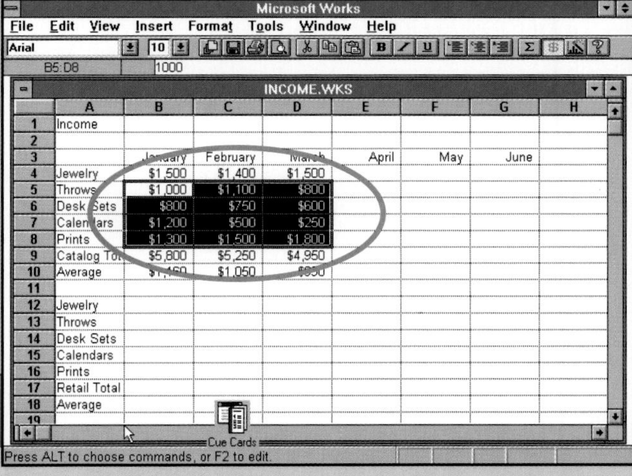

5 Select from cell **B5** down to **B8** and over to **D8**. Works highlights the selected cells. You will remove the dollar signs from the values in the selected cells.

6 Click on **Format** in the menu bar and click on the **Number** command. This step opens the Number dialog box.

Task 33: Choosing a New Number Format

7 Click on **Comma**. This action selects the Comma number format, which adds thousands separators but not dollar signs.

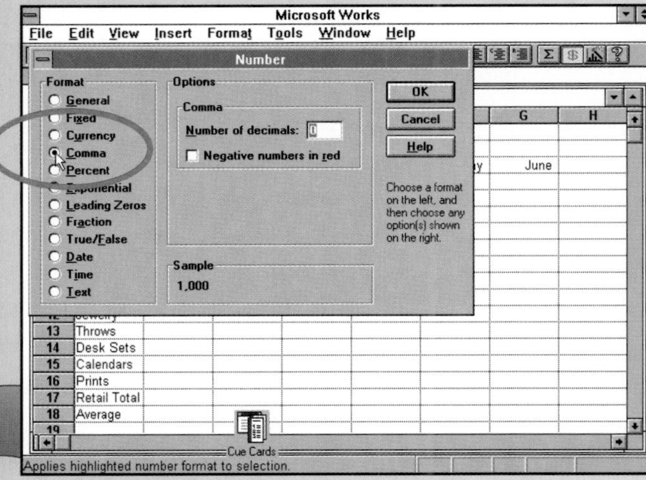

8 Click on **OK**. Works changes the number format for the selection.

9 Click anywhere on the screen to turn off the highlight.

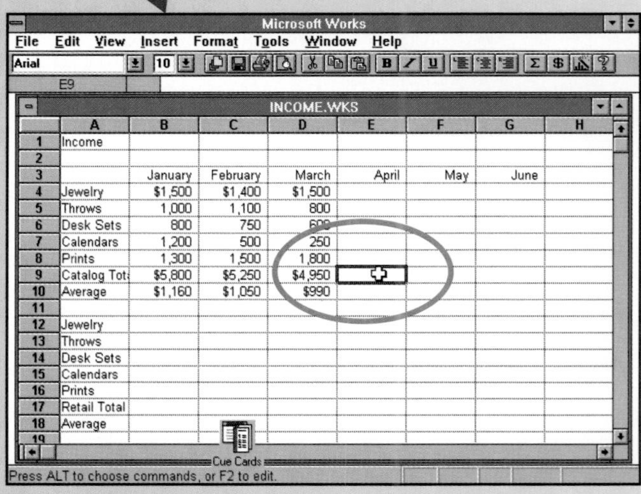

TASK 34

Editing the Contents of Cells

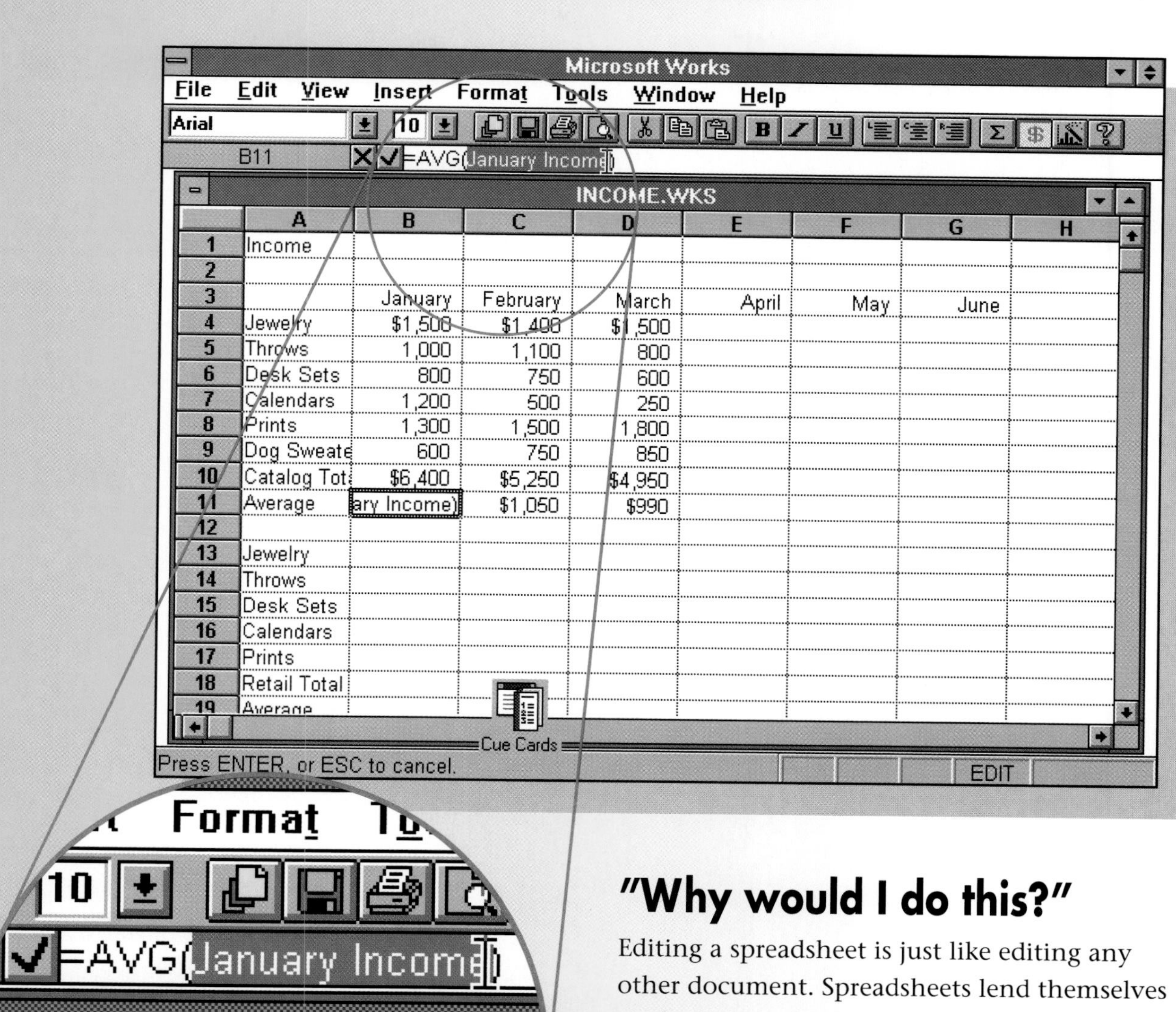

"Why would I do this?"

Editing a spreadsheet is just like editing any other document. Spreadsheets lend themselves to changing values, and sometimes changing values lead to your modifying formulas, text, and numbers. In this task, you'll learn how to edit a cell by using the formula bar.

This task assumes that a spreadsheet, such as the one you used in the last task, appears on-screen.

Task 34: Editing the Contents of Cells

1 Click on the number **9** at the left border of the spreadsheet and drag the pointer down to number **10**. This step selects rows 9 and 10.

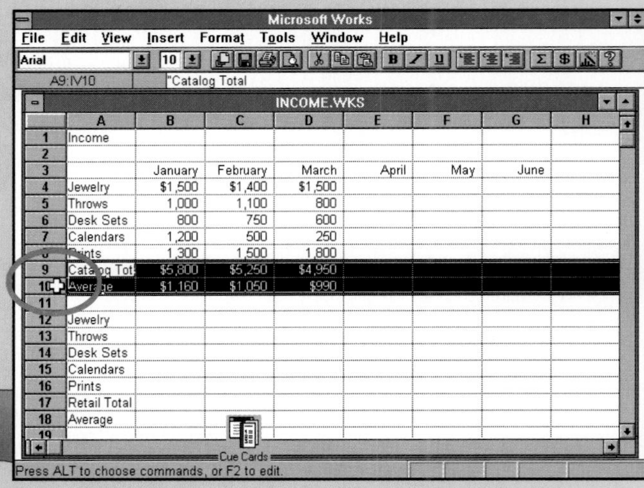
Microsoft Works

File Edit View Insert Format Tools Window Help

A9:IV10 "Catalog Total

INCOME.WKS

	A	B	C	D	E	F	G	H
1	Income							
2								
3		January	February	March	April	May	June	
4	Jewelry	$1,500	$1,400	$1,500				
5	Throws	1,000	1,100	800				
6	Desk Sets	800	750	600				
7	Calendars	1,200	500	250				
8	Prints	1,300	1,500	1,800				
9	Catalog Tot	$5,800	$5,250	$4,950				
10	Average	$1,160	$1,050	$990				
11								
12	Jewelry							
13	Throws							
14	Desk Sets							
15	Calendars							
16	Prints							
17	Retail Total							
18	Average							

Cue Cards

Press ALT to choose commands, or F2 to edit.

2 Drag the selected rows down one cell. This step inserts another row above the selected rows.

Microsoft Works

File Edit View Insert Format Tools Window Help

A9:IV10 "Average

INCOME.WKS

	A	B	C	D	E	F	G	H
1	Income							
2								
3		January	February	March	April	May	June	
4	Jewelry	$1,500	$1,400	$1,500				
5	Throws	1,000	1,100	800				
6	Desk Sets	800	750	600				
7	Calendars	1,200	500	250				
8	Prints	1,300	1,500	1,800				
9	Catalog Tot	$5,800	$5,250	$4,950				
10	Average	$1,160	$1,050	$990				
11								
12	Jewelry							
13	Throws							
14	Desk Sets							
15	Calendars							
16	Prints							
17	Retail Total							
18	Average							

Cue Cards

Drag mouse to position data. Press ESC to cancel.

3 Click on cell **A9**. This makes cell A9 the active cell.

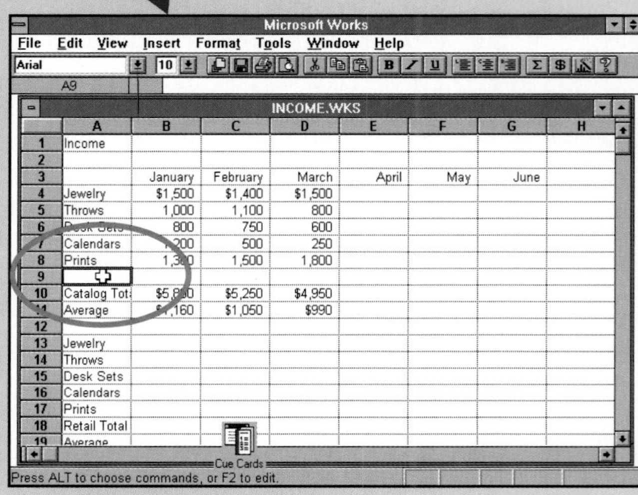
Microsoft Works

File Edit View Insert Format Tools Window Help

A9

INCOME.WKS

	A	B	C	D	E	F	G	H
1	Income							
2								
3		January	February	March	April	May	June	
4	Jewelry	$1,500	$1,400	$1,500				
5	Throws	1,000	1,100	800				
6	Desk Sets	800	750	600				
7	Calendars	1,200	500	250				
8	Prints	1,300	1,500	1,800				
9								
10	Catalog Tot	$5,800	$5,250	$4,950				
11	Average	$1,160	$1,050	$990				
12								
13	Jewelry							
14	Throws							
15	Desk Sets							
16	Calendars							
17	Prints							
18	Retail Total							
19	Average							

Cue Cards

Press ALT to choose commands, or F2 to edit.

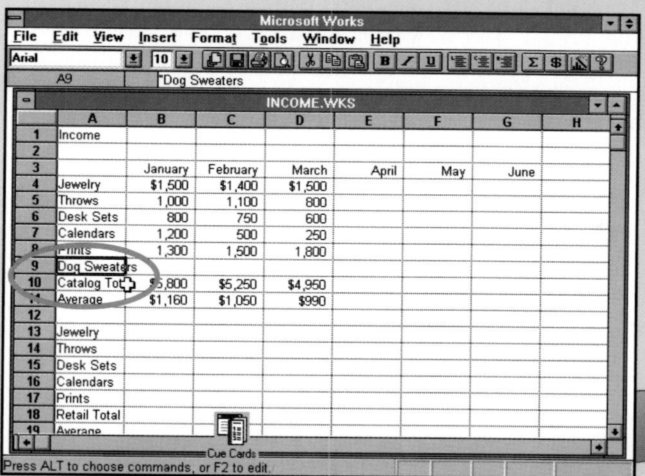

4 Type **Dog Sweaters** and press **Enter**. This gives the new row a label. The entry *Dog Sweaters* is wider than cell A9 and appears to take space in cell B9. When you put data into cell B9, however, Works restricts *Dog Sweaters* to cell A9.

5 Click on cell **B9**, type **600**, and press →.

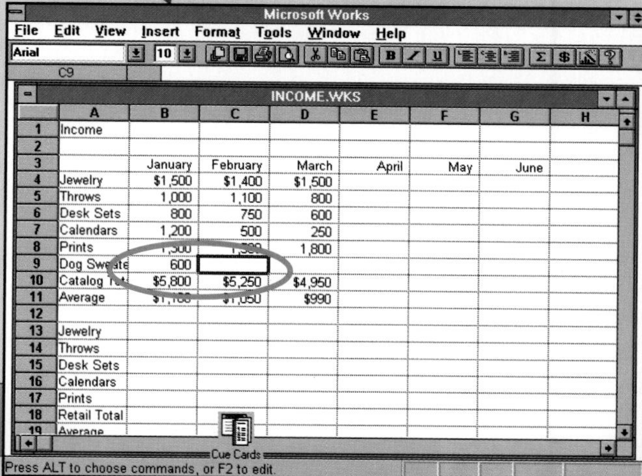

6 Type **750** in cell C9 and press →.

Task 34: Editing the Contents of Cells

7 Type **850** in cell D9 and press **Enter**.

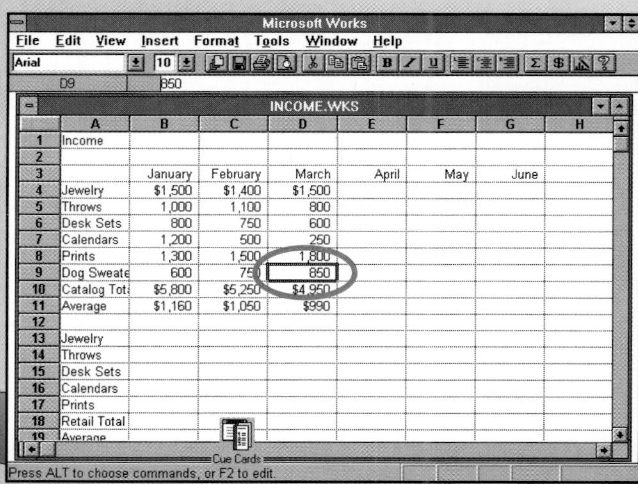

Microsoft Works

File Edit View Insert Format Tools Window Help

B10 =SUM(January Income)

INCOME.WKS

	A	B	C	D	E	F	G	H
1	Income							
2								
3		January	February	March	April	May	June	
4	Jewelry	$1,500	$1,400	$1,500				
5	Throws	1,000	1,100	800				
6	Desk Sets	800	750	600				
7	Calendars	1,200	500	250				
8	Prints	1,300	1,500	1,800				
9	Dog Sweate	600	750	850				
10	Catalog Tot	$5,800	$5,250	$4,950				
11	Average	$1,160	$1,050	$990				
12								
13	Jewelry							
14	Throws							
15	Desk Sets							
16	Calendars							
17	Prints							
18	Retail Total							
19	Average							

Cue Cards

Press ALT to choose commands, or F2 to edit.

8 Click on cell **B10**. In the formula bar, Works displays the formula stored in cell B10.

9 Select the text **January Income** within the parentheses in the formula bar.

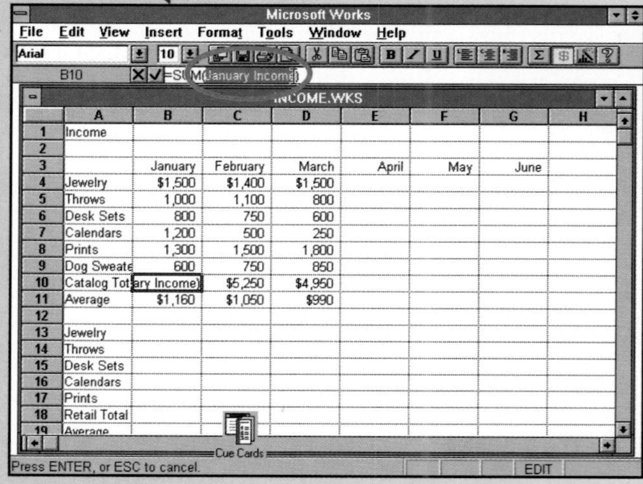

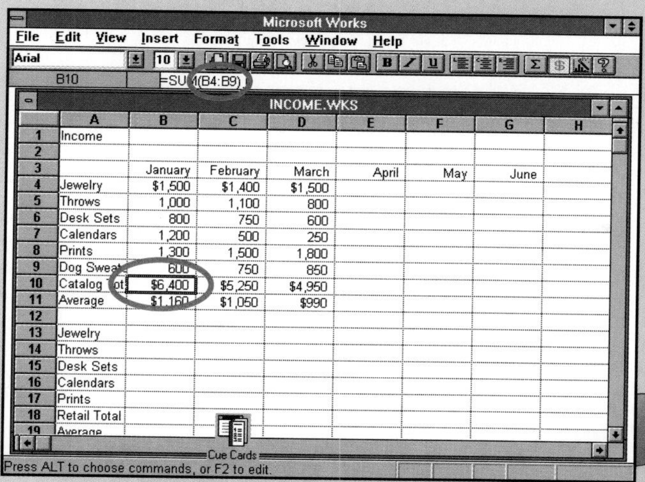

10 Type **B4:B9** within the parentheses and press **Enter**. Works calculates the edited formula and displays the result in cell B10.

11 Click on cell **B11.** In the formula bar, Works displays the formula stored in cell B11.

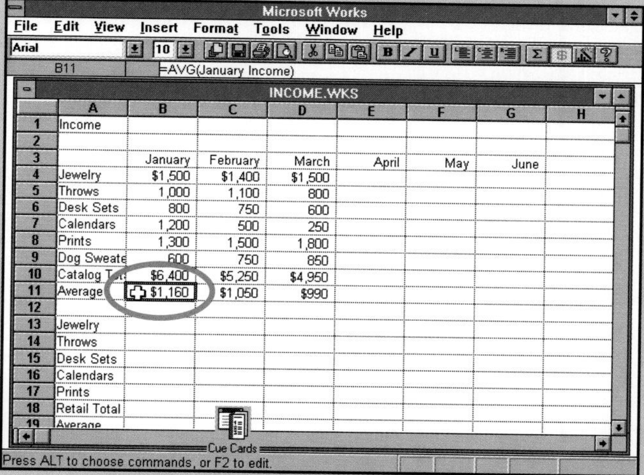

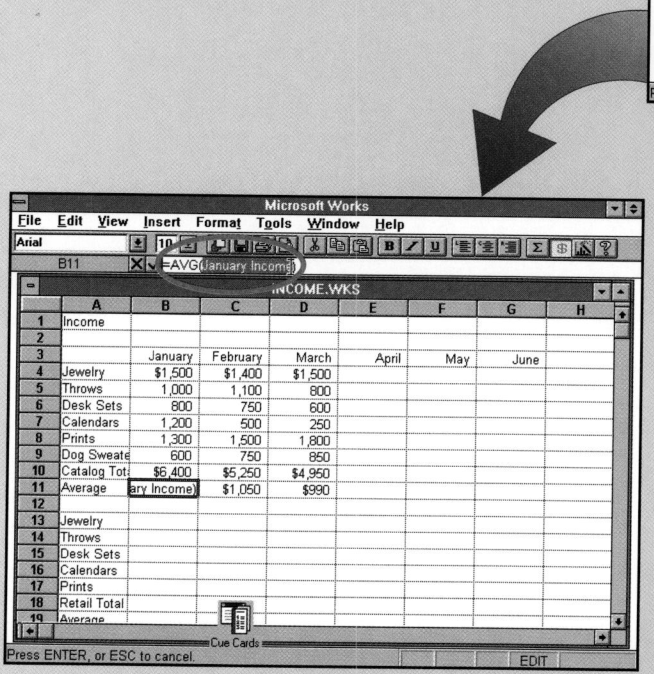

12 Select the text **January Income** within the parentheses in the formula bar.

Task 34: Editing the Contents of Cells

13 Drag from cell **B4** to **B9**. Works highlights the cells and, in the formula bar, replaces `January Income` with `B4:B9`.

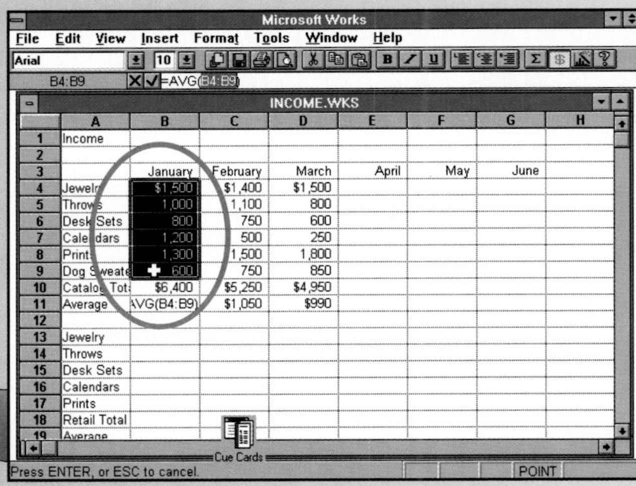

14 Press **Enter**. Works calculates the edited formula and displays the result in cell B11.

NOTE

The formula editing in this task points out how valuable it is to name ranges. One of the ways to decrease the amount of cell-by-cell editing in this task is to redefine the range *January Income* to include the new cell B10.

15 Select the range **B10:D10**, click on **Edit** in the menu bar, and click on **Fill Right**. This step copies the formula across all three rows and recalculates the totals.

NOTE

Continue editing the formulas until they are all correct. Remember that you should change the formulas in cells B11, C11, and D11.

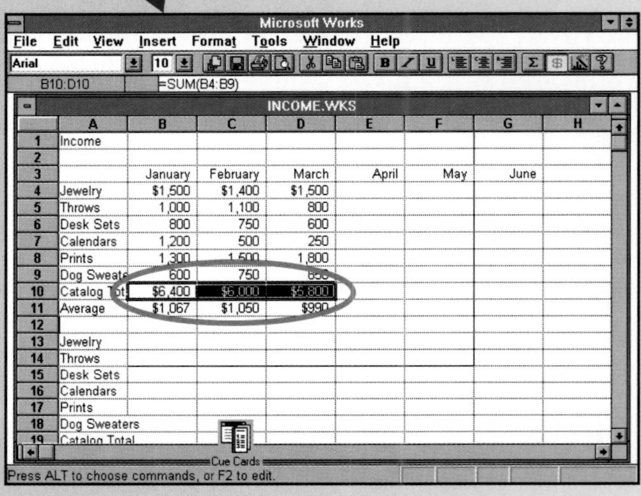

TASK 35

Adjusting Column Width and Row Height

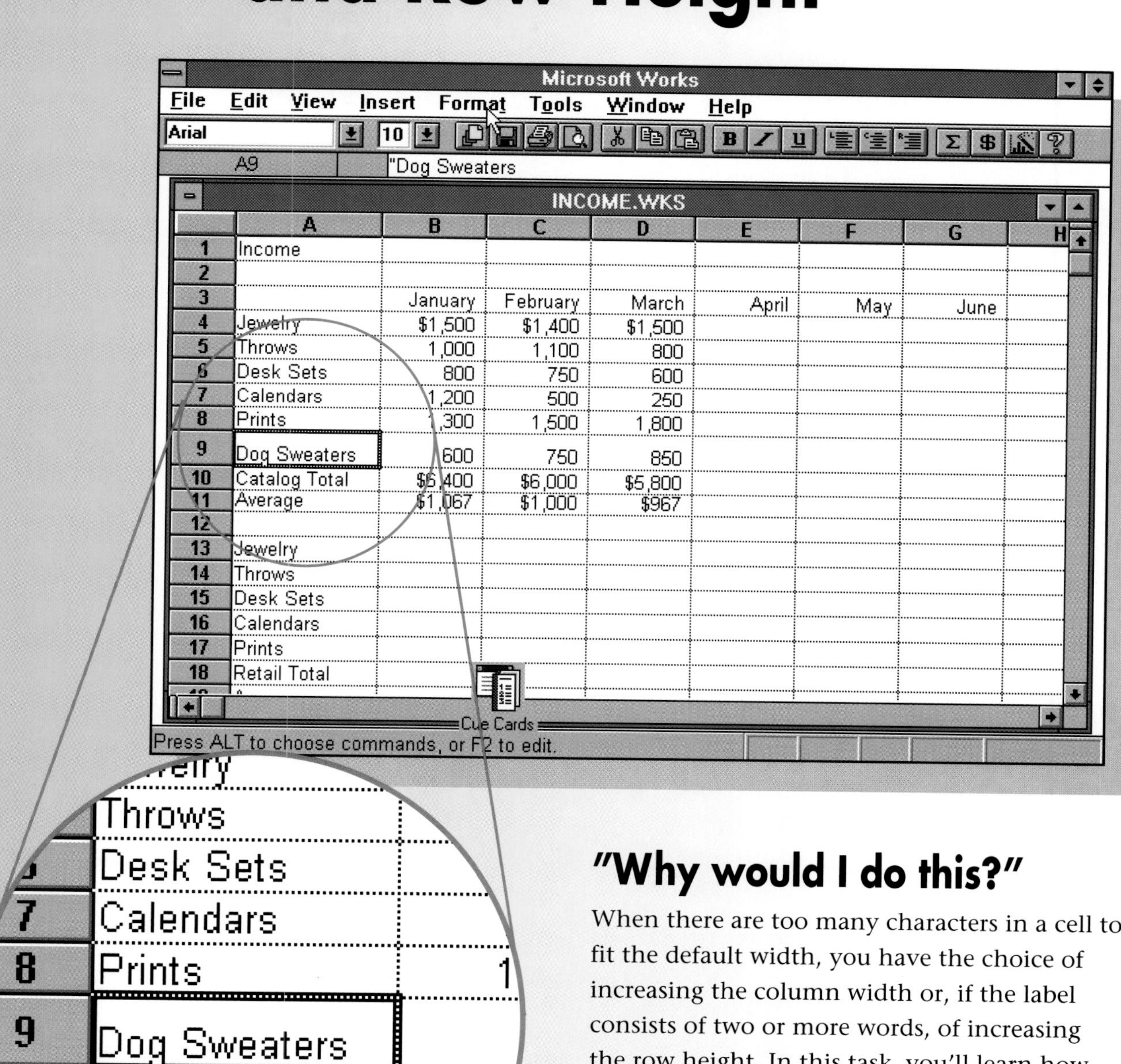

"Why would I do this?"

When there are too many characters in a cell to fit the default width, you have the choice of increasing the column width or, if the label consists of two or more words, of increasing the row height. In this task, you'll learn how to adjust column width and row height.

This task assumes that a spreadsheet, such as the one you used in the last task, appears on-screen.

Task 35: Adjusting Column Width and Row Height

1 Move the mouse pointer to the border between columns A and B until the pointer changes to a double-headed arrow. The tail of the mouse pointer says ADJUST.

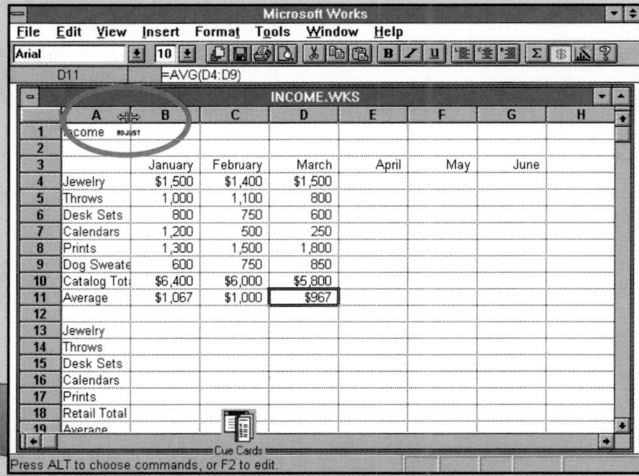

WHY WORRY?

If the contents of a cell display #####, either the cell is not wide enough to display all the characters in the entry, or you tried to apply an invalid number format. You must widen the column or apply a valid format.

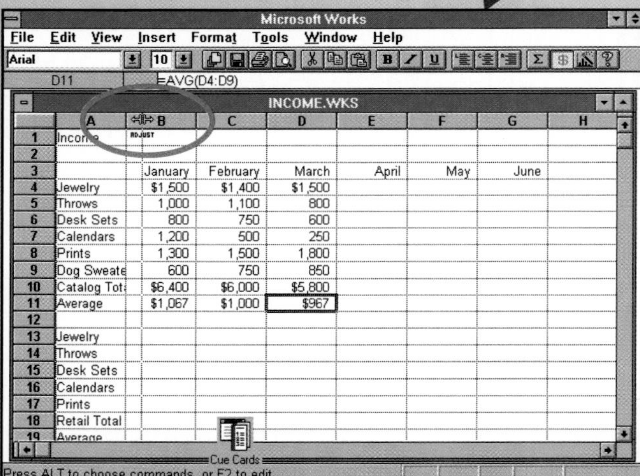

2 Drag the pointer toward the right side of the screen and release the mouse button. Works displays a line to indicate your present position as you drag and adjusts the width of the column when you release the mouse button.

3 Move the mouse pointer to the border between rows 9 and 10 until the pointer changes to a double-headed arrow.

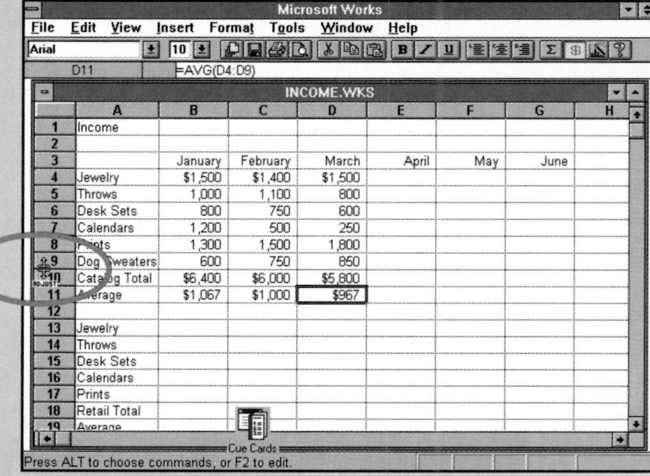

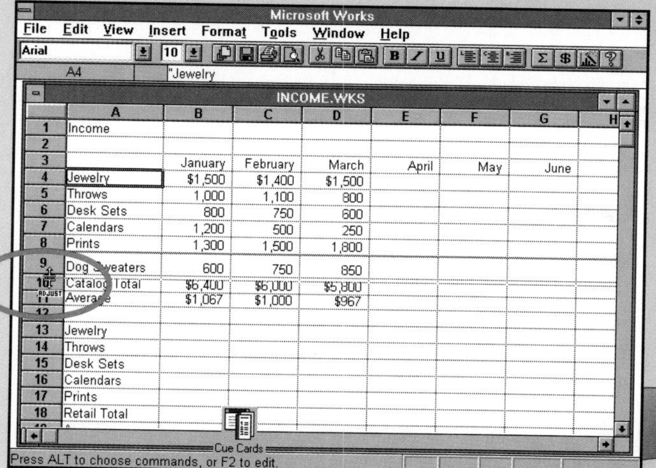

4 Drag the pointer down until the row is the desired height. Works displays a line indicating your current position as you drag.

> **NOTE**
>
> You also can adjust column width or row height by double-clicking on a column letter or row number. Works adjusts the column width or row height to fit the widest or highest items.

5 Click on cell **A9**. This makes cell A9 the active cell.

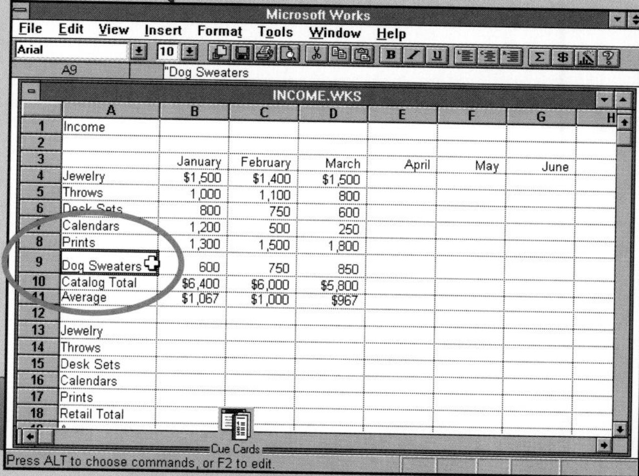

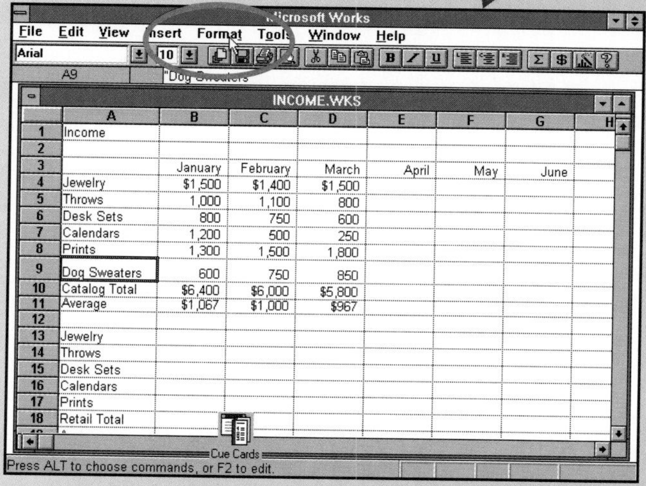

6 Click on **Format** in the menu bar. This opens the Format menu.

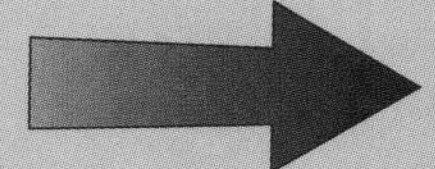

7 Click on **Row Height**. This step opens the Row Height dialog box.

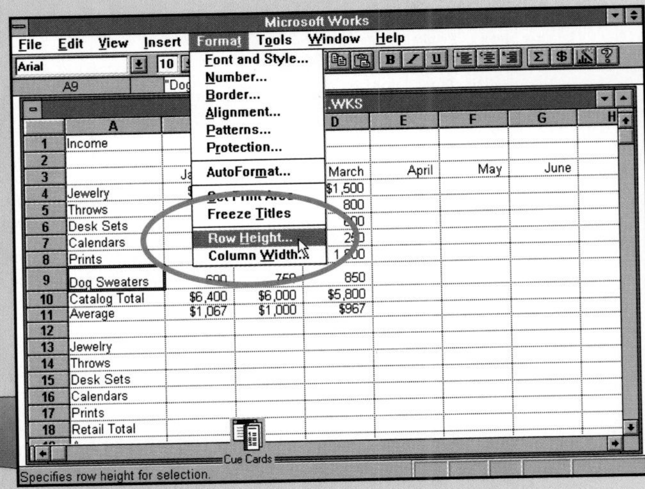

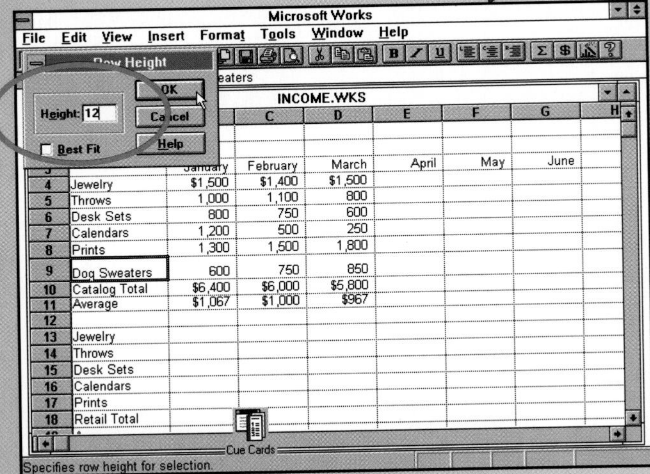

8 Type **12** in the Row Height dialog box and click on **OK**. Works returns row 9 to the default height of 12.

TASK 36

Inserting and Deleting Rows and Columns

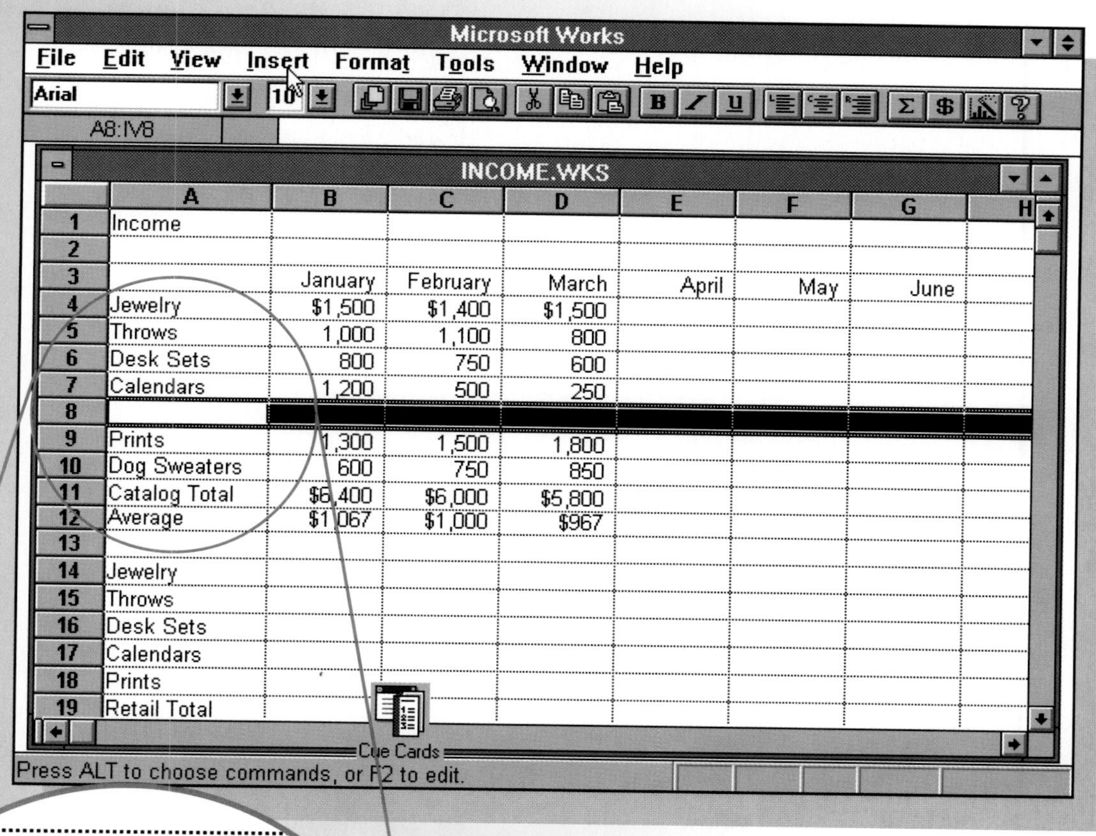

"Why would I do this?"

Over time, you'll need to make changes to your spreadsheet that involve adding and removing rows and columns, changes such as buying a new television set or paying off a car. In this task, you'll learn how to insert a column and row and then delete them.

This task assumes that a spreadsheet, such as the one you used in the last task, appears on-screen.

Task 36: Inserting and Deleting Rows and Columns

1 Click on **8** at the far left side of the spreadsheet. This action highlights row 8.

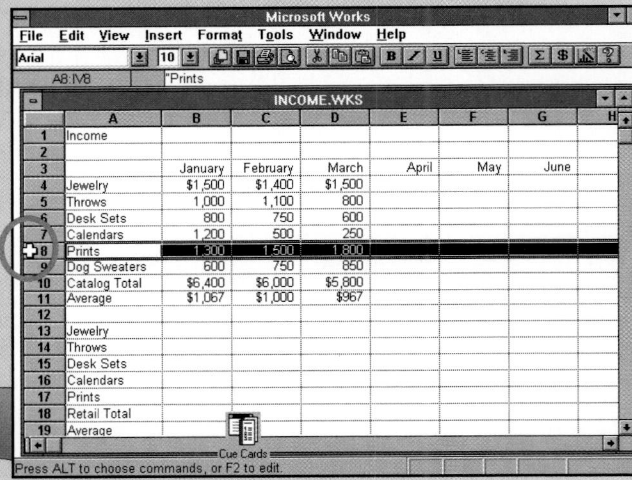

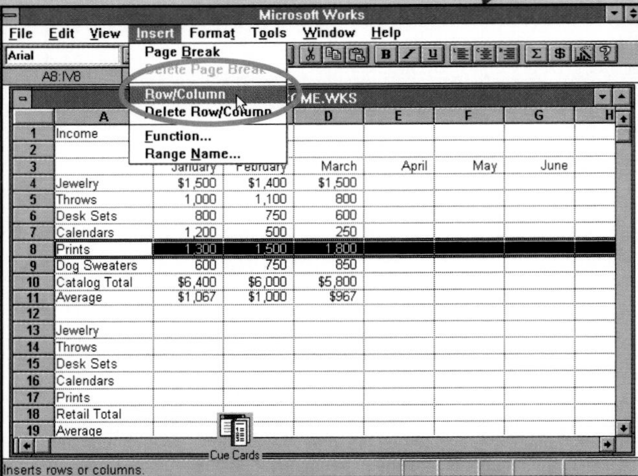

2 Click on **Insert** in the menu bar and click on **Row/Column**. This step adds a row before the selected row; all the rows below the new one are pushed down the spreadsheet. (Works adds a row because you selected a row.)

WHY WORRY?

Because of relative reference, Works automatically changes every formula to show the new cell addresses that have been pushed down or over by the addition of the new row or column.

3 Click on **Insert** in the menu bar and click on **Delete Row/Column**. This action deletes the selected row and returns the formulas to their previous state.

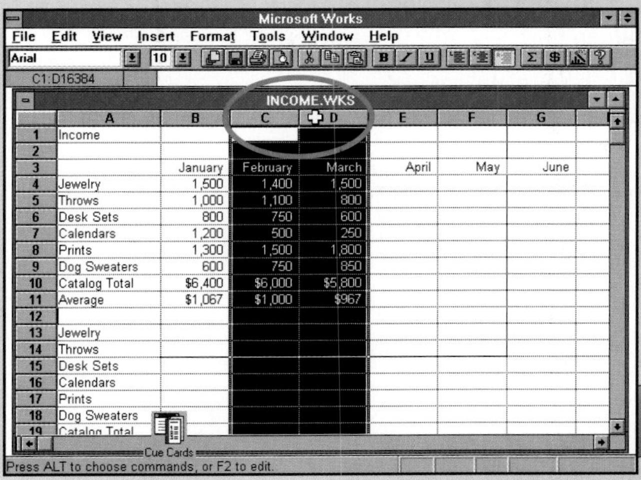

4 Click on the **C** above the February column at the top of the spreadsheet and drag the mouse pointer to column **D**. This step selects columns C and D.

5 Click on **Insert** in the menu bar and click on **Row/Column**. Works adds two new columns (the same number of columns you selected) and pushes the remaining columns toward the right.

NOTE

Formulas to the right of the new columns now reflect new cell addresses, just as formulas below a new row change.

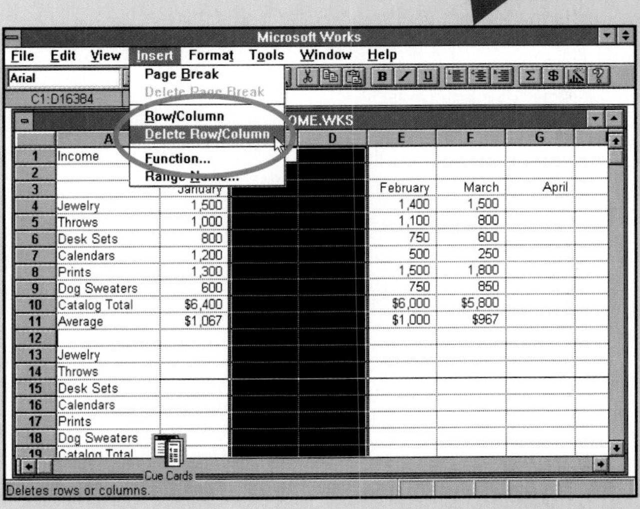

6 Click on **Insert** in the menu bar and click on **Delete Row/Column**. Works deletes the new columns and changes affected formulas back to their previous state.

TASK 37

Creating a Chart

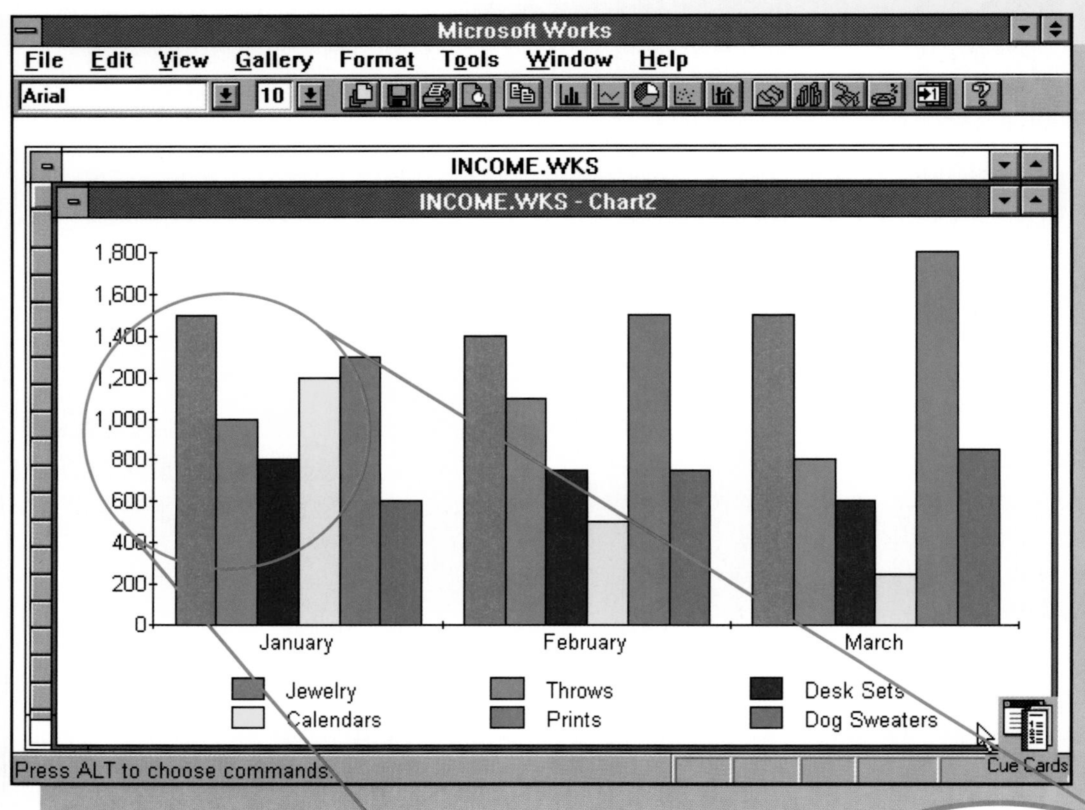

"Why would I do this?"

A chart is a picture of your data. When you want to emphasize a point, a chart is the way to go. In this task, you'll use Works charting feature to create a chart with the default settings.

This task assumes that a spreadsheet, such as the one you used in the last task, appears on-screen.

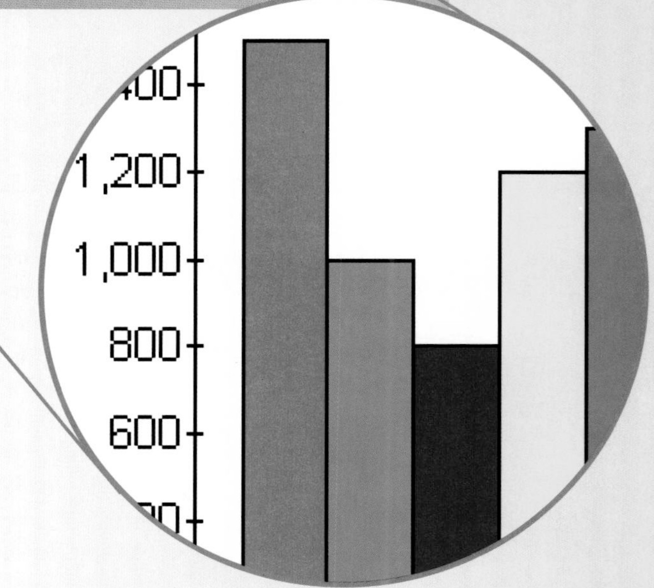

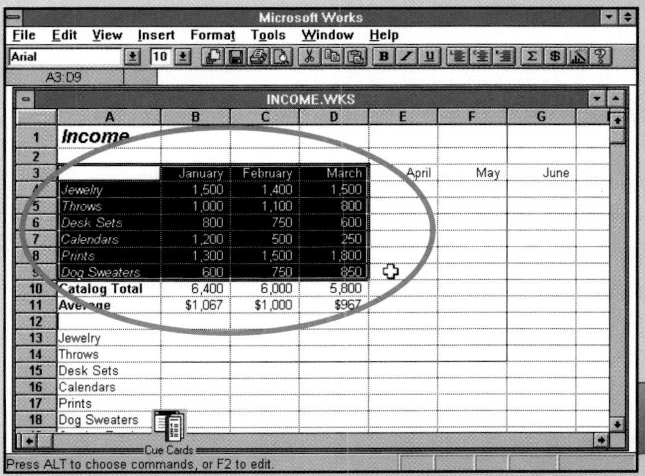

1 Select the range of cells from **A3** down to **A9** and over to **D9**. This step selects the cells for January, February, and March. Be sure to include the row and column labels so that Works will use them in the chart.

NOTE

Create a separate chart for the totals, if needed. Mixing the amounts that lead to totals with the totals themselves results in a very inaccurate chart.

2 Click on the **New Chart** toolbar button. This opens the New Chart dialog box, which displays a sample of your chart. Clicking on the New Chart toolbar button is the same as choosing Tools Create New Chart from the menu.

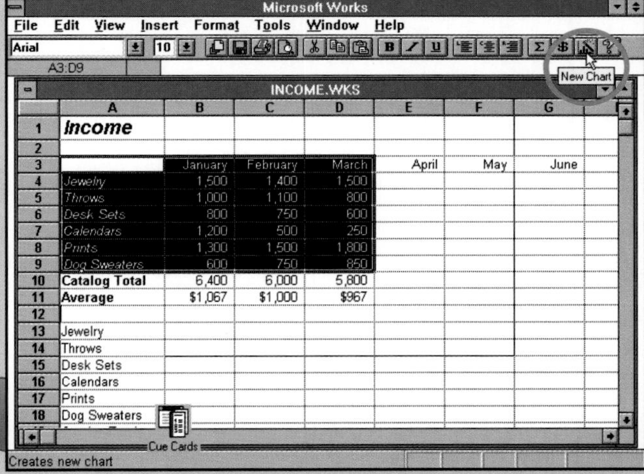

3 Click on **OK**. Works displays the chart in a chart window and restores the minimized Cue Cards.

Task 37: Creating a Chart

4 Click on the **Minimize** button in the Cue Cards window. This step closes the Cue Cards so that you can see the complete chart.

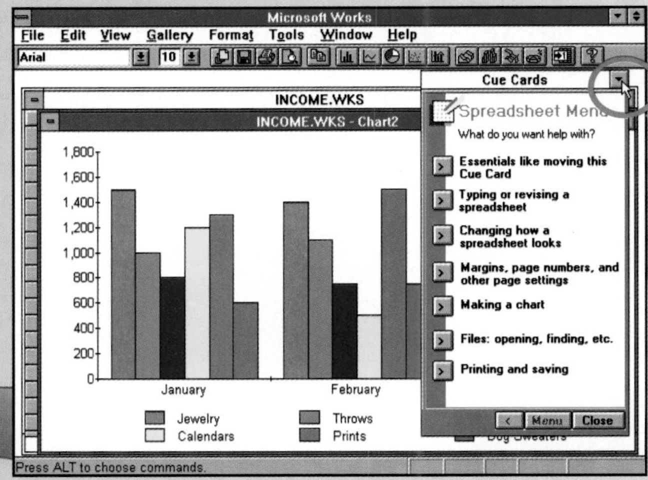

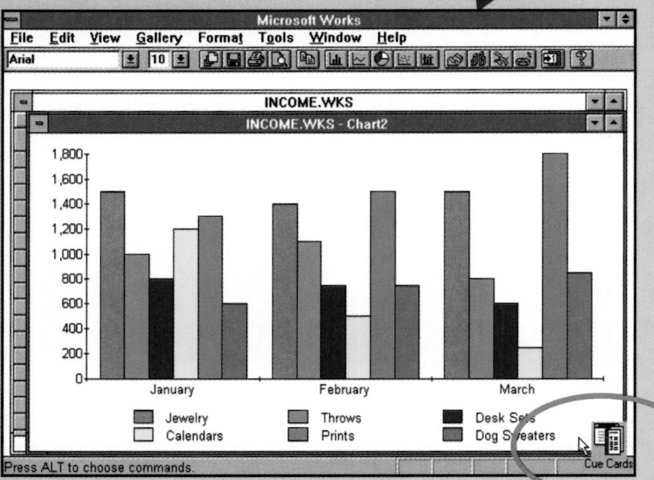

5 Drag the Cue Cards icon to the bottom right side of the screen. You are now ready to format and edit the chart.

TASK 38

Adding Titles, Labels, Legends, and a Grid

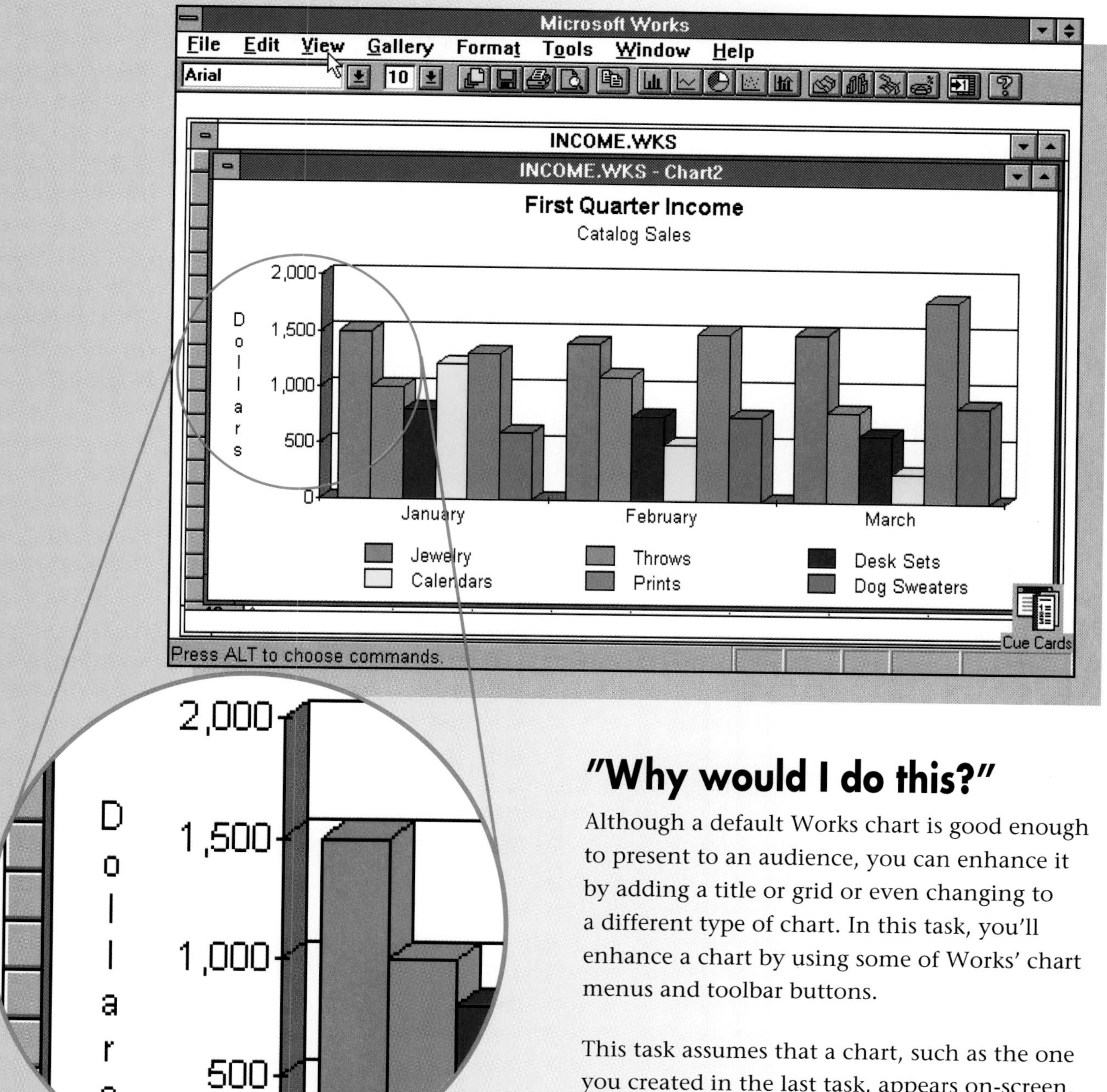

"Why would I do this?"

Although a default Works chart is good enough to present to an audience, you can enhance it by adding a title or grid or even changing to a different type of chart. In this task, you'll enhance a chart by using some of Works' chart menus and toolbar buttons.

This task assumes that a chart, such as the one you created in the last task, appears on-screen.

Task 38: Adding Titles, Labels, Legends, and a Grid

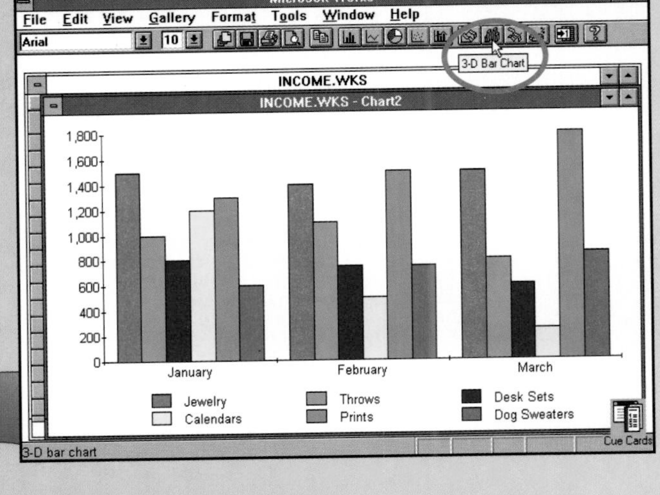

1 Click on the **3-D Bar Chart** toolbar button. Works displays the 3-D Bar dialog box, which allows you to choose the type of 3-D bar chart you want.

NOTE

The toolbar has other chart buttons: Bar Chart, Line Chart, Pie Chart, Scatter Chart, Mixed Chart, 3-D Area Chart, 3-D Line Chart, and 3-D Pie Chart.

2 Click on **OK**. This step chooses the default 3-D bar chart type, which is labeled *1* and highlighted in the 3-D Bar dialog box.

3 Click on **Edit** in the menu bar and click on **Titles**. Works opens the Titles dialog box, in which you can type several titles for the chart.

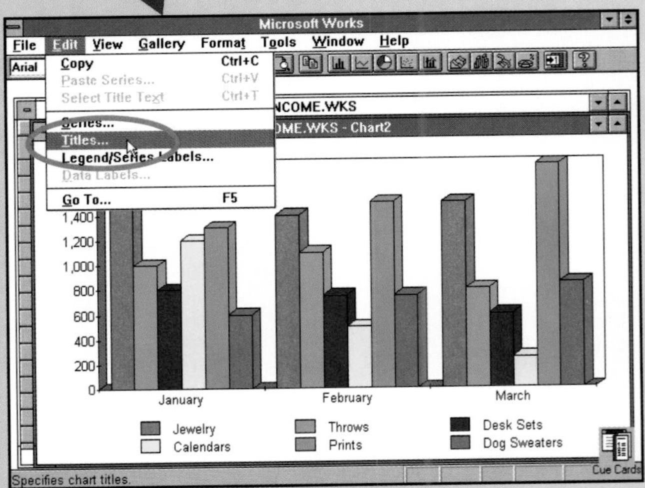

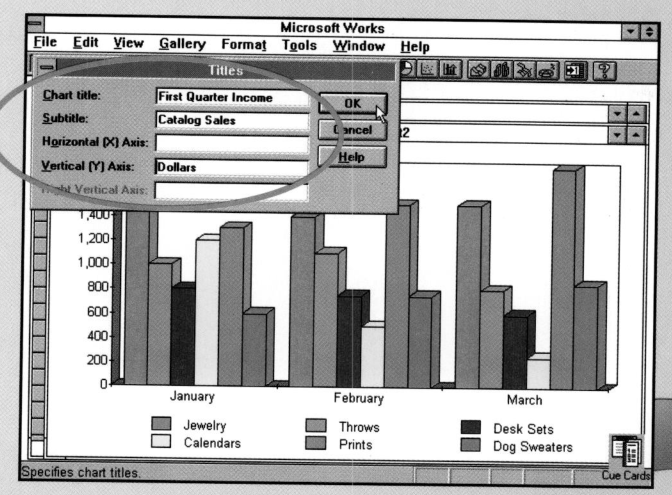

4 Type **First Quarter Income** in the Chart Title text box, type **Catalog Sales** in the Subtitle text box, type **Dollars** in the Vertical (Y) Axis text box, and click on **OK**. Press Tab to move from text box to text box. Works closes the dialog box and inserts the titles in the chart.

5 Click on **Format** in the menu bar and click on **Vertical (Y) Axis**. Works displays the Vertical Axis dialog box.

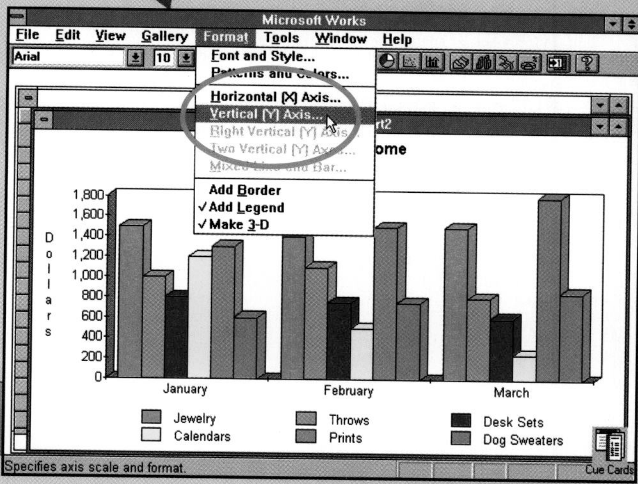

6 Click on the **Show Gridlines** check box to select it. Selecting this check box tells Works that you want to add horizontal gridlines that run between the y axes.

7 Click on **OK**. Works closes the dialog box and adds gridlines to the chart.

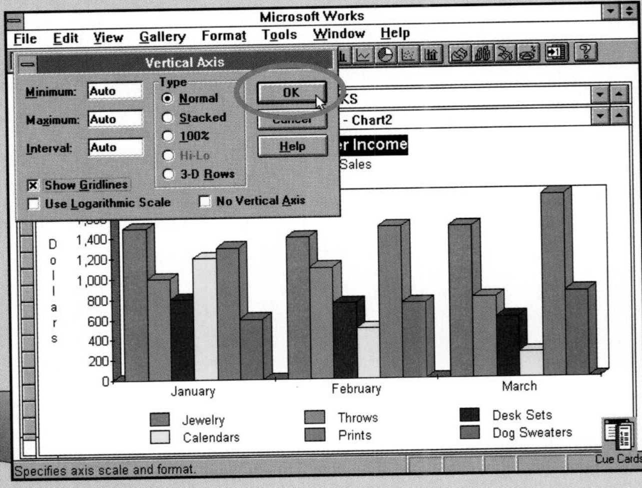

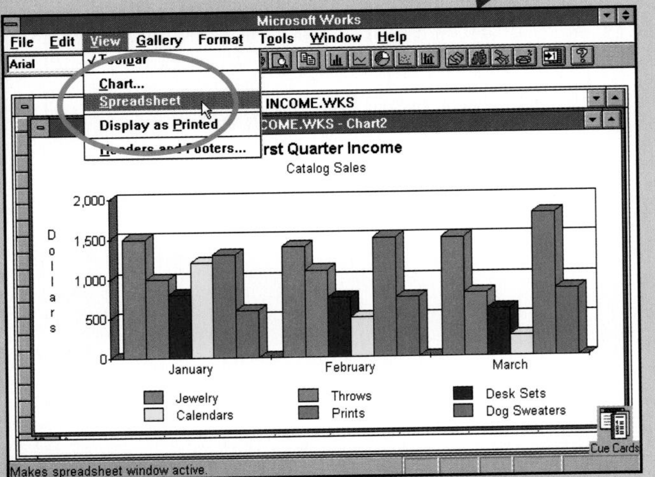

8 Click on **View** in the menu bar and click on **Spreadsheet**. Works returns you to the spreadsheet.

NOTE

To return to the chart, choose View Chart from the menu. If you have created more than one chart, select the chart you want to view in the Charts dialog box and click on OK.

Microsoft Works
File Edit View Insert Format Tools Window Help
OK to delete data in this field? (Cannot Undo this operation.)
You tried to delete a field, or were renaming a field and forgot to type a colon. Choose OK to delete the field and all of its contents or choose Cancel to cancel the command. You will not be able to undo this operation.
OK
Cancel
First Name:
Address1:
Address2:
City:
Voice Phone:
State:
ZIP:
Cue Cards
CUSTLIST.WDB
Customers
Last Name:
Fax:
RESIZE
Times New Roman
Last Name: Roe
First Name: Rochelle
Address1: 63 Main Street
Address2: RFD #1
City: Anytown
Voice Phone: 5555551328
Fax: 5555553651
State: NY
ZIP: 11000
Price: 150
Tax: 0.07
Total:
type text followed by : to create field.
Date
Time
Text

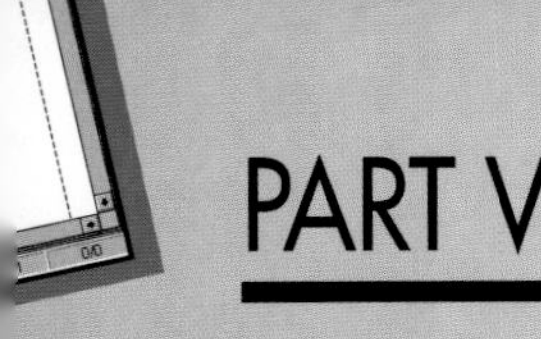

PART VI

Creating a Database

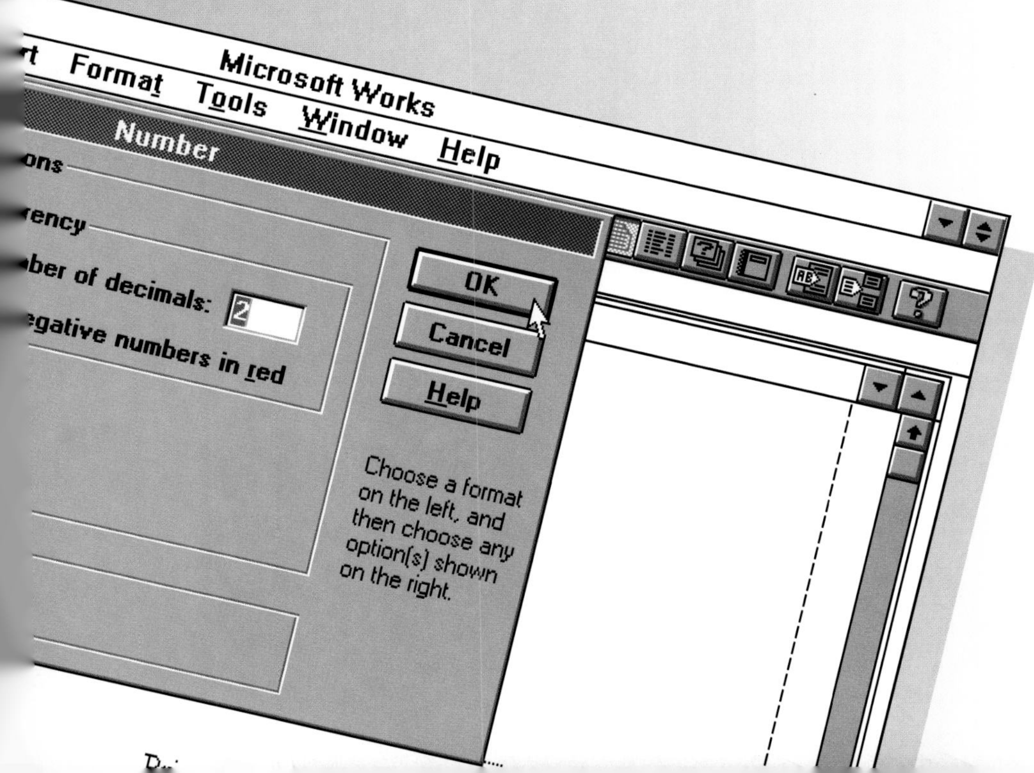

The Database tool enables you to keep track of information such as your customers, inventory, and personal addresses and telephone numbers. A *database* is an organized collection of related information. Databases are groups of *records* (all the information for one customer or one inventory item). Records are made up of *fields*, the smallest piece of information in a database. A field holds a single piece of information, such as a last name, a city, a telephone number, or a short memorandum.

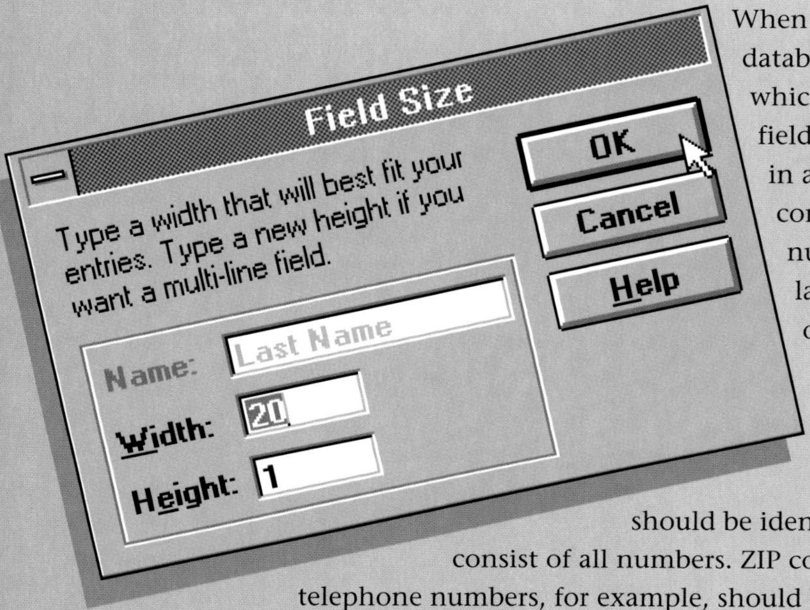

When you enter information into a database, you type into an *input form*, which is a layout of fields, each one with a field name that identifies it. When you fill in a field, the Database tool evaluates its contents and labels the field as text, a number, or a formula. You can also label fields as text or as a specific type of number (currency, date, time, fixed, exponential, and so on). You can calculate numbers, money, dates, and times values and place the results in fields. Most information should be identified as text, although it might consist of all numbers. ZIP codes, Social Security numbers, and telephone numbers, for example, should be labeled text—you'll never calculate them. Values in number fields are right-aligned, and values in text fields are left-aligned.

X5.67"

Y3.83"

You can either view a database one record at a time (in form view) or several records at a time in a spreadsheet format (in list view). In either mode, you can add, edit, and delete records.

After you create a database and enter records, you can query the database to retrieve records that meet certain criteria. Then you can compile the retrieved information into a report, or you can create and send out form letters to your selected audience.

In this part, you'll create a database, identify the fields in each record, design an input form, and enter text, numbers, and a formula.

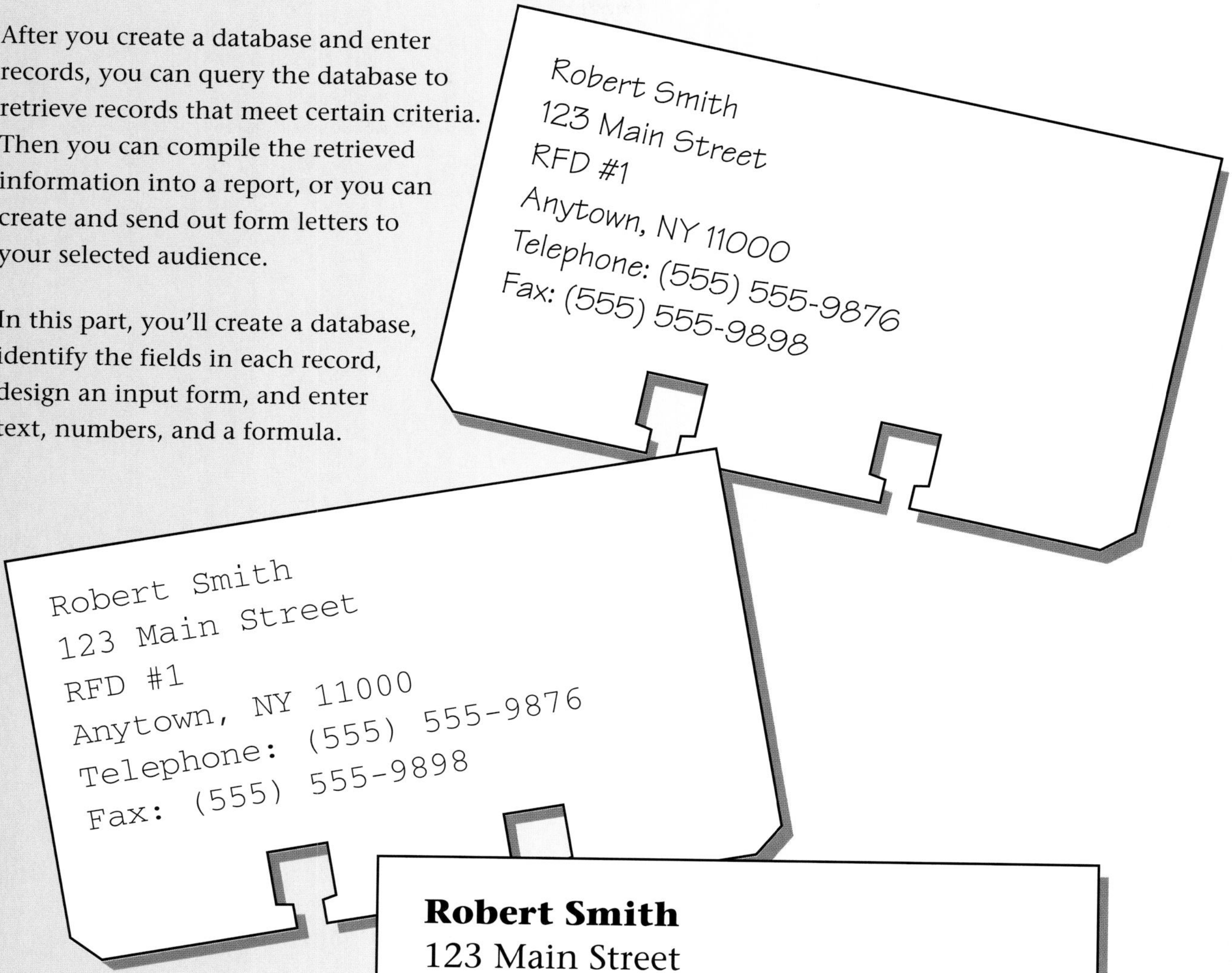

Robert Smith
123 Main Street
RFD #1
Anytown, NY 11000
Telephone: (555) 555-9876
Fax: (555) 555-9898

Robert Smith
123 Main Street
RFD #1
Anytown, NY 11000
Telephone: (555) 555-9876
Fax: (555) 555-9898

Robert Smith
123 Main Street
RFD #1
Anytown, NY 11000
Telephone: (555) 555-9876
Fax: (555) 555-9898

TASK 39

Creating a Form

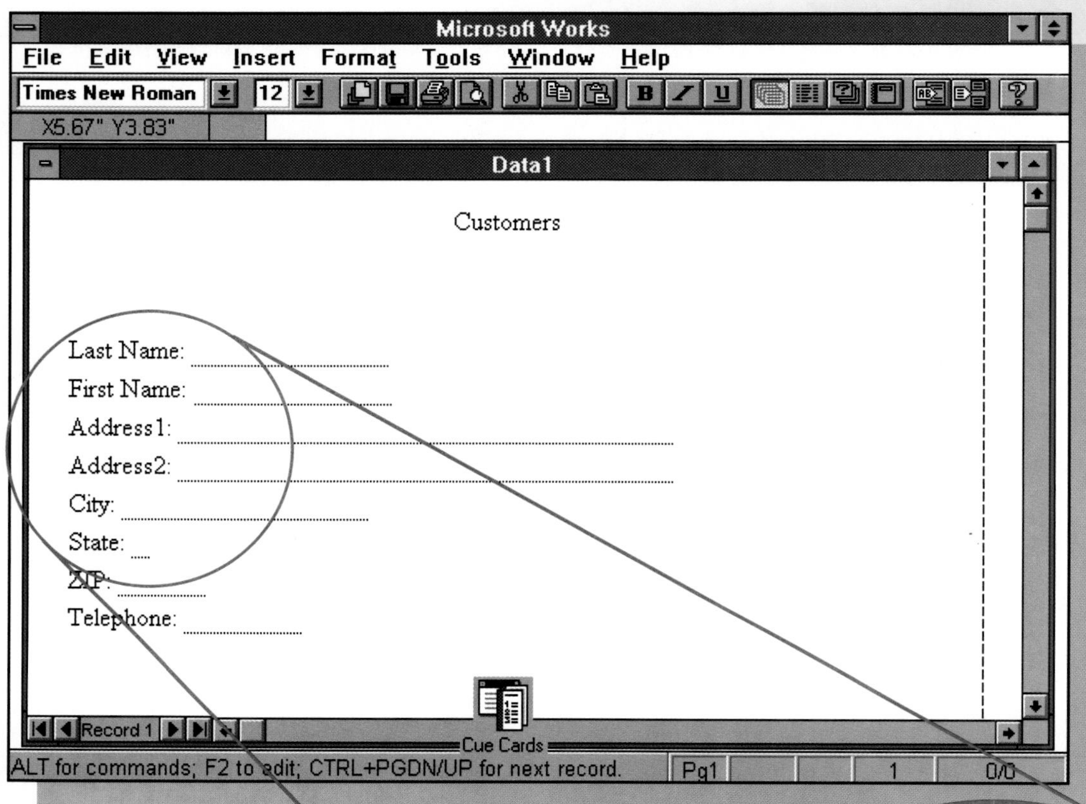

"Why would I do this?"

To enter records in a database, you have to design an input form. An *input form* is the screen in which you type data. In this task, you'll create an input form and enter field names.

This task assumes that you have started the Database tool and that your screen is empty.

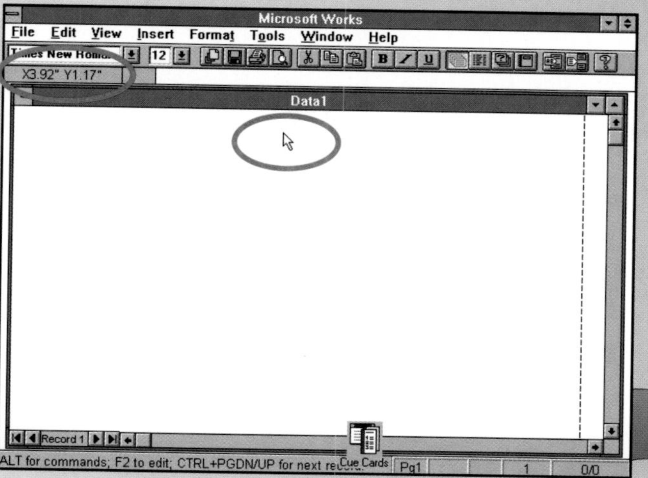

1 Click at the top of the form, right under the name of the window. This step places the insertion point in the position in which you want to type the title of the database. In the formula bar, `X3.92"` tells you the horizontal position of the insertion point near the center of the screen; `Y1.17"` tells you the insertion point's vertical position near the top of the screen. Whenever you move the insertion point, X and Y reflect its new position.

2 Type **Customers** and press **Enter**. Works displays the name *Customers* in the formula bar and inserts it in both the form and the database file.

NOTE

In the formula bar, `Customers` is preceded by a quotation mark, which indicates that Works considers the characters that you typed to be text.

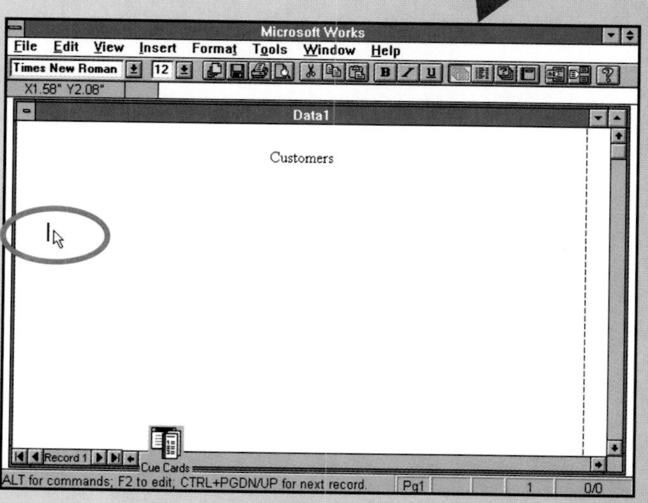

3 Place the insertion point near **X1.50" Y2.00"**. To move the insertion point exactly to those coordinates, either move the mouse pointer and click repeatedly until you find the coordinates, or press any combination of ←, →, ↓, and ↑. Each time you press one of these keys, the insertion point moves approximately 0.08".

4 Type **Last Name:** and press **Enter**. This step enters a field name, which describes the contents of the field. The colon at the end tells Works that this entry is a field name. (If you forget to type the colon, Works thinks that the entry is a title.) Works displays the Field Size dialog box.

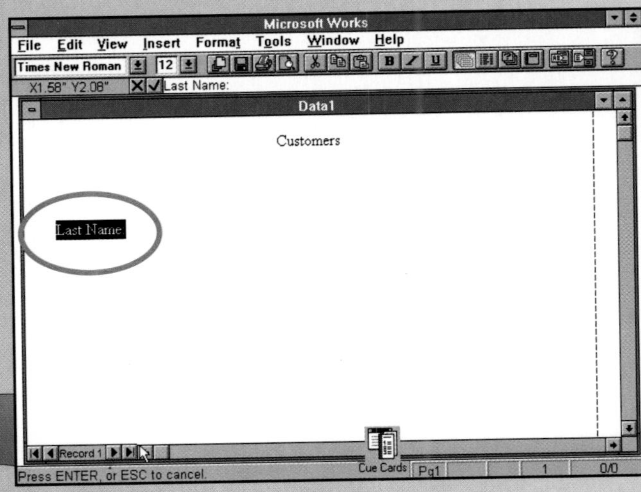

5 Click on **OK**. In the Field Size dialog box, you define the width of the field. Clicking on OK means that you accept the default value of 20 characters. Works adds a dotted line to the entry, to show the field width. Works also moves the insertion point to the next line.

6 Type **First Name:** and press **Enter**. Pressing Enter accepts the entry, enters the field name, and opens the Field Size dialog box.

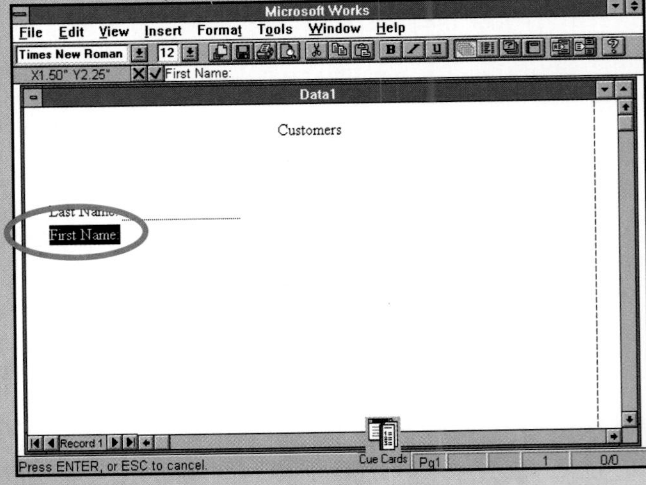

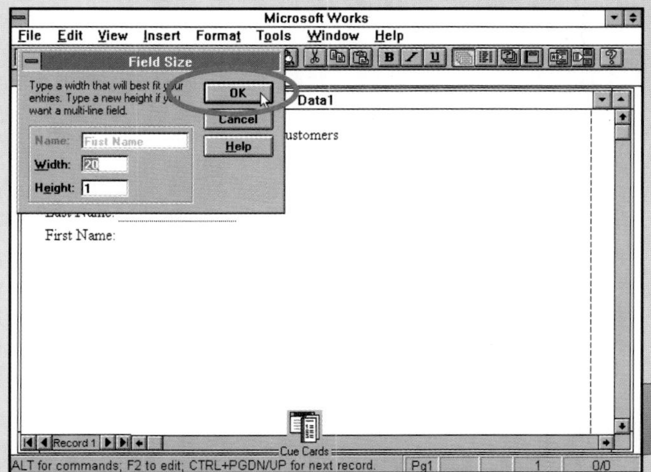

7 In the Field Size dialog box, click on **OK** to accept the default field width of 20.

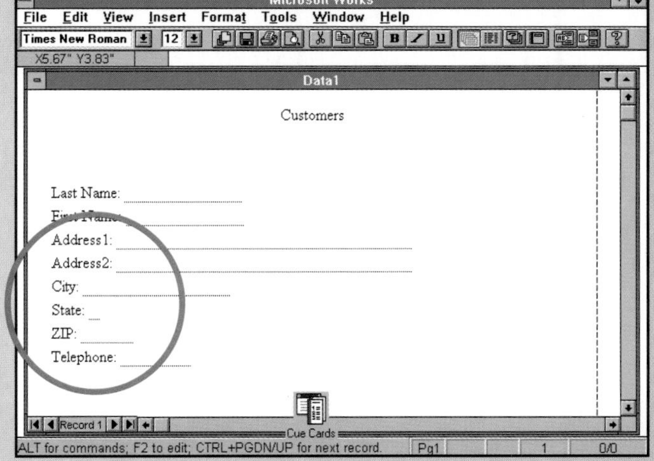

8 Add the remaining fields, using 1.50" as the X position and using the Y position and field width listed here:

Field Name	Y"	Field Width
Address1:	2.50"	**50**
Address2:	2.75"	**50**
City:	3.00"	**25**
State:	3.25"	**2**
ZIP:	3.50"	**9**
Telephone:	3.75"	**12**

NOTE

To help you line up fields, the Database tool shows you the coordinates at which the insertion point is located. The X coordinate tells you the insertion point's side-to-side (horizontal) location, and the Y coordinate tells you its top-to-bottom (vertical) location. The combination of X and Y coordinates tells you the exact location of the insertion point.

TASK 40

Adding, Modifying, Moving, and Deleting Fields

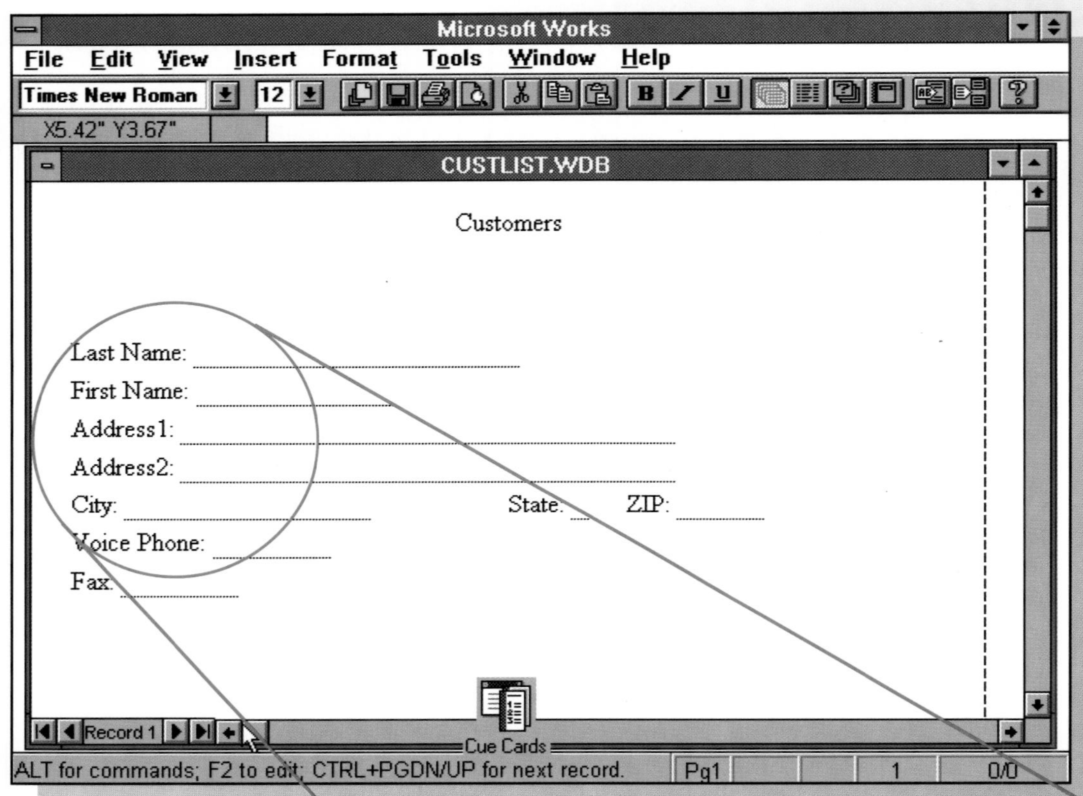

"Why would I do this?"

A database isn't set in stone right after you create it. Over time, you'll add or rename fields, move fields around for more efficient data entry, add more room for some fields, and get rid of fields that aren't needed any more. In this task, you'll insert, edit, relocate, delete, and change the size of fields.

This task assumes that you have started the Database, created an input form, and saved it.

Task 40: Adding, Modifying, Moving, and Deleting Fields

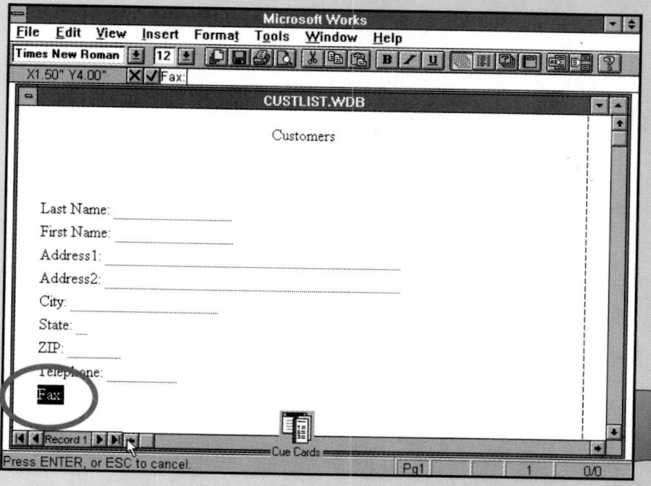

1 Move the insertion point to **X1.50" Y4.00"**, type **Fax:** (be sure to add the colon), and press **Enter**.

2 In the Field Size dialog box, type **12** in the Width text box and click on **OK**. Adding a new field is exactly like adding a field to a new input form. All you have to do is move the insertion point to an empty area in the form.

NOTE

The default field size is 20 characters—that is, the field will hold no more than 20 characters.

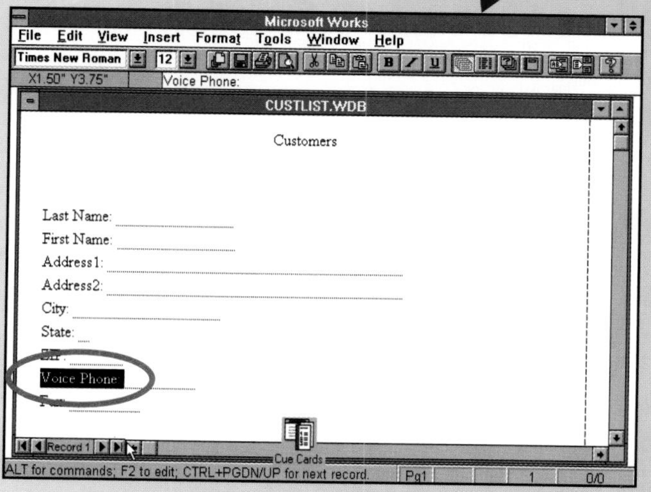

3 Click on **Telephone** to select it, type **Voice Phone:**, and press **Enter**. This step replaces the old field name with the new.

Task 40: Adding, Modifying, Moving, and Deleting Fields

4 Click on **State**. Works highlights the field. Notice that the word DRAG is attached to the mouse pointer tail.

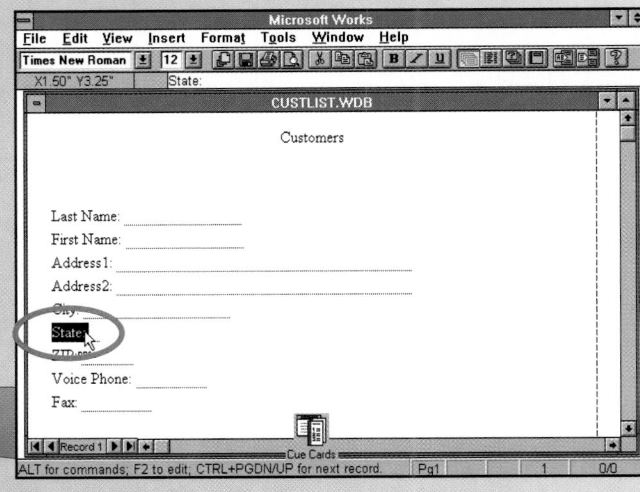

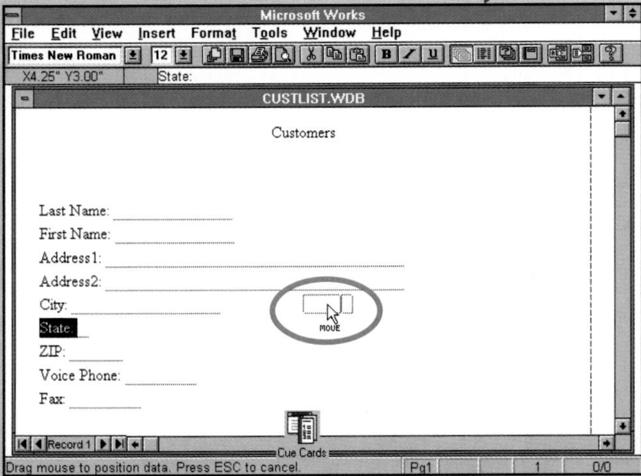

5 Drag the pointer to **X4.25" Y3.00"** and release the mouse button. This step relocates the State field.

6 Drag the **ZIP** field to **X5.00" Y3.00"**, drag the **Voice Phone** field to **X1.50" Y3.25"**, and drag the **Fax** field to **X1.50" Y3.50"**.

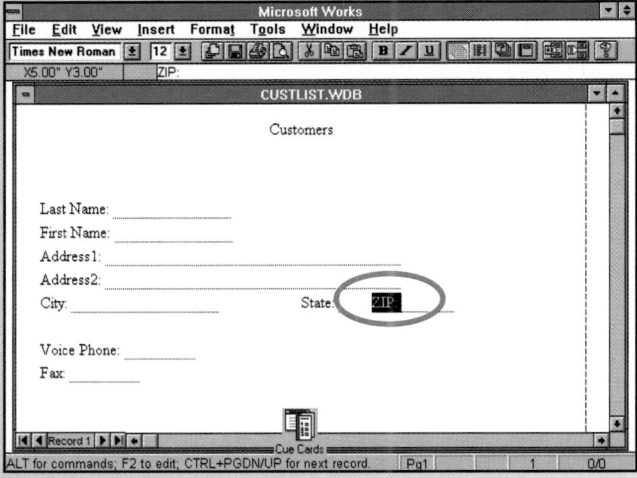

WHY WORRY?

To move the field back to its original location, select it and drag it back. Pressing Ctrl+Z or choosing Edit Undo does not reverse this action.

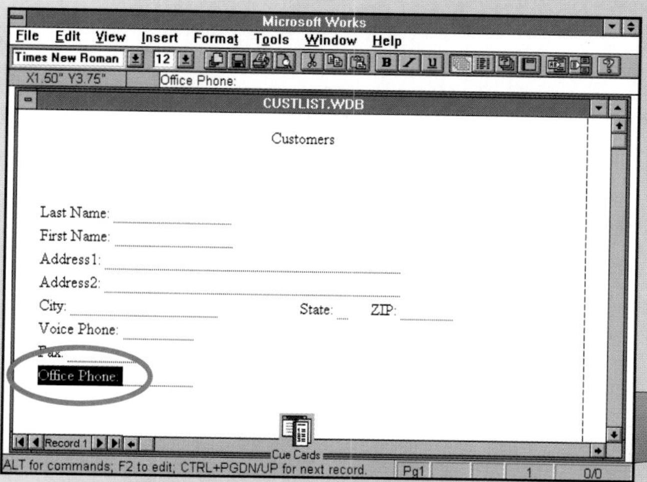

7 Move the insertion point to **X1.50" Y3.75"**, type **Office Phone:**, and use a field width of **12**.

8 Click on **Office Phone** if it isn't selected, click on **Insert** in the menu bar, and click on **Delete Selection**. Works displays a message box to make sure that you really want to delete the selected field.

NOTE

As a shortcut, you can press Delete rather than choosing the Insert Delete Selection command.

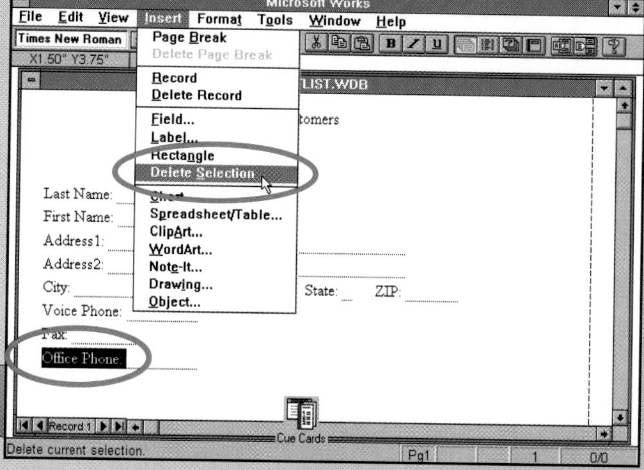

Microsoft Works

OK to delete data in this field? (Cannot Undo this operation.)

You tried to delete a field, or were renaming a field and forgot to type a colon. Choose OK to delete the field and all of its contents or choose Cancel to cancel the command. You will not be able to undo this operation.

OK Cancel

9 Click on **OK**. Works removes the field from the database.

NOTE

Deleting a field from a database can be destructive. If the field contains data, you will lose it permanently. Before deleting a field, save the database under a different name. That way, you'll have an extra copy.

10 Click on the **dotted line** next to `Last Name`. Works highlights the line and displays three handles in the box.

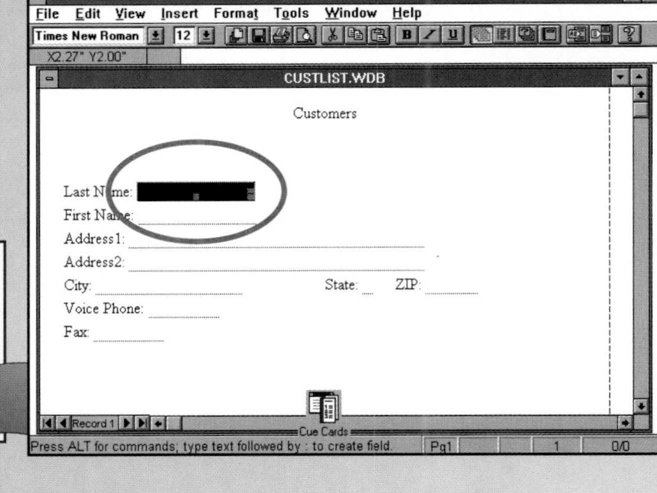

NOTE

Handles are small blocks that appear on any selected object. They allow you to change the object's size or to move it. Click on a handle and drag the mouse pointer to move or resize the selected object.

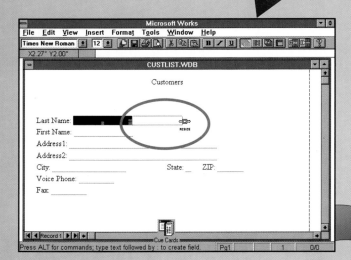

11 Click on the **top handle** at the right side of the highlighted line and drag toward the right margin. This step will provide more room for characters in the field.

NOTE

To allow enough space for data entry in each field, regardless of the field length you defined, you should increase the field length as you finalize your input form design.

12 Release the mouse button and click anywhere outside the selected field. Works displays a longer dotted line for the Last Name field.

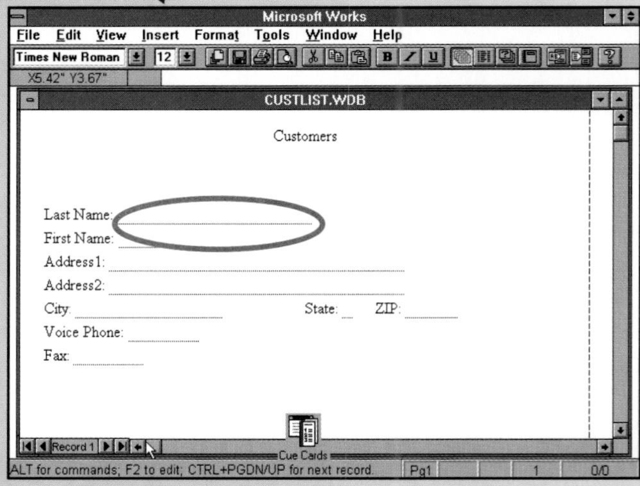

NOTE

To squeeze even more information on your form, consider using a smaller point size or a thinner font. To change the point size or font of a field, choose the Font and Style command from the Format menu.

TASK 41

Entering Text and Numbers

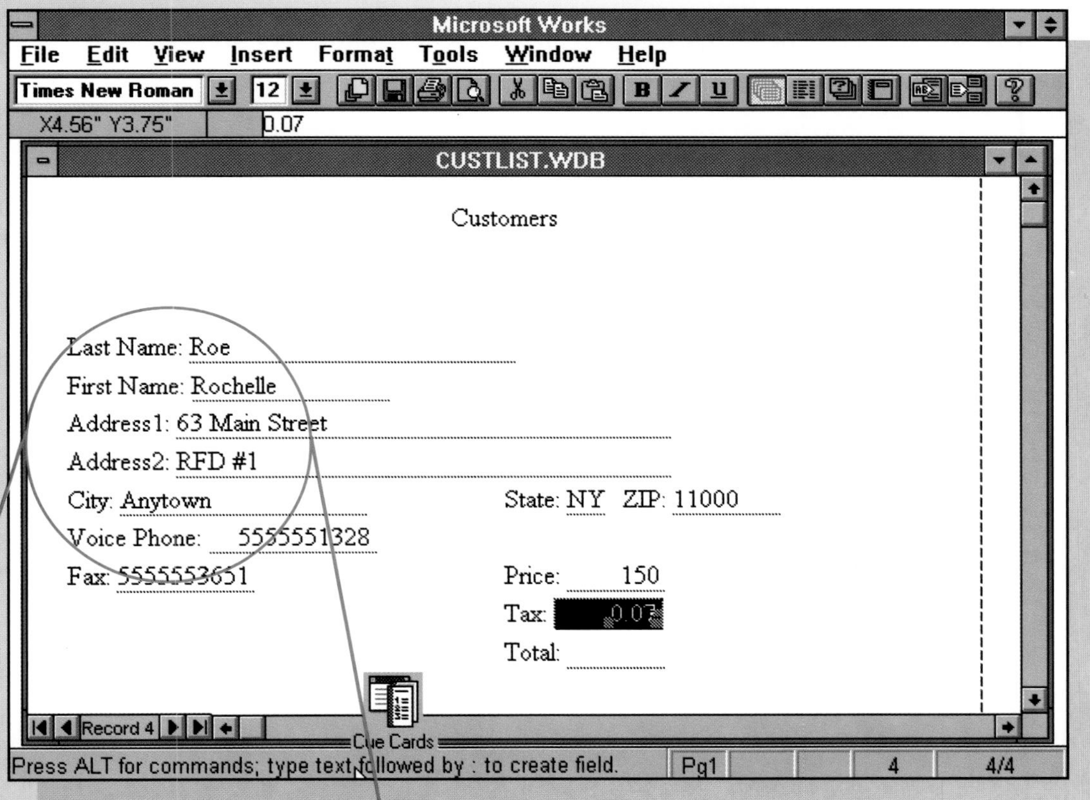

"Why would I do this?"

You create a database to store information. It's important to be able to enter both text and numbers easily and efficiently. In this task, you'll enter text and numbers in an input form. Be sure to add the new fields as instructed in the first step.

This task assumes that you have started the Database, created an input form, and saved it.

Task 41: Entering Text and Numbers

1 In the input form, add the following new fields, using 4.25" as the X position for each field:

Field Name	Y"	Field Width
Price:	4.25"	**10**
Tax:	3.75"	**11**
Total:	4.00"	**10**

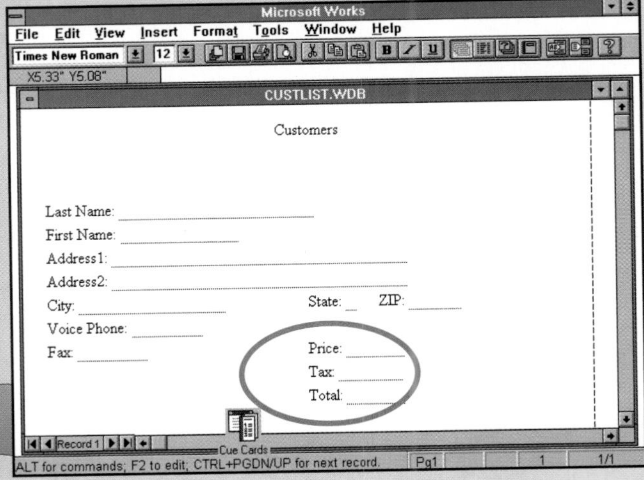

2 Click on the **dotted line** next to `Last Name`. This step gets the field ready to accept information.

3 Type **Craig** and press **Tab**. Pressing Tab moves the highlight to the next field.

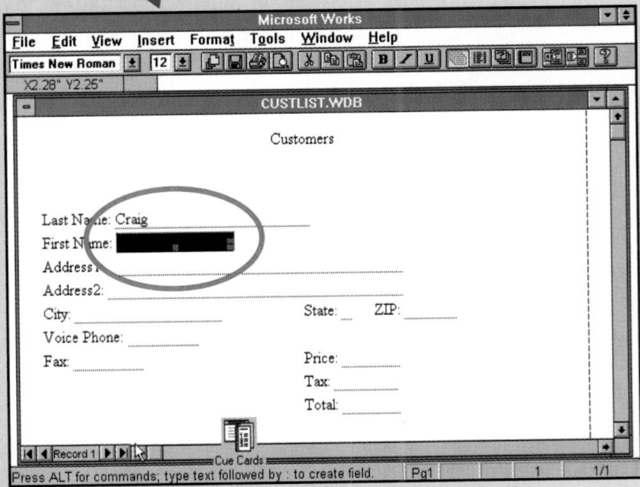

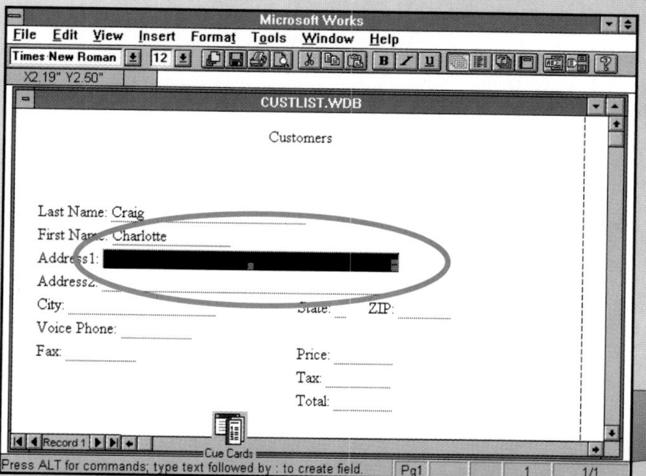

4 Type **Charlotte** and press **Tab**.

WHY WORRY?

Even if a field appears too small as you enter data, it still contains the data. If you need to change a field's dimensions while you are entering data, go ahead. Changing the size of the highlight makes it easier to view the field.

5 Type **100 Broadway** in the Address1 field and press **Tab twice**; type **Anytown** in the City field and press **Tab**; type **NY** in the State field and press **Tab**; then type **11000** in the ZIP field and press **Tab**.

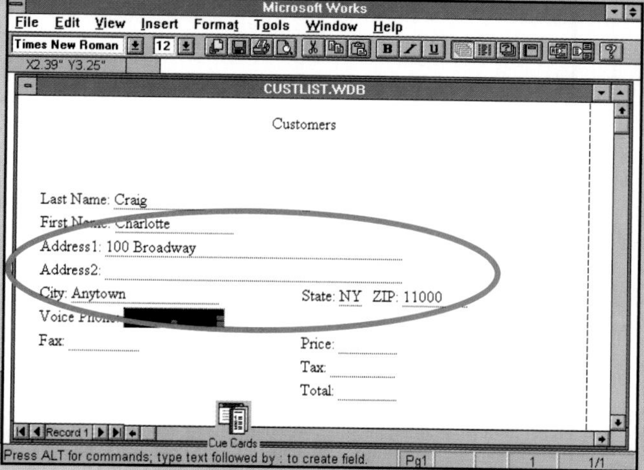

WHY WORRY?

If you type a ZIP code that starts with a zero, Works may treat the ZIP code as a number and remove the leading zero. To correct this, choose Format Number. In the Number dialog box, click on Text and click on **OK**.

6 Type **5555555555** in the Voice Phone field and press **Tab**; then type **5555555554** in the Fax field and press **Tab**. If Works converts the number to scientific notation, just drag the field to make it wider.

7 Type **125** in the Price field and press **Tab**.

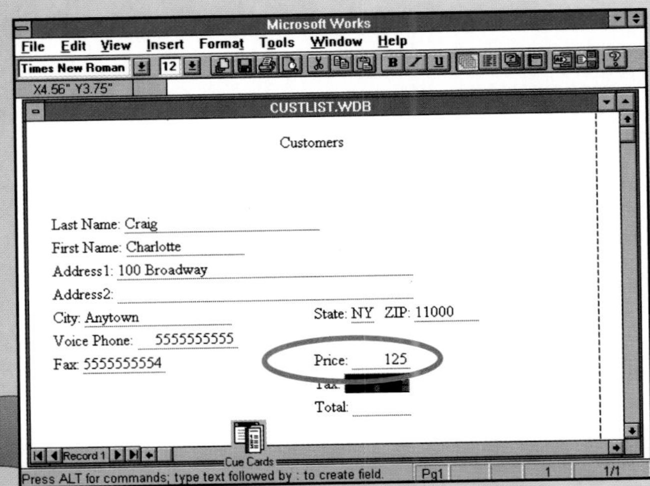

8 Type **0.07** in the Tax field, press **Enter**, and click on the **right-arrow** button to the right of `Record 1` in the status bar. Works displays a blank record, and `Record 2` appears in the status bar.

9 Repeat steps 2-8 for each record you want to add to your database.

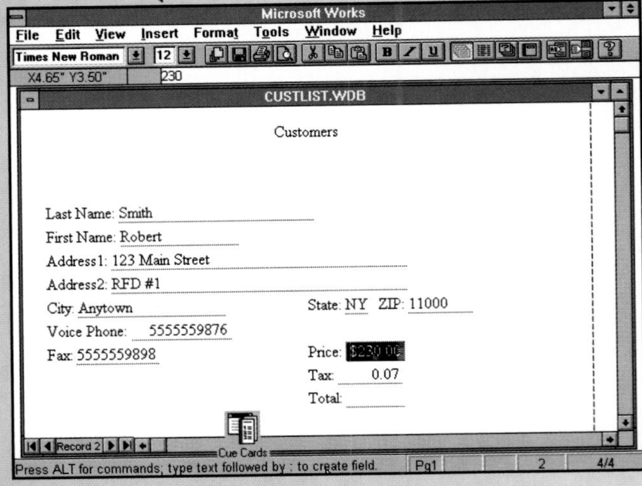

TASK 42

Entering Formulas and Formatting Number Fields

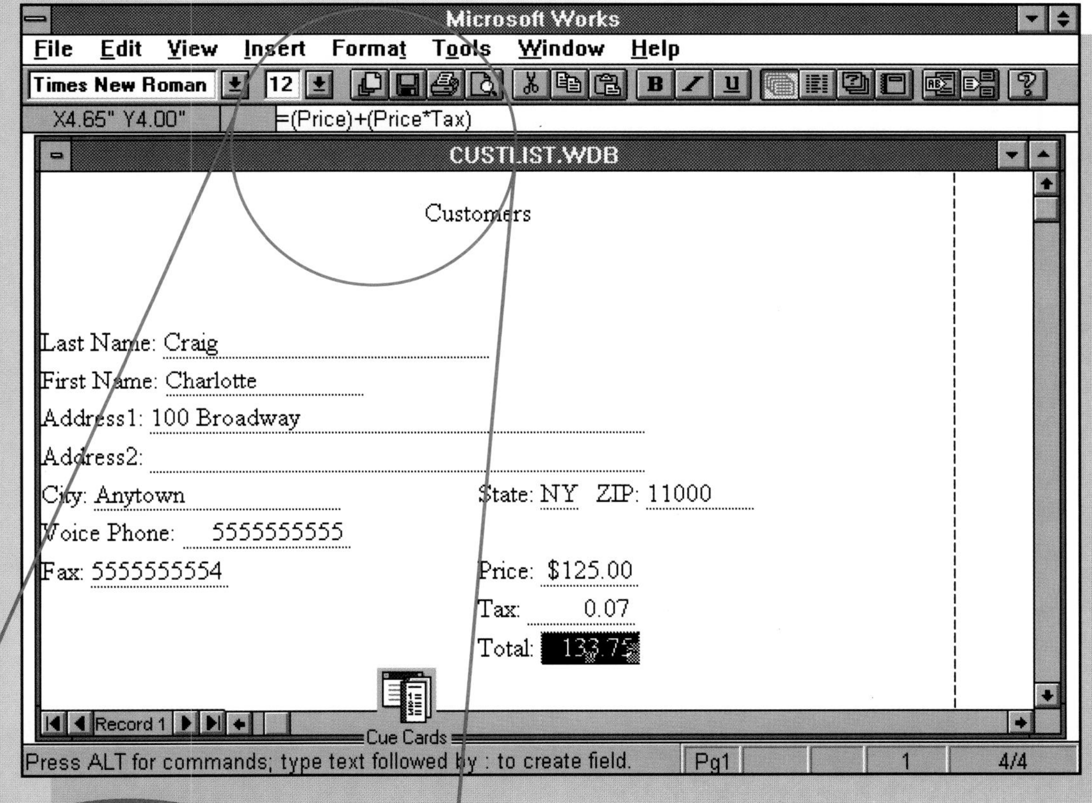

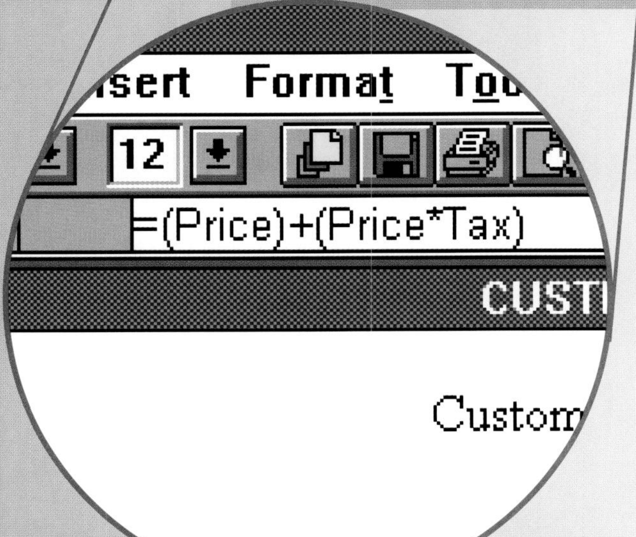

"Why would I do this?"

In databases as well as spreadsheets, you can calculate the contents of number fields. You can quickly calculate a sales tax and a grand total, subtract the starting date from the current date to compute an anniversary, and so on. In this task, you'll format number fields and learn how to enter a formula.

This task assumes that you have started the Database and have entered records in an input form.

Task 42: Entering Formulas and Formatting Number Fields

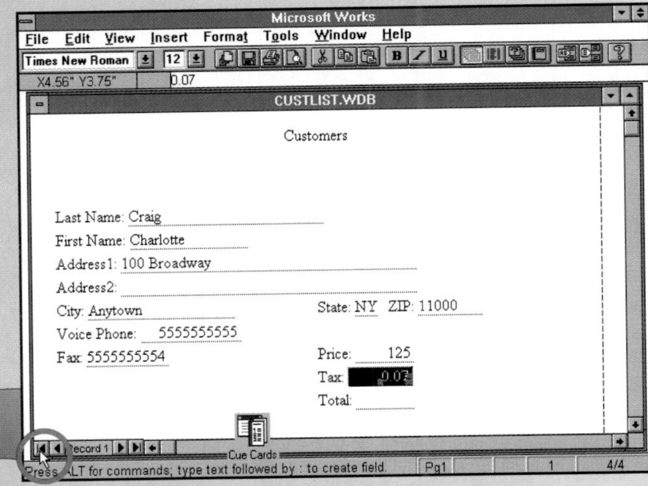

1 Click on the **leftmost arrow** button in the status bar. Works displays `Record 1` in the status bar and the first record you entered on-screen.

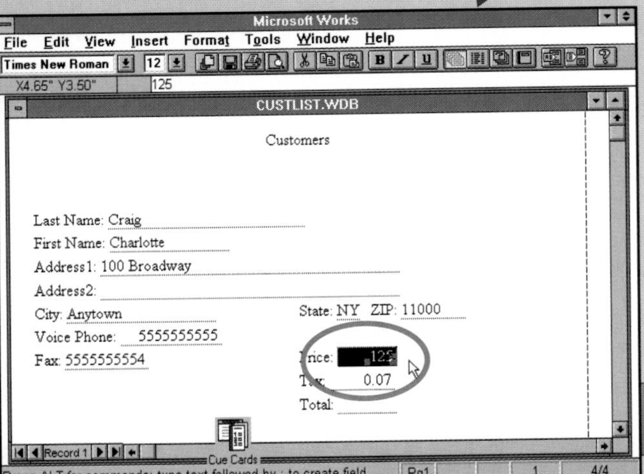

2 Click on **125** in the Price field.

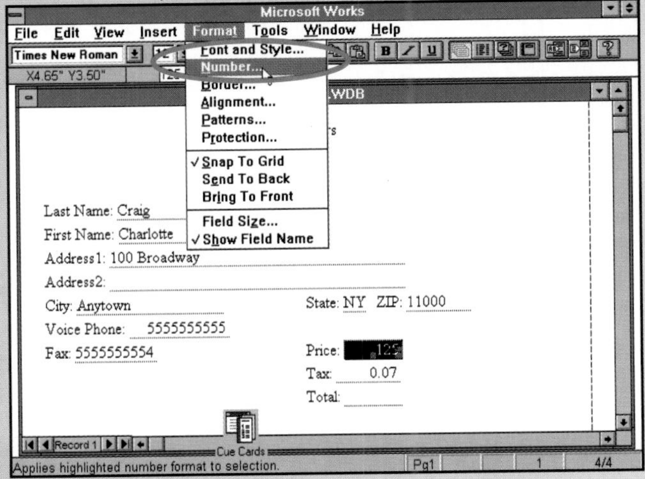

3 Click on **Format** in the menu bar and click on **Number**. Works displays the Number dialog box.

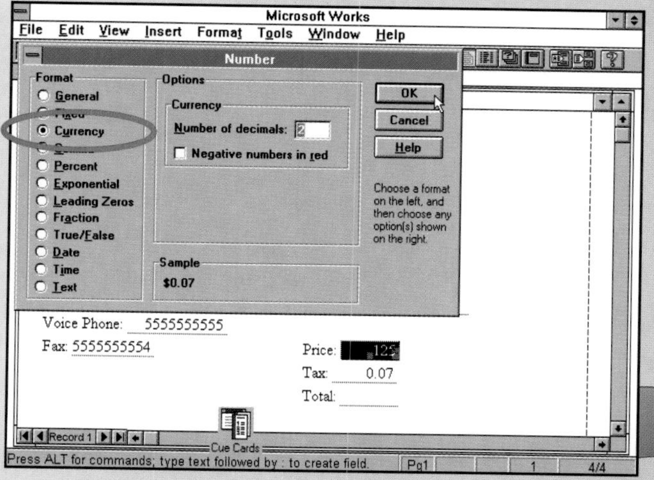

4 Click on **Currency** and click on **OK**. This step applies the Currency format to the Price field and accepts the default number of decimals (2). Works uses this format to display all numbers in this field in every record.

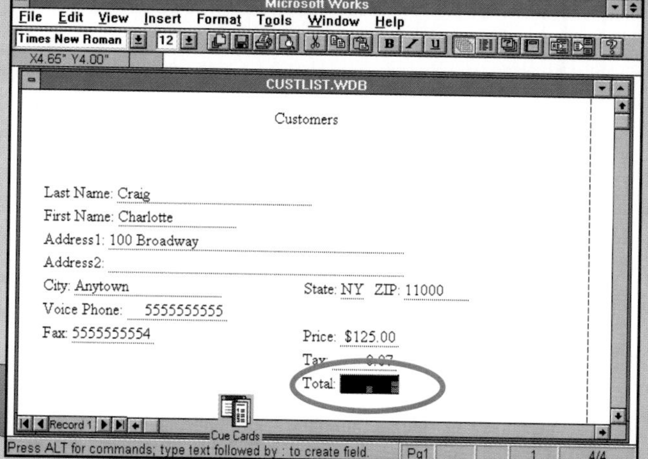

5 Click on the **dotted line** next to `Total`. Works highlights the Total line and makes it active. You will add a formula to this field.

NOTE

When typing a database formula, always type an equal sign before typing the rest of the formula. To enter a field name in a formula, enclose it in parentheses so it won't be confused with text.

6 Type **=(Price)+(Price*Tax)** and press **Enter**. This formula computes the sales tax, adds it to the price, and places the total in the Total field for each record in this database.

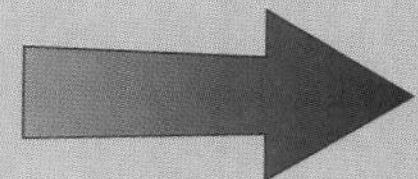

7 Click on **Format** in the menu bar and click on **Number**. Works displays the Number dialog box.

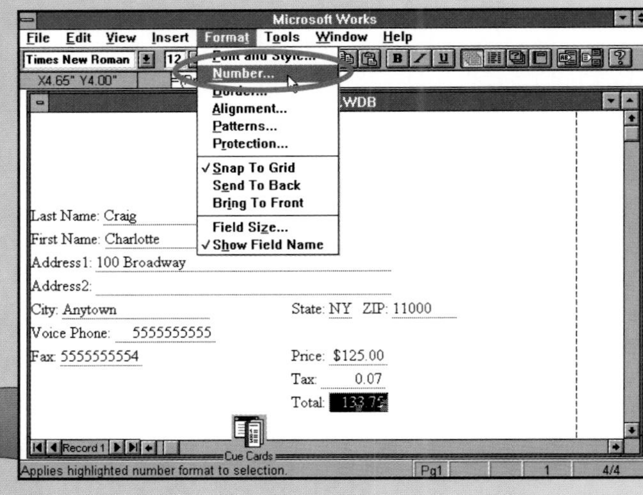

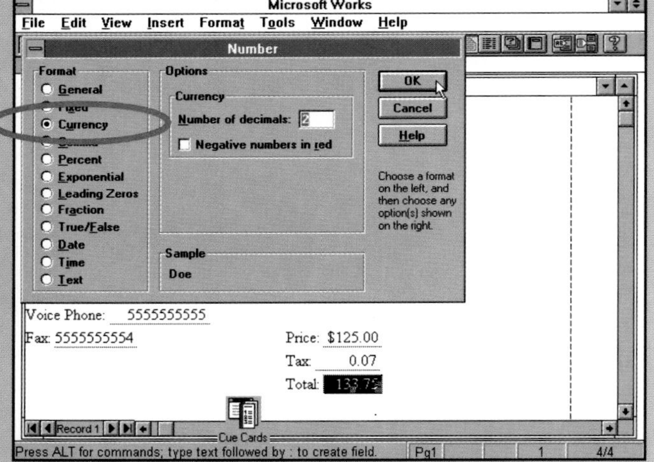

8 Click on **Currency** and click on **OK**. This step defines the Total field as Currency with two decimal places.

Microsoft Works
File Edit View Insert Format Tools Window Help
Arial
10
CUSTLIST.WDB
City State ZIP Voice Phon Facsimile Price Tax Tota
Anytown NY 11000 5555555555 5555555554 $125.00 0.07 $133
Anytown NY 11000 5555559876 5555559898 $230.00 0.07 $246
Anytown NY 11000 5555556111 5555559500 $35.00 0.07 $37
Anytown NY 11000 5555551328 5555553651 $150.00 0.07 $160
Last Name First Name Address1 Address2 City State ZIP Voice Phon
Craig Charlotte 100 Broadway Anytown NY 11000
Smith Robert 123 Main Street RFD #1 Anytown NY 11000
Doe Douglas 4 Arch Street P. O. Box 1 Anytown NY 11000
Roe Rochelle 63 Main Street RFD #1 Anytown NY 11000
"Crane
Craig
Crane Charlotte 100 Broadway
Smith Lewis 101 Point Place
Doe Robert 123 Main Street
Roe Douglas 4 Arch Street
Rachel 63 Main Street
choose commands, or F2 to edit.
Cue Cards
Last Name First Name MI Address1 Address2 City State ZIP
Craig Charlotte 100 Broadway RFD #1 Anytown NY 11000
Smith Robert 123 Main Street P. O. Box 1 Anytown NY 11000
Doe Douglas 4 Arch Street RFD #1 Anytown NY 11000
Roe Rachel 63 Main Street Anytown NY 11000
Cue Cards
commands, or F2 to edit.

PART VII

Using the Database

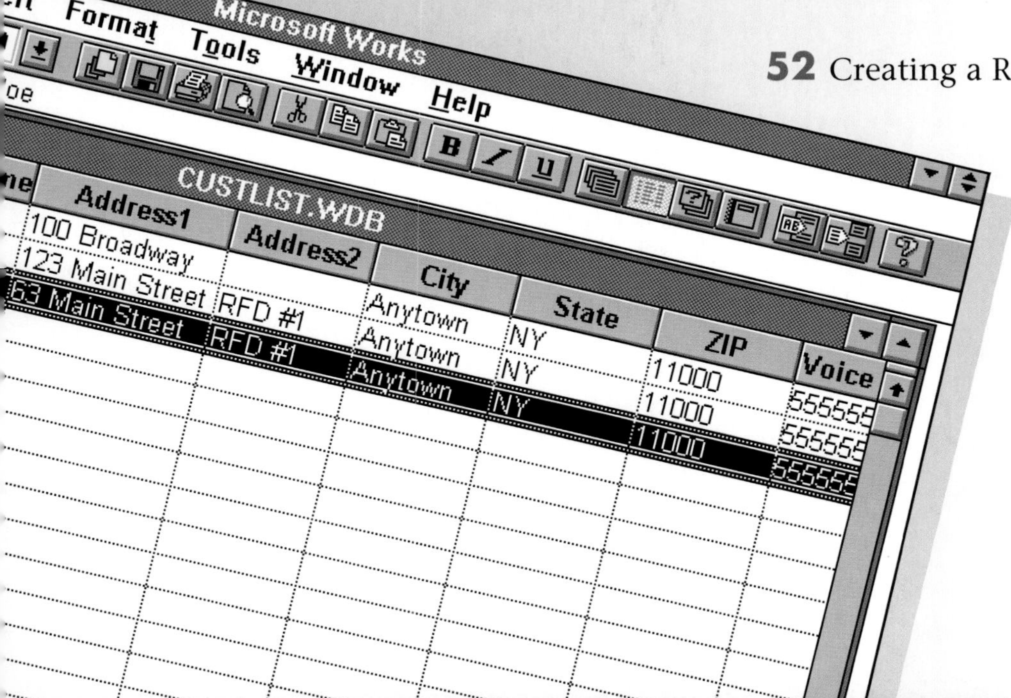

Up to this point, you have used the Database tool to create a database, design an input form, and enter text, numbers, and a formula. Once you have entered a group of records, you can edit or delete them, and of course, you can add new records to the database.

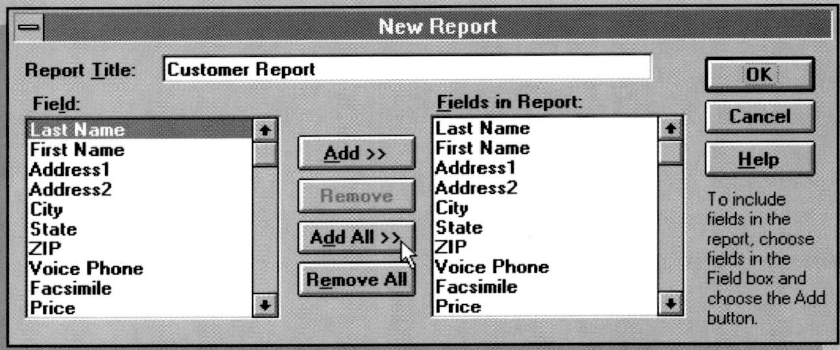

In this part, you learn how to use the Database tool in list view, and you expand your knowledge of form view. You change the width of a field and the name of a field. You learn how to find a record and replace a field in a record. You find out how to insert, move, and delete records and fields, how to hide and reveal records and fields, and how to annotate a form using two separate methods. You learn how to retrieve specific records, sort the records in a database, and create and edit a report.

List view allows you to view several records at once. You can view a database either one record at a time (in form view) or several records at a time in a spreadsheet format (in list view). In either mode, you can add, edit, and delete records.

Once you have created a database and entered records, you can *query* the database to retrieve records that meet certain criteria. Then you can compile the retrieved information into a report, or you can create and send out form letters to your selected audience.

When you query a database, you ask Works to compare values in the query with the contents of one or more fields. Comparison and logical operators used to retrieve a set of records are:

Is Equal To. This comparison operator checks to see whether the value in the database field matches the value in the query. If the values match, Works retrieves the record. For example, if the entered value is NY, the field must contain NY; all other fields are ignored.

Is Less Than. This comparison operator checks to see whether the value in the database field is less than the value in the query. If so, Works retrieves the record. For example, if the entered value is 9, the field must contain a negative value or 0 to 8.

Is Greater Than. This comparison operator checks to see whether the value in the database field is greater than the value in the query. If so, Works retrieves the record. For example, if the entered value is 99, the field must contain a value of 100 or more.

Is Not Equal To. This comparison operator checks to see whether the value in the database field is not equal to the value in the query. If the values are not equal, Works retrieves the record. For example, if the entered value is ME, the field can contain anything but ME.

Is Less Than or Equal To. This comparison operator checks to see whether the value in the database field either matches or is less than the value in the query. If so, Works retrieves the record. For example, if the entered value is 99, the field can contain any value up to and including 99.

Is Greater Than or Equal To. This comparison operator checks to see whether the value in the database field either matches or is greater than the value in the query. If so, Works retrieves the record. For example, if the entered value is 99, the field can contain any value from 99 or greater.

Contains. This comparison operator checks to see whether the value in the database field contains the value in the query. If so, Works retrieves the record. For example, if the entered value is *the,* the field can contain *other, them, othello, together, therapy,* and so on.

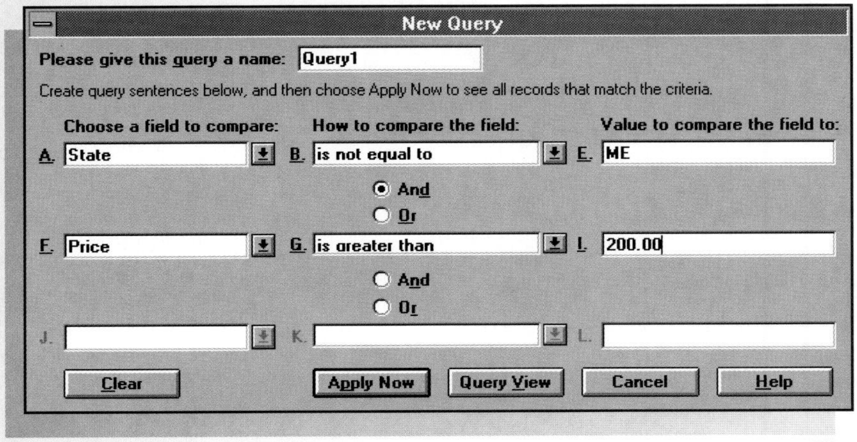

And. This logical operator checks condition 1 and condition 2 and condition 3. All conditions must be met for a record to be retrieved.

Or. This logical operator checks condition 1 or condition 2 or condition 3. At least one of the conditions must be met for a record to be retrieved.

TASK 43

Working with a List of Records

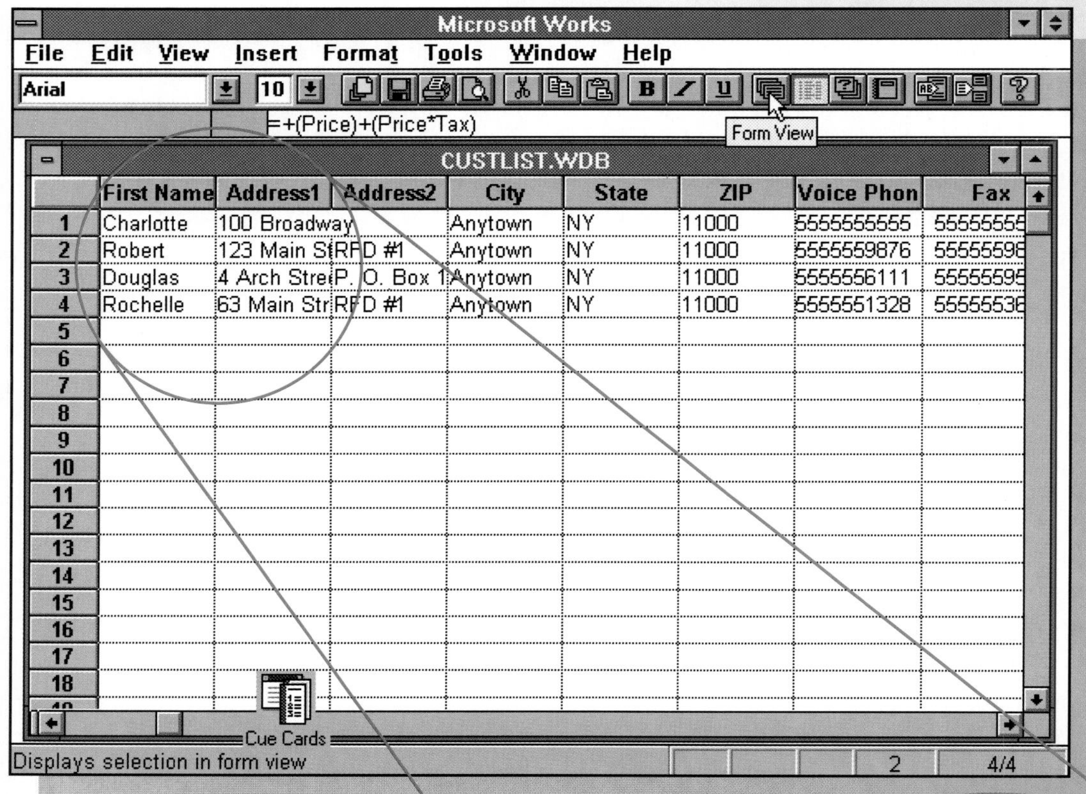

"Why would I do this?"

Displaying several database records at a time has its advantages. You can edit more quickly, and you can see more fields at once. In this task, you switch from form view to list view and back again.

This task assumes that you have started the Database tool, that a database is open, and that you have entered records in an input form.

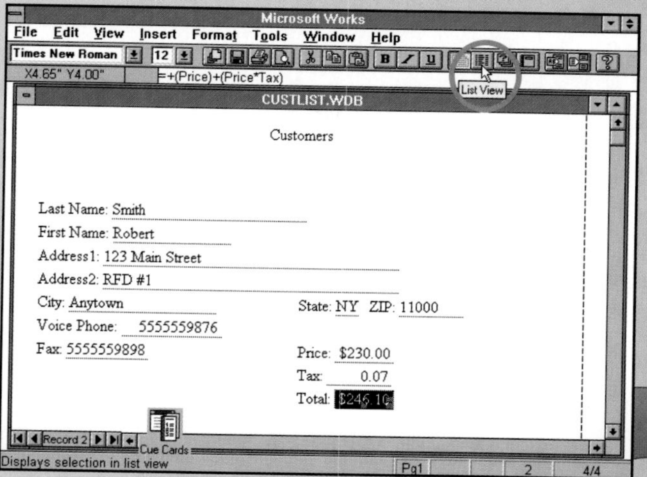

1 Click on the **List View** button on the toolbar. This is the same as choosing the List command from the View menu or pressing F9. Works switches to list view, which shows several records in a table format.

WHY WORRY?

Use the vertical scroll bar to see any *records* that don't fit in the window; use the horizontal scroll bar to see any *fields* that don't fit.

2 Click on the **Form View** toolbar button. This is the same as choosing the Form command from the View menu or pressing F9. Works switches back to form view, where you view one record at a time.

NOTE

F9 is a toggle key. When you are in form view, press F9 to go to list view, and when you are in list view, press F9 to return to form view.

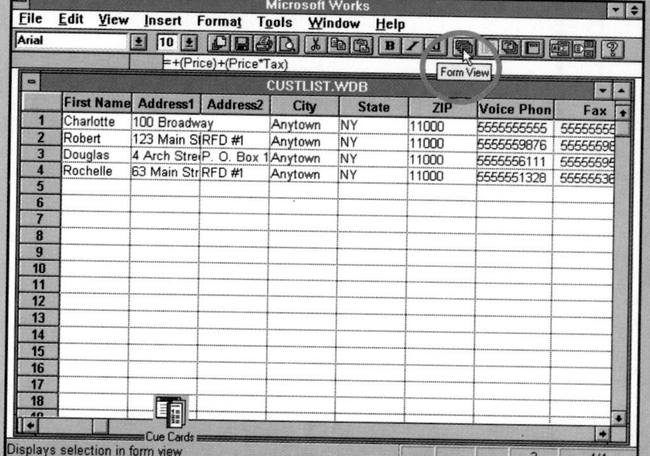

TASK 44

Changing the Width of a Field

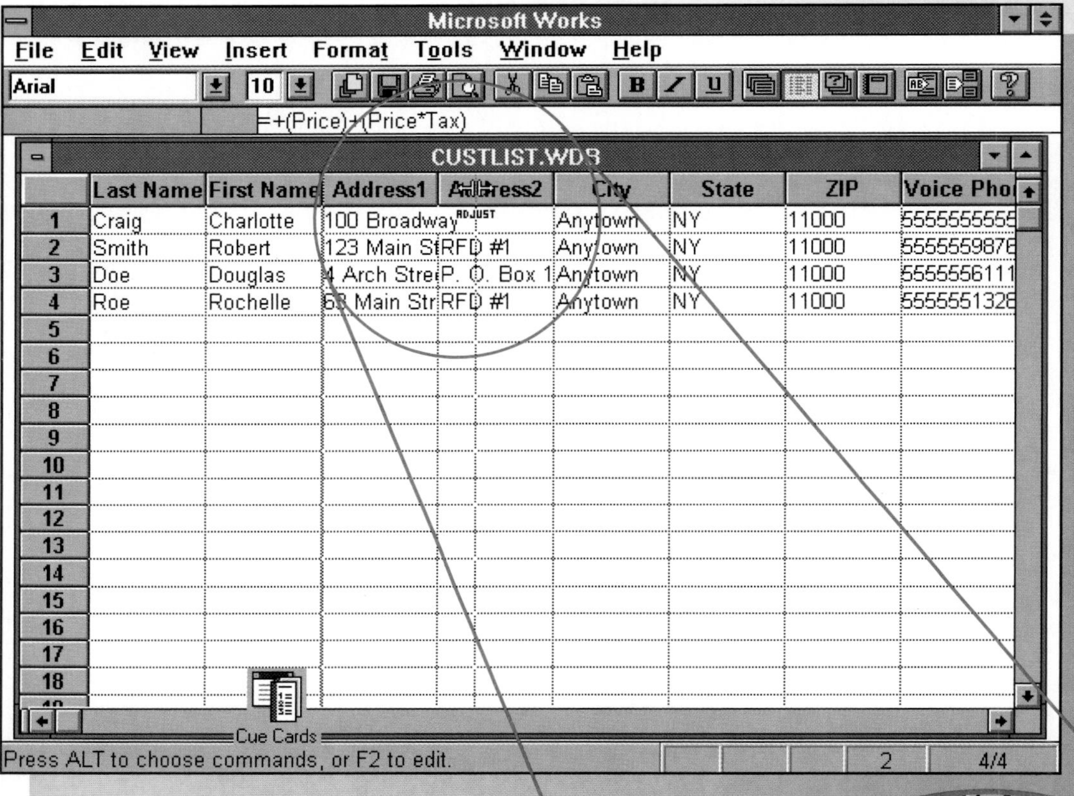

"Why would I do this?"

When you display a database in list view, quite often you need to adjust columns so that you can see the complete column heading or the longest field in a column. In this task, you change the width of a field containing a long entry so that you can see every character in it.

This task assumes that the Database tool is active and that a database is displayed in list view.

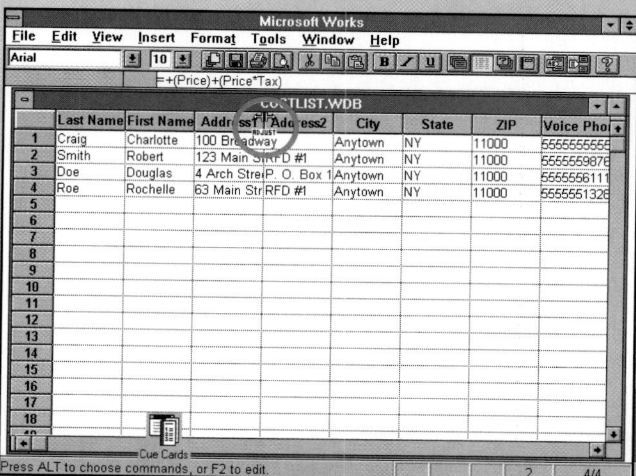

1 Move the mouse pointer to the border between `Address1` and `Address2`, until the mouse pointer changes to a double-headed arrow. This pointer indicates that you can move the border between two columns.

2 Drag the border toward the right side of the screen. A vertical line indicates the current width of the column. As you drag, you can look at the line and decide whether the column is the appropriate width.

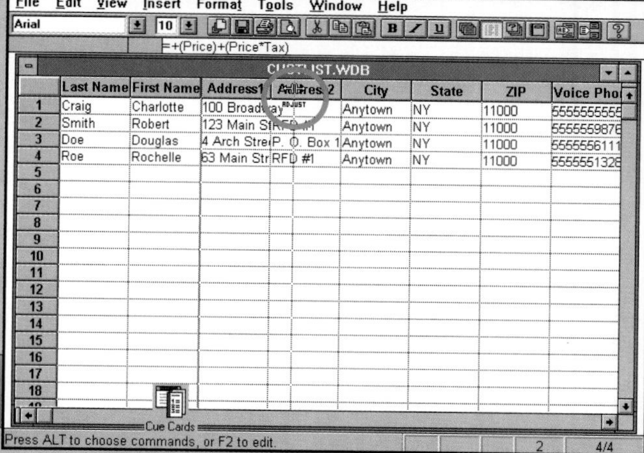

NOTE

To quickly adjust the column width, double-click on the right side of the cell you want to adjust.

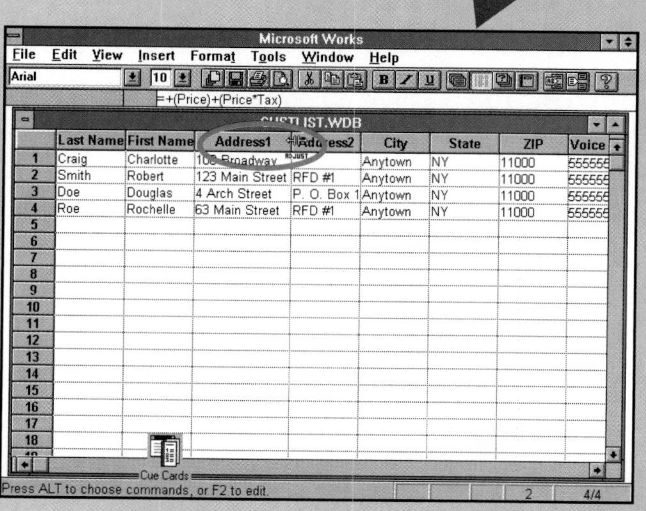

3 Release the mouse button. The column width is set.

NOTE

You can also change column width by choosing the Field Width command from the Format menu and entering a specific value in the Field Width dialog box. To adjust the column width to the value with the most characters, select the Best Fit check box.

TASK 45

Changing a Field Name

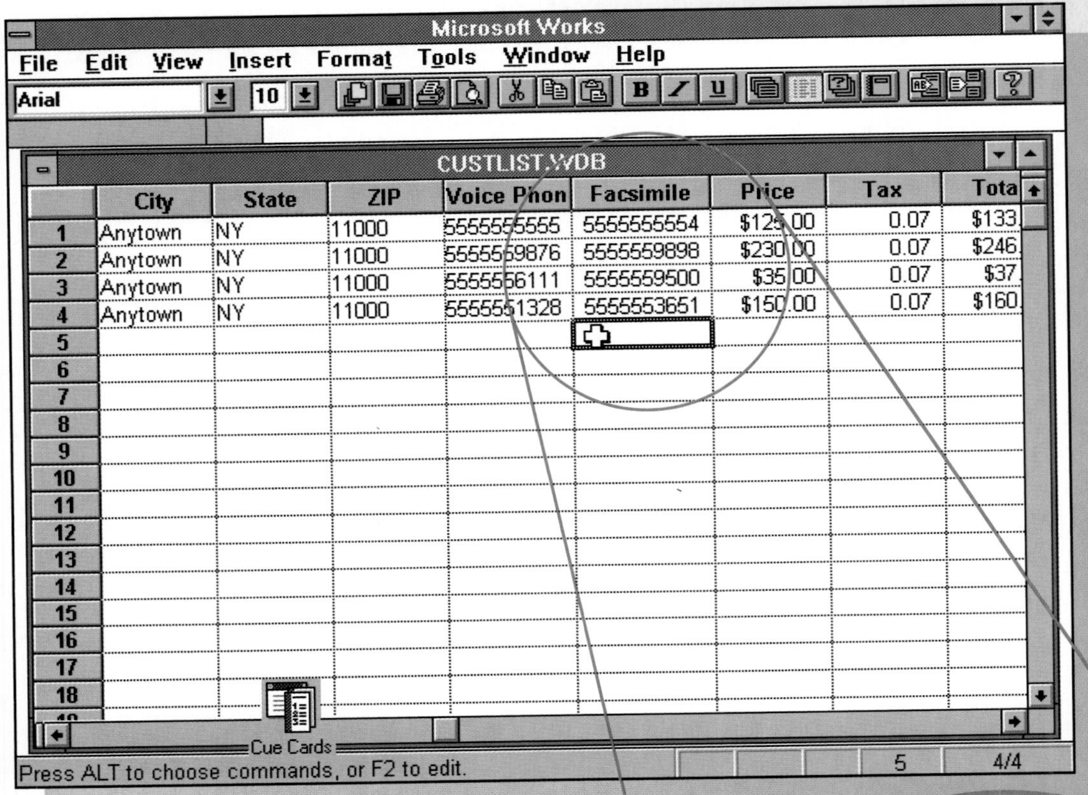

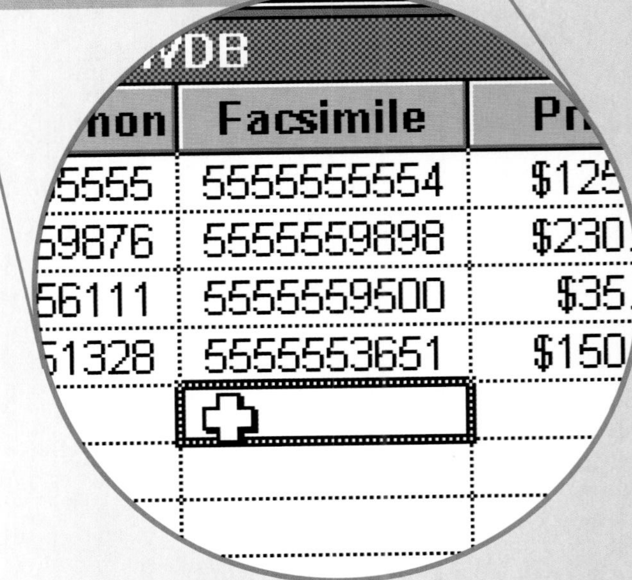

"Why would I do this?"

You may want to change a field name so that it more accurately describes the field's contents. You may want to correct a misspelling or just change the field name so that it fits better with the other field names that serve as report headings. In this task, you change the name of a field.

This task assumes that the Database tool is active and that a database is displayed in list view.

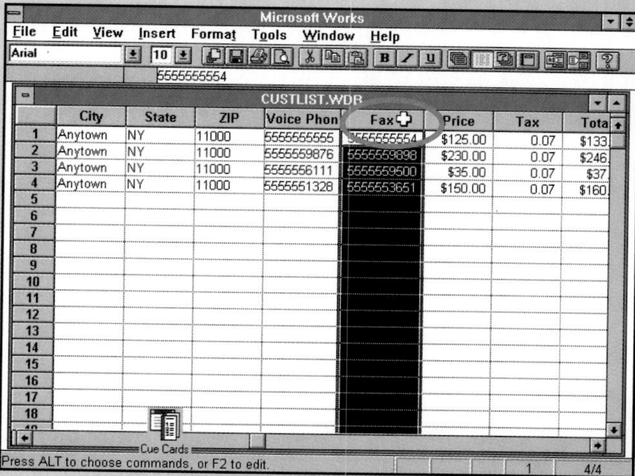

1 Click on the **Fax** column label. This step selects the entire Fax field.

2 Click on **Edit** in the menu bar and click on **Field Name**. This opens the Field Name dialog box.

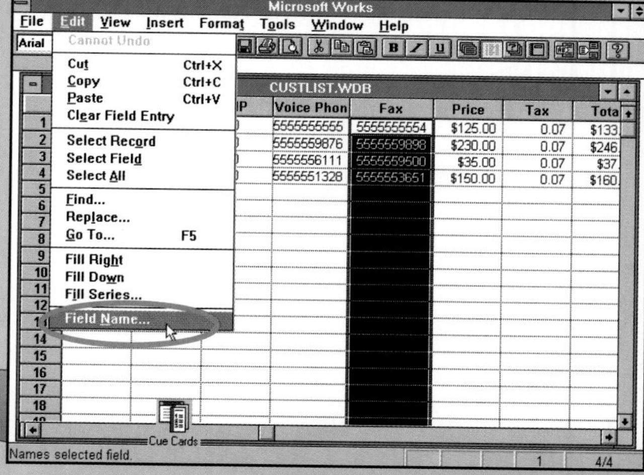

Microsoft Works
Field Name
Name: Facsimile
OK
Cancel
Help
CUSTLIST.WDB
Names selected field.

3 Type **Facsimile** in the Name text box and click on **OK**. This closes the dialog box and changes the field name from *Fax* to *Facsimile*.

Inserting, Moving, and Deleting a Record in a List

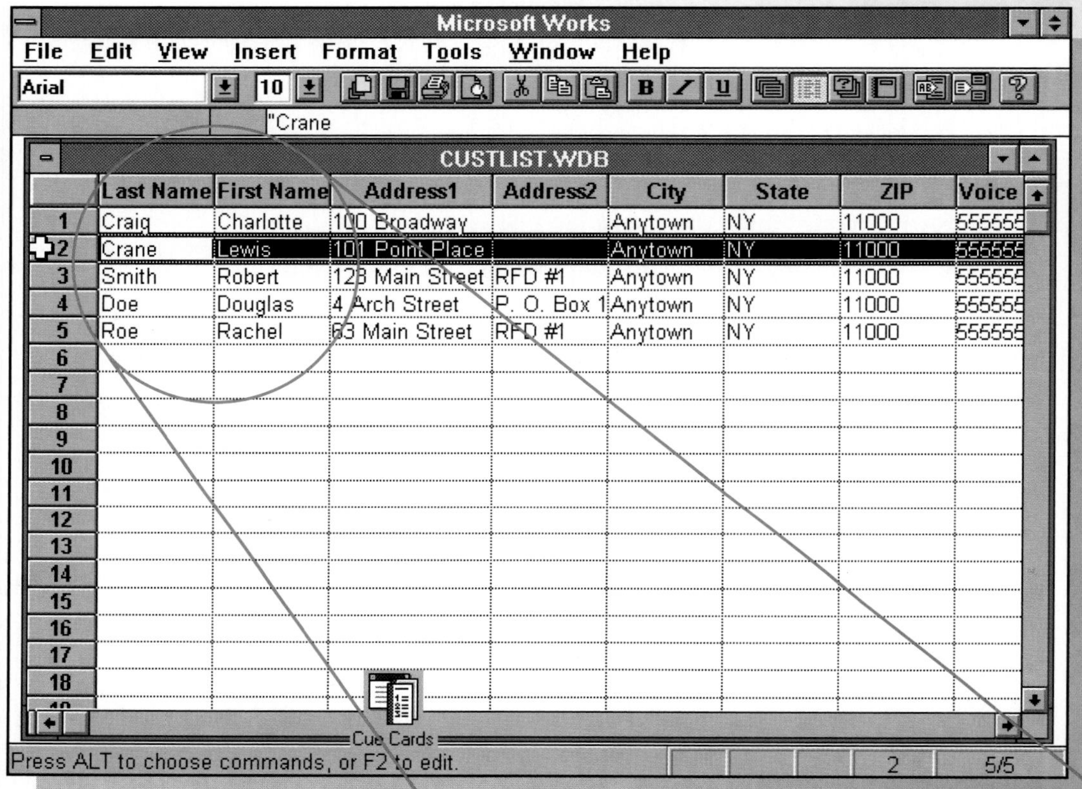

"Why would I do this?"

Databases are made to be changed. In a regularly used database, you constantly insert new records, change the content or location of existing records, and delete unneeded records. In this task, you insert a new record, move it, and delete it. When you insert a new record, you're actually adding a new row to the list.

This task assumes that the Database tool is active and that a database is displayed in list view.

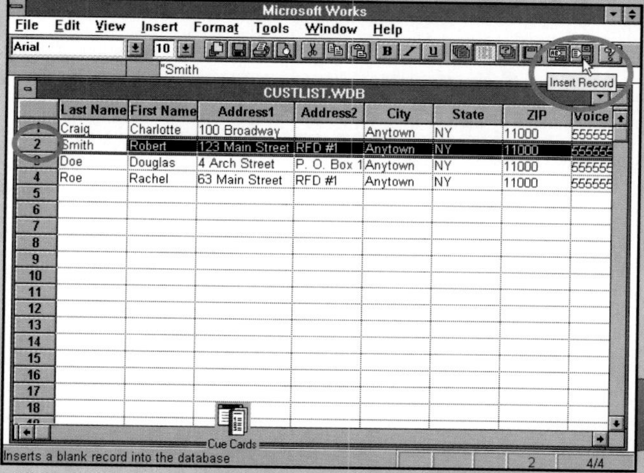

1 Click on the row label for **Record 2**; then click on the **Insert Record** toolbar button. Works inserts a new record above the selected record and renumbers the rows accordingly. This toolbar button is the same as the Insert Record/Field command.

NOTE

When selecting a record, if you don't click on the row label, you highlight the contents of a field rather than the entire record.

2 Type **Crane, Lewis, 101 Point Place, Anytown, NY, 11000, 5555555558, 5555555511, 52.50, 0.07**, pressing Tab to move from field to field. For this record, don't type any text in the Address2 field. You don't need to enter anything in the last field; Works calculates its contents.

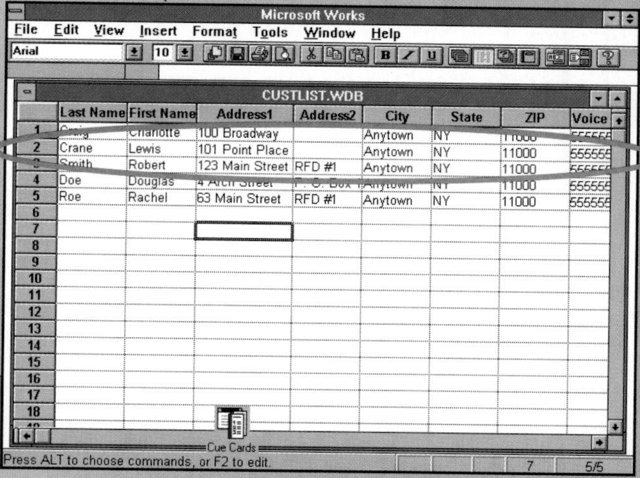

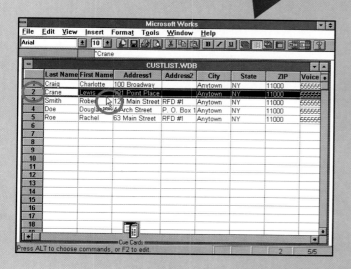

3 Click on the row label for **Record 2** to select it; then move the mouse pointer toward a border of the selection, until the mouse pointer changes to an arrow with DRAG attached to its tail.

Task 46: Inserting, Moving, and Deleting a Record in a List

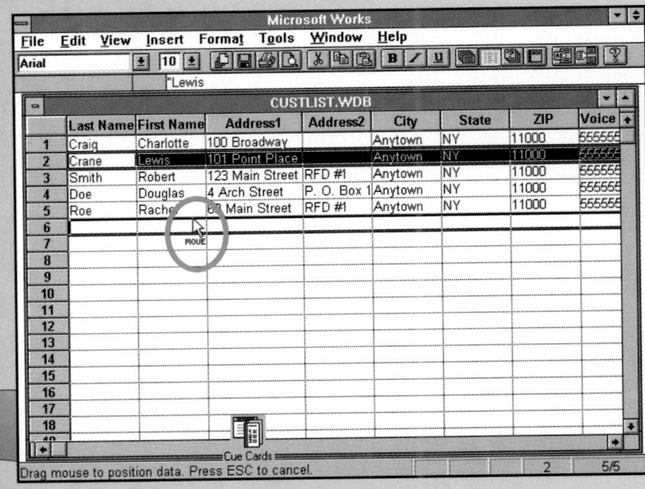

4 Drag the record to the bottom of the list of records. Notice that DRAG changes to MOVE. The heavy border indicates where the record will be placed when you release the mouse button.

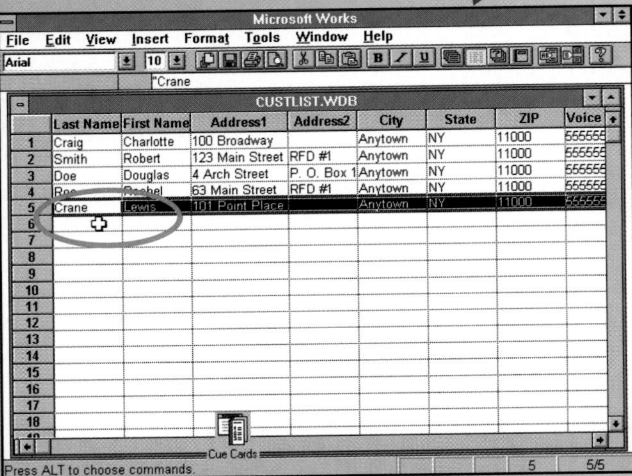

5 Release the mouse button. Works moves the record to the bottom of the database and renumbers the rows from 2 to 5.

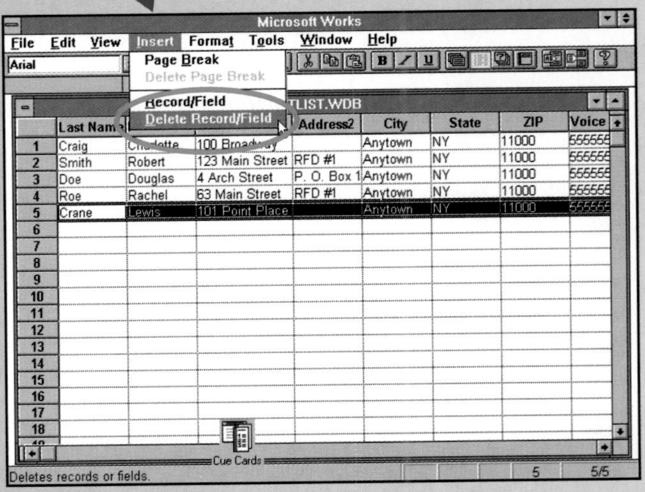

6 Click on **Insert** in the menu bar and click on **Delete Record/Field**. Works deletes the selected record. Pressing the Delete key also deletes a selected record.

WHY WORRY?

To "undelete" a record that you just deleted, press Ctrl+Z or choose Edit Undo. Remember that you must undo an action immediately after taking it. Keep in mind that any type of deletion is destructive; always think twice before deleting.

TASK 47

Inserting, Moving, and Deleting a Field in a List

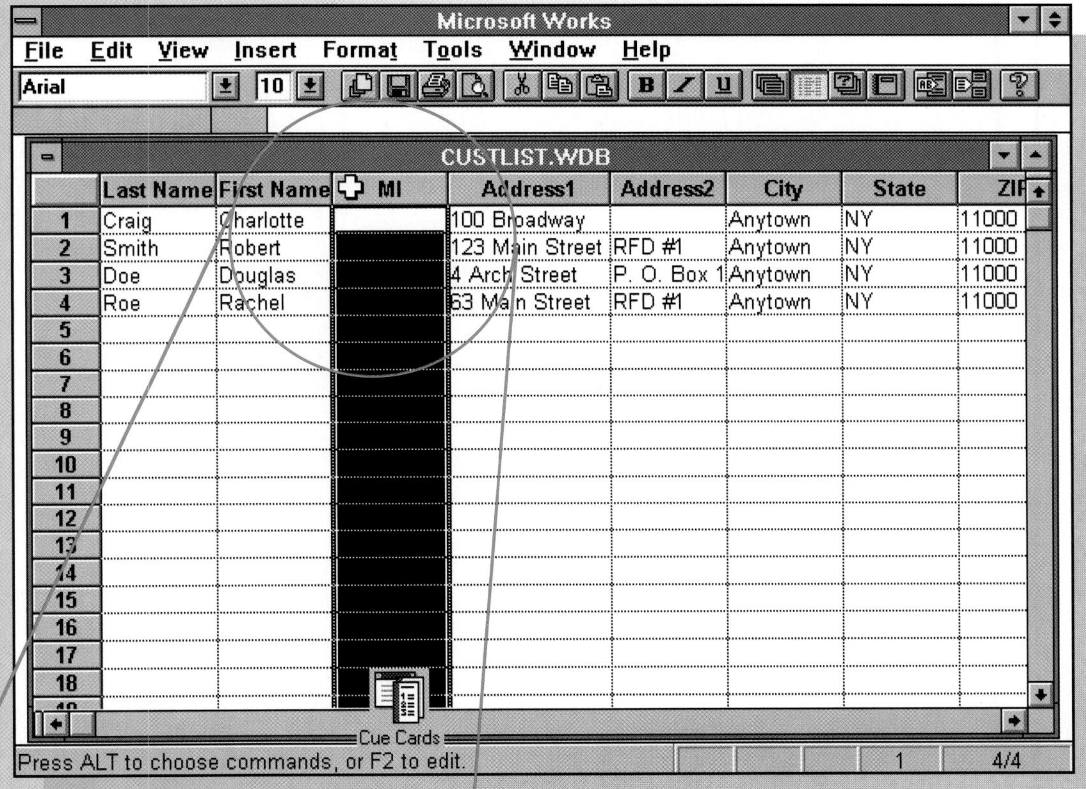

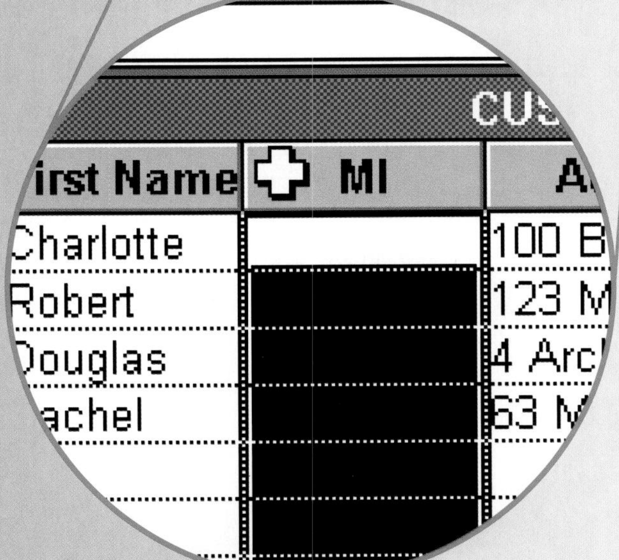

"Why would I do this?"

In the process of refining a database's design, you need to add, modify, and delete fields. In this task, you insert a new field, move the field to a new location, and delete the field. When you insert a new field into a database, you're actually adding a new column to the list.

This task assumes that the Database tool is active and that a database is displayed in list view.

Task 47: Inserting, Moving, and Deleting a Field in a List

1 Click on the **Address1** column label and click on the **Insert Field** toolbar button. Works inserts a new column (field) to the left of the selected column. Using this toolbar button is the same as choosing the Insert Record/Field command.

NOTE

Another way to add a field is to select a column, move the mouse pointer until it changes shape and displays DRAG at its tail, and drag it toward the right. Works creates a new column.

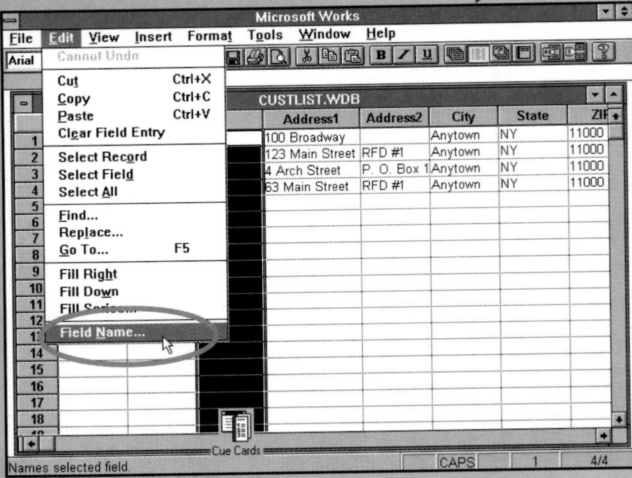

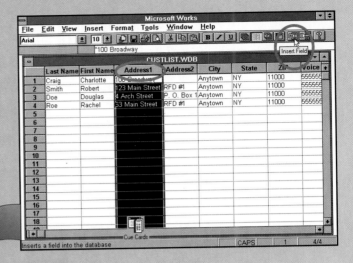

2 Click on **Edit** in the menu bar and click on **Field Name**. Works opens the Field Name dialog box.

3 Type **MI** in the Name text box and click on **OK**. Works inserts `MI` at the top of the new field column.

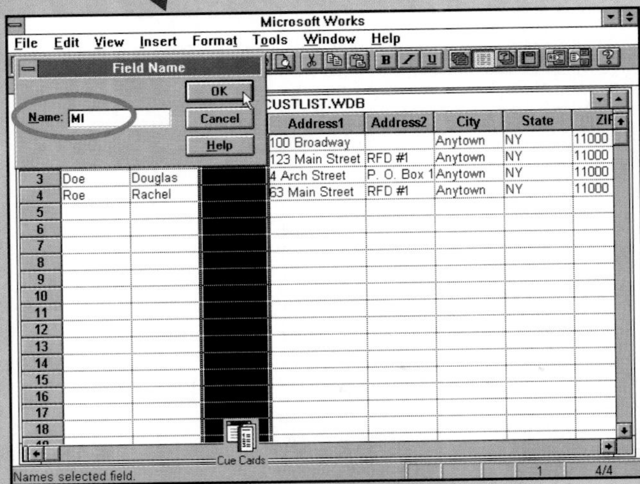

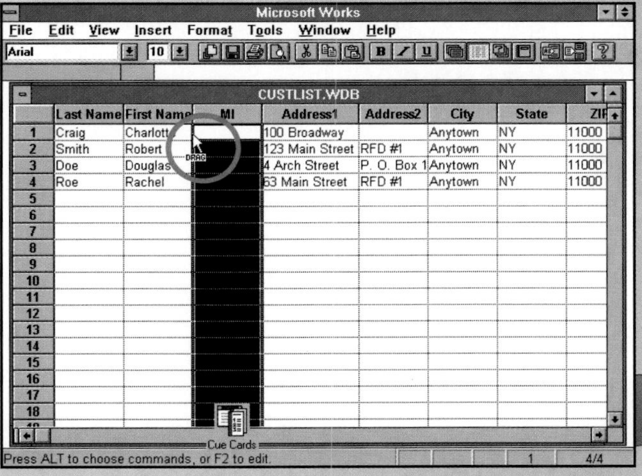

4 Position the mouse pointer on the border between the First Name and MI columns, but not on the column labels. The mouse pointer changes to an arrow displaying DRAG at its tail.

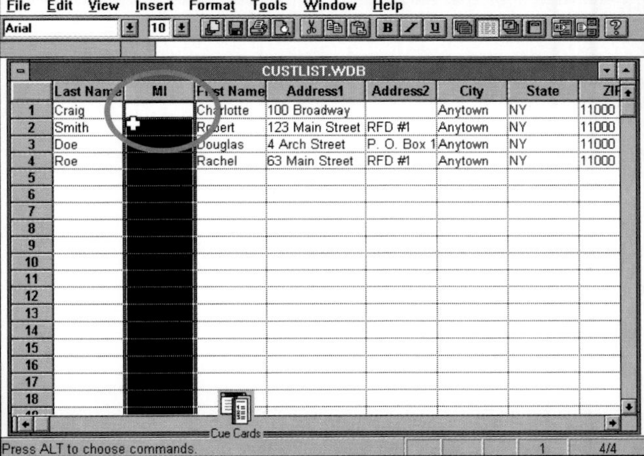

5 Drag the column toward the left side of the screen and, when it jumps left to the next column, release the mouse button. The mouse tail displays MOVE as you drag the column. Works moves the column to its new position, left of the First Name column.

WHY WORRY?

You cannot press Ctrl+Z or choose the Edit Undo command to undo the move; however, you can drag the column back to its old position.

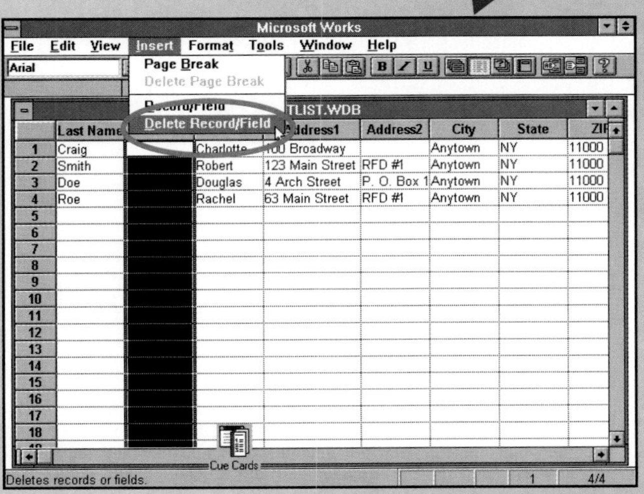

6 Click on **Insert** in the menu bar and click on **Delete Record/Field**. Works deletes the new MI field from the database.

NOTE

If you delete a field that contains data, you lose that data, so be very careful when deleting a field. Deletion can be destructive.

TASK 48

Hiding and Revealing Fields and Records

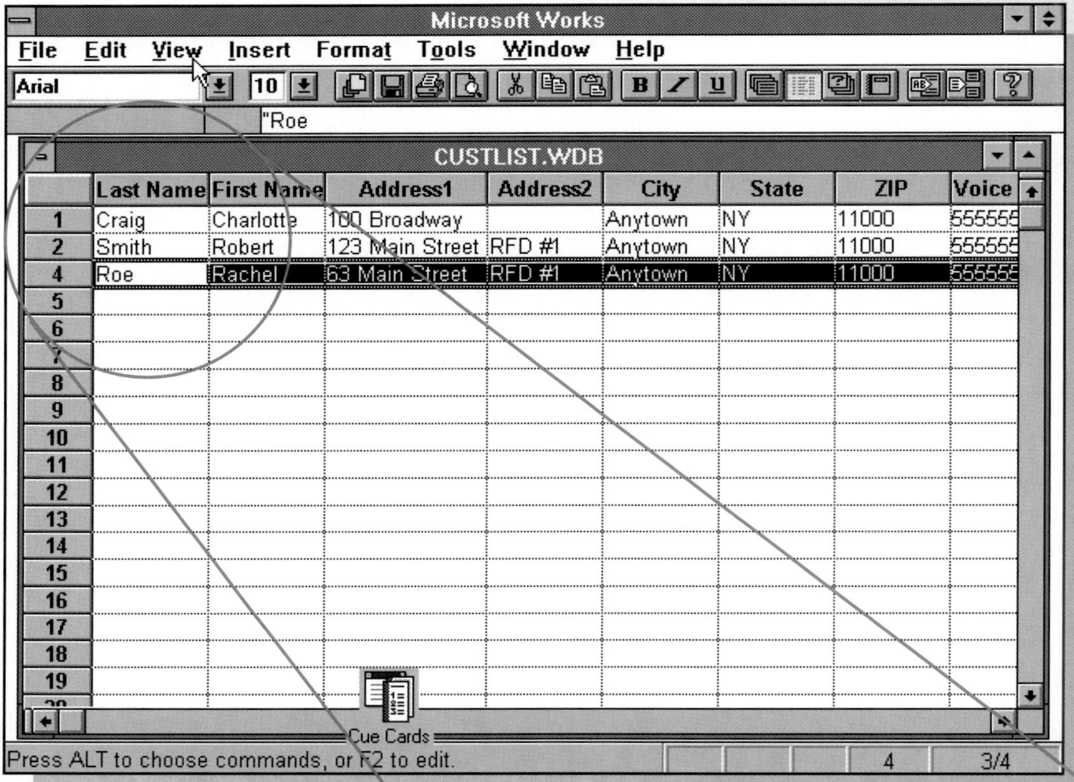

"Why would I do this?"

Hiding records and fields allows you to keep sensitive information confidential and enables you to view noncontiguous fields side by side so that you can compare them without having to scroll back and forth. In this task, you hide and reveal a field, hide a record, display only the hidden record, and reveal all the records.

This task assumes that the Database tool is active and that a database is displayed in list view.

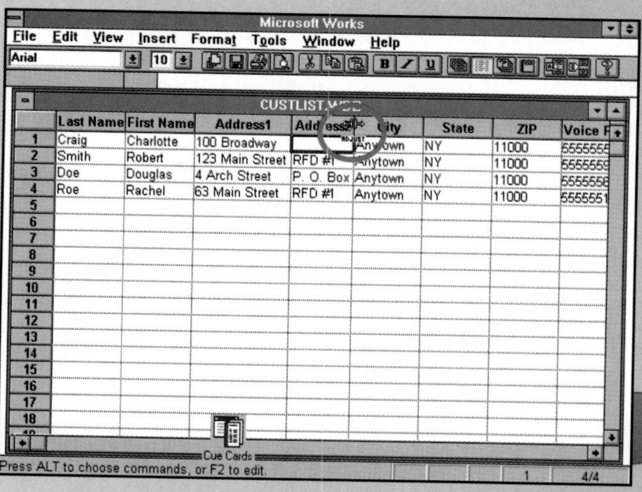

1 Move the mouse pointer to the border between the column labels for `Address2` and `City`. Make sure that the pointer is in the label, not in a record. Works changes the mouse pointer to a double-headed arrow displaying `ADJUST` at its tail.

2 Drag the pointer left, toward the `Address1` label. Works displays a vertical line that indicates the right border of the Address2 field.

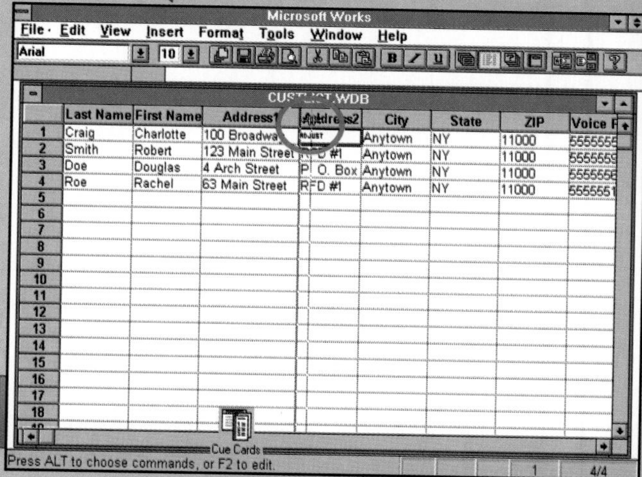

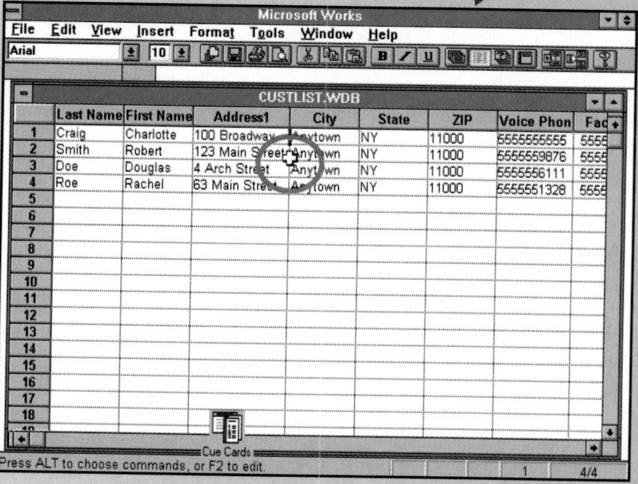

3 Release the mouse button when the border you are dragging is on top of the right border of the Address1 field. Works hides the Address2 field, making its width zero. Notice that the border is slightly heavier than usual, indicating that the hidden field is selected.

Task 48: Hiding and Revealing Fields and Records

4 Click on **Edit** in the menu bar and click on **Go To**. Works displays the Go To dialog box.

You can also press F5 to display the Go To dialog box.

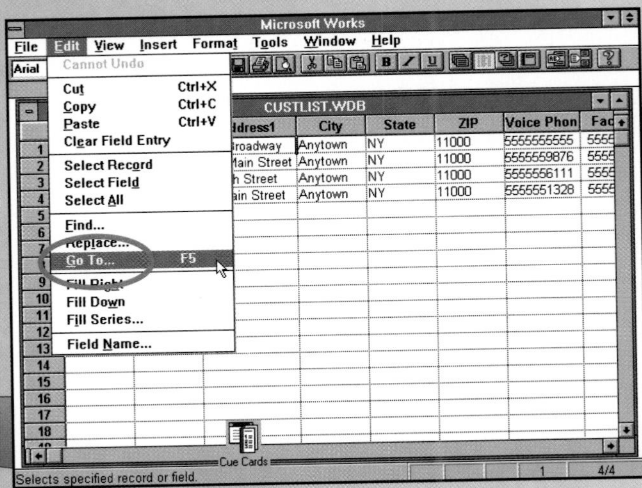

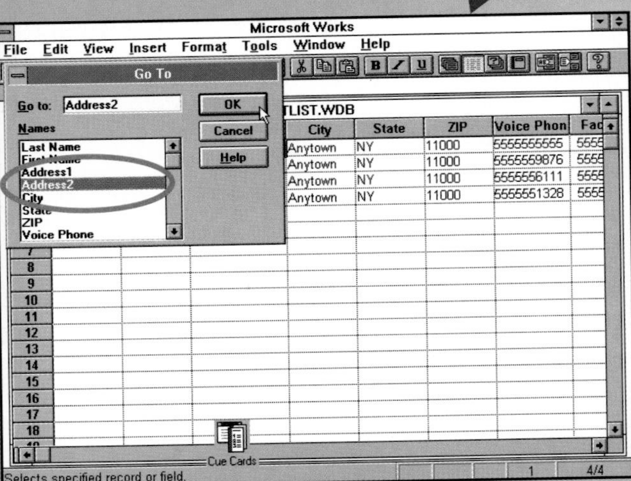

5 Click on **Address2** in the Names list and click on **OK**. Works closes the Go To dialog box and returns to the database. Although there doesn't appear to be any changes to the database, the hidden field is selected.

6 Click on **Format** in the menu bar and click on **Field Width**. Works displays the Field Width dialog box.

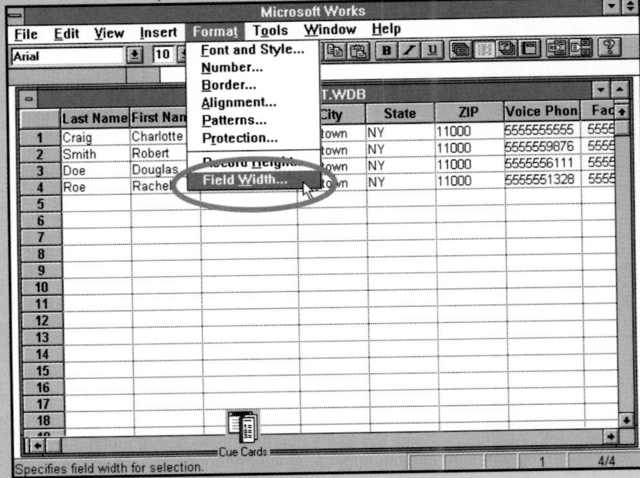

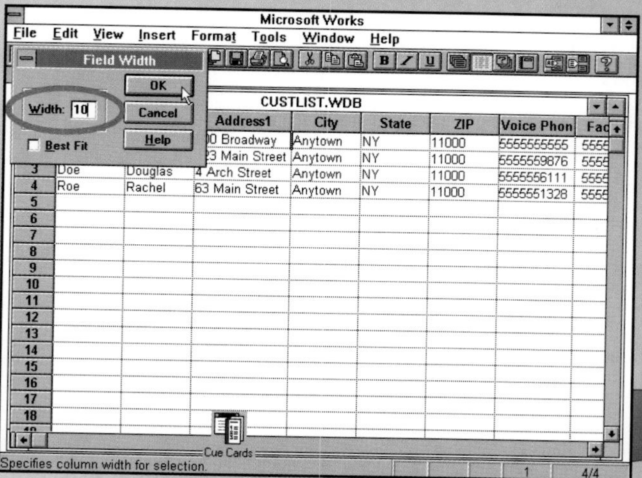

7 Type **10** in the Width text box and click on **OK**. The default width for a field is 10. This step closes the dialog box and displays the formerly hidden field.

NOTE

To hide a field or reveal a hidden field in form view, choose the Format Show Field Name command.

8 Click on the row label for **Record 3**, click on **View** in the menu bar, and click on **Hide Record**. This step selects Record 3 and then hides it. Notice that Works does not renumber the records.

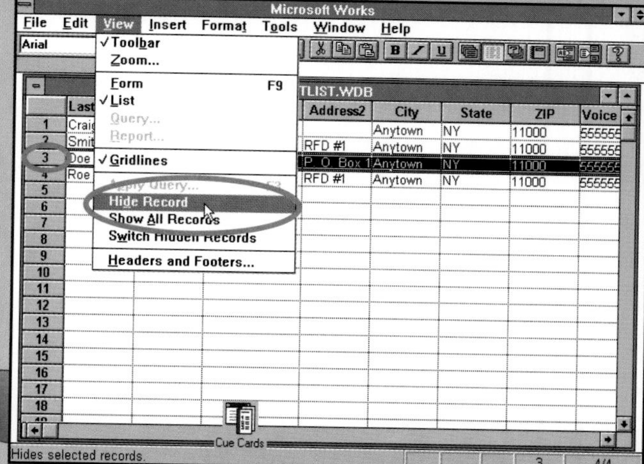

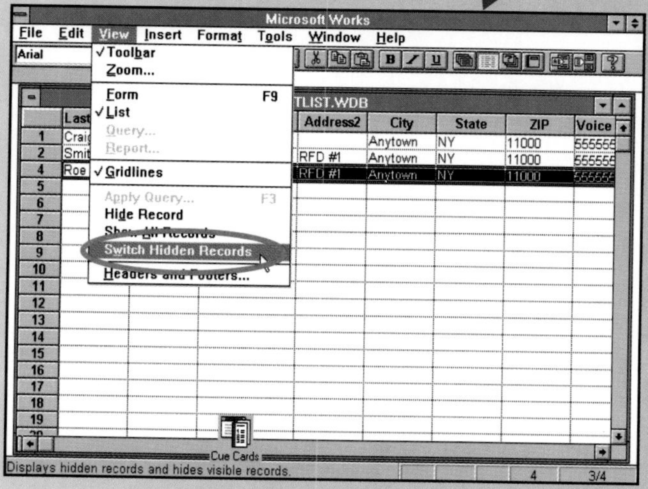

9 Click on **View** in the menu bar and click on **Switch Hidden Records**. Works displays the hidden record and hides all the other records.

NOTE

Click on the Show All Records command in the View menu to reveal all the records (although not all records are displayed at this point).

TASK 49

Finding a Record and Replacing a Field

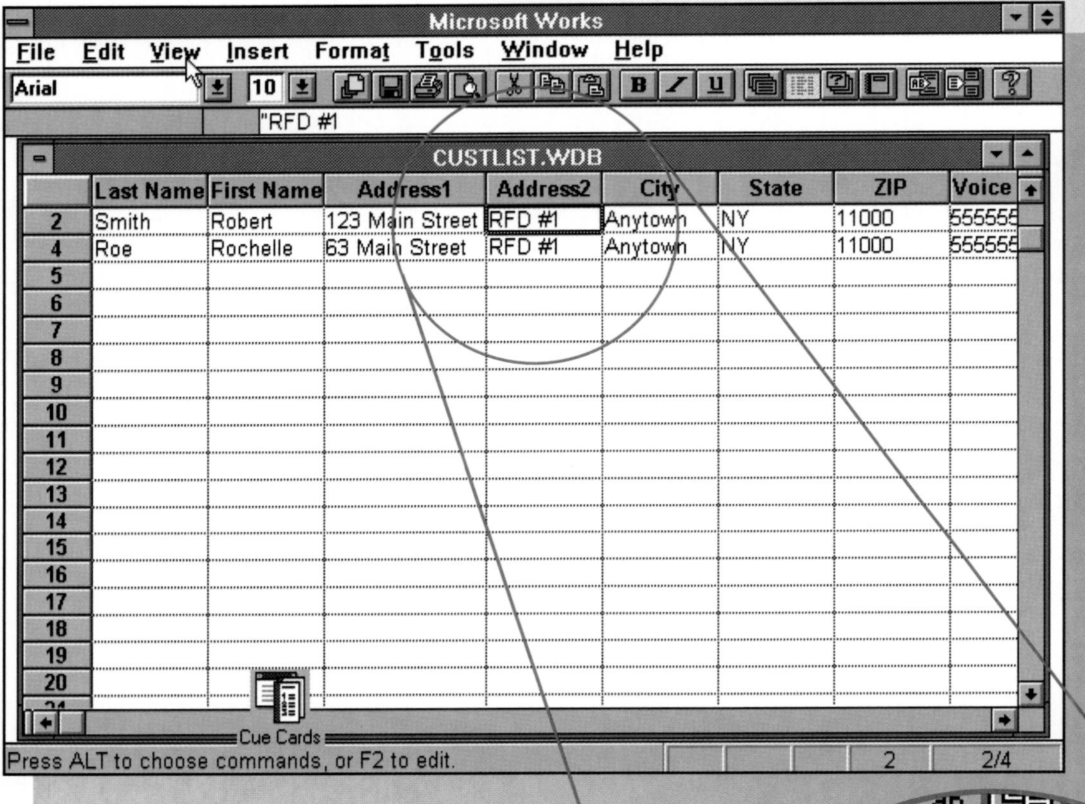

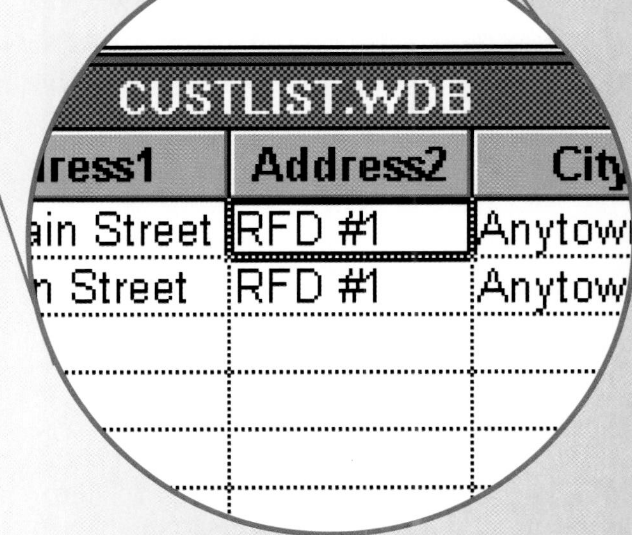

"Why would I do this?"

Finding one record or several records, especially in a very large database, can save you the time and effort of searching through records page by page. In this task, you instruct Works to search for the next record that has RFD listed in the Address2 field. Then you search for a name and replace it.

This task assumes that the Database tool is active and that a database is displayed in list view.

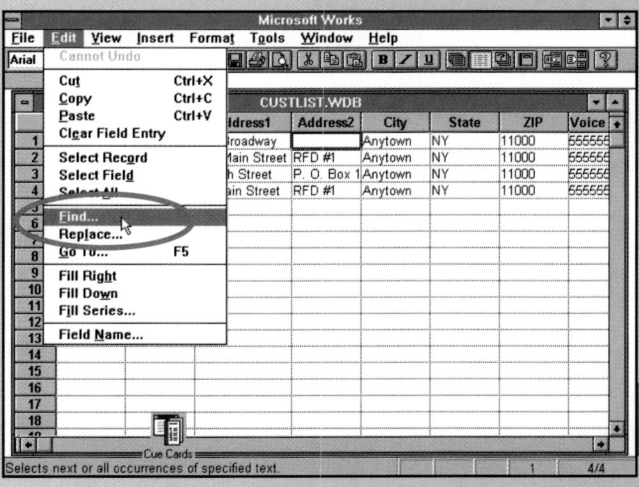

1 Click on **Edit** in the menu bar and click on **Find**. This action displays the Find dialog box.

2 Type **RFD** in the Find What text box. Typing RFD means that you want Works to search for records that contain the word RFD.

NOTE

Works searches for characters regardless of their case; therefore, whether you type *rfd, Rfd,* or *rFd,* Works will find the word *RFD.*

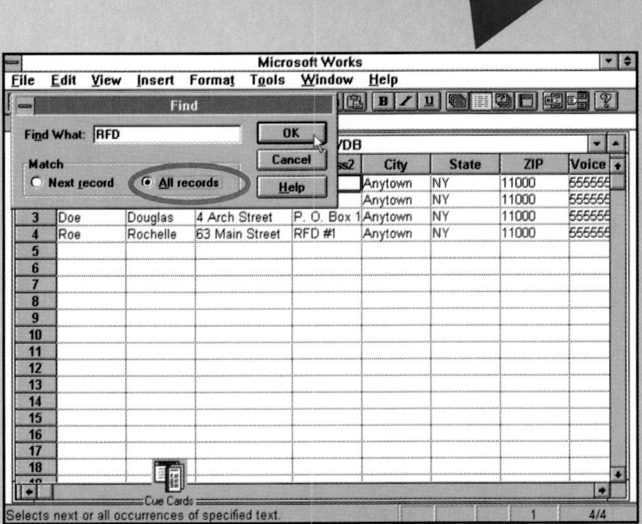

3 Click on the **All Records** option button and click on **OK**. All Records tells Works to search through every record in the database. Works displays the two records that contain the word RFD.

NOTE

The Next Record option button tells Works to search only for the next record containing the specified word.

Task 49: Finding a Record and Replacing a Field

4 Click on **View** in the menu bar and click on **Show All Records**. Works redisplays all the records in the database.

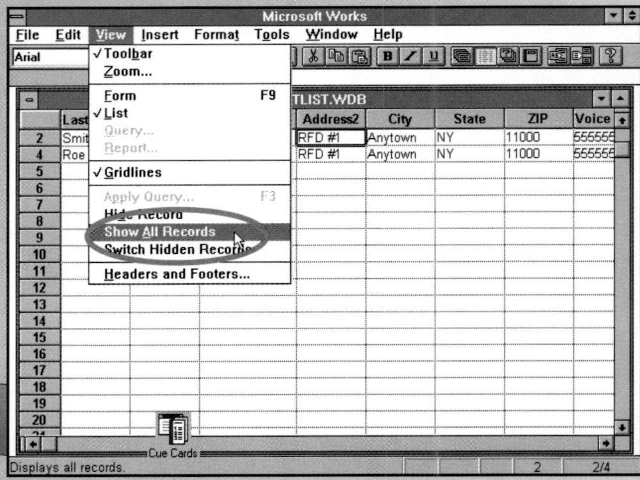

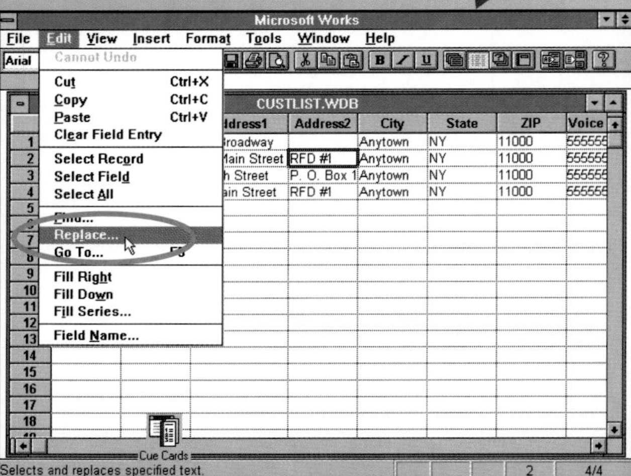

5 Click on **Edit** in the menu bar and click on **Replace**. This step displays the Replace dialog box.

NOTE

If you have already searched for and replaced text in the current work session, the Find What and Replace With text boxes are already filled in; for instance, this example displays RFD in the Find What text box. Just replace the previous values with new text.

6 Type **Rochelle** in the Find What text box. The word *Rochelle* is called the *search string,* the text for which you are searching.

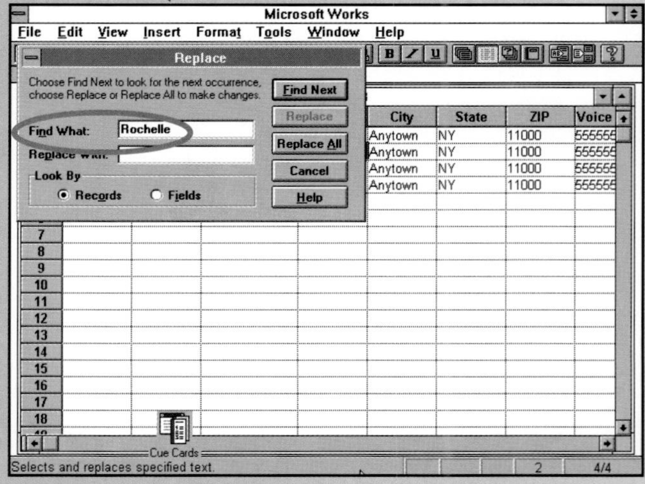

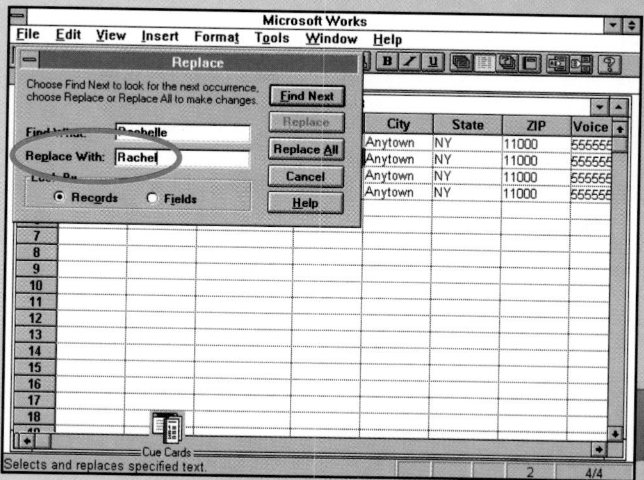

7 Type **Rachel** in the Replace With text box. The word *Rachel* is the *replace string,* the text with which Works replaces search strings that it finds.

NOTE

When the Records option button in the Look By group is selected, Works will search from left to right through all records. If you select Fields instead, Works will search all records field by field, in a top to bottom direction.

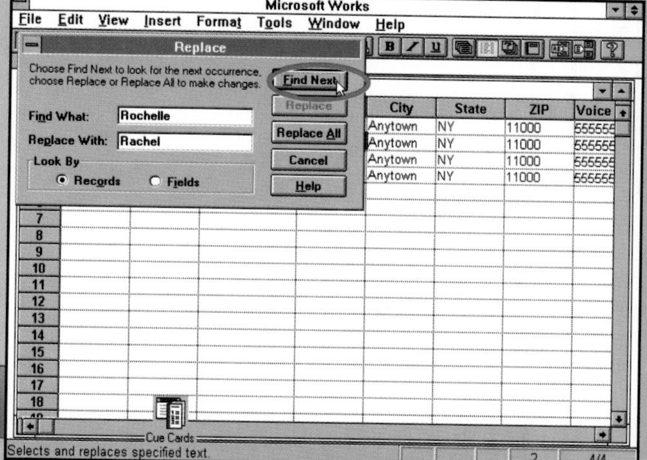

8 Click on **Find Next**. This step starts the search. When Works finds the first occurrence of the search string, it highlights the text in the record.

NOTE

Sometimes you won't be able to see the highlighted search string because the Replace dialog box is in the way. To ensure that Works actually found the search string, move the dialog box by dragging its title bar.

9 Click on **Replace**. This step replaces the search string with the replace string.

Rather than choosing the Replace button, you can click on Cancel to close the dialog box without any further action, click on Find Next to find the next occurrence of the search string, or click on Replace All to replace every occurrence of the search string with the replace string.

TASK 50

Querying the Database

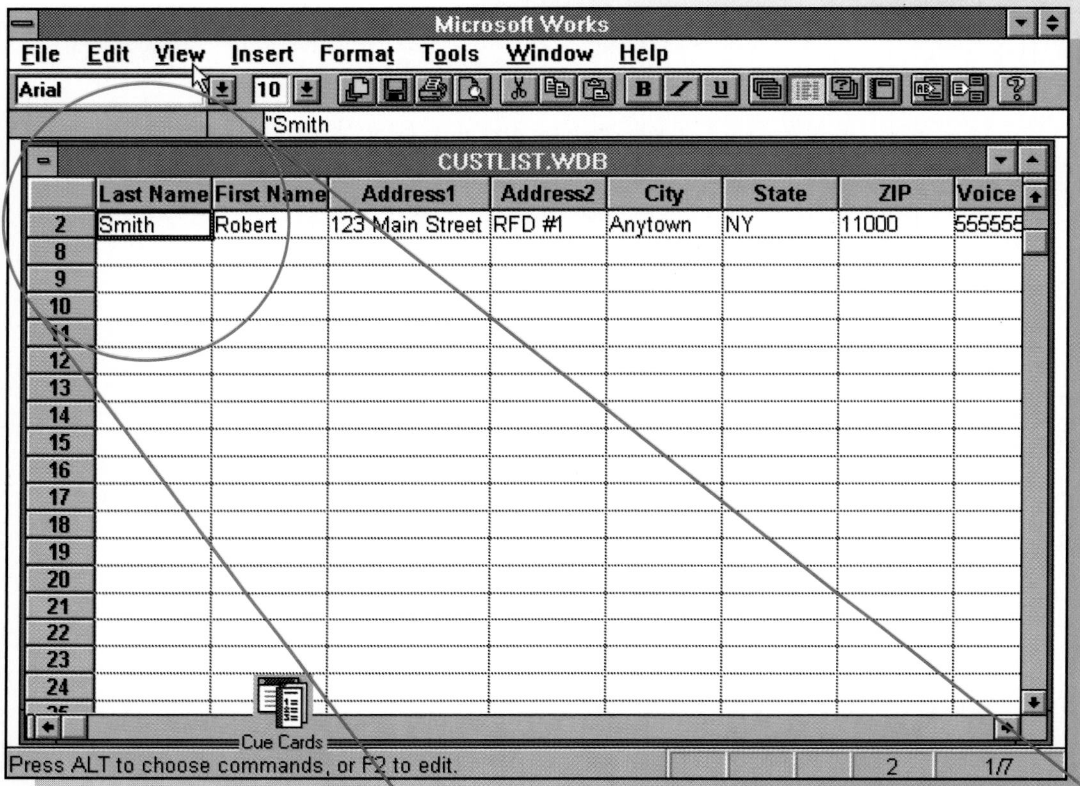

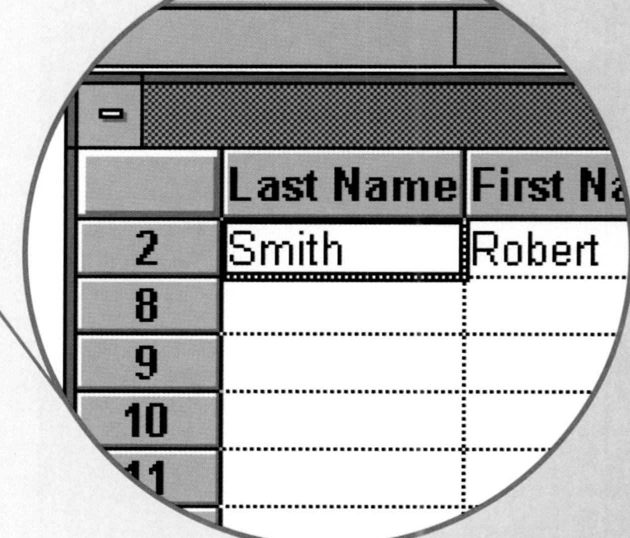

"Why would I do this?"

Querying the database retrieves records that contain specific information. Queries find matches in specific fields and can use multiple criteria to do so. In this task, you add three new records in either form view or list view, and then you perform a query in list view.

This task assumes that the Database tool is active and that a database is displayed in form view (click on the Form View button in the toolbar).

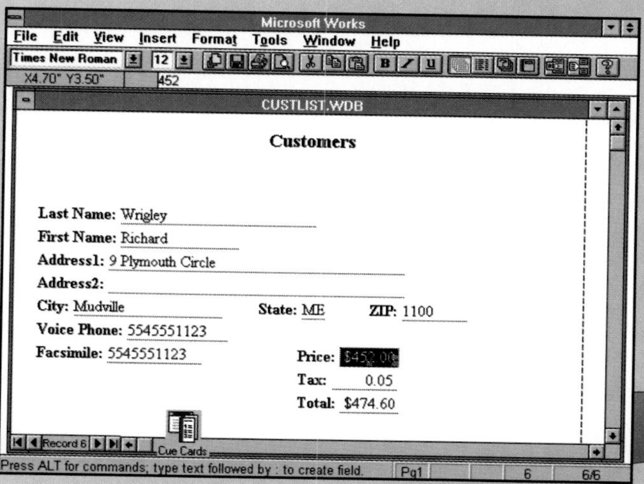

1 Add these three records to the sample database, skipping the Address2 field: (1) **Jones, Mary, Jones Lane, Mudville, ME, 01100, 5545552091, 5545551122, 325.00, 0.05**; (2) **White, Wanda, 555 Whitney Road, Mudville, ME, 01100, 5545559524, 5545559524, 37.00, 0.05**; and (3) **Wrigley, Richard, 9 Plymouth Circle, Mudville, ME, 01100, 5545551123, 5545555982, 452.00, 0.05**.

2 Click on **Tools** in the menu bar and click on **Create New Query**. Works opens the New Query dialog box.

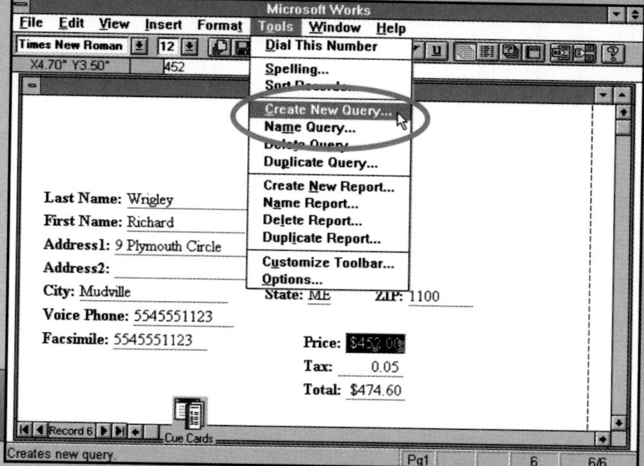

3 Select **State** from the Choose a Field to Compare drop-down list box. This step indicates that you want Works to query the State field to retrieve specific records.

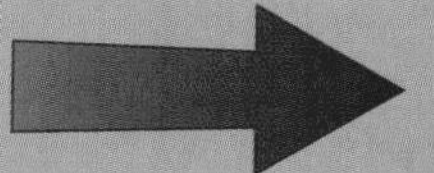

Task 50: Querying the Database

4 Select **Is Not Equal To** in the How to Compare the Field drop-down list box. You're checking to see whether the State field is *not* equal to a certain value.

NOTE

Although you can name a query, you can accept Works' suggested query name, *Query1*. Choose the Tools Name Query command whenever you want to name a query.

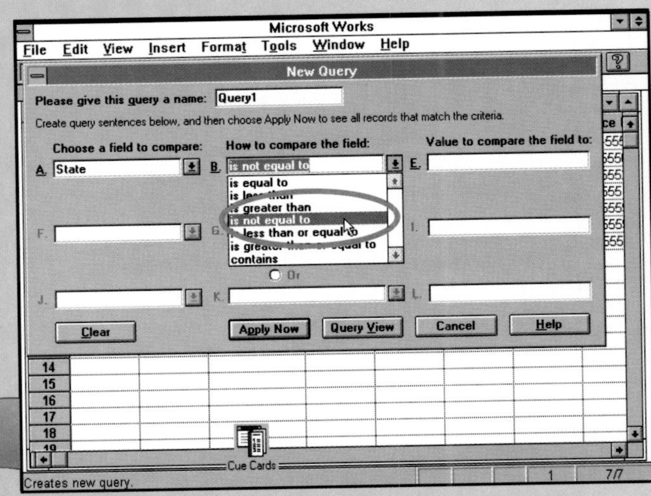

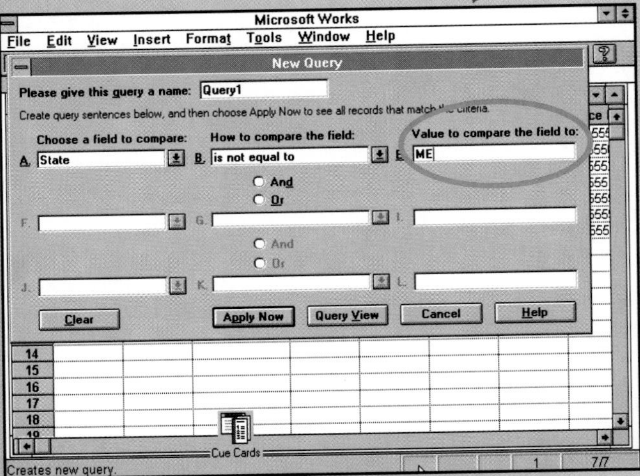

5 Type **ME** in the Value to Compare the Field To text box. You have finished building the first half of the query, which tells Works to retrieve the records in which the State field is not equal to Maine.

NOTE

You can begin the query now by clicking on the Apply Now button, or you can enter a second set of criteria.

6 Click on the **And** option button. This means that both criteria must be satisfied for a record to be retrieved. If you click on the Or option button instead, Works will retrieve all records that meet either the first or second set of criteria.

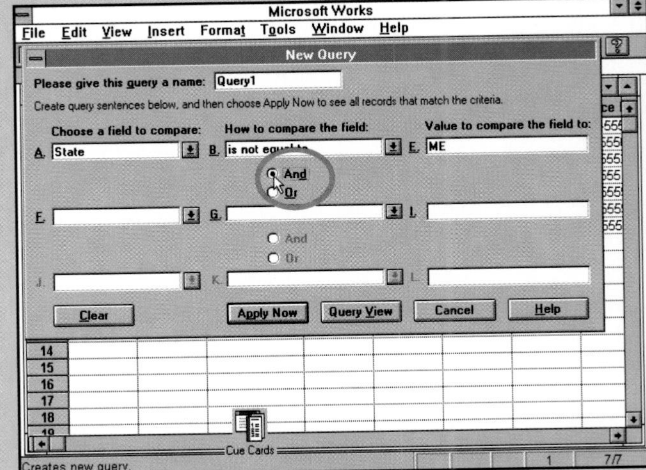

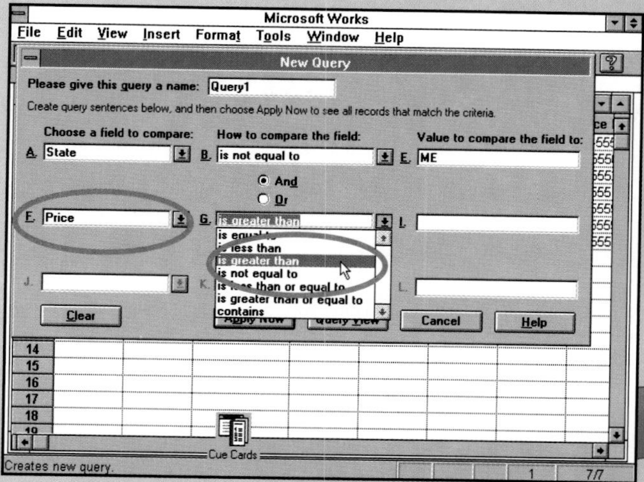

7 Select **Price** in the second Choose a Field to Compare drop-down list box and select **Is Greater Than** in the second How to Compare the Field drop-down list box.

8 Type **200.00** in the second Value to Compare the Field To text box. You have finished building your query, which tells Works to retrieve the records in which the State field is equal to any value but Maine and in which the Price field is greater than $200.

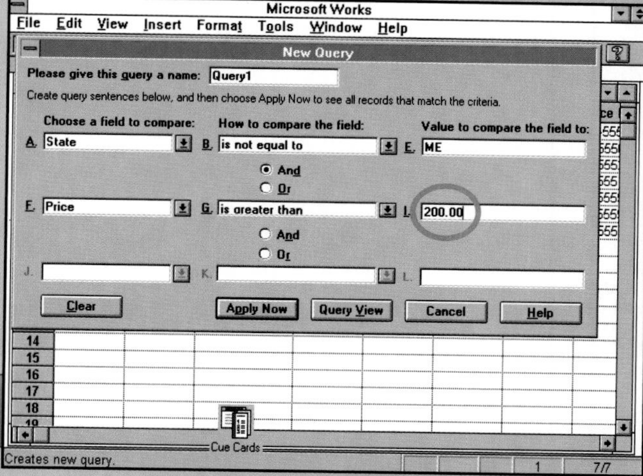

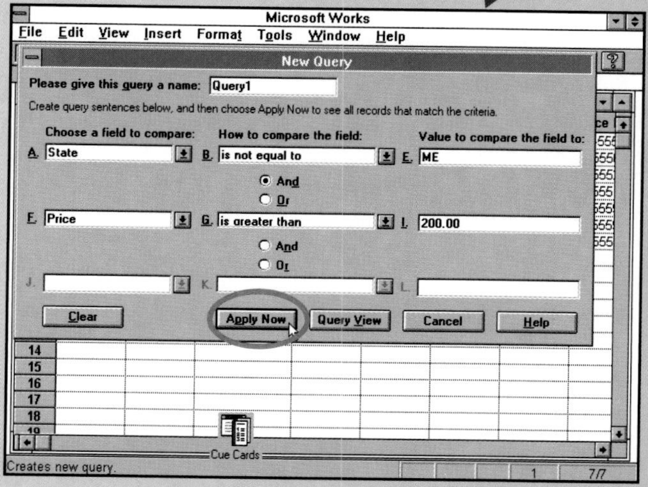

9 Click on **Apply Now**. Works finds one record that meets both criteria.

NOTE

After completing a query, if you want to retrieve all the records that don't match, and hide all the records that do match, open the View menu and choose the Switch Hidden Records command.

TASK 51

Sorting Records

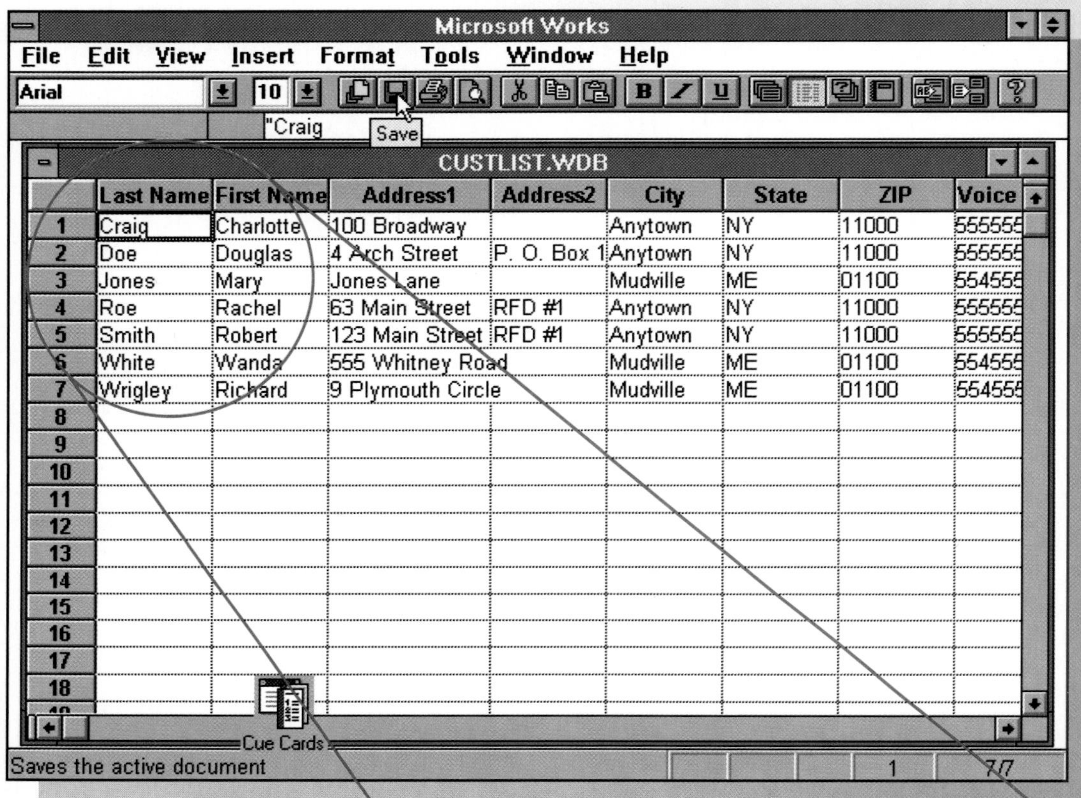

"Why would I do this?"

When you add new records to a database, you enter data as it comes along, not in any particular order. Sorting enables you to arrange records alphabetically or numerically by a selected field. In this task, you perform a sort.

This task assumes that the Database tool is active and that a database is displayed in list view.

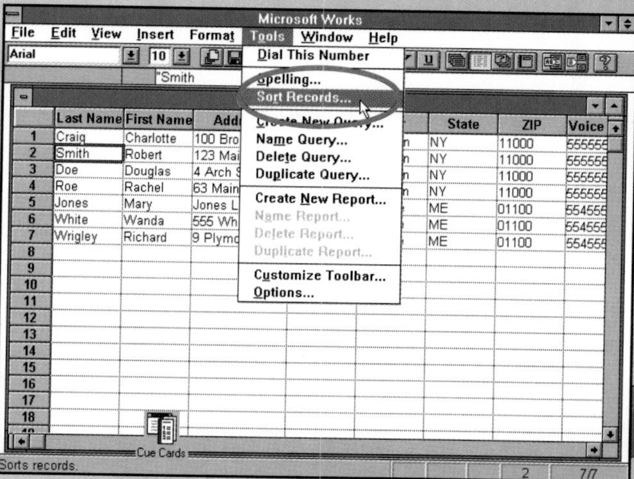

1 Click on **Tools** in the menu bar and click on **Sort Records**. The Sort Records dialog box opens.

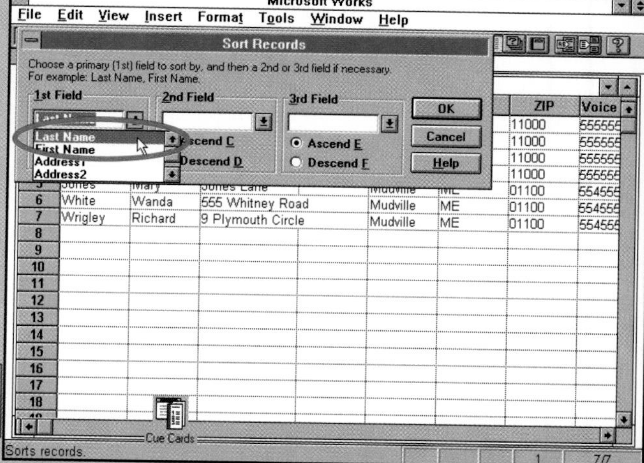

2 Click on **Last Name** in the 1st Field drop-down list box. This is the first field in the database and, therefore, the default. Clicking on Last Name means that Works will sort the records by the contents of the Last Name field.

NOTE

In large databases, you may need to sort by two or even three fields. For example, if your database has several records with *Smith* as the last name, you should also sort by first name.

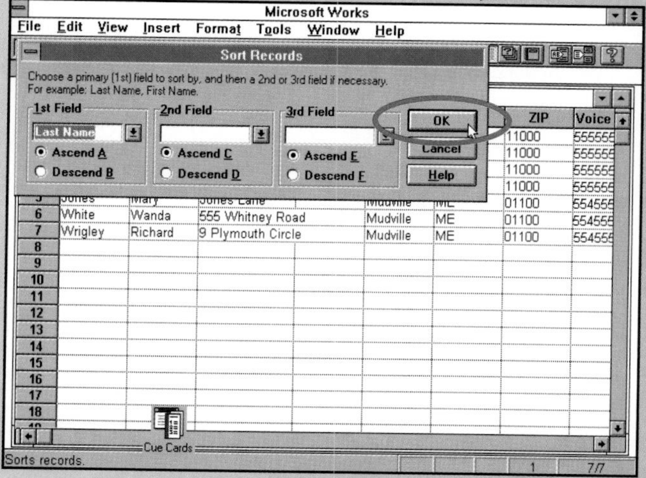

3 Click on **OK**. This step selects the default sort order, Ascend A, which tells Works to sort from A to Z. Works closes the dialog box and sorts all the records by the contents of the Last Name field.

NOTE

After completing a sort, if you save the database, Works remembers the sort and displays the records in that order the next time you open the database.

TASK 52

Creating a Report

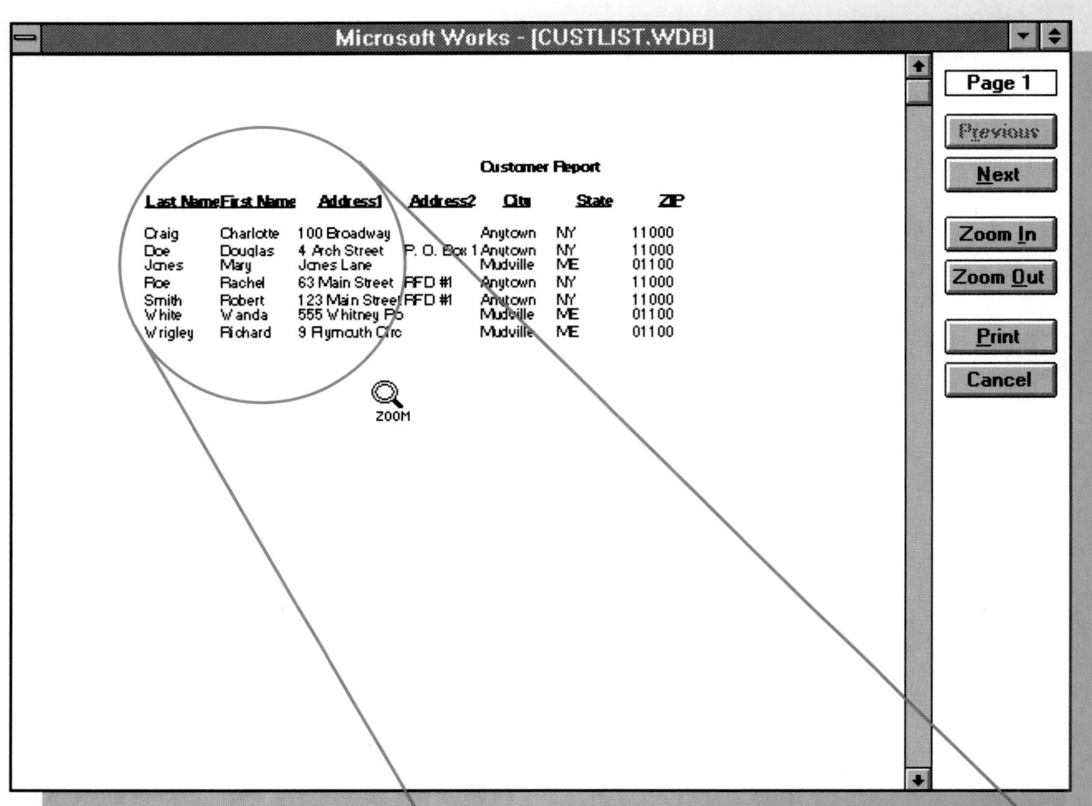

"Why would I do this?"

Reports show sorted and retrieved records in an attractive way that an audience can easily understand. In this task, you create a simple report.

This task assumes that the Database tool is active and that a database is displayed in list view.

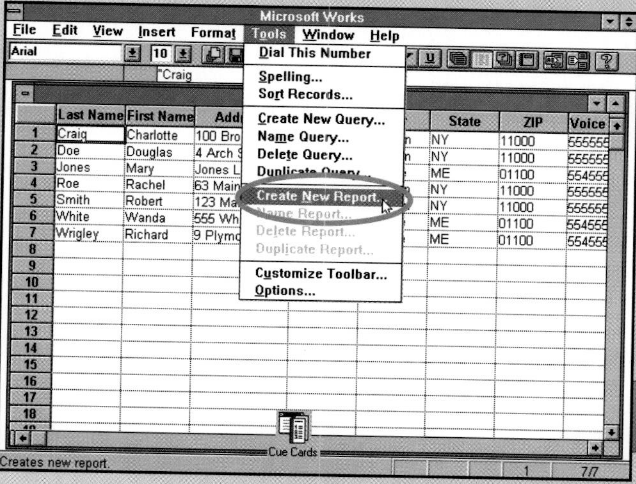

1 Click on **Tools** in the menu bar and click on **Create New Report**. Works displays the New Report dialog box.

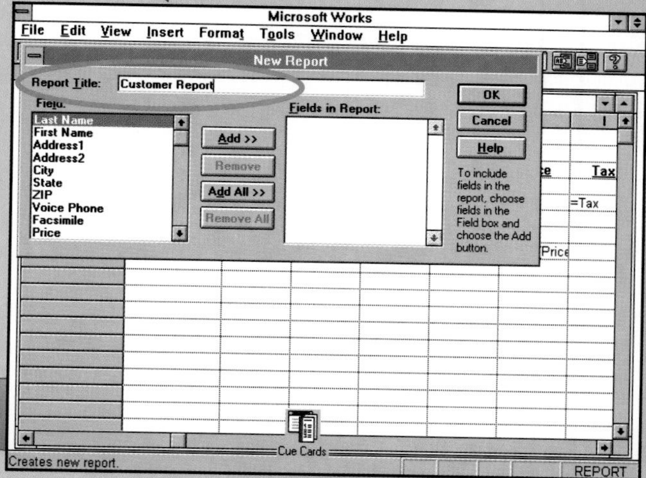

2 Type **Customer Report** in the Report Title text box. This step adds a title to the report.

3 Click on the **Add All** button. This step tells Works that you want to add all fields to your report.

NOTE

When you want most of the database's fields in your report, it's easier to add all the fields and then remove the few that you don't want.

4 Click on **Voice Phone** in the Fields in Report scroll box and click on the **Remove** button. This step removes the Voice Phone field from the report.

WHY WORRY?

When you remove a field from a report, you are not removing it from the database.

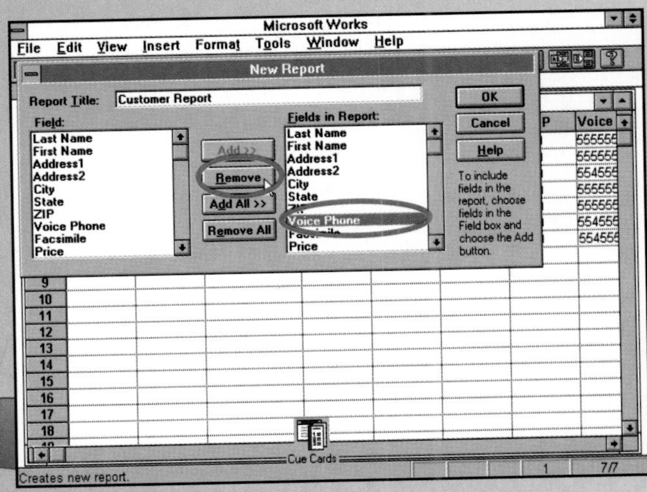

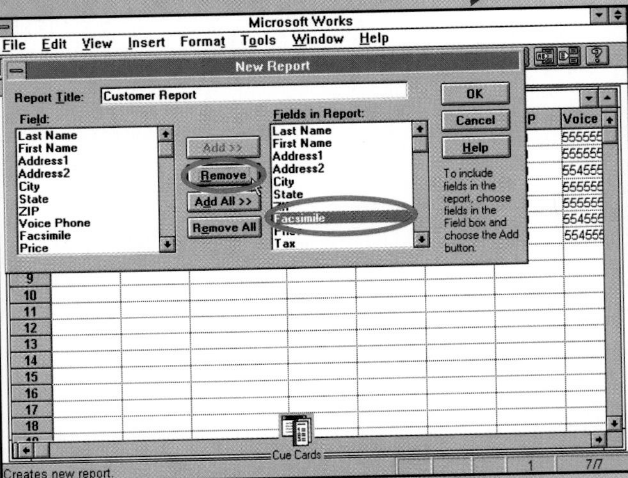

5 Click on **Facsimile** in the Fields in Report scroll box, click on the **Remove** button, and click on **OK**. This step removes the Facsimile field from the report, closes the New Report dialog box, and opens the Report Statistics dialog box.

6 Click on **Price** in the Fields in Report list box, and click on the **Sum** check box to select it. This step tells Works that you want to compute a total for the list of prices in the database.

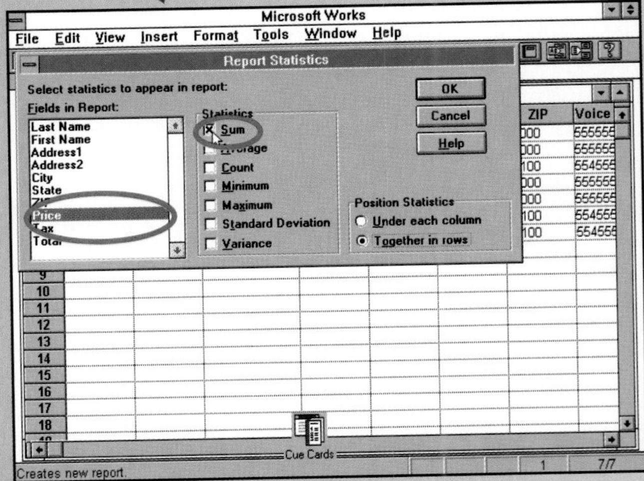

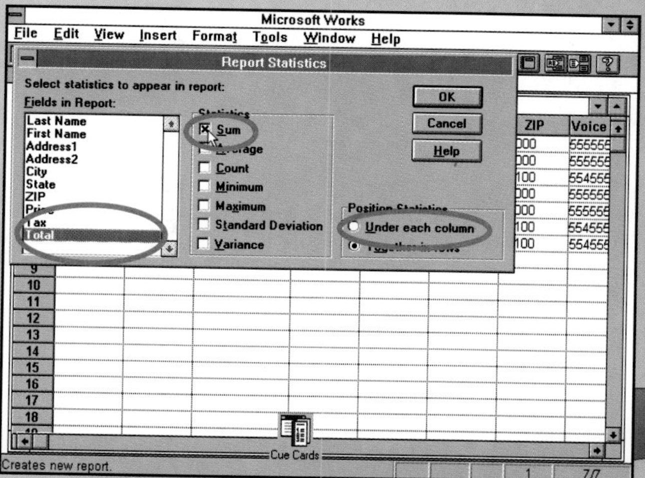

7 Click on **Total** in the Fields in Report list box, and click on the **Sum** check box to select it. This step tells Works that you want to sum all the Total fields in the database. Click on the **Under Each Column** option button to place the totals under the Price and Total columns in the report; then click on **OK**.

8 Works creates a report definition and displays a message box. Click on **OK** to close the message box.

NOTE

A *report definition* shows the elements of your report. You can understand a report definition by comparing the row labels on the left with the rest of the row.

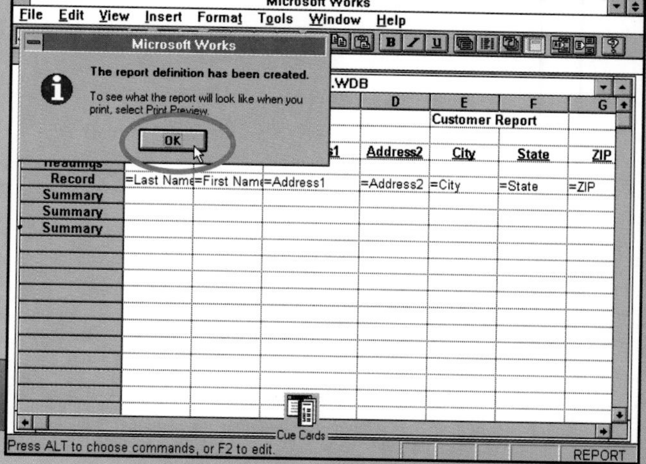

9 Click on the **Print Preview** button on the toolbar.

NOTE

Click the mouse pointer to "zoom" (magnify the view of) the report. Click on the Next button to see the next page.

PART VIII

Using the Communications Tool

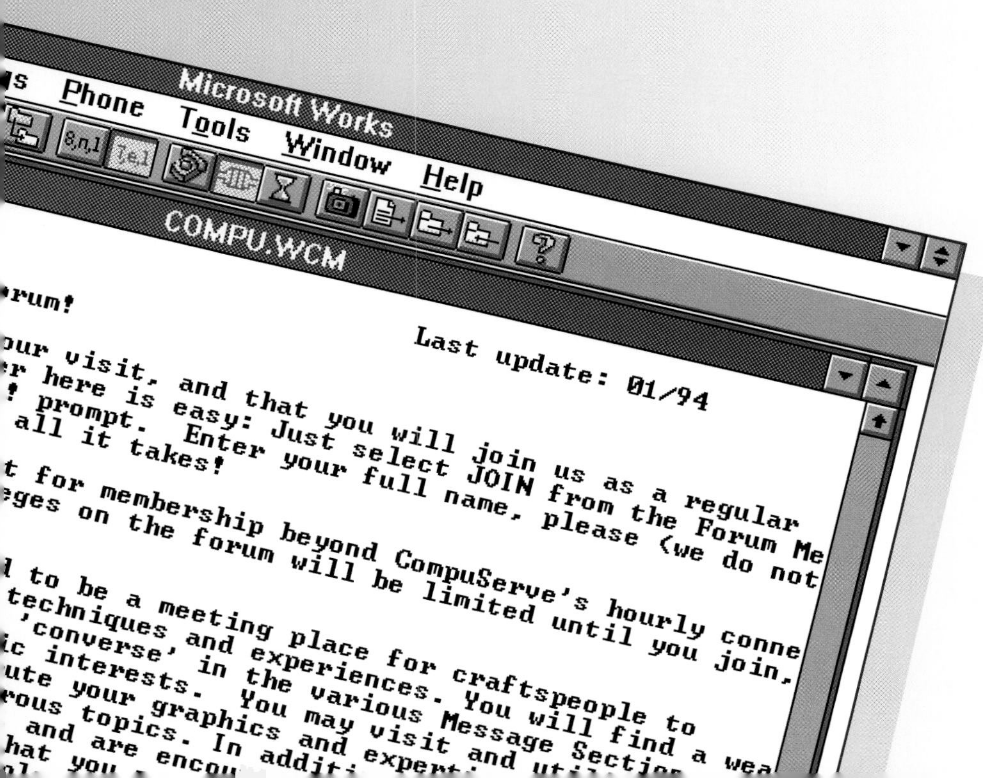

Microsoft Works' Communications tool allows you to communicate with the outside world via your computer—sending and receiving files and messages, doing research, reading newspapers and magazines, and even shopping.

Using the Communications tool to communicate this way, you must have a modem attached to or installed in your computer and also attached to a telephone line.

Communication between two computers requires that the computers understand each other and match in the following ways:

Baud Rate. The rate of data transfer through your computer's communications port. Baud rates vary from as low as 110 to 19,200 and beyond. Typical baud rates used by on-line services are 1200, 2400, and 9600.

Data Bits. The number of bits used to represent one character. Works supports settings of 7 and 8 (the default is 8).

Parity. An error-checking procedure in which an extra parity bit is added to each group of transmitted data bits. As the remote computer receives each group of data, it checks to see whether the 1's in the data bits match. Works supports None (the default), Even, Odd, Mark, and Space. *None* indicates that no parity bit is used. *Even* sets the parity bit to 1 if an even number of 1's is needed. *Odd* sets the parity bit to 1 if an odd number of 1's is

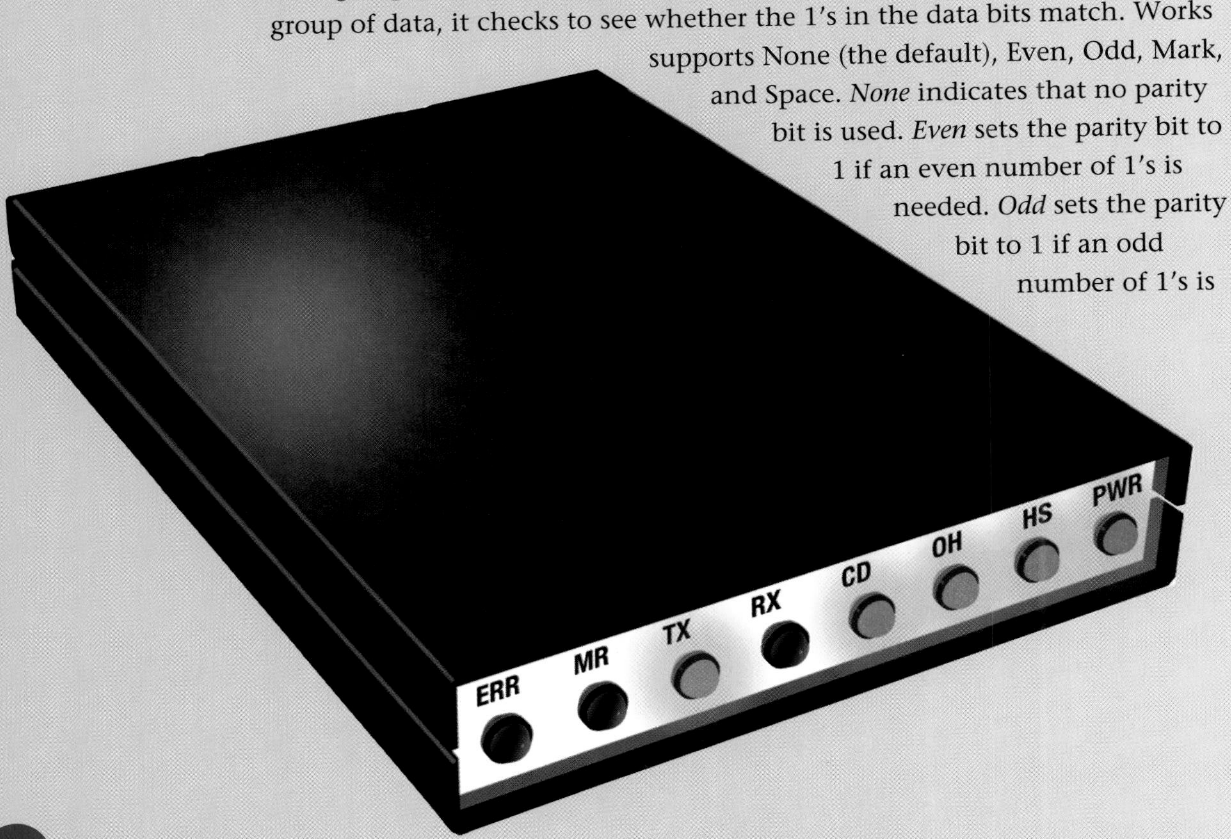

needed. *Mark* always has a parity bit, which is set to 1. *Space* always has a parity bit set to 0. The most common settings are None, Even, and Odd.

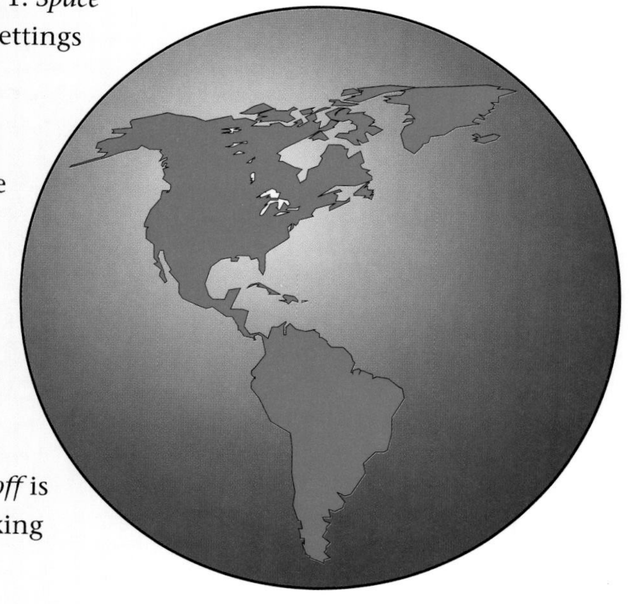

Stop Bits. Indicators of the time between the end of the transmission of one bit and the beginning of the transmission of the next bit. Works supports settings of 1 (the default) and 2.

Handshake. The communication between two computers to establish how the data flow is handled when buffers (data storage areas) are full. Works supports None, Xon/Xoff, and Hardware. *None* (the default) means that there is no handshaking, *Xon/Xoff* is handshaking via software, and *Hardware* is handshaking via hardware.

Your modem must be capable of operating at the selected baud rate, and the baud rate for both communicating computers must be identical. In most cases, the Handshake setting should be set to None. For most communications, Data Bits should be 8, Parity should be None, and Stop Bits should be 1; this setup is known as *8N1*. Many other communications services, however, use 7 Data Bits, Even Parity, and 1 Stop Bit—a setup known as *7E1*. When you log on to a remote computer for the first time, if the characters on your screen are garbled, switch from one set of data bits/parity/stop bits, such as 8N1, to another, such as 7E1.

In this part, you learn how to log on to the on-line service called *CompuServe*; however, all on-line services work in different ways. Although Works commands and communications features look and behave the same, regardless of the on-line service you use, the commands you issue within a particular service vary a great deal. For information about how to use a specific on-line service, refer to its documentation. The best way to learn how the Communications tool works with a particular service is to take the time to experiment.

TASK 53

Starting the Communications Tool

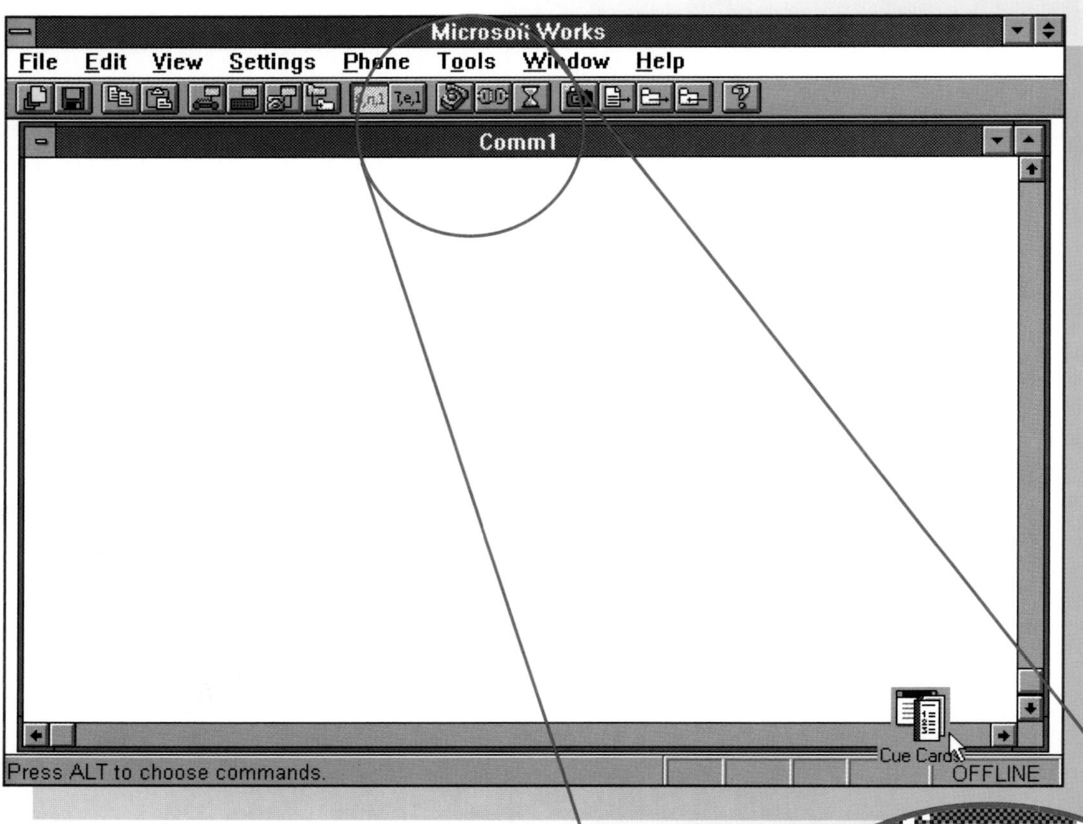

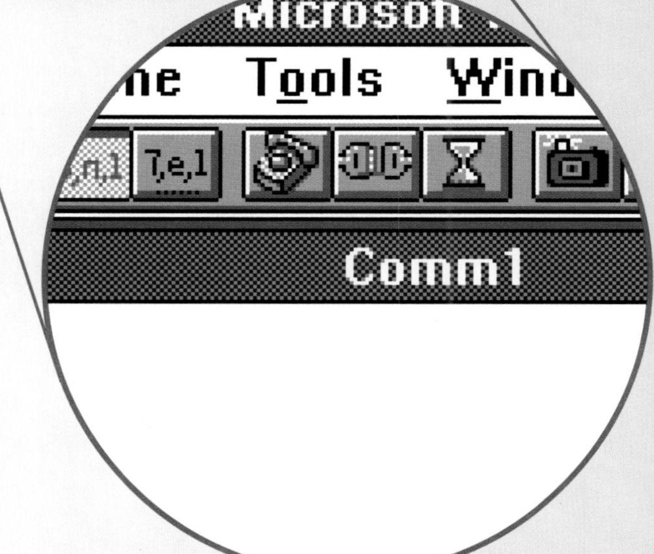

"Why would I do this?"

The Communications tool allows you to communicate with the outside world. You can send one of your Works documents, spreadsheets, or database files to a business colleague or just chat with a friend. In this task, you start the Communications tool for the first time and watch as Works checks your modem.

This task assumes that you have started Works and that the New & Recent Documents Startup dialog box is open.

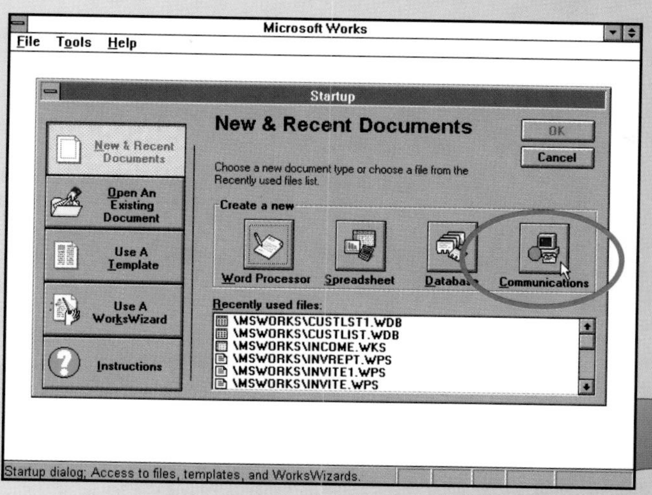

1 Click on the **Communications** button. (Because the New & Recent Documents button at the left side of the dialog box is active—it looks pressed down—you don't need to click on it.) Works displays the Modem Setup dialog box.

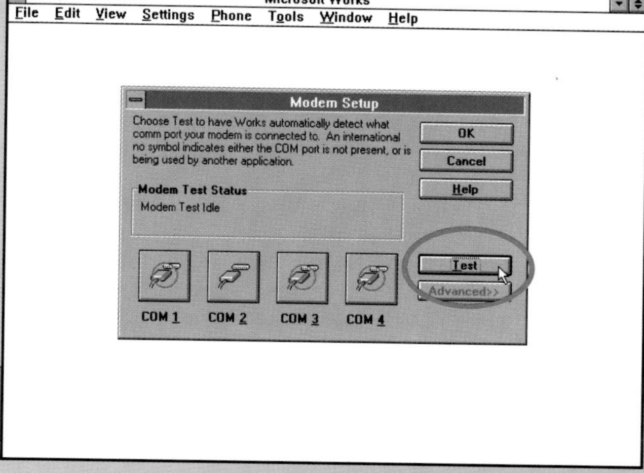

2 Click on **Test**. Works checks your computer system to see which communications port your modem is attached to. In this example, Works finds that the modem is attached to COM 2.

WHY WORRY?

Your modem might not be attached to COM 2. Communicating with other computers relies on having a modem properly attached to your computer and having good communications software installed.

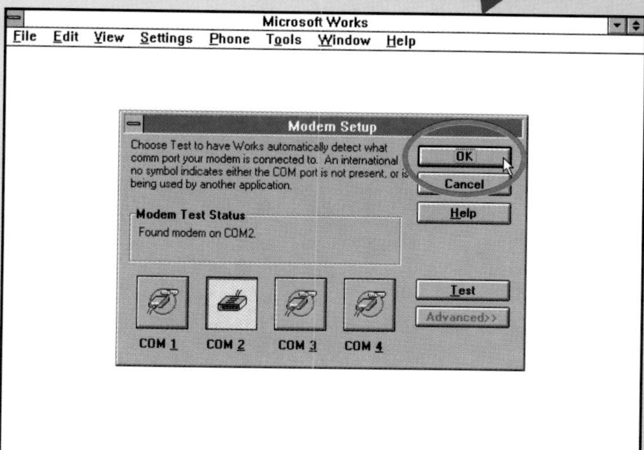

3 Click on **OK**. Works closes the dialog box and opens the Communications window. Minimize the Cue Cards window to get it out of the way.

NOTE

Works checks your modem only the first time you start the Communications tool. After that, Works displays the Easy Connect dialog box, where you specify the phone number of the computer you want to communicate with.

TASK 54

Adjusting Communications Files and Settings

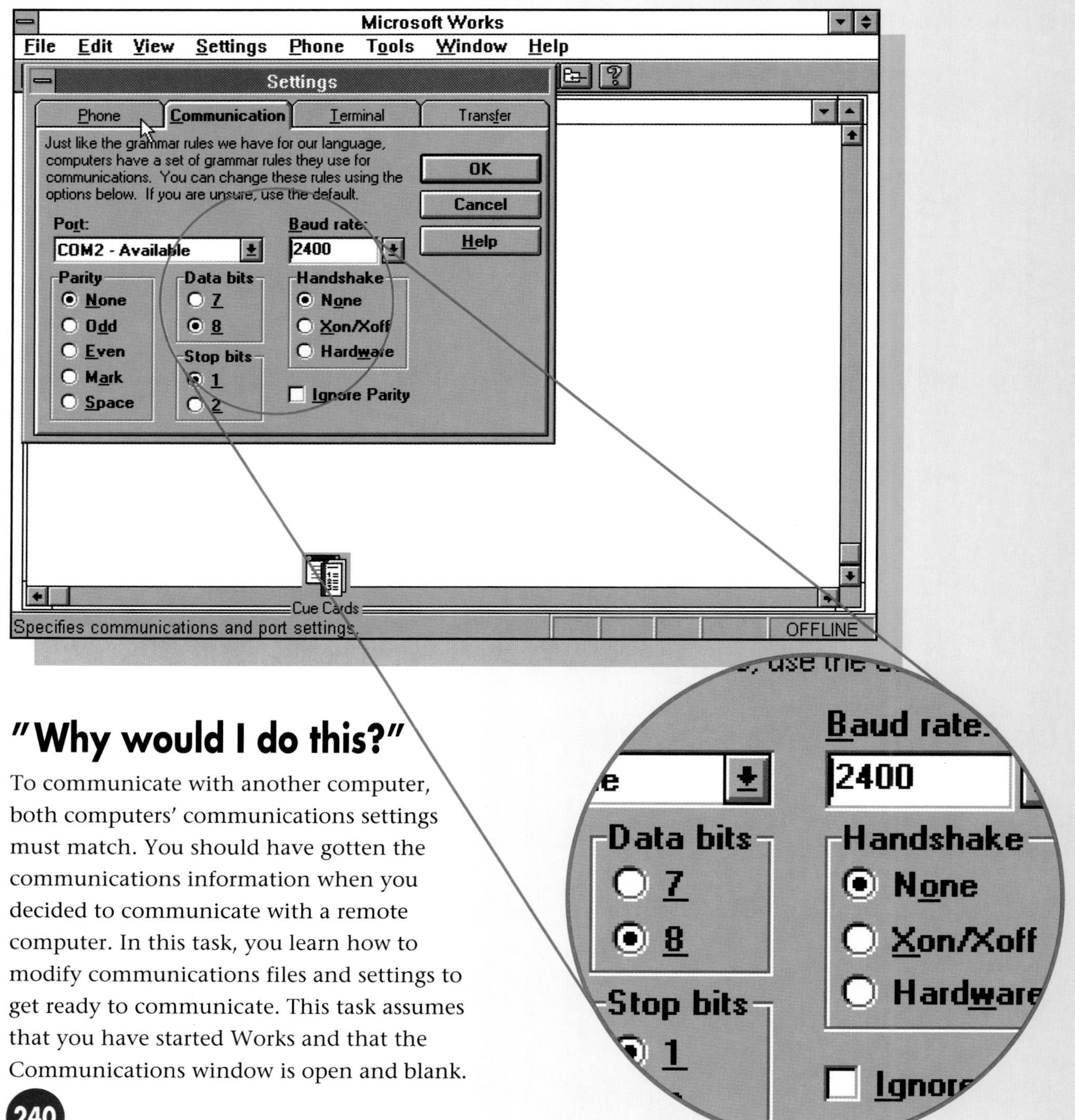

"Why would I do this?"

To communicate with another computer, both computers' communications settings must match. You should have gotten the communications information when you decided to communicate with a remote computer. In this task, you learn how to modify communications files and settings to get ready to communicate. This task assumes that you have started Works and that the Communications window is open and blank.

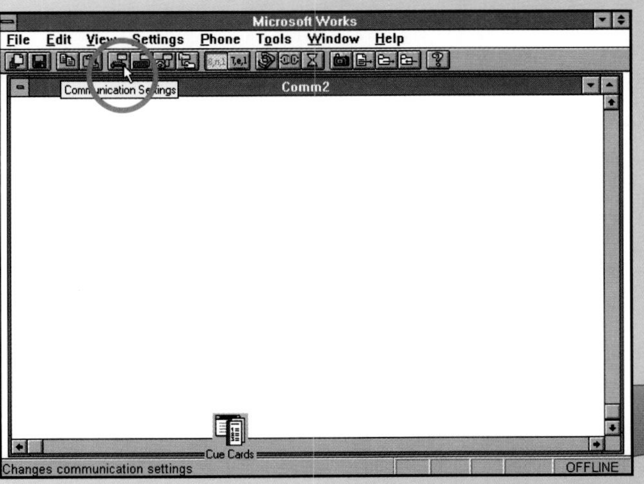

1 Click on the **Communication Settings** button on the toolbar. Works opens the Settings dialog box.

NOTE

The three buttons to the right of the Communication Settings button on the toolbar open the same dialog box; however, the button you choose determines which part of the dialog box appears. In this example, the Communication part appears because you clicked on the Communication Settings button.

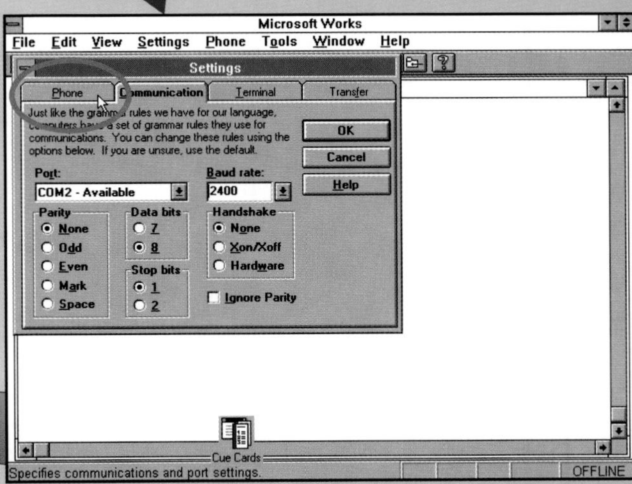

2 Check the options in this area of the dialog box and click on the **Phone** tab. Works opens the Phone area of the Settings dialog box. Make sure that the selected options match the settings that the remote computer requires.

3 In the Phone Number text box, type the telephone number of the computer you want to connect to, such as **555-5555**, and press **Tab**. Works moves the insertion point to the Name of Service text box.

4 Type the name of the service that the telephone number is associated with, such as **CompuServe**.

NOTE

In general, you should accept the options in the rest of the dialog box. However, if your telephone is not touch tone, click on the Pulse option button.

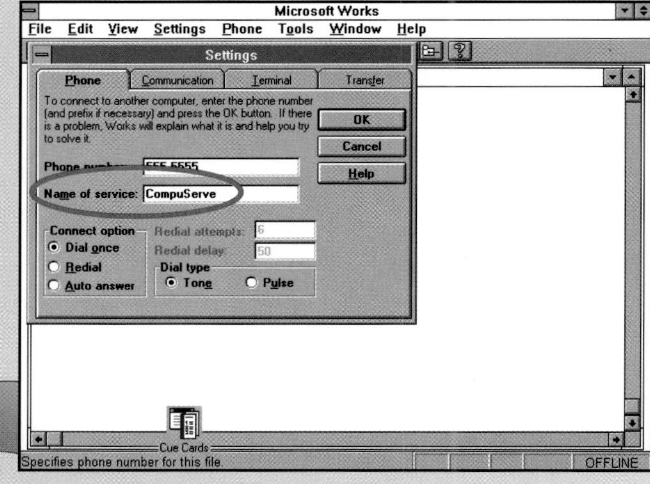

5 Click on **OK**. Works closes the dialog box and returns to the Communications window. You should save the communications file by choosing the File Save command. Works displays the Save As dialog box.

6 Type a file name, such as **compu**, in the File Name text box and click on **OK**. Works closes the dialog box.

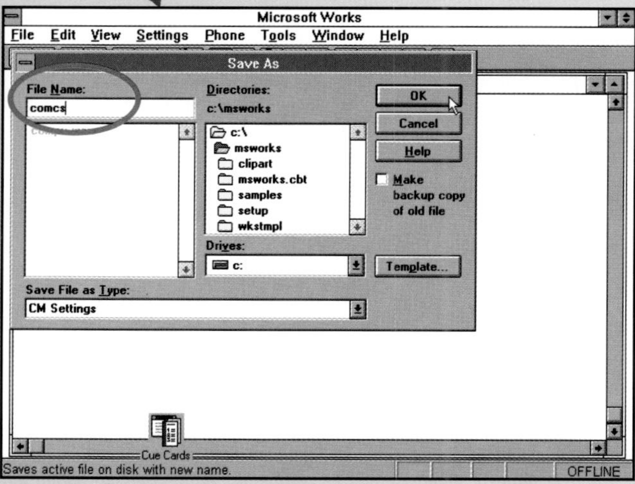

TASK 55

Dialing Another Computer

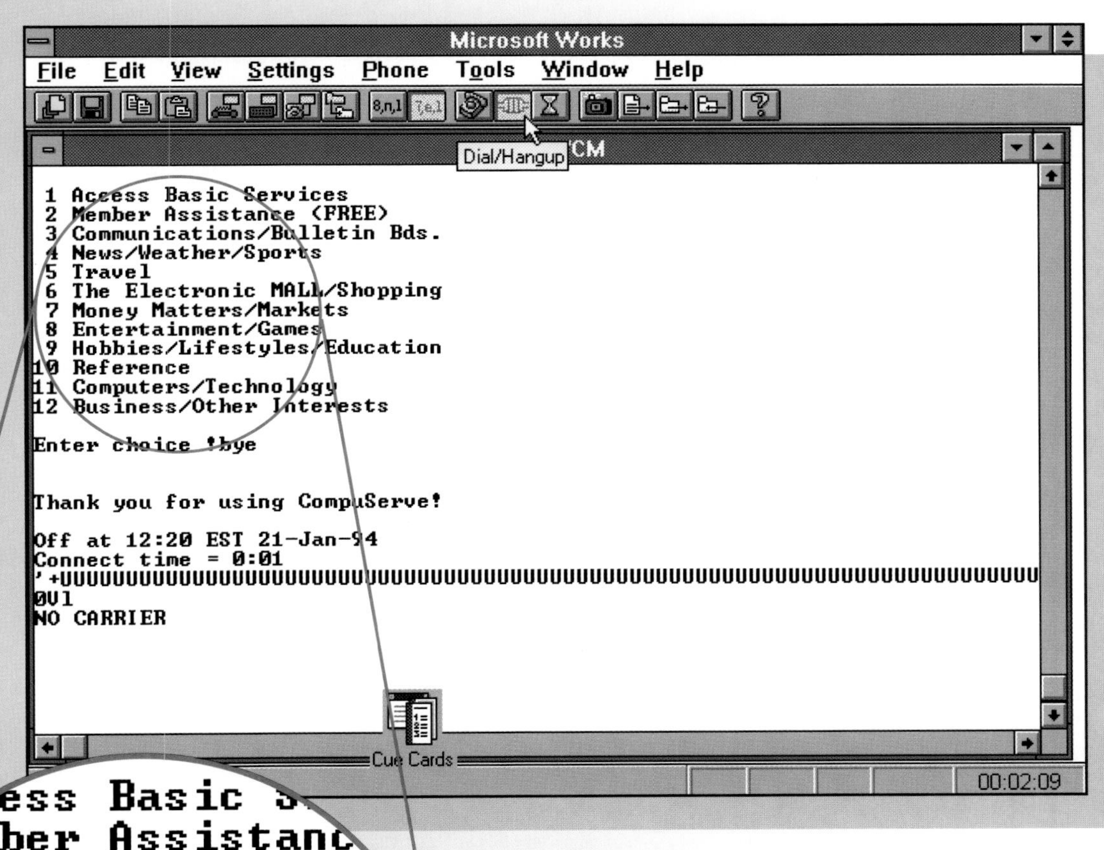

"Why would I do this?"

The only way to communicate with another computer is to call it or wait for it (or its operator) to call you. In this task, you dial a computer, log on, and log off.

This task assumes that you have started Works, that you have defined and saved your communication settings, and that the New & Recent Documents Startup dialog box is open.

Task 55: Dialing Another Computer

1 Select the communications file for the computer you want to call, such as **COMPU.WCM**, by clicking on its name in the Recently Used Files scroll box, or by clicking on the Open an Existing Document button and clicking on the file name in the File Name scroll box. Click on **OK**. Works opens the Communications tool, opens the Cue Cards window, and displays a message box. Before you continue, minimize the Cue Cards window.

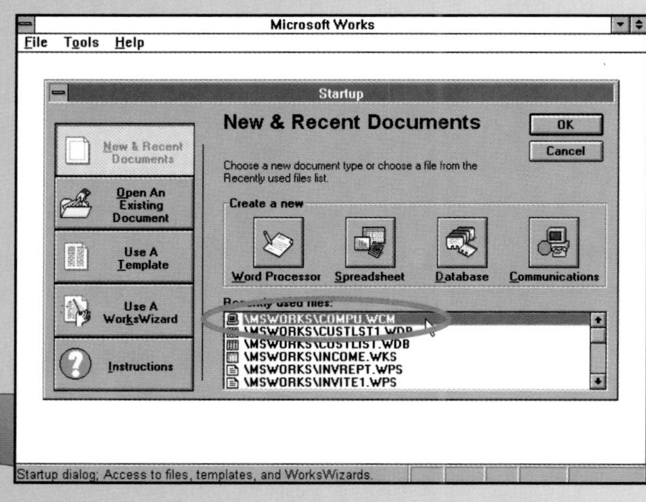


```
Microsoft Works
File  Edit  View  Settings  Phone  Tools  Window  Help
COMPU.WCM
Visitor Announcement                              Last update: 01/94

Welcome to the Crafts forum!

We hope you will enjoy your visit, and that you will join us as a regular
member.  Becoming a member here is easy: Just select JOIN from the Forum Me
or type JOIN at any forum! prompt.  Enter your full name, please (we do not
handles here), and that's all it takes!

There is no additional cost for membership beyond CompuServe's hourly conne
time charges.  Your privileges on the forum will be limited until you join,
we encourage you to do so!

The Crafts Forum is designed to be a meeting place for craftspeople to
congregate and share ideas, techniques and experiences. You will find a wea
of information here. You may 'converse' in the various Message Sections wit
others who share your specific interests.  You may visit and utilize the
Libraries, as well as contribute your graphics and expertise. We have regul
scheduled conferences on numerous topics. In addition, members are welcome
arrange their own conferences, and are encouraged to arrange a variety of
exchanges and swaps.  We ask that you not post any public messages with you
home address or phone number, please.

Press <CR> for more:
Cue Cards
Press ALT to choose commands.                                   00:05:18
```

2 After your computer connects to the other computer, a status screen may appear. Conduct your on-line session—go shopping, look at the weather or news, or chat with a friend.

3 Choose the Logoff or Bye command from the on-line menus. The on-line service tells you that you have logged off and hangs up the phone line.

NOTE

Click on the Dial/Hangup toolbar button if it looks pressed down, indicating that you're still connected. Then click on OK in the message box. This ensures that you are disconnected.

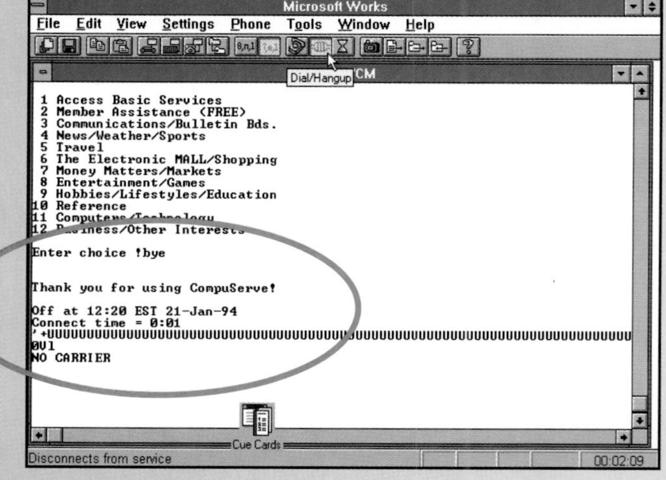

Index

A-C

D

E-F

Index

G-H

I

J-L

M-N

O-P

Q-R

Finding Common Tasks

The following table shows you where in this book you can find information on completing common Works tasks. For a more detailed listing of all tasks covered in *Easy Works 3 for Windows,* refer to the Table of Contents at the front of this book.

When you need help with...	Turn to page...
Starting a Works tool	15
Moving around a document, spreadsheet, or database	49
Selecting blocks of text or data	53
Printing your work	62
Checking your spelling and words in a document, spreadsheet, or database	75
Entering text and numbers in a spreadsheet	132
Creating a chart	170
Creating a database form	182
Querying a database	224
Communicating with another computer	243